C#

A Beginner's Guide

About the Author

Pat McGee (Vancouver, British Columbia) is a software development instructor and curriculum developer at the British Columbia Institute of Technology. A former game programmer, McGee has co-authored books on Microsoft XNA Game Studio and is a recipient of Microsoft's Most Valuable Professional award for DirectX and XNA. You may contact the author at http://HandsOnCoding.net.

About the Technical Editor

Adam Barney is a nerd. After buying a Commodore 64 with money from his paper route in the fourth grade, he's never stopped learning about computers and how to make these stupid machines do cool things. Adam is now a Microsoft MVP (C#) and ASPInsider, and runs his own independent consulting company, Barney Consulting, in Lincoln, Nebraska.

C#
A Beginner's Guide

Pat McGee

New York Chicago San Francisco
Athens London Madrid Mexico City
Milan New Delhi Singapore Sydney Toronto

Library of Congress Cataloging-in-Publication Data

McGee, Pat (Software development instructor)
C# 5.0 : a beginner's guide / Pat McGee.
pages cm
ISBN 978-0-07-183583-1 (paperback)
1. C++ (Computer program language) I. Title.
QA76.73.C153M338 2015
005.13'3—dc23 2014042771

McGraw-Hill Education books are available at special quantity discounts to use as premiums and sales promotions, or for use in corporate training programs. To contact a representative, please visit the Contact Us pages at www.mhprofessional.com.

C#: A Beginner's Guide

1 2 3 4 5 6 7 8 9 0 DOC DOC 1 0 9 8 7 6 5 4

ISBN 978-0-07-183583-1
MHID 0-07-183583-0

Sponsoring Editor Brandi Shailer
Editorial Supervisor Janet Walden
Project Manager Namita Gahtori, Cenveo® Publisher Services
Acquisitions Coordinator Amanda Russell
Technical Editor Adam Barney
Copy Editor William McManus
Proofreader Lisa McCoy
Indexer Claire Splan
Production Supervisor Jean Bodeaux
Composition Cenveo Publisher Services
Illustration Cenveo Publisher Services
Art Director, Cover Jeff Weeks
Cover Designer Jeff Weeks

Special thanks to my wife, son, mom, and dad—for their love and support.

Contents at a Glance

Contents

PART IV Data-Driven Development

Acknowledgments

I wish to thank several people who have offered assistance or guidance, or who have been especially helpful during my career: Brian Anderson, Elsie Au, John Blackwell, Erik Benson, John Bowyer-Smyth, Stephen Cawood, Kevin Cudihee, Marlene Delanghe, Dr. Kim Dotto, Steve Eccles, Medhat Elmasry, Rhonda Ewashko, Lorraine Fentie, Dr. Mirela Gutica, Dr. Dean Hildebrand, Beata Kozma, Jason Harrison, Richard Hart, Uwe Helm, Bill Howorth, Thomas Lane, Shebia Leung, Kate Maclean, Paul Mills, Orrett Morgan, Jeff Parker, Brian Pidcock, Marilyn Stevenson, Ron Terencio, Marlena Vanderwal, Dr. Kimberly Voll, Michael Whyte, Debra Williams, and Dr. Benjamin Yu.

Introduction

This book offers a simple step-by-step approach to learning object-oriented programming with C# and the .NET Framework while also preparing readers for data-driven development. The content is comprehensive and to the point so that you can learn it quickly. Over 150 examples provide clear references to help you through the material with ease. For hands-on experience, over 150 self test questions throughout the book offer extra practice to solidify your understanding of the material learned. An additional 46 exercises are mixed in with the content throughout the book to help you focus on the most relevant concepts as they are discussed.

A thorough coverage of both LINQ-based and traditional database development is provided so that you can perform an adequately full range of queries and joins that any data-driven developer needs. Additional coverage of file input/output, XML handling, and JSON handling also offers you the flexibility you require to handle alternative sources of data with C#.

This book is great for the new programmer because it covers topics from the ground up, with no prior developer experience required. In addition, experienced programmers who are endeavoring to learn C# will get the no-frills language low-down they need to begin developing advanced data-driven applications in ASP.NET, Windows, or any other C#-based platform.

What This Book Covers

This book covers an introduction to Visual Studio for development and debugging, C# programming basics, a solid object-oriented programming foundation, collections and advanced C# structures, LINQ for database development, and traditional database development, as well as file, XML, and JSON handling.

To get the most from this book, read it sequentially and try all examples in Microsoft Visual Studio whenever possible. Visual Studio is the software required to write, edit, and run C# applications. If you do not have a paid edition, Microsoft Visual Studio 2013 Express for Desktop is free and will run all examples in the book as long as you have Windows 7 or later.

Also, to improve your understanding during the discussions in each chapter, complete the *Try This* exercises when you encounter them. These exercises offer hands-on practice with the topics currently presented. To further your knowledge of each topic, complete the self test questions at the end of the chapter.

Digital Resources for This Book

All solutions to the self-test questions at the end of each chapter are provided in an online appendix available for download at

www.mhprofessional.com/computingdownload

In addition, you will find the code for all examples plus the *FoodStore* database SQL and .mdf files. This *FoodStore* database is used in the data-driven examples and exercises that are contained within Chapters 13 through 18. (The appendix included in this book shows the entity relationship diagram and conceptual view for the *FoodStore* database.)

How Is This Book Organized?

Topics in this book are organized sequentially to quickly build your knowledge in a way that is comprehensive but not overly challenging.

Part I covers programming basics. Chapter 1 introduces the code editor and debugger and provides exercises to practice using these tools. Then, modest programming continues in Chapter 2 with variables, constants, enumerations, and arrays. In Chapter 3, use of variables is expanded further with math operators. Chapter 4 then shows how to organize and group instructions with methods. To enable more complex and iterative logic, Chapter 5 discusses conditional structures and loops. Chapter 6 examines the fundamental topic of how to create, format, search, and extract useful information from strings of text. Then, Chapter 7 shows how to format, parse, compare, and calculate differences for dates and times.

After you have explored programming basics, object-oriented structures are introduced in Part II, "Object-Oriented Programming." Part II begins at Chapter 8 with explanations of classes, structs, constructors, properties, and encapsulation with access modifiers. Once you have this knowledge, Chapter 9 explains how to extend classes and structs with inheritance. Chapter 10 discusses how to further extend objects with generic types. Chapter 10 then moves on to explain how to manage multiple objects at once using collections of various types.

Part III, "Advanced Structures," introduces more techniques to control class encapsulation and extensibility. Chapter 11 explains how delegates and anonymous functions enable event handling within a class. This coverage of delegates and anonymous functions also serves to prepare you for understanding how LINQ extension methods work when they are discussed later, in Chapter 16. Next, Chapter 12 looks at designing classes with interfaces. The topic of interfaces is also especially helpful later for explaining how to optimize queries with LINQ to Entities.

Part IV, "Data-Driven Development," explores various ways to manage database and data alternatives. To prepare initially, Chapter 13 discusses how to connect to the database and how to examine data within it using Microsoft Visual Studio. Then, to get ready for using LINQ with databases, Chapter 14 introduces the Entity Framework to bridge your C# code with the database. After setting up with the Entity Framework, Chapters 15 and 16 both cover LINQ to Entities using query syntax and method-based syntax to manage database content from your C# code. Then Chapter 17 explains how to perform the really challenging queries, which involve columns from multiple tables. For the times when you do not want LINQ to manage your database content, Chapter 18 explains how to execute raw SQL scripts and stored procedures from your code. Various ways to enable file input and output are covered in Chapter 19. Handling alternative sources of data is discussed next. Chapter 20 covers XML, and Chapter 21 covers JSON.

Part V, "Stand-alone Topics," ties up loose ends by covering structures that you likely will see later as a C# developer. Chapter 22 discusses how attributes are created and used. You will want to understand attributes when you get to C# development for either Windows or web development. Chapter 23 explains operator overloading. You probably won't use operator overloading in most business applications, but you likely will want to use it in game development or any application that applies math with vectors. The two chapters in Part V may not be very useful for you now, but they are easy to follow if you ever need a good reference.

And, as mentioned earlier, the appendix shows the entity relationship diagram and the conceptual view for the *FoodStore* database.

Part I

Programming Basics

Chapter 1

Introduction to C# Coding and Debugging

Key Skills & Concepts

- Brief History of C#
- Understanding Basic Code Terminology
- Writing and Running a Program
- Using the Integrated Development Environment
- Incorporating Debugging Techniques

At this point you must be anxious to get coding—me too! To prepare, after a brief history of C#, we will begin with a discussion on code terminology. Then we are going to write and run some simple programs while getting familiar with the development environment and debugging tools. When this chapter is done, you will be ready to immerse yourself in code for the rest of the book.

Brief History of C#

C#, pronounced *C sharp,* is a multipurpose language that can be used to develop console, windows, web, and mobile applications. C# was first introduced as part of the Microsoft .NET Framework, which was announced and demonstrated in July 2000 at Microsoft's Professional Developers Conference. C# became an official language specification in 2002 with the official release of .NET 1.0. C# is popular due to its ease of use on different Windows platforms, its well-organized object-oriented methodology, and its C-style syntax that is familiar to most software developers today.

C# is a programming language that is enabled through the .NET Framework. The .NET Framework is a common environment and toolset for creating, building, and running Windows applications, Windows services, web applications, and web services with the Microsoft platform. The .NET Framework also includes common class libraries that provide functionality and structures for all languages that use the .NET Framework. Other languages within this framework include Visual Basic .NET (VB.NET) and Managed C++.

Understanding Basic Code Terminology

To begin our discussion of C# as a programming language, let's define some basic code structures:

- **Variables** Variables are user-defined named references to stored data. Variable names are usually nouns that describe the items stored. Properly named variables help to narrate your code.
- **Methods** Methods are groups of instructions that perform a routine. Method names are usually verbs that describe the action they perform. Methods help reduce duplicate code by enabling code reuse in addition to making programs easier to read and debug.
- **Classes** Classes are templates that provide a related grouping of methods, data, and other constructs. Classes are used to create objects.
- **Namespaces** Namespaces are logical groupings of classes. Referencing namespaces (with "using" statements) at the top of your code file lets you use their classes in that file. In addition to using the namespaces provided by the .NET Framework, you will routinely want to create your own namespaces to organize your classes. In every example within this book, you will see a reference to at least one library of the .NET Framework. Most often, the *System* namespace is referenced in the examples to access the *Console* class for enabling writing to the console window. Namespaces also prevent conflicts that occur when classes have identical names. When more than one class share the same name, the namespace of the class is used in combination with the class name to identify it.

Comments

In addition to making sure that you use proper naming of variables, methods, classes, and namespaces, you will at times want to add comments to narrate your code. Comments are visible to anyone who reads the code. Comments are not included in the executable application. There are three ways to write comments in C#:

- **Single-line comments** Single-line comments are preceded by two forward slashes, //. For example:

```
// Comments about the code structure go here.
```

- **Multiple-line comments** Multiple-line comments begin with /* and end with */, as shown next. This comment style may be used for narrative paragraphs.

```
/* Information about the code
   structure belongs here. */
```

- **XML tag comments** XML tag comments are preceded by triple forward slashes, ///, at the start of each line. This comment style enables auto-generation of HTML documentation for code blocks in your application through a transformation that is enabled in Microsoft Visual Studio. XML tag comments also enable tooltip hints for describing code blocks. The nine main comment tags are <remarks>, <summary>, <example>, <exception>, <param>, <permission>, <returns>, <seealso>, and <include>. XML tag comments may precede a method to provide a summary of its parameter and list return type. An example follows:

```
/// <summary>
/// Method description goes here.
/// </summary>
/// <param name=''varName''>Parameter description.</param>
/// <returns>Return value description.</returns>
```

Syntax

Syntax defines the set of rules for structural correctness of a programming language. When writing code, aside from comments, every semicolon, brace, parenthesis, word, and letter case must be accurate. Improper syntax will stop your code from compiling into an executable program.

Indentation

Opening and closing curly braces are required to enclose structures such as classes, methods, and more. For readability and by convention, it is essential that you indent and left-align your code within each pair of curly braces. Structures inside structures must also be indented and left-aligned:

```
namespace ConsoleApplication1 // Namespace declaration.
{
    class Program             // Class inside namespace.
    {
        static void Main()    // Method inside class.
        {
        }
    }
}
```

The material in this book often implements a common variation of code indentation to present code instructions in fewer lines by placing the opening curly brace at the end of the loop header, method header, or class header:

```
namespace ConsoleApplication1 { // Namespace declaration.
    class Program {             // Class inside namespace.
        static void Main() {    // Method inside class.
        }
    }
}
```

Writing and Running a Program

When you write code, you are writing human-readable instructions. C# is considered a high-level language because the instruction set is user friendly.

Writing and Editing Your Code

Normally you will want to write and edit your C# code inside some edition of Microsoft Visual Studio, since it integrates several different tools to help you to edit, manage, and compile your code solution. A *solution* is a collection of projects. It is possible to have more than one project in a solution, but the solutions in this book always include only one project. Figure 1-1 shows a solution within the Visual Studio integrated development environment (IDE) that contains a project named ConsoleApplication1. By default, the code editor is displayed in the large section on the left. The Solution Explorer is on the right. The Solution Explorer provides easy viewing and navigation for code files and other resources. Also, on the bottom right in Figure 1-1, you can see the Properties window. The Properties window provides a summary of the properties for any file or resource that is selected within the project. In this case, the Properties window displays the file name and path of the Program.cs file which is selected in the Solution Explorer. An Error List window also exists at the bottom of the IDE in Figure 1-1. The Error List window displays any errors that prevent your code from running. This window will be discussed in more detail later in this chapter during the section on debugging techniques.

NOTE

Until we begin Part II, all classes, methods, and variables that are declared at the class level must be declared with a static modifier. Variables that are declared within methods are nonstatic. The static modifier will be explained in Chapter 8.

Program Compilation and Execution

After you finish writing your C# instructions, you then need to compile them before you can run your program. When you compile your C# code, you are actually converting the instructions into a bytecode-style format that runs on Windows.

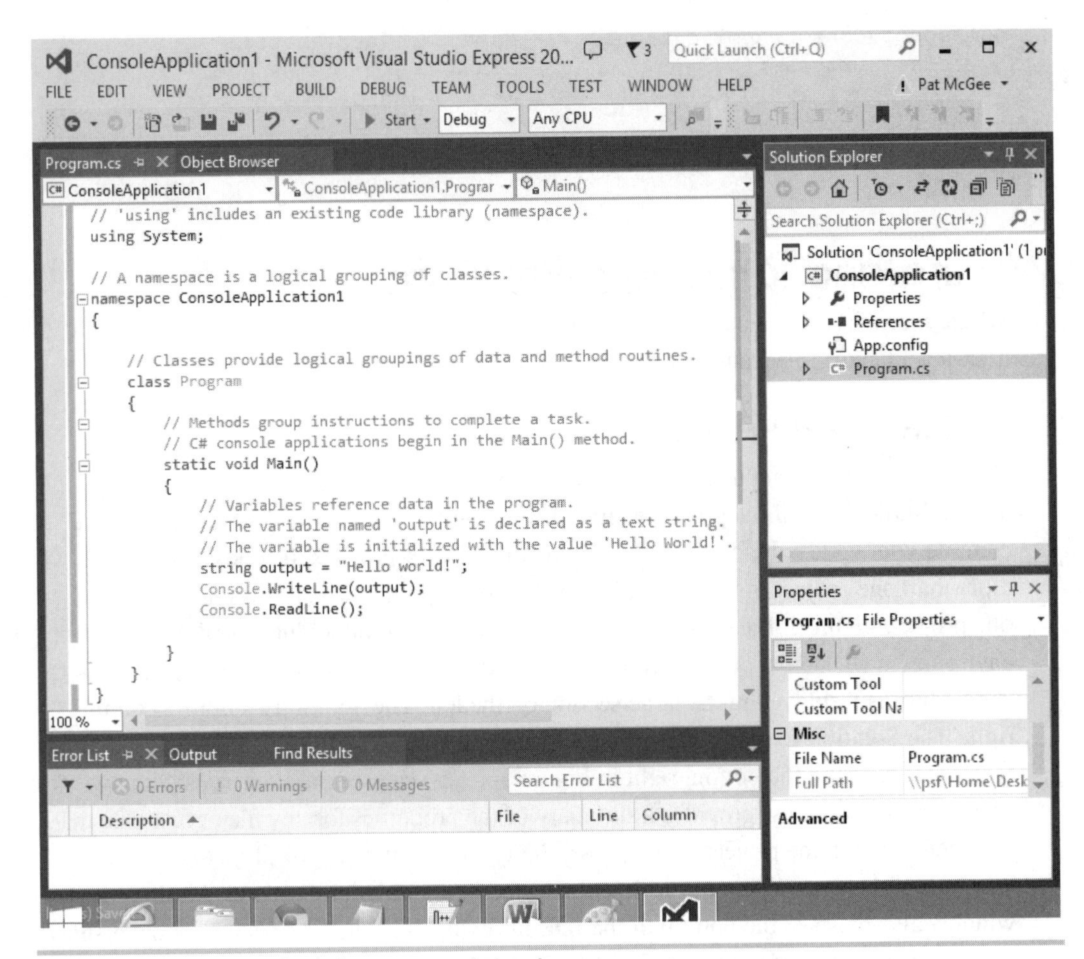

Figure 1-1 The Visual Studio integrated development environment

Try This 1-1 Creating Your First C# Program

This section provides your first opportunity to practice writing code and using Visual Studio to compile and run it. In this walkthrough, you will write a program that prints "Hello world!" to a console window.

1. Launch Microsoft Visual Studio from the Start menu.
2. Once Visual Studio is open, select File | New | Project. In the New Project dialog that opens, expand the Templates node and select the Visual C# node on the left. From there select Console Application from the list that appears in the center of the New Project dialog, as shown in Figure 1-2.

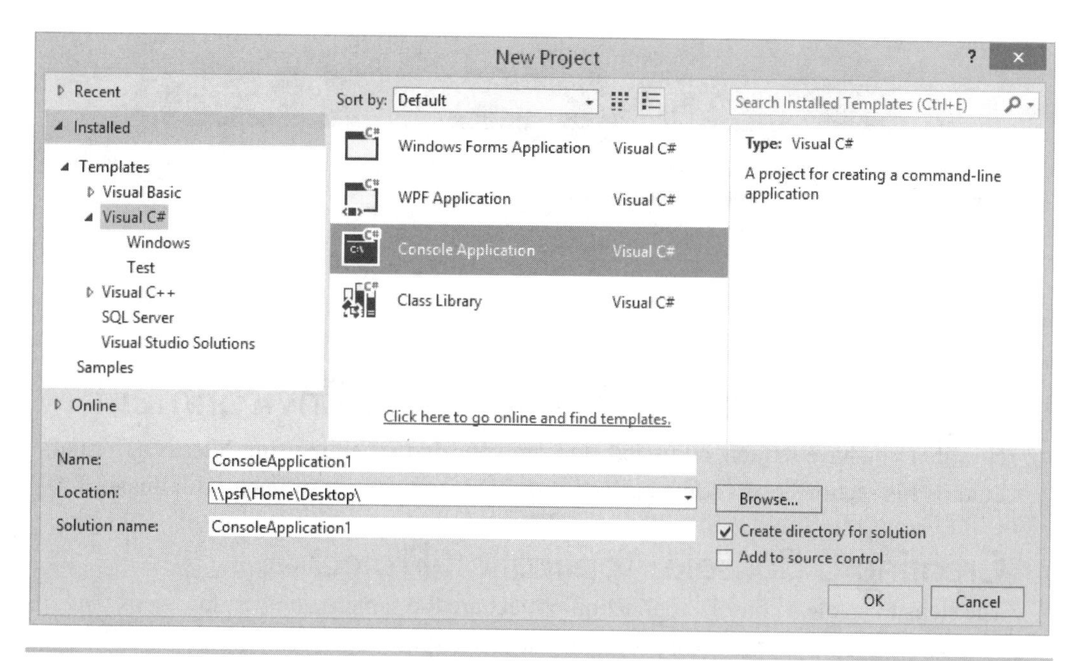

Figure 1-2 Creating a console application

NOTE

All examples in this book run in a console application project. When not stated, code that is presented for an example belongs in the Program.cs file.

3. Once the project has been created, double-click the Program.cs file in the Solution Explorer panel on the right to view the code. Replace the contents of Program.cs with the written instructions that are displayed in Figure 1-1. Comments are not compiled, so you are not required to include them.

CAUTION

Remember that the spelling, letter case, and punctuation used in your code must all be correct or your program will not compile and run.

4. After writing your code, compile and run the program. To do this, either click the green arrow button, labeled Start, which is located in the Visual Studio toolbar (refer to Figure 1-1), or press F5. Running the program launches the console window to display the message "Hello world!" (see Figure 1-3).
5. You may terminate the program by either pressing ENTER in the console application or pressing SHIFT-F5 when in Visual Studio.

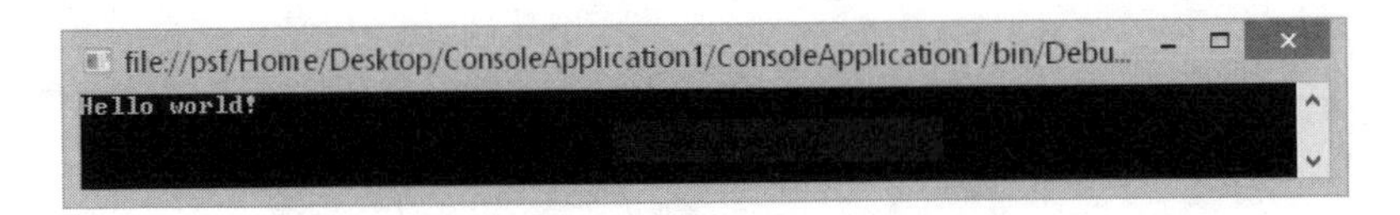

Figure 1-3 Output from the console application

Using the Integrated Development Environment

Now that you have written, compiled, and run your first program using Microsoft Visual Studio, this section covers some basics for managing your code projects with this tool.

Creating a Console Application Project

The steps to create a console application project are the same as the first few steps you followed to create your first C# program. Launch Visual Studio, select File | New | Project, and, under the Templates node, select Visual C#. From there, select Console Application from the list in the center of the New Project dialog (refer to Figure 1-2).

Compiling and Running a Program

Compiling a program refers to the process of converting C# human-readable instructions to a bytecode format that can be executed. To compile and run a program from Visual Studio, select Debug | Start Debugging or press the F5 key. Alternatively, just click the Start button in the Visual Studio toolbar, as shown earlier in Figure 1-1.

Stopping the Application

When running the program from Visual Studio, you can stop its execution by placing your cursor in the Microsoft Visual C# code editor window and then pressing SHIFT-F5. You can also stop the program by clicking the toolbar button with the small red square icon. This button is only visible in Visual Studio while the program is running.

Unless specified, the console will close automatically when a program finishes running. When you're running a console application, to stop the command window from closing when the application finishes, you can add the instruction *Console.ReadLine()* at the end of the program to force it to wait for the user to press ENTER before terminating.

Saving the Solution

By default, the act of compiling code from Visual Studio will automatically save any code changes. To save one file at a time while viewing each code file, select File | Save or press CTRL-S. Also, to save all code and resource changes in your solution, select File | Save All or press CTRL-SHIFT-S.

Exiting the Solution

When the application is not running, you may exit the Visual Studio environment by navigating to File | Exit.

Opening the Solution

To open a Visual Studio solution with one of your code projects in it, navigate to the folder where your project is stored and double-click the solution file. The solution file is generated whenever you create a console application. The solution file has a .sln extension. Double-clicking the solution file will launch Visual Studio with your code project inside it. When Visual Studio is running, you can open a solution from the File | Open menu. You can also use the CTRL-O shortcut from Visual Studio to launch the Open File dialog, which you can use to navigate to the .sln file.

Renaming a Code File

To rename a code file, right-click the code file name in the Solution Explorer and then choose Rename in the drop-down list. You will be prompted to enter a new name for your code file. Alternatively, while the file is selected, press F2 and rename it when prompted.

Renaming Code Structures

Renaming variables, methods, classes, and namespaces is a very important part of development. Good coders rely heavily on proper names for variables, methods, and classes to accurately describe how the code works. Due to the iterative nature of code development, you will often think of better names for your structures much later, after declaring them. For these reasons, you will want to use both the Find and Replace dialog and the Rename dialog to rename your variables, methods, and classes as you think of better names.

The Find and Replace Dialog

To launch the Find and Replace dialog, select Edit | Find and Replace | Replace In Files or use the keyboard shortcut CTRL-SHIFT-H. Figure 1-4 shows dialog settings used to rename a

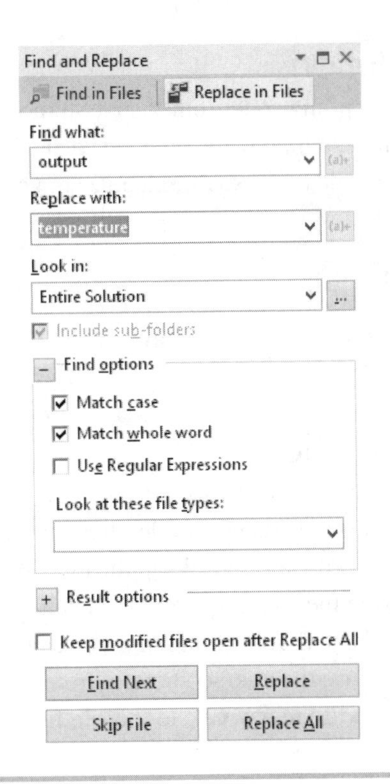

Figure 1-4 The Find and Replace dialog

variable called *output* to *temperature*. You can apply changes to one reference at a time, to a code block such as a method, to an entire code page, or to the entire solution, depending on which option you select from the Look In drop-down menu. If you are applying changes one at a time, then you must click Replace. Clicking Replace applies the change and advances the cursor to the next reference that matches the search criteria. If you do not wish to change the currently selected text, click Find Next to advance the cursor to the next reference. When searching an entire solution while replacing text, you can also click Skip File to avoid making further changes to the current file. To apply changes to all references in a defined range, click Replace All.

Sometimes you may not know the case or full spelling of a structure that you must locate but you know part of the spelling. You can adjust your search in these situations by toggling the Match Case and Match Whole Word check boxes. For additional search flexibility, you can also select the Regular Expressions check box to search based on a regular expression in the Find What area. Regular expressions define matching patterns, and they are discussed in Chapter 6.

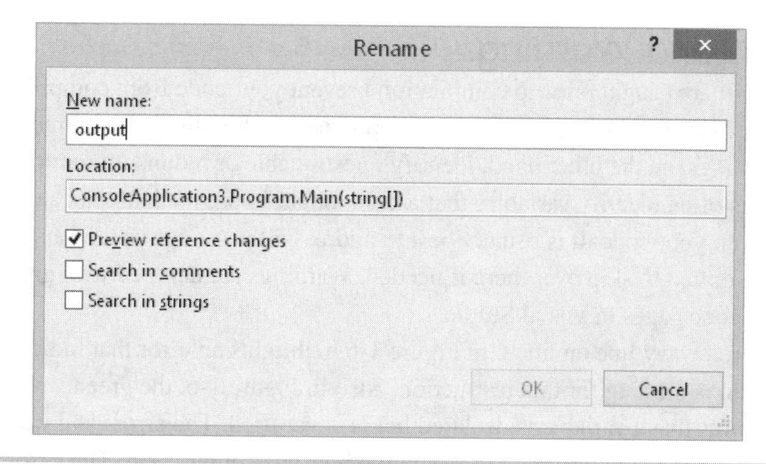

Figure 1-5 Refactoring with the Rename dialog

Refactoring with the Rename Dialog

The Rename dialog offers a focused way to rename code structures within their program context. For example, renaming a namespace with the Find and Replace dialog may bluntly change the namespace name, the assembly reference, comments, and other similarly named structures. The Rename dialog, on the other hand, provides more relevant options to change only the code references to it. To launch the Rename dialog, right-click the text to be renamed and then select Refactor | Rename. The shortcut CTRL-R-R also launches the Rename dialog with the selected text in it. You can also open this dialog by choosing Edit | Refactor | Rename. Figure 1-5 shows the Rename dialog with text that is to be renamed in the New Name field.

Incorporating Debugging Techniques

Debugging is the process of eliminating errors. To be effective at debugging, you must be able to combine several different techniques to track bugs in your code. There are times when you will need to be creative in your bug-tracking efforts, so familiarity with many debugging techniques will prove to be valuable.

Understanding how the IDE can help you debug your code will make you far more productive as a developer. Some errors may be caught prior to run time, but others will be apparent only when the program runs. For C# developers, Visual Studio provides a rich set of tools to help identify and understand errors in either case.

Errors and Warnings

Errors that are caught prior to compilation prevent your code from compiling. In Visual Studio, errors that are caught prior to compilation are highlighted with red wavy lines.

Warnings, on the other hand, identify questionable or redundant sections of code. Warnings often identify variables that are no longer in use so that you can get rid of them to clean up your code. It is usually best to address all warnings as they appear, but you have the option to skip over them if needed. Warnings are denoted with green wavy lines on your code pages in Visual Studio.

The red wavy line on line 6 in Figure 1-6 highlights an error that indicates that a semicolon is missing for this instruction. Also in Figure 1-6, the green wavy line on line 5 warns that a variable is declared but is never used. The errors and warnings are summarized in the Error List window at the bottom of Figure 1-6. The Error List window appears by default, but if it is not displayed, you can open it by selecting View | Error List or by pressing CTRL-W-E.

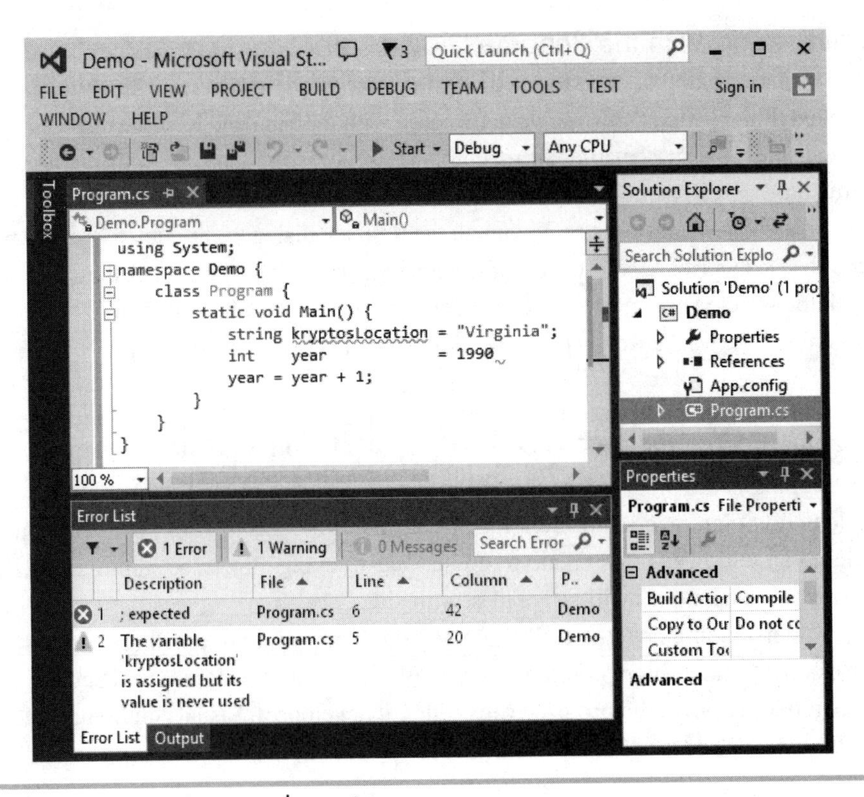

Figure 1-6 Viewing errors and warnings

TIP

The most critical errors are listed at the top of the Error List window, so fix those first when debugging. You can navigate to the line where the error occurs by double-clicking the error description in the Error List.

Breakpoints

Breakpoints allow you to halt your program at any instruction you choose. When stopping your program at a breakpoint in the code, you can inspect the variable values at that point in the application, or you can step through your code from that point one line at a time. In Figure 1-7, breakpoints are set at lines 9 and 13.

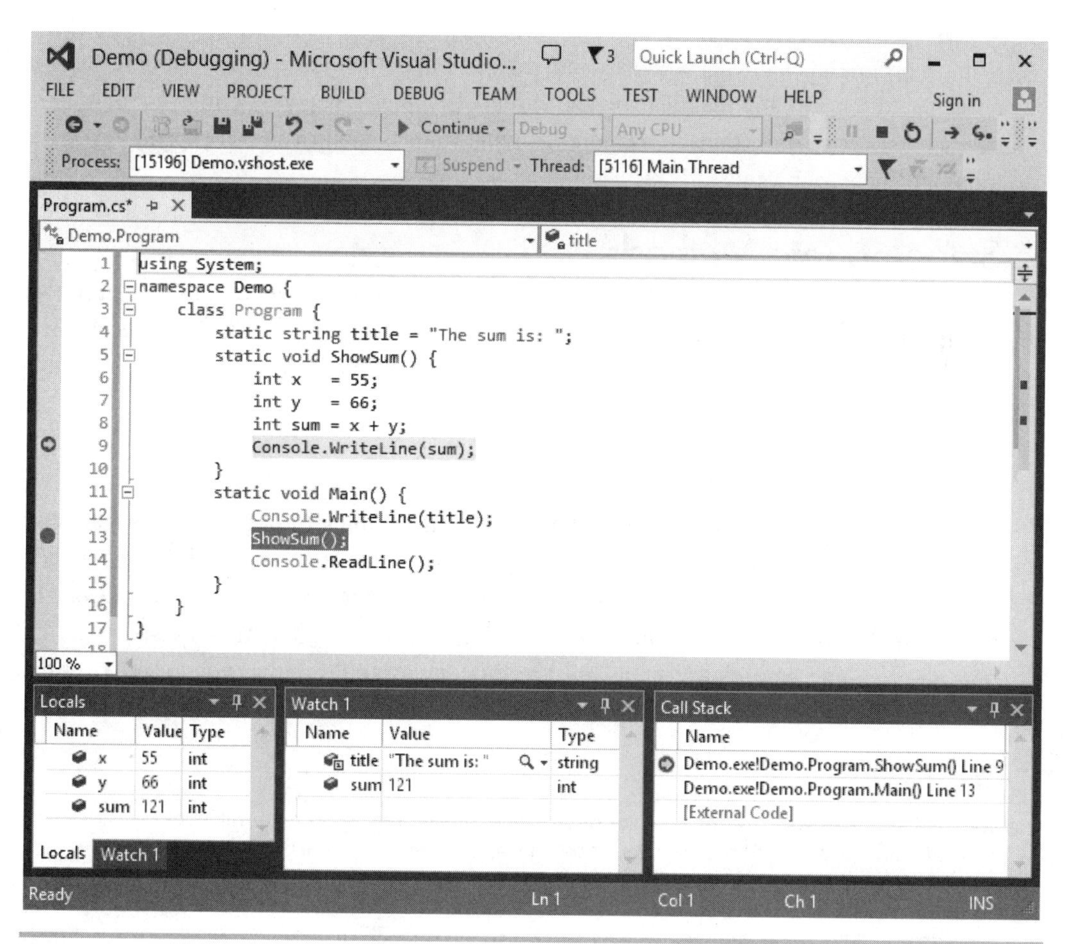

Figure 1-7 Viewing local variables and the call stack while halted

To set breakpoints, click in the gray margin, also called the *gutter,* beside the instruction where the program is halted. You can set or clear breakpoints by placing the cursor beside the instruction where the program is to halt and then pressing F9. Toggling F9 at the breakpoint location clears and sets the breakpoint. When you run the program, it will stop at the breakpoint until you take further action.

Resuming Program Execution

When your program is halted, or when you are stepping through your code, you can return to normal program execution by pressing F5. You may also resume program execution by selecting Debug | Continue, or you could instead click the Continue button in the toolbar.

Tooltips

While a program is halted at a breakpoint, you can hover the cursor over a variable's reference to see a tooltip that displays the variable's value. When your cursor is hovering over a complex variable that stores more than one value, usually you can expand the tooltip to show each value.

Stepping into Methods

When stepping through your code, you can step into a method from the calling instruction by pressing F11 or by selecting Debug | Step Into. To resume the program, press F5. At the breakpoint on line 13 in Figure 1-7, for example, you would need to press F11 to step into the *ShowSum()* method.

Stepping over Methods

During debug sessions, you do not want to waste time stepping through methods that you know already work properly. You can skip past proven or irrelevant methods, or methods defined in the framework, by pressing F10 at the calling instruction or by selecting Debug | Step Over. To resume the program, press F5. In Figure 1-7, the program first halts at line 13. To avoid stepping through the *ShowSum()* method, pressing F10 allows you to step over the calling instruction so you can advance to line 14.

TIP

To speed up inspection of your variables and routines while debugging, you will want to memorize the keyboard shortcuts for stepping into and stepping over code. Here is a memory trick: First, remember that both routines are triggered with the F10 and F11 keys. To remember that F10 is for Step Over, think of the zero as the letter "O" in Over. To remember that F11 is for Step Into, think of the one as the letter "I" in Into.

The Call Stack Window

When debugging, you may sometimes want to know where a method was called if it can be called from several locations. Or, you might want to know the sequence of the methods that were accessed prior to the failing instruction. The Call Stack window shows where the calling instruction is located and shows the most recently accessed methods in sequence of access. The Call Stack window appears only while the program is running. To view the Call Stack window while debugging, select Debug | Windows | Call Stack or press ALT-F7. Visual Studio's display of the call stack appears at the bottom right of Figure 1-7.

The Locals Window

When stepping through your code, the Locals window automatically displays the current values of all variables that are declared locally in the method. By default, the Locals window is positioned at the bottom left of the development environment, as shown in Figure 1-7. If you do not see the Locals window, you can launch it while the program is halted at a breakpoint by choosing Debug | Windows | Locals or pressing ALT-F4.

Try This 1-2 Inspecting Your Code

This exercise offers practice for

- Creating and writing a console application program
- Setting breakpoints
- Examining code line by line while the program is halted
- Stepping into methods
- Stepping over methods
- Examining variable values with tooltips and the Locals window

Try stepping through your code and examining the variable values at run time:

1. Open Visual Studio and create a console application project, as outlined earlier in the chapter.
2. Replace all code in the Program.cs file with the code that appears in Figure 1-8.
3. Set a breakpoint beside the call to the *MultiplyTwoNumbers()* method and run the program until it halts.

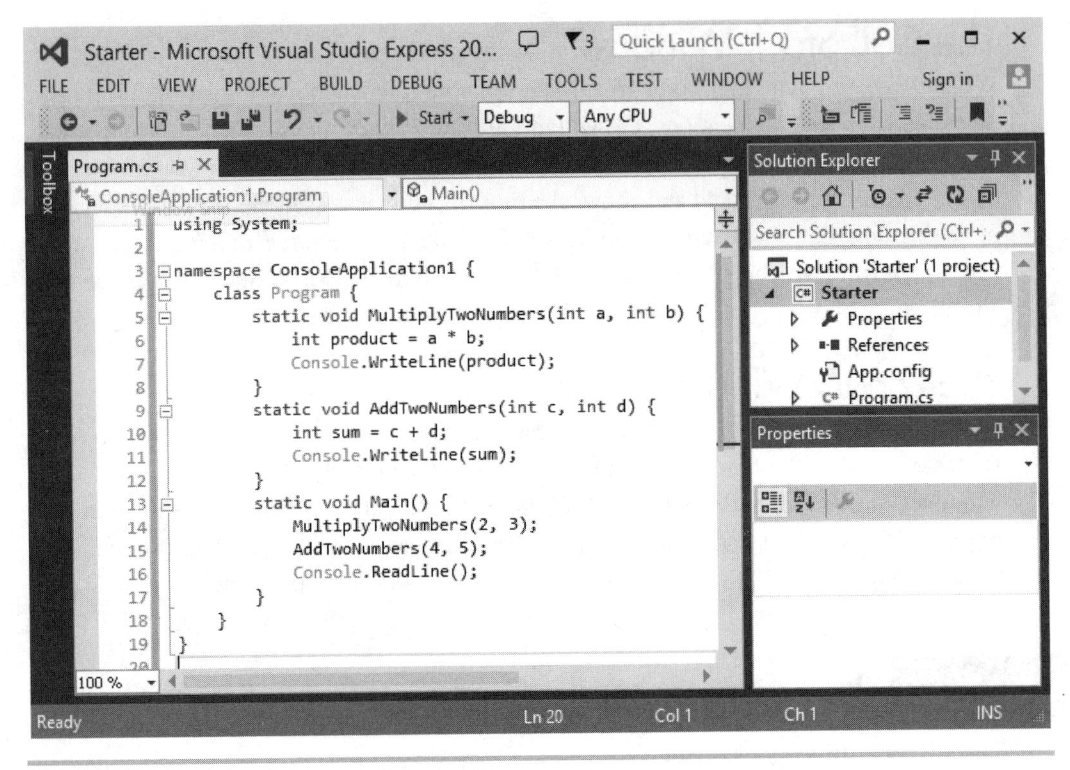

Figure 1-8 Code inspection project

4. Step into the *MultiplyTwoNumbers()* method with the F11 shortcut.
5. When inside *MultiplyTwoNumbers()*, press F10 repeatedly to advance line by line to the end of this method.
6. While halted inside the *MultiplyTwoNumbers()* method, notice how the variables *a, b,* and *product* appear in the Locals window. Also, hover your cursor over each variable reference and observe how values stored in each variable appear inside a tooltip.
7. Press F10 to advance line by line out of the *MultiplyTwoNumbers()* method, and press F10 again to advance over the call to *AddTwoNumbers()*.
8. To shut down the program, allow it to run until completion by pressing F5 to resume execution. Press ENTER when prompted.

The Watch Window

The Watch window allows you to customize the list of variables and their corresponding values when you are halted at a breakpoint. The Watch window is different from the Locals window because it shows both local and class-level variables simultaneously. The Watch window can only be viewed at run time. The Watch window does not appear by default. To launch it and to create a list, first halt the program at a breakpoint, then right-click a variable name and select Add Watch from the pop-up menu. The window appears as shown at the bottom middle of Figure 1-7. You can delete an item from the watch list by right-clicking the item and selecting Delete Watch.

NOTE

By default, Visual Studio runs with debugging. At times, you might choose to run the project without debugging to avoid having to disable breakpoints. While not relevant for the material in this book, extremely large solutions can take much longer to start when debugging is enabled. To run the project without debugging, select Debug | Start Without Debugging or press CTRL-F5.

Try-Catch Blocks

To avoid program crashes and to generate helpful responses for critical errors, you may place your suspect or vulnerable code inside a try-catch block. When an error is encountered in the try block, the application skips the remaining instructions in the block and resumes execution in the catch block. Code implemented in the catch block can display or log information about the error and also provide a suitable response for the error. The program then resumes after leaving the catch block.

The Exception Class

The *Exception* class, from the *System* namespace, creates an object that stores and provides information about errors when they are caught. The catch block can be set up to receive an *Exception* object that contains information about the error. Here is a simplified view of the try-catch syntax:

```
try {                                   // 'try' block header.
    // Code that may lead to run-time errors is placed here.
}
catch (Exception e) {                   // 'catch' block header receives
                                        // the Exception object named ''e''.
    // Respond to the error.
    Console.WriteLine(e.Message); // Display error information with the
                                        // 'Message' property.
}
```

Property	Description
Data	Gets user-defined information about the error.
HelpLink	Gets or sets a link to information associated with a specific exception.
InnerException	Gets the System.Exception instance that caused the error.
Message	Gets a relatively user-friendly message that describes the error.
Source	Gets or sets the name of the application that caused the error.
StackTrace	Displays a listing of items on the call stack that led to the error.
TargetSite	Gets the name of the method that throws the error.

Table 1-1 Properties of the Exception Class

The *Exception* class provides properties that offer additional information about errors that are found in a catch block. These properties are listed and described in Table 1-1. Note that not all of the properties in Table 1-1 apply to every run-time error.

Example 1-1 Setting Up a Try-Catch Block

This example shows how to set up a try-catch block to prevent a crash from a divide-by-zero error. While the code in the try block is trivial, the solution offers a simple demonstration of how to quickly set up run-time error handling.

When the error in this example is encountered in the try block, the catch block is entered and information about the error is obtained with an *Exception* object named *e*. Error details are printed with the help of the *Exception* object's *StackTrace* and *Message* properties.

```
using System;

namespace Starter {
    class Program {
        public static void Main() {
            // 'try' block contains vulnerable code.
            try {
                int x = 0;
                int y = 1;
                int z = y / x; // Invalid operation.
            }
            // 'catch' block handles error and
            // provides information about the error.
            catch (Exception e) {
```

```
                Console.WriteLine("Error:" + e.StackTrace);
                Console.WriteLine(e.Message);
            }
            Console.ReadLine();
        }
    }
}
```

When you run this program, as soon as the application encounters the fatal error, it enters the catch block. Information about the location of the error in the program is displayed with the *StackTrace* property. Detail about the error is printed with the *Message* property.

```
Error:   at Starter.Program.Main() in C:\ConsoleApplication\Program.cs:line 10
Attempted to divide by zero.
```

NOTE

This example can be rewritten without a try-catch block to avoid a program crash. However, try-catch blocks are especially helpful for catching errors and preventing crashes when referencing external resources such as files or database content.

Logging Data

For really large programs, where hundreds or thousands of lines of code must execute first to create conditions where errors may occur, it can sometimes be very difficult to determine where the error occurred. For example, a variable value may fall outside a valid range. Stepping through your code to find this error might not be feasible since potentially thousands of instructions must execute to find the stray value. In a situation like this during development, you might consider writing your output to a log file to track changes in your data values so that you can run your application at normal speed.

C# allows you to quickly output text to a file with the *StreamWriter* class, which is defined in the *System.IO* namespace. There are several ways to create a *StreamWriter* object. The syntax we will use, shown next, defines the object with two parameters. The first parameter is a string that represents the file location. The second parameter is a Boolean value that indicates whether the object overwrites the existing file or appends output to any data in the existing file:

```
StreamWriter streamWriter = new StreamWriter(string fileLocation, bool append);
```

When the *StreamWriter* object is created, if a file does not exist at the location specified, then one is created.

Example 1-2 Logging Data

This example program generates a simple log file in the same directory where the project code files are stored. It then writes error details in the file when an error occurs.

```
using System;    // Namespace of Console and Exception classes.
using System.IO; // Namespace of StreamWriter class.

namespace Starter {
    class Program {
        public static void Main() {
            // 'try' block contains vulnerable code.
            try {
                int x = 0;
                int y = 1;
                int z = y / x; // Invalid operation.
            }
            // 'catch' block handles error and
            // provides information about the error.
            catch (Exception e) {
                LogError(e);
                Console.WriteLine("Error logged to file.");
            }
            Console.ReadLine();
        }

        public static void LogError(Exception e) {
            const string FILE_NAME = "log.txt";
            const bool APPEND = true;
            string filePath = "../../" + FILE_NAME;

            // Create writer and append to file.
            StreamWriter sw = new StreamWriter(filePath, APPEND);

            // Show output.
            sw.WriteLine(e.StackTrace);
            sw.WriteLine(e.Message);
            sw.Close();
        }
    }
}
```

When you run the project, you will notice a text file named log.txt is generated inside the directory where the code exists. Every time you run the program, you will see an additional line of text that reads "Here is some log data." when viewing the log file with a text editor such as Notepad.

Chapter 1 Self Test

The following questions are intended to help reinforce your comprehension of the concepts covered in this chapter. The answers can be found in the accompanying online Appendix B, "Answers to the Self Tests."

1. Fill in the blanks:

- **A.** A __________ is a logical group of instructions.
- **B.** __________ are templates that provide logical groupings of methods and data.
- **C.** __________ are logical groupings of classes.
- **D.** __________ reference stored data.

2. Indicate whether this statement is true or false:

____ It is usually more effective to fix errors at the top of the Error List window before fixing other errors in the list.

3. List shortcuts for the following routines:

- **A.** ____ Stopping the program.
- **B.** ____ Setting or clearing a break point.
- **C.** ____ Stepping into a method.
- **D.** ____ Stepping over a calling instruction.
- **E.** ____ Resuming program execution.

4. Write a program that prints your name in the console window.

5. List at least two techniques you can follow to write more readable code.

6. Describe ten debugging techniques discussed in this chapter and briefly describe an advantage of each one.

7. Select the most definitive statement:
   - A. Commenting is an essential part of any functional program.
   - B. A divide-by-zero error is an example of a syntax error.
   - C. Indentation of code within C# structures will not help you write a better program.
   - D. Try-catch blocks allow programs to gracefully handle errors when referencing external resources such as files or database content.
8. What variables and corresponding values appear in the Locals window while halted at line 11 of Figure 1-8?

Chapter 2

Variables, Constants, Arrays, and Enumerations

Key Skills & Concepts

- Data Types
- Variables
- Constants
- Arrays
- Enumerations

When you are managing data, it is important to consider which type of data structure is the most effective one for the job. C# enables many structures for managing data within the application. This chapter discusses variables, constants, arrays, and enumerations, which are some of the simplest C# structures for managing data.

- **Variables** Variables are uniquely named references to stored data. Variable values can change at run time.
- **Constants** Constants are uniquely named references to values. Constant values cannot change after they are assigned when the constants are declared.
- **Arrays** Arrays store multiple values of the same data type.
- **Enumerations** Enumerations are sets of named constants called *enumerators*. This customizable type offers a reader-friendly reference to a group of constant values.

Data Types

When selecting a data structure, you will always need to consider the format of the data to be stored. This format is referred to as the data type.

C# is a strongly typed language. This means that once a data structure is defined with a given data type, the structure is unable to hold a value of a different type. For example, C# will not let you store alphabetical values in references that are designed for numeric values, nor will C# allow you to directly store a fractional value in a reference that is designed for whole numbers only.

The C# library has many predefined data types. Table 2-1 shows a handful of popular C# data formats.

Type	Definition	Suffix/Numeric Literal	Range/Example
byte	Stores 8 bits.		0 to 255
int	Stores whole numbers.		−2,147,483,648 to 2,147,483,647
long	Stores really large whole numbers.	l or L	−9,223,372,036,854,775,808 to 9,223,372,036,854,775,807
float	Stores large fractional numbers.	f or F	−3.402823e38 to 3.402823e38 Requires `f` suffix for non-whole number.
double	Stores really large fractional numbers.	d or D	−1.79769313486232e308 to 1.79769313486232e308
decimal	Stores a 128-bit value that has a smaller range but greater precision than a float.	m or M	−79228162514264337593543950335 to79228162514264337593543950335 Requires `m` suffix for non-whole number.
bool	Stores true or false and nothing else.		true, false
char	Stores single characters.		'a', '1', '&'
string	Stores groups of characters.		"hi there" , "abc123", "$*1k2"
DateTime	Stores all time units from year to milliseconds as well as options for setting the time zone and calendar. Also see Chapter 7 for additional details on formatting DateTime values.		11/2/2011 7:59:33 AM

Table 2-1 Common Data Types

Numeric Literals

When looking at Table 2-1, note that several numeric data types also have suffixes, which are also called numeric literals. These numeric literals help to distinguish one numeric data type from another. The suffixes may also be capitalized, but usually they are written in lowercase.

To demonstrate how suffixes are used, here are examples of valid and invalid instructions for declaring and initializing float variables:

```
// Height in Meters
float cnTower              = 553;    // Valid
float empireStateBuilding = 443.1;  // Causes error
float burjKhalifa          = 829.8f; // Valid
```

Notice that fractional numeric values require a suffix of `f` to distinguish them as float types. Whole numbers can be assigned to float types because the float type is large enough to store any valid whole number.

On a similar note, here is a comparison of valid and invalid instructions that declare and initialize decimal variables:

```
// Net Worth in US dollars
decimal amancioOrtega = 51700000000;      // Valid
decimal ingvarKamprad = 39900000000.79m; // Valid
decimal leeShauKee    = 22300000000.34   // Causes error
```

Notice that whole numbers can be assigned to decimal variables because the decimal format is large enough to store any whole number. On the other hand, the format of a fraction value must be clarified with the numeric literal `m` before the number can be assigned to a decimal variable.

Variables

As mentioned at the start of this chapter, variables are uniquely named references to stored data. Variable values can be changed at run time.

Variable Types

Two types of variables exist:

- **Value type** Value type variables store simple types that are predefined in the C# library, such as integer, float, and decimal types. Value type variables reference a location in memory that stores the data.
- **Reference type** Variables that reference custom objects made using classes or collections of data are reference type variables. Reference type variables refer to a location in memory that contains the starting address where the data is stored.

Variable Syntax

Variables are declared with a data type followed by a variable name. The variable is initialized when a value is first assigned to it.

Variables can be declared separately and then initialized later:

```
int totalOutlets; // Declare the variable.
totalOutlets = 4; // Initialize the variable.
```

Variables can also be declared and initialized on the same line:

```
int totalOutlets = 4;
```

Variable Names

A variable's name uses a word or word combination to describe the variable's data. Generally, variable names are written in *camelCase,* meaning the first letter of the name is lowercase and then, after the first word, each consecutive word in the variable name begins with an uppercase letter. All other letters in the name are lowercase, and no spaces are permitted in a variable's name. A camelCase variable name with only one word is all lowercase.

NOTE

Most C# developers use camelCase names when the variable's access level is private or protected. With this same standard, if the variable access level is public, the variable name is written in *PascalCase,* meaning each word in the name starts with an uppercase letter while all other letters are lowercase. Usually, though, variables are not created with a public access level. We will discuss private, protected, and public access levels in Chapter 8.

Example 2-1 Data Types and Variables

This example shows how to declare, initialize, and use variables to manage references to data in memory. To create this program, create a new console application (as described in Chapter 1) and replace the existing C# code in Program.cs with the following code:

```
using System;

namespace Starter {
    class Program {
        public static void Main() {
            // Variable declarations and initialization (assignment).
            int venusMoonCount = 0;
            float windSpeed     = 450.0f;
            string venusFact    = "Venus is the only planet "
                                + "that rotates clockwise.";
            // Display the variable values.
            Console.WriteLine(venusFact);
            Console.Write("Total moons = ");
            Console.WriteLine(venusMoonCount);

            Console.Write("Venusian windspeed = ");
```

```
                Console.WriteLine(windSpeed + " miles/hr.");

                Console.ReadLine();
            }
        }
    }
```

When you run this program, the output shows the values that are referenced with each variable:

```
Venus is the only planet that rotates clockwise.
Total moons = 0
Venusian windspeed = 450 miles/hr.
```

Constants

Similar to variables, constants are uniquely named references to values. Constants are different from variables, though, because constant values cannot change after they are initialized. Since constant values are fixed, the constant reference prevents unwanted data tampering throughout the program. In addition, the constant's name provides a reader-friendly reference for the data value.

Constant Syntax

Constants are declared and initialized in a manner similar to variables. However, to ensure the constant values remain constant at run time, a constant declaration is preceded with the keyword *const*:

```
const string FUN_FACT = "Facts about Venus";
```

Constant Names

For consistency in naming standards, most C# developers write constant names entirely with uppercase letters. The constant name is made from a word or group of words. If more than one word is used in the constant name, then the words are usually separated by an underscore.

TIP

Whenever your code uses arbitrary fixed numbers, store these values in a constant. The constant structure will stop unintentional changes to the original number. The constant's descriptive name will also help to narrate the code.

Try This 2-1 Practice with Variable and Constant Structures

Practice working with variable and constant structures. This exercise offers a simple way to observe differences between the two structures.

1. Start with the solution presented in Example 2-1.
2. At the start of the *Main()* method, add a constant declaration that references the title "Fun Facts About Venus," and on the line that follows, add an instruction to display the title:

```
const string TITLE = "* Fun Facts About Venus *";
Console.WriteLine(TITLE);
```

3. At the end of the *Main()* method, just before the *Console.ReadLine()* instruction, add code to reassign the *windSpeed* variable value with the same measure in kilometers per hour, and on the two lines that follow, add instructions to display this new output:

```
const float KM_PER_MILE = 1.609f;
windSpeed = windSpeed * KM_PER_MILE;
Console.Write("Venusian windspeed = ");
Console.WriteLine(windSpeed + " km/hr.");
```

4. Run the new version of your program. Your program should now display the new information with the help of the constant title and *windSpeed* variable:

```
* Fun Facts About Venus *
Venus is the only planet that rotates clockwise.
Total moons = 0
Venusian windspeed = 450 miles/hr.
Venusian windspeed = 724.05 km/hr.
```

5. Now observe what happens if you change the *windSpeed* declaration to be constant. To make this change, replace the instruction that declares and initializes the *windSpeed* variable with this instruction:

```
const float windSpeed    = 450.0f;
```

Notice after the change that an error appears at the line of the program when a new value is assigned to *windSpeed*. The error appears at run time because constant structure values cannot be modified after their declaration.

Explicit Variable Conversion (Casting)

When working with numeric values, if you need to assign a value from a variable with a type that has more storage space into a variable type with a similar format but less storage, you must perform a *cast*. When assigning a variable to the new type, the original variable is preceded by the new type in parentheses. Truncation of data may occur during the cast. For example, when casting –386.8f from a float format to an integer, the digits on the right side of the decimal are lost:

```
float distance         = -386.8f;
int   distanceInMiles  = (int)distance; // Stores -386
```

Implicit Variable Conversion

When working with similar numeric data types, if you assign a value to a variable with a data type that has more storage space, then an implicit conversion occurs. The number may be altered slightly when it is assigned into the larger format. The next two instructions highlight a slight alteration when a float value is assigned to a double variable:

```
float  distance        = -67.7f;
double distanceInMiles = distance;       // Converts to -67.6999969482422
```

Arrays

The variable structure we have discussed so far only references one data value. Sometimes, though, you will need more complex structures to manage larger data sets. One of the more basic structures for storing and accessing multiple data values is the array. Arrays store multiple values of the same data type.

Array Syntax

Each value within the array is stored inside an *element* of the array. Elements of the array are referenced sequentially with an *index*. Arrays usually have only one dimension, but they can have more dimensions if needed. For single-dimensional arrays, each element is referenced with a unique index value. By default, the first element of a single-dimensional array has a numeric index of 0. All elements that follow are referenced with an incremented index. This instruction declares an array of strings and stores eight string values in it:

```
string[] island = new string[] {"Hawaii", "Maui", "Oahu", "Kauai", "Molokai",
                                "Lanai", "Niihau", "Kahoolawe"};
```

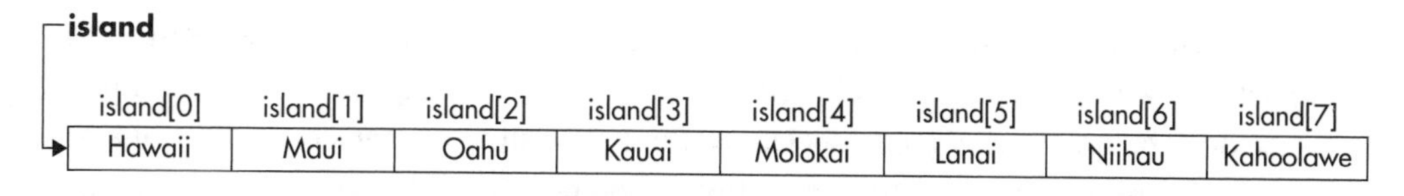

Figure 2-1 Array address, indexes, and elements

Figure 2-1 shows how the array references the address of the first element value in memory. Every element value in the array is referenced with an index.

When declaring arrays, you must define the type and name like any other variable. Then, to initialize the array, an assignment is required with the *new* keyword followed by the data type. This assignment initializes the array with a fixed amount of space to store a predetermined number of elements. Three common ways to declare arrays are to state

- Type, name, and array size together
- Type and name first and then size allocation later
- Type, name, and size inferred while initializing element values when the array is declared

Declaring Array Type, Name, and Size Together

The following code example shows a declaration for an array of string objects with enough space for three elements, after which each element of the array is assigned a string value separately:

```
string[] name = new string[3];
name[0] = "Hawaii"; // first element referenced at index '0'
name[1] = "Maui";   // second element referenced at index '1'
name[2] = "Oahu";   // third element referenced at index '2'
```

Declaring Array Type and Name First and Size Allocation Later

Sometimes you will need to declare an array before you can determine the total elements to be stored. Once your program determines the required size, you can then allocate the space. With this syntax in mind, an array of island names could first be declared as an array of string objects, and then, later, space can be allocated for three elements:

```
string[] name;
   name = new string[3];
name[0] = "Hawaii"; // first element referenced at index '0'
name[1] = "Maui";   // second element referenced at index '1'
name[2] = "Oahu";   // third element referenced at index '2'
```

Declaring Array Type, Name, and Size While Initializing Element Values

Sometimes you will see array declarations where values are assigned on the same line as the declaration. If you were to declare and initialize an array that stores all the main islands of Hawaii in one line, the instruction would be

```
string[] island = new string[] { "Hawaii", "Maui", "Oahu", "Kauai",
                                 "Molokai", "Lanai", "Niihau", "Kahoolawe"};
```

Example 2-2 Array Introduction

Here is a full example that demonstrates the three common ways to declare single-dimensional arrays:

```
using System;

namespace Starter {
    class Program {
        public static void Main() {
            const int NUM_ISLANDS = 3;
            const int HAWAII = 0; const int MAUI = 1; const int OAHU = 2;

            // Part A:  Assigning size in the declaration.
            string[] name = new string[NUM_ISLANDS];
            name[HAWAII]  = "Hawaii"; // 1st element at index '0'
            name[MAUI]    = "Maui";   // 2nd element at index '1'
            name[OAHU]    = "Oahu";   // 3rd element at index '2'

            // Part B:  Assigning size later in the program.
            int[] population;
            population = new int[NUM_ISLANDS];
            population[HAWAII]  = 187200;
            population[MAUI]    = 145000;
            population[OAHU]    = 955000;

            // Part C:  Initializing the array and size in the declaration.
            float[] squareMiles = new float[] { 4028.0f, 727.2f, 596.7f };

            int island = MAUI;
            Console.WriteLine("* Statistics for " + name[island] + " *");
            Console.WriteLine("Population: " + population[island]);
            Console.WriteLine("Square miles: " + squareMiles[island]);

            Console.ReadLine();
        }
    }
}
```

Since the arrays in this example are designed to store statistical data about each island in a predetermined sequence, generating statistical information for each island is easy. The output for Maui is taken from each array when running this example:

```
* Statistics for Maui *
Population: 145000
Square miles: 727.2
```

Try This 2-2 Practice with Arrays

This section gives you some practice working with arrays. In this exercise you will work with the array declaration, sizing, initialization, and index reference.

1. Create a console application and replace the auto-generated code in the Program.cs file with this code:

```
using System;

namespace Starter {
    class Program {
        public static void Main() {
            string[] teams = new string[2];
            teams[0] = "Hawaii Hammerheads";
            teams[1] = "Hawaiian Islanders";
            Console.WriteLine("The first team is " + teams[0]);
            Console.WriteLine("The second team is " + teams[1]);
            Console.ReadLine();
        }
    }
}
```

2. Try adding the team Honolulu Hurricanes to the array. You will need to increase the array size to create room for the new team.
3. Add an instruction to display the name of the third team.
4. Run the new version of this program. The final output should appear as:

```
The first team is Hawaii Hammerheads
The second team is Hawaiian Islanders
The second team is Honolulu Hurricanes
```

Array Length

When you use arrays, you will often need to know how many elements each array stores. Fortunately, each array instance exposes a *Length* property to obtain the number of elements in the array.

Example 2-3 Array Length

This code example shows how to use the *Length* property to retrieve the array size for an array that contains names of the main islands of the Hawaiian Islands:

```
using System;

namespace Starter {
    class Program {
        public static void Main() {
            string[] island = new string[] { "Hawaii", "Maui", "Oahu",
                    "Kauai", "Molokai", "Lanai", "Niihau", "Kahoolawe" };
            Console.Write("The total main Islands of Hawaii is ");
            Console.WriteLine(island.Length);
            Console.ReadLine();
        }
    }
}
```

Once you build and run this program, the number of items in the array is displayed:

```
The total main Islands of Hawaii is 8
```

Sorting Arrays

Single-dimensional arrays can be sorted with the *Sort()* method:

```
void Sort(arrayType[] array);
```

Example 2-4 Sorting Arrays

Here is an example that sorts Hawaiian surfing destinations in alphabetical sequence:

```
using System;

namespace Starter {
    class Program {
```

```
        public static void Main() {
            string[] surfDestinations = new string[]
            { "Ehukai Beach Park", "Laniakea", "Backyards",
              "Hookipa", "Honolua"};
            Array.Sort(surfDestinations);
            Console.Write(
            "Top 5 Hawaiian surf destinations in alphabetical order:  ");
            Console.WriteLine(surfDestinations[0] + ", "
                            + surfDestinations[1] + ", "
                            + surfDestinations[2] + ", "
                            + surfDestinations[3] + ", "
                            + surfDestinations[4] + ".");
            Console.ReadLine();
        }
    }
}
```

The output shows the destinations in alphabetical order:

```
Top 5 Hawaiian surf destinations in alphabetical order:  Backyards, Ehukai Beach
 Park, Honolua, Hookipa, Laniakea.
```

Multidimensional Arrays

For flexibility, you can create a hierarchy of arrays. A hierarchy of arrays is a multidimensional array. Figure 2-2 shows a multidimensional array that stores low and high temperature data for a five-day weather forecast. The *forecast* array references the starting address for

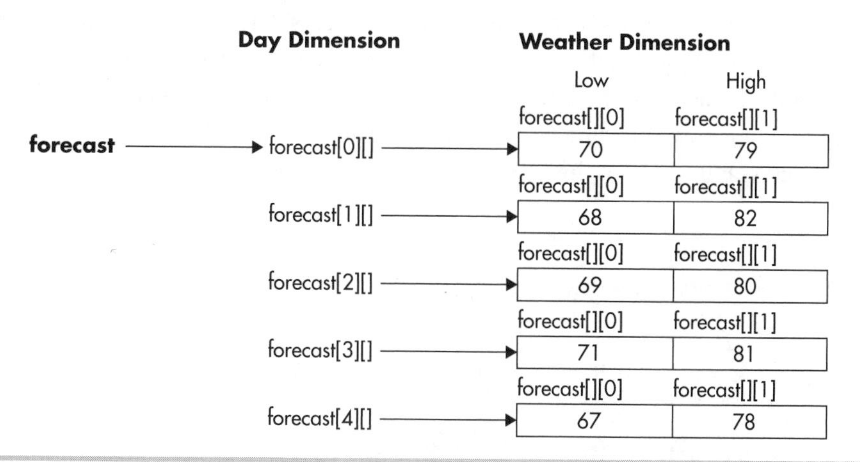

Figure 2-2 Multidimensional array

the day elements. Each day element references the starting address of a weather array that contains daily low and high temperature values.

Each array in the hierarchy is a dimension. Elements of each dimension are referenced with a numeric index. The first element of each dimension is referenced with an index of zero. Consecutive indexes of elements that follow are incremented by one, in sequential order.

Multidimensional Array Syntax

When declaring a multidimensional array, you must also declare the type and name of the array. In the square brackets following the type declaration, use a comma to separate the dimensions. All dimensions are fixed in size.

```
int[,] forecast    = new int[NUM_DAYS, NUM_WEATHER_STATS];
```

To assign values to elements in a multidimensional array, you must identify the correct index for each dimension:

```
forecast[WED, LOW]  = 69;
forecast[WED, HIGH] = 80;
```

The index of each dimension must also be used to reference the desired data:

```
Console.WriteLine("Wednesday's forecast is for a low temperature of "
                + forecast[WED, LOW] + " and a high temperature of "
                + forecast[WED, HIGH] + ".");
```

Example 2-5 Multidimensional Arrays

This example shows a two-dimensional array that stores daily low and high temperatures for a five-day forecast. The first dimension of the array references the day of the week. The second dimension of the array references the high and low temperatures of the day. When assigning or referencing an element of the array, both indexes for the day and temperature reading are required:

```
using System;

namespace ConsoleApplication1 {
    class Program {
        static void Main() {
            const int MON = 0, TUE = 1, WED = 2, THU = 3, FRI = 4;    // Day.
            const int LOW = 0, HIGH = 1;                            // Temperature.

            const int NUM_DAYS = 5, NUM_WEATHER_STATS = 2;     // Dimension sizes.

            // Declare and initialize array.
```

```
            int[,] forecast     = new int[NUM_DAYS, NUM_WEATHER_STATS];

            // Assign values to each element in array.
            forecast[MON, LOW] = 70; forecast[MON, HIGH] = 79;
            forecast[TUE, LOW] = 68; forecast[TUE, HIGH] = 82;
            forecast[WED, LOW] = 69; forecast[WED, HIGH] = 80;
            forecast[THU, LOW] = 71; forecast[THU, HIGH] = 81;
            forecast[FRI, LOW] = 67; forecast[FRI, HIGH] = 78;

            // Show Wednesday's forecast.
            Console.WriteLine("Wednesday's forecast is for a low temperature of "
                        + forecast[WED, LOW] + " and a high temperature of "
                        + forecast[WED, HIGH] + ".");

            Console.ReadLine();
        }
    }
}
```

The output displays the low and high temperatures for Wednesday:

```
Wednesday's forecast is for a low temperature of 69 and a high temperature of 80.
```

Multidimensional Array Length

When working with multidimensional arrays, you will sometimes want to use the *GetLength()* method to dynamically obtain the size of a dimension:

```
int GetLength(int dimension);
```

When considering Example 2-5, *GetLength()* could be used to determine the size of the day dimension:

```
const int DAY_DIMENSION     = 0;
Console.WriteLine(forecast.GetLength(DAY_DIMENSION));      // Outputs 5.
```

Using the same example, *GetLength()* could also determine the size of the temperature dimension:

```
const int WEATHER_DIMENSION = 1;
Console.WriteLine(forecast.GetLength(WEATHER_DIMENSION));  // Outputs 2.
```

Enumerations

To finish our coverage of basic C# data structures, let's discuss enumeration types. An enumeration type defines a list of related constant values. Enumerations offer reader-friendly code with protection against unwanted changes to values in the list.

Enumeration Syntax

Enumeration types are defined using the *enum* keyword. The enumeration is followed by a list of enumerators contained within curly braces. By default, enumerators are associated with integer values that represent their position in the list, but enumerators can reference values of any integer-based data type. Zero is the default starting value of an enumerated list when no value is assigned. Unless specified, the enumerator value is incremented by one at each next position in the list. In this case, the enumerator named *Jupiter* takes on a default value of 0:

```
enum PlanetSize {
    Jupiter, Saturn, Uranus, Neptune, Earth, Venus, Mars, Mercury, Pluto
};
```

Enumerator values can be assigned manually too. Here the diameter in miles is assigned to each enumerator:

```
enum PlanetDiameter {
    // Diameter in miles.
    Jupiter=88800, Saturn=74900, Uranus=31763, Neptune=34500,
    Earth=7926, Venus=7500, Mars=4200, Mercury=3030, Pluto=1480
};
```

When you need to obtain a value associated with the enumerated item, a cast is required:

```
int jupiterSize = (int)PlanetDiameter.Jupiter;
```

Enumeration Naming

Enumeration names are most commonly written using PascalCase, meaning each word in the name starts with an uppercase letter while all other letters are lowercase. That is the convention used for this book.

Enumeration Methods

You can obtain the name of an enumerator with a cast using the enumeration type and the value of the enumerator. With the enumeration declaration

```
enum {
    Jupiter, Saturn, Uranus, Neptune, Earth, Venus, Mars, Mercury, Pluto
};
```

the enumerator name can be obtained using the enumerator's value:

```
Planet enumerator = (Planet)4;
string name = enumerator.ToString(); // Assigns 'Earth'.
```

Determining the Enumerator Count

To dynamically determine the total enumerators in an enumeration, you can first convert the enumerator list into an array. Then you can use the *Length* property of the array to get the count.

All enumerator names can be retrieved into a string array with the *GetNames()* method of the *Enum* class. The *GetNames()* method requires the enumeration type as a parameter. To obtain this custom enumeration type, you can use a *typeof* expression with the name of the enumeration as the parameter. The *typeof* expression result can then serve as the data type for the *GetNames()* method parameter:

```
string[] planetNames = Enum.GetNames(typeof(Planet));
```

Once the enumerator names are stored in a string array, you can obtain their count by checking the *Length* property of the array:

```
int totalPlanet = planetNames.Length;
```

Example 2-6 Enumerations

This short example demonstrates how to create an enumeration that orders planets by their diameter size in descending order:

```
using System;
namespace Starter {
    class Program {
        const int FIRST = 1;
        // Define Planet enumeration with enumerators in descending order.
        enum Planet {
            Jupiter = FIRST, Saturn, Uranus,
            Neptune, Earth, Venus, Mars, Mercury, Pluto
        };

        public static void Main() {
            // Store all planet names in an array and output the length.
            string[] planetNames = Enum.GetNames(typeof(Planet));
Console.WriteLine("Total planets: "     + planetNames.Length);
            // Display size ranking for Earth.
```

```
                Console.WriteLine("Earth size rank = "  + (int)Planet.Earth);

                // Show planet name associated with the top size ranking.
                Planet planetName = (Planet)FIRST;
                Console.WriteLine("The largest planet is "
                                + planetName.ToString() + ".");
                Console.ReadLine();
            }
        }
}
```

The output generated when running this program is

```
Total planets: 9
Earth size rank = 5
The largest planet is Jupiter.
```

Given all of the setup required to create and reference an enumeration, their usefulness may not initially be apparent when learning to code. As the complexity of your code grows, though, the benefit of having a list of named constants will help to strengthen your code while also making it reader friendly.

Example 2-7 Enumerations with Arrays

This example shows how to implement the solution for Example 2-2 with an enumeration instead of separately declared constants. In this example, the declaration and use of an array is demonstrated as before. This time, though, the enumerators are used as indexes instead of constants to reference the array elements.

```
using System;

namespace Starter {
    class Program {
        enum Islands { Hawaii, Maui, Oahu } // Define enumeration.
        public static void Main() {
            // Store Island names in array and get enumerator count.
            string[] islandNames = Enum.GetNames(typeof(Islands));
            int      islandCount = islandNames.Length;

            // Part A:  Assigning array size in the declaration.
            string[] name = new string[islandCount];
            name[(int)Islands.Hawaii]  = "Hawaii";
            name[(int)Islands.Maui]    = "Maui";
            name[(int)Islands.Oahu]    = "Oahu";
```

```
            // Part B:  Assigning array size later in the program.
            int[] population;
            population = new int[islandCount];
            population[(int)Islands.Hawaii] = 187200;
            population[(int)Islands.Maui]   = 145000;
            population[(int)Islands.Oahu]   = 955000;

            // Part C:  Initializing the array and size in the declaration.
            float[] squareMiles = new float[] { 4028.0f, 727.2f, 596.7f };

            int island = (int)Islands.Maui;
            Console.WriteLine("* Statistics for " + name[island] + " *");
            Console.WriteLine("Population: " + population[island]);
            Console.WriteLine("Square miles: " + squareMiles[island]);

            Console.ReadLine();
        }
    }
}
```

The output obtained uses the Maui enumerator to reference the correct element in each array:

```
* Statistics for Maui *
Population: 145000
Square miles: 727.2
```

Chapter 2 Self Test

The following questions are intended to help reinforce your comprehension of the concepts covered in this chapter. The answers can be found in the accompanying online Appendix B, "Answers to the Self Tests."

1. What is the difference between declaring a variable and initializing a variable?
2. Why does this instruction cause an error?

   ```
   float distance = 1047.3;
   ```

   How can you fix it?
3. Venus's year lasts 224.7 Earth days, because it takes Venus 224.7 days to revolve around the Sun. Write a short program that stores this total number of days in a double variable. Output the variable value with a description about the number in the console window.
4. Modify the code from Example 2-2 to display the population and square mileage of Oahu.

5. Declare a new array in the code for Example 2-2 to store the location of the highest elevation on each of the Hawaiian Islands. Hawaii's highest point is at the Mauna Kea Volcano. Maui's highest elevation is at the East Maui Volcano. Oahu's highest point is in the Waianae Mountains. Show data from the new array in your output for one of the islands.
6. Modify the code for Example 2-5 to show the low and high temperature for Thursday.
7. Write a short program that declares an enumeration for college semesters, which include fall, winter, and spring terms. Dynamically obtain the value associated with the spring term enumerator and display it. Then, use this value to obtain and display the associated enumerator name. Next, dynamically retrieve all enumerator names in an array and then display each name by referencing the array. Design your program so it provides the following output:

```
Spring value: 2
The enumerator name associated with 'springValue' = Spring
Enumerators include: Fall, Winter, Spring
```

8. Modify the multidimensional array in Example 2-5 to include a chance of rain in the second dimension. Percentages to store over five days, starting with Monday, include 30, 75, 98, 80, 34. After making the necessary adjustments, print out the weather forecast for Friday. Your output should resemble the following:

```
Friday's forecast is for a low temperature of 67 and a high temperature of 78.
The chance of rain is 34%.
```

Chapter 3

Numeric Operators and Routines

Key Skills & Concepts

- Basic Calculations
- Increment Operator
- Decrement Operator
- Randomization

This brief chapter discusses simple but essential C# math operators and methods. Coverage of numeric operators and math methods may seem trivial, but understanding these topics is essential for implementing programming logic. While we are on the topic of operations with numbers, this chapter also provides a modest introduction to randomizing numbers.

Basic Calculations

Let's first examine operators and methods that allow you to write routines that you would find in most basic calculators.

Addition

Addition uses the + operator. As you would expect, addition is performed by placing both operands at opposite sides of the + operator. Also, the compound operator, +=, reassigns a variable on the left with its starting value plus the right operand value.

```
const int A = 9;   const int B = 3;
int sum   = A + B;               // sum =  9 + 3 = 12
    sum += B;                    // sum = 12 + 3 = 15
```

Subtraction

Subtraction requires the – operator. Obviously, in an equation you can subtract an operand on the right of the – operator from the operand on the left. The minus assignment operator combination, –=, reassigns a variable with its starting value minus the right operand.

```
const int A = 9;   const int B = 3;
int difference  = A - B;       // difference = 9 - 3 = 6
    difference -= B;           // difference = 6 - 3 = 3
```

Multiplication

The multiplication operator is represented with *. You can calculate a product of two numbers by placing each number at opposite sides of the * operator. The multiplication assignment operator, *=, reassigns a variable on the left with its original value multiplied by the right operand.

```
const int A = 9;   const int B = 3;
int product  = A * B;          // product =  9 x 3 = 27
    product *= B;              // product = 27 x 3 = 81
```

Division

The division operator is /. Division is performed by placing the numerator on the left of / and the denominator on the right. The /= combination reassigns a variable at the left with its starting value divided by the right operand.

```
const int A = 9;   const int B = 3;
int quotient  = A / B;         // quotient = 9 ÷ 3 = 3
    quotient /= B;             // quotient = 3 ÷ 3 = 1
```

Remainder

The modulus operator, %, is used to calculate the remainder during division. It is also possible to implement a self-assignment using a compound combination of %=.

```
const int A = 9;   const int B = 7;
int remainder = A % B;         // remainder of 9 ÷ 7 = 2

float c = 9.0f;
c %=  B;                       // remainder of 9.0 ÷ 7 = 2.0
```

Exponentiation

The *System* namespace of the .NET Framework provides a *Math* class that offers methods for more advanced calculations. To automate exponentiation, the *Math* class offers a *Pow()* method that receives the base value and exponent as parameters. The *Pow()* method returns the result as a double type. This example shows how *Pow()* raises 3 to the power of 2:

```
double result = Math.Pow(3, 2); // 3² = 9
```

Square Root

The *Math* class provides the *Sqrt()* method to calculate square roots:

```
double result = Math.Sqrt(9);    // √9 = 3
```

Increment Operator

The increment operator, ++, adds 1 to a numeric type variable. Placement of this operator before or after a variable determines when the variable value is updated. Understanding how this operator works is essential to becoming a skilled programmer because it is a fundamental feature of most mainstream programming languages. The increment operator's importance will be apparent when we discuss *for* loops in Chapter 5.

Pre-Increment Expressions

Placing the ++ operator before a numeric variable creates a pre-increment expression. A pre-increment expression immediately adds 1 to the variable value when the instruction is executed:

```
int number = 5;
Console.WriteLine(++number); // Displays 6
```

Post-Increment Expressions

Placing the ++ operator after a numeric variable creates a post-increment expression. A post-increment expression adds 1 to the variable on the line after this instruction is executed:

```
int number = 5;
Console.WriteLine(number++); // Displays 5
Console.WriteLine(number);   // Displays 6
```

Try This 3-1 Operator Practice

This exercise offers a chance to observe the difference between the operators +, +=, and ++ (in both pre-increment and post-increment expressions).

1. In a brand new console application, declare an integer variable and initialize it with the value of 7.
2. Using a combination of +, +=, and ++ pre-increment and post-increment operators, write four instructions that increment the variable value by 1. Each instruction must increment the variable in a manner that is unique when compared to all other instructions in the program.

3. Design your program so the output generated looks like the following:

```
Original value: 7
Incremented value: 8
Incremented value: 9
Value during post-increment execution: 9
Incremented value: 10
Incremented value: 11
```

Decrement Operator

The decrement operator, `--`, reduces a variable value by 1. Similar to the increment operator, placement of the decrement operator before or after the variable determines when the variable is actually decremented.

Pre-Decrement Expressions

When the decrement operator is placed before a numeric variable, the value is reduced by 1 immediately:

```
int number = 5;
Console.WriteLine(--number); // Displays 4
```

Post-Decrement Expressions

When the decrement operator is placed after a numeric variable, the value is decremented on the line after the post-decrement instruction:

```
int number = 5;
Console.WriteLine(number--); // Displays 5
Console.WriteLine(number);   // Displays 4
```

TIP

When reassigning variable values while adding, subtracting, multiplying, or dividing, always use compound assignment, pre-/post-increment expressions, or pre-/post-decrement expressions. It easier to write +=, -=, *=, /=, ++, or -- compared to writing the longhand form. Expressions using compound shorthand assignments are more efficient because the variable being reassigned needs to be evaluated only once. Any experienced programmer who reads your code and sees a long expression like x = x + 1 may interpret this as a sign of inexperience.

Randomization

You may at times need to generate random numbers. Random number generation is useful and necessary for implementing security routines, randomizing video game play, and creating unique identifiers for objects in your application. One of the easiest ways to perform randomization is with the *Random* class from the *System* namespace.

The Default Random Constructor

The default *Random* constructor generates a number that is based on the system clock. A random variable is created with a new instance of the *Random* class.

CAUTION

Since the random variable is instantiated with the system clock, creating multiple *Random* objects in quick succession can generate repeating random number sequences that are not random. It is acceptable, however, to use the default *Random* constructor to generate *Random* objects if one *Random* object instance is used to create many random numbers over time.

Generating Random Integer Numbers

Three methods exist in the *Random* class to generate random integers. The *Next()* method with no parameters generates an integer that is greater than or equal to 0 and less than 2,147,483,647:

```
Random rnd    = new Random();
int    random = rnd.Next();
```

The *Next()* method with an integer parameter generates an integer between 0 and the exclusive upper bound that is specified by the parameter. Since the upper bound is exclusive, in the following case, numbers generated may include 0 to 999999998:

```
Random rnd    = new Random();
const int MAX = 999999999;
int    random = rnd.Next(MAX);
```

The *Next()* method with two parameters generates an integer between an inclusive minimum and an exclusive upper bound. For the following case, numbers that might be generated with a minimum of 100,000,000 and an upper bound of 999,999,999 could include any number from 100,000,000 to 999,999,998:

```
Random rnd     = new Random();
const int MIN = 100000000;
const int MAX = 999999999;
int     random = rnd.Next(MIN,MAX);
```

Generating Random Double Numbers

The *NextDouble()* method of the *Random* class generates a double-precision floating point number greater than or equal to 0.0 and less than 1.0:

```
Random rnd     = new Random();
double random = rnd.NextDouble();
```

Example 3-1 Default Random Generation

This example shows how a default *Random* object may be declared to generate many random values. Each time that you run the program, a random number is generated with a different method to restrict the number type and range:

```
using System;

namespace ConsoleApplication1 {
    class Program {
        static Random rnd = new Random();

        static void Main() {
            const int MIN = 40; const int MAX = 50;

            Console.WriteLine("0   <= num < 2,147,483,647: " + rnd.Next());
            Console.WriteLine("0   <= num < 50:            " + rnd.Next(MAX));
            Console.WriteLine("40  <= num < 50:            " + rnd.Next(MIN,MAX));
            Console.WriteLine("0.0 <= num <  1.0:          " + rnd.NextDouble());
            Console.ReadLine();
        }
    }
}
```

The output from running this program will be similar to the following text:

```
0   <= num < 2,147,483,647: 1721183231
0   <= num < 50:            10
40  <= num < 50:            46
0.0 <= num <  1.0:          0.942834792166406
```

Example 3-2 Improper Random Number Generation

As mentioned earlier, creating multiple instances of a *Random* object to generate random numbers in quick succession leads to repeating number sequences. Here is a poorly written program that fails to create truly random numbers:

```
using System;

namespace ConsoleApplication1 {
    class Program {
        static void Main() {
            Random randomA = new Random();      // New Random object.
            Console.WriteLine(randomA.Next());

            Random randomB = new Random();      // New Random object.
            Console.WriteLine(randomB.Next());

            Random randomC = new Random();      // New Random object.
            Console.WriteLine(randomC.Next());

            Console.ReadLine();
        }
    }
}
```

When you run the program, you may see some unique numbers, but you will likely see repeated numbers:

```
1056405274
1056405274
1056405274
```

The Seeded Random Constructor

Another technique that is used for avoiding repeating number sequences when generating random numbers involves passing a random integer value, called a seed, to the *Random* class constructor. The seed is used to calculate the starting point for the number sequence:

```
static Random random = new Random(int seedValue);
```

Generating a Random Seed

When the seed is always the same, the sequence is always repeated. If the seed is random, then the sequence will be unpredictable.

Try This 3-2 Reusing a Seed Value

This exercise shows how improperly seeded *Random* objects will not generate random numbers.

1. Write a program that creates two *Random* objects with a seed value of 5.
2. Generate random numbers with each object using the *NextDouble()* method.
3. Notice that both numbers that are generated are identical.

How can you create a random seed when you are trying to create a random number? Microsoft suggests generating a random array of bytes with the help of the *RNGCryptoServiceProvider* class from the *System.Security.Cryptography* namespace. The byte array can then be converted to a random string, which in turn can be converted to an integer, which may then be used as the seed.

To generate a random array of bytes, you first need to create a byte array:

```
// Create byte array.
const int TOTAL_BYTES                =   4;
byte[]    byteArray                  = new byte[TOTAL_BYTES];
```

Then, after referencing the *System.Security.Cryptography* namespace, an instance of the *RNGCryptoServiceProvider* class is required:

```
// Generate Cryptography class object.
RNGCryptoServiceProvider crypto = new RNGCryptoServiceProvider();
```

Now the *GetBytes()* method of the *RNGCryptoServiceProvider* class can generate and store the random byte array:

```
crypto.GetBytes(byteArray);
```

The *ToInt32()* method of the *BitConverter* class from the *System* namespace can convert the random byte array to the integer seed value. The first parameter of the *ToInt32()* method receives the byte array, and the second parameter is the starting index of the byte array:

```
int seed = BitConverter.ToInt32(byteArray, 0);
```

Example 3-3 Generating a Random Number with a Random Seed

This example shows all of the steps needed to create a random seed, which can then be used to generate a *Random* object:

```
using System;
using System.Security.Cryptography;

namespace ConsoleApplication1 {
    class Program {
        static void Main() {
            // Create byte array.
            const int TOTAL_BYTES           =   4;
            byte[]    byteArray             = new byte[TOTAL_BYTES];

            // Generate Cryptography class object.
            RNGCryptoServiceProvider crypto = new RNGCryptoServiceProvider();

            // Generate a random byte array and store it.
            crypto.GetBytes(byteArray);

            // Convert the byte array to an integer.
            int seed = BitConverter.ToInt32(byteArray, 0);

            // Display the seed.
            Console.WriteLine("Seed value: " + seed);

            // Generate a random object with the random seed.
            Random random          = new Random(seed);

            // Generate a random number between 1 and 99.
            const int MIN          =   1;
            const int MAX          = 100;
            int randomInteger      = random.Next(MIN, MAX);
            Console.WriteLine("Random integer between 1 and 99: "
                             + randomInteger);
            Console.ReadLine();
        }
    }
}
```

The output shows the random seed value and the random integer between 1 and 99:

```
Seed value: 643640352
Random integer between 1 and 99: 84
```

Chapter 3 Self Test

The following questions are intended to help reinforce your comprehension of the concepts covered in this chapter. The answers can be found in the accompanying online Appendix B, "Answers to the Self Tests."

1. In the equation $V_{final} = V_{initial} + a * t$
   - V = velocity (meters per second)
   - a = acceleration (meters per second squared)
   - t = time taken (seconds)

   Using this equation, write a program to calculate the velocity of an object after 20 seconds when V_{inital} = 10 m/s and acceleration has remained constant at 0.5 m/s^2.
2. Examine this code:

   ```
   int x = 55;    x *= 2;    x -= 70;    x %= 13;
   Console.WriteLine(++x);
   ```

   Without the help of a computer, determine the number that is written to the window.
3. Examine this code:

   ```
   int x = 55;    ++x;    x -= 15;    x--;     x += 5;    x++;
   Console.WriteLine(x--);
   ```

   Without the help of a computer, determine the number that is written to the window.
4. What two techniques are recommended for generating random numbers when multiple random numbers are required?
5. Create a new program that generates two random numbers with *Random* objects that are created using random seeds that are generated with the *RNGCryptoServiceProvider* class. Each number must be greater than or equal to 1 and less than or equal to 21. Display the results.

Chapter 4

Methods and Scope

Key Skills & Concepts

- Method Syntax
- Method Overloads
- Passing Arguments by Value and by Reference
- Scope

As your programs increase in size, you will need to organize your instructions into routines called methods. Methods group instructions that are related by their function. Methods also enable code reuse and prevent code duplication since each method can be executed as many times as needed. Most often, developers will declare method names that are verbs or word combinations starting with a verb to describe the method's purpose. All instructions within the method must serve the single purpose described by this name. With well-named methods, it is easy to glance at the code and understand what it does. In the end, the many benefits of methods make your code reader friendly and less prone to errors.

Method Syntax

To examine method syntax, let's look at the structures that define a method (refer to Figure 4-1):

- **Header** The method header, also known as a method signature, is the first line of a method. It contains, at a minimum, the name of the method, a return type, and a parameter list.

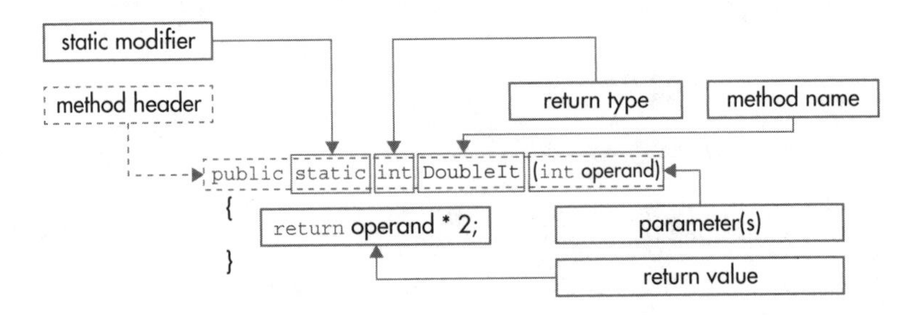

Figure 4-1 Method structures

- **Name** Methods are named with a verb or word combination that describes its function. Most C# developers start all method names with an uppercase letter and then use an uppercase letter to start each subsequent word, if any, in the name. This common PascalCase naming style for methods is also used in this book.
- **Return value** Methods often perform a routine that returns data to the line of code that called the method. This data value is the return value. The keyword *return* followed by a reference to the data terminates the method's execution and passes the data back to the calling instruction.
- **Return type** A method's return type declares the data type of the value returned by the method to the calling instruction.
- **Void type** If a method does not return data to the calling instruction, the method return type is assigned the *void* type.
- **Parameters** Parameters are variables that are declared inside the method header. When one or more method parameters exist, the calling instruction must either pass variable values or pass references to the method in the same sequence as their declaration in the method header. Values that are passed to parameter declarations in the header are called arguments.
- **Static modifier** So far, all methods discussed in this book have used a static modifier, as shown in Figure 4-1. Static methods can only call other static methods without an object reference. We will start omitting the static modifier in Chapter 8 when we begin creating customized objects and types. Until then, we need to continue using the static modifier for all methods we create.

NOTE

It is normal if you are new to programming and you are still uncertain about how and when you need to use a static modifier when declaring your methods. Details about how and when to use static references are explained in Chapter 8.

Calling a Method

To execute a method's instructions, you must call the method. To call a method, you must type the method name and include the required arguments within parentheses. Here is a method called *CalculateCircumference()* that expects a float parameter:

```
// Receive diameter parameter and return circumference.
static float CalculateCircumference(float diameter) {
    const float PI = 3.14159265358979f;
    return diameter * PI;
}
```

Next is an example of a statement that calls *CalculateCircumference()* to calculate the circumference of a circle that has a diameter of 6.0 units. The diameter is included as an argument in the call statement.

```
const float DIAMETER = 6.0f;
float circumference  = CalculateCircumference(DIAMETER);
```

Indentation

All of a method's instructions are indented and aligned within the opening and closing curly braces that follow the method header. Usually, the opening curly brace is placed on a new line:

```
static float ConvertToLiters(float quarts)
{
    const float LITERS_PER_QT = 0.94635f;
    return quarts * LITERS_PER_QT;
}
```

Sometimes developers will place the starting curly brace for a method on the same line as the method header. Developers might use this style to see more code on one page:

```
static float ConvertToKg(float pounds) {
    const float KG_PER_LB = 0.454f;
    return pounds * KG_PER_LB;
}
```

Example 4-1 Creating and Implementing Methods

This example demonstrates how to create and call two methods. *ConvertToKM()* receives a float parameter named *miles* and returns the equivalent total kilometers as a float value. Since *ConvertToKM()* returns a float value, the declared return type of this method is also float. *ShowDistance()* receives both the total miles and the total kilometers as parameters and displays these values in a reader-friendly format. *ShowDistance()* does not return any value to the calling instruction, so this method's return type is void.

```
using System;

namespace ConsoleApplication1 {
    class Program {
        // Console applications always start in the Main() method.
        static void Main() {
            const float MILEAGE = 98.0f;
            float kilometers    = ConvertToKM(MILEAGE); // Calling instruction.
```

```
            ShowDistance(MILEAGE, kilometers);          // Calling instruction.
            Console.ReadLine();
        }

        // Display the mile to km conversion in a reader friendly format.
        static float ConvertToKM(float miles) {
            const float KM_PER_MILE = 1.60934f;
            return miles * KM_PER_MILE;                 // Returns a float.
        }

        // Convert miles to km and show the result.
        static void (float miles, float km) {
            Console.WriteLine(miles + " miles = "
                            + km + " km.");
        }
    }
}
```

When running the program, the total kilometers is calculated using the mileage provided. The output printed from the void *ShowDistance()* method presents a reader-friendly comparison of these distance measures:

```
98 miles = 157.7153 km.
```

Try This 4-1 Method Implementation Practice

This exercise offers practice for creating your own methods with proper use of parameters and return types.

1. Create a new console application project, as described in Chapter 1.
2. Replace all of the code inside of Program.cs with the following:

```
using System;

namespace ConsoleApplication1 {
    class Program {
        static void Main() {
            const float  MATH_GRADE        = 80.0f;
            const float  BIOLOGY_GRADE     = 80.0f;
            const float  PROGRAMMING_GRADE = 92.0f;
            const string STUDENT_NAME      = "G. Treele";
            // Call CalculateAverage() to calculate the average grade.
            float average = CalculateAverage(MATH_GRADE, BIOLOGY_GRADE,
                                             PROGRAMMING_GRADE);
```

```
                // Call ShowAverage() to display the student name and overall average.
                ShowAverage(STUDENT_NAME, average);
                Console.ReadLine();
            }
        }
    }
```

3. Create the missing methods *CalculateAverage()* and *ShowAverage()* so they receive the arguments that are passed from the existing calling instructions.
4. Design *CalculateAverage()* so it returns the calculated average of equally weighted course grades.
5. Design *ShowAverage()* so the output displays the following:

```
G. Treele average: 84
```

Method Overloads

Method overloading allows you to create methods with identical names as long as each method has a unique arrangement of parameter types. Overloading can make your code more reader friendly when these methods perform similar routines.

Example 4-2 Method Overloading

This example shows how method overloading can be applied with two methods named *DisplayContact()*. Both versions of *DisplayContact()* show address information. Different versions of the *DisplayContact()* method are invoked depending on whether or not a fax machine number is provided. To avoid code duplication, the overload that receives the fax machine number calls the other *DisplayContact()* overload to perform the initial part of the routine:

```
using System;

namespace ConsoleApplication1 {
    class Program {
        static void Main() {
            // Call overload with no fax.
            DisplayContact("Banana Republic Women", "735 State Street",
                           "Santa Barbara", "CA", "93101");
            Console.WriteLine();
```

```
            // Call overload with fax.
            DisplayContact("Legal Aid Society", "1223 West Sixth Street",
                           "Cleveland", "OH", "44113", "216-586-3220");
            Console.ReadLine();
        }

        // Overload with no fax.
        static void DisplayContact(string orgName, string street,  string city,
                                   string state, string zip) {
            Console.WriteLine(orgName);
            Console.WriteLine(street);
            Console.WriteLine(city + ", " + state);
            Console.WriteLine(zip);
        }

        // Overload with fax.
        static void DisplayContact(string orgName, string street, string city,
                                   string state, string zip, string fax) {
            // Use DisplayContact() overload with no fax.
            DisplayContact(orgName, street, city, state, zip);
            Console.WriteLine("fax: " + fax);                   // Show fax.
        }
    }
}
```

When running the program, contact information for organizations with and without fax numbers are displayed in a professional format:

```
Banana Republic Women
735 State Street
Santa Barbara, CA
93101

Legal Aid Society
1223 West Sixth Street
Cleveland, OH
44113
fax: 216-586-3220
```

Passing Arguments by Value and by Reference

Arguments can be passed to methods in two ways: by value or by reference. When the argument is passed by value, changes to the argument in the method have no effect on the original value in the calling instruction. When the argument is passed by reference, changes to the argument in the method also affect the original value in the calling instruction.

Passing Arguments by Value

When parameters are passed to a method by value, a copy of the variable is made. Changes to the variable copy inside the method do not affect the original variable value outside the method. In Chapter 2, we discussed how different data types are classified as value types or reference types. By default, arguments that are declared with a value type format are also passed by value to the method. In other words, original values for float, integer, and decimal type arguments are not altered by method changes.

Passing Arguments by Reference

When passing arguments by reference to a method, the starting address for the data value is given to the method. Any changes made inside the method to the values referenced by this object are also applied to the object's values outside the method. Variables with complex data types such as arrays or instances of a class are passed by reference.

NOTE

The string format is a special case to consider when passing by value or by reference. The string is a reference type that is passed to the method by reference. However, the string is *immutable*, which means it cannot be changed. Any assignment or modification to a string within a method actually creates a new string that gets passed back to the calling instruction. In other words, the string is a reference type and it is passed by reference, but the default behavior appears as if the string is passed by value to a method.

Example 4-3 Passing by Value vs. Passing by Reference

This example shows the contrast in how argument values are affected when passed by value or by reference. In this example, an array of prices is declared. A single element of the array is passed by value to an *AddTax()* method. Changes applied to the copy inside *AddTax()* do not affect the array values where the call is made. When the array is passed by reference to the *Inflate()* method, adjustments for inflation within the method affect the original array in the calling instruction.

```
using System;

namespace ConsoleApplication1 {
    class Program {
        const int FIRST_PRICE = 0;
        static void Main() {
            decimal[] prices = { 9.99m };
            ShowPrices(prices);
            AddTax(prices[FIRST_PRICE]);     // Pass by value.
```

```
            ShowPrices(prices);                   // Pass by reference.
            Inflate(prices);                      // Pass by reference.
            ShowPrices(prices);                   // Pass by reference.

            Console.ReadLine();
        }

        // Receives argument by reference.
        static void ShowPrices(decimal[] price) {
            Console.WriteLine("Value in calling method: "
                            + price[FIRST_PRICE].ToString("C"));
        }

        // Receives argument by value.
        static void AddTax(decimal price) {
            const decimal TAX_RATE = 1.07m;
            price *= TAX_RATE;
            Console.WriteLine("After tax: " + price.ToString("C"));
        }

        // Receives argument by reference.
        static void Inflate(decimal[] prices) {
            const decimal INFLATION_RATE = 1.01m;
            prices[FIRST_PRICE] *= INFLATION_RATE;
            Console.WriteLine("After inflation: "
                            + prices[FIRST_PRICE].ToString("C"));
        }
    }
}
```

The following output from this example shows how the *AddTax()* method does not affect the values of the array because a single array element is passed to it by value. The *Inflate()* method, however, has affected the original array values because the array is passed by reference.

```
Value in calling method: $9.99
After tax: $10.69
Value in calling method: $9.99
After inflation: $10.09
Value in calling method: $10.09
```

Passing Arguments Explicitly by Reference

It is possible to explicitly pass prebuilt C# types by reference to a method. You may wish to do this if you need to modify more than one variable at once within a method.

A *ref* keyword is also required before each argument that is explicitly passed by reference:

```
AdjustForInflation(ref house, ref salary);
```

Example 4-4 Explicitly Passing Arguments by Reference

This example shows how two arguments can be passed explicitly by reference so they can both be updated with an inflationary increase:

```
using System;

namespace ConsoleApplication1 {
    class Program {
        static void Main() {
            float house  = 200000.0f;
            float salary = 75000.0f;

            // Explicitly pass variables by reference
            AdjustForInflation(ref house, ref salary);
            Console.WriteLine("** Values After Inflation Adjustment **");
            Console.WriteLine("Home:    " + house);
            Console.WriteLine("Income: " + salary);
            Console.ReadLine();
        }

        // Receive arguments explicitly by reference.
        static void AdjustForInflation(ref float home, ref float income) {
            const float RATE = 1.03f;
            home   *= RATE;
            income *= RATE;
        }
    }
}
```

Results displayed verify that the original arguments are inflated within the method when received explicitly by reference:

```
** Values After Inflation Adjustment **
Home:    206000
Income: 77250
```

Passing Uninitialized Variables by Reference

Normally, whenever you pass an argument by value or by reference, it must already be initialized. However, when the *out* keyword is included in a parameter declaration, an uninitialized variable can be passed to the method by reference: You can also pass an initialized variable as well when using the *out* keyword. The method with the variable reference can then initialize the variable or overwrite it. Here is a sample method header that includes the *out* keyword:

```
static void GetAccrualRate(out double interest , double years)
```

An instruction that passes a variable to a method like the one defined earlier also denotes this variable with the *out* keyword:

```
GetAccrualRate(out accrualRate, TOTAL_YEARS);
```

Example 4-5 Passing Uninitialized Variables by Reference

Here is a full example that shows declaration of the variable *accrualRate,* which is then passed in an uninitialized state to the method by reference:

```
using System;

namespace ConsoleApplication1 {
    class Program {
        static void Main() {
            const double TOTAL_YEARS = 5;
            double accrualRate;

            // Pass uninitialized rate explicitly by reference.
            GetAccrualRate(out accrualRate, TOTAL_YEARS);
            Console.WriteLine("Accrual rate: " + accrualRate);
            Console.ReadLine();
        }

        // Receive uninitialized interest rate explicitly by reference.
        static void GetAccrualRate(out double interest , double years) {
            const double INTEREST_RATE = 1.05;
            interest = Math.Pow(INTEREST_RATE, years);
        }
    }
}
```

The output from the *GetAccrualRate()* method is displayed as follows:

```
Accrual rate: 1.2762815625
```

Scope

A variable or object's scope describes the region of code where the variable can be accessed. The term scope is often called visibility since a program recognizes variables and objects when they are in scope.

Class Scope

Class scope defines the accessibility for variables and objects declared at the class level. These variables and objects can be edited or read anywhere within the class. Class-level declarations are convenient if several methods within the class must reference the item. However, class-level scope is more error prone than localized scope since class-level items can be modified anywhere in the class for as long as the class instance exists.

Method Scope

Variables and objects that are declared inside a method are accessible for edits and reads only within the method. Method-only variable and object recognition is referred to as method scope. The lifetime of a variable or object that is declared inside a method is much shorter than the lifetime of class-level variables and objects. Method-level items exist from the point they are declared in the method to the time the method exits. The local variables or objects in the method must be reinitialized whenever the method is called again. In other words, local method variables and objects are born during each visit to the method, and they die when the method exits.

Block Scope

Block scope is an even more refined level of scope than method scope. Block scope refers to the accessibility of a variable or object that is declared inside a conditional structure or loop. We will discuss these structures in Chapter 5. A variable or object declared inside a code block is not recognized outside the block where it is defined. Restricting the existence of a variable or object to a block of code strengthens your algorithms by preventing unwanted value tampering at other places within the method. Block scope also makes your code more reader friendly because the variables or objects are declared at the exact location where they are used.

TIP

Ideally, the range of availability for reading or editing should be as local as possible to prevent unwanted changes that could lead to errors. Localization will also make your code more readable since variables are declared and used within the same region where they are used.

Variable Precedence

You may declare a variable within a method that has the same name and type as a variable that is declared at the class level. The local variable always takes precedence. As a result, whenever you reference a variable name that exists both locally and at the class level, the locally declared variable is used.

Example 4-6 Scope and Precedence

This example shows how the more local scope takes precedence over class-level scope. When printing data from a method where a variable is declared both at the class level and method level, the method variable value is output. When printing data from a block where the variable is declared at the class level and block level, the block-level value is printed. When printing data where only the class-level variable is accessible, only the class-level variable value is output.

```
using System;

namespace ConsoleApplication1 {
    class Program {
        static int classAndMethodLevel = 3000; // Class level declarations.
        static int classAndBlockLevel  = 3333;

        static void Main() {
            Console.WriteLine("Class Level:  " + classAndMethodLevel);
            Console.WriteLine("Class Level:  " + classAndBlockLevel);
            ShowLocalizedValues();
            Console.ReadLine();
        }

        // Receive uninitialized interest rate explicitly by reference.
        static void ShowLocalizedValues() {
            const bool ENTER_CONDITION = true;
            int classAndMethodLevel     = 200;  // Method level declaration.
            Console.WriteLine("Method Level:  " + classAndMethodLevel);
            if (ENTER_CONDITION) {
                int classAndBlockLevel = 10;   // Block level declaration.
                Console.WriteLine("Block Level:    " + classAndBlockLevel);
            }
        }
    }
}
```

The output shows that the variable with the most local scope is always printed:

```
Class Level:   3000
Class Level:   3333
Method Level:   200
Block Level:     10
```

Try This 4-2 Examining Scope

This exercise shows how variable accessibility differs according to the location where it is defined.

1. Starting with the solution for Example 4-6, set breakpoints
   - Just before the *if* statement inside *ShowLocalizedVariables()*
   - Inside the *if* block
   - Just before the *ReadLine()* instruction inside *Main()*
2. Compare the variable names and values that appear in the Locals window when halted at each breakpoint.

To avoid situations where scope conflicts may occur, you are better off using descriptive and unique names for all variables. The naming conventions you use to distinguish class-level variables from method-level variables can also help to eliminate this problem.

Chapter 4 Self Test

The following questions are intended to help reinforce your comprehension of the concepts covered in this chapter. The answers can be found in the accompanying online Appendix B, "Answers to the Self Tests."

1. Write a program that implements a method that calculates and returns the surface area of a sphere when the value of the radius is passed to the method. Output the radius and surface area from the *Main()* method. The formula for calculating the surface area of a sphere is $4 \pi r^2$, where r is the radius $\pi = 3.14159$. Implement another method to display the surface area value.

2. Indicate whether each statement is true or false.

   A. ____ A void method does not return a data value to the calling instruction.

   B. ____ It is possible to have the following two methods within the same class:

   ```
   static void PerformCalculation(int a, int b) { }
   static void PerformCalculation(int c, int d) { }
   ```

   C. ____ It is possible to have the following two methods within the same class:

   ```
   static void PerformCalculation(int a, int b) { }
   static void PerformCalculation(int c, float d) { }
   ```

   D. ____ It is usually better to pass a float argument to a method by reference.

   E. ____ Class-level variables have precedence over method-level variables with the same name.

   F. ____ Variables that are declared at the method level reference values in memory for the life of the class.

3. In your own words, explain why locally declared variables and objects are usually preferred over class-level declarations.

4. Starting with Example 4-2, add another overloaded *DisplayContact()* method that receives a phone number and displays it. This method also receives a fax number as a parameter. Test your new method by calling it.

5. If you were to declare a new variable inside *ShowLocalizedValues()* called *gravity,* why would you receive an error if you tried to display this variable with the instruction *Console.WriteLine(gravity);* from the *Main()* method?

6. Fill in the blanks.

   A. The instruction *CalculateSpeed(out float speed, float time)* passes *time* by ________.

   B. The instruction *CalculateSpeed(out float speed, float time)* passes *speed* by ________.

7. Modify Example 4-4 to also explicitly pass a reference to the *annualFoodCost* variable to adjust the value for inflation. Show the final result in *Main()* after the adjustment. The initial *annualFoodCost* value is $10,000 prior to calling *AdjustForInflation()*.

Chapter 5

Conditional Structures and Loops

Key Skills & Concepts

- Control Structures
- Comparison Operators
- Conditional Structures
- Loops

This chapter introduces the two main types of control structures, conditional structures and loops. Conditional structures enable decision making for code execution. Loop structures enable repetitive code execution.

Control Structures

Both conditional structures and loops are control structures because they rely on conditional *expressions* to select branches of code for execution. The conditional expression in a conditional structure or loop evaluates to either a true or false result. For example, if an expression is true, such as when the value of *x* is greater than 5, the code block enclosed by the control structure is executed:

```
if (x < 5)
{
    // Execute instructions within the curly braces.
}
```

Indentation and Alignment

Each control structure usually begins with a header that contains an expression for evaluation. While there are exceptions, normally, the block of code to be executed follows the control structure header. This code block is contained within opening { and closing } curly braces. Code within the curly braces is indented and left-aligned.

Usually, the opening curly brace is placed on the line after the control structure header, like this:

Conditional Structure Example **Curly brace on the line after the header**	**Loop Example**

`if (counter < 5)`
`{`
`    Console.WriteLine(counter);`
`}`
	`while (counter < 5)`
	`{`
	`    Console.WriteLine(counter);`
	`    counter++;`
	`}`

To save space, curly braces may be placed after the control structure header on the same line, like this:

Conditional Structure Example **Curly brace on the same line as the header**	**Loop Example**

`if (counter < 5) {`
`    Console.WriteLine(counter);`
`}`
	`while (counter < 5) {`
	`    Console.WriteLine(counter);`
	`    counter++;`
	`}`

When only one line of code exists in the control structure block, the curly braces are optional, as shown here:

Conditional Structure Example **No curly braces**	**Loop Example**
`if (counter < 5)` `    Console.WriteLine(counter);`	`while (counter++ < 5)` `    Console.WriteLine(counter);`

TIP

To help keep your code readable and easier to debug, you are better off using proper indentation and alignment of your control structures as you write your code. Your teammates will expect this from you too.

Nesting

It is possible to place control structures within control structures, a practice called *nesting*. In this case, a conditional statement is placed within a conditional statement:

```
if (counter < 5) {
    Console.WriteLine(counter);
    if (counter < 2) {
        Console.WriteLine("Below minimum");
    }
}
```

Comparison Operators

To enable conditional structures and loops, comparison operators allow you to create Boolean expressions that are used in either structure type. The conditional expressions generate either true or false outcomes that allow the program to decide whether or not to execute code within the conditional block or loop block. In this section we will examine the common comparison operators.

Equals and Not Equals Operators

The equals operator, = =, determines if two operands of the same data type are equal. The equals operator uses two equal signs because the use of only one equal sign is interpreted as an assignment. In other words, *c* = *d* assigns the value of *d* to *c*. However, *c* = = *d* implies a comparison is being made.

To determine if two operands of the same data type are not equal, use the not equals operator, !=. The exclamation mark is a negation operator, which is usually called *not*. Placing ! before a true expression makes it false. Since two negatives make a positive, placing ! before a false expression makes it true. Table 5-1 shows how the equals and not equals operators are used in Boolean expressions.

Less Than and Greater Than Operators

C# uses less than (<), greater than (>), less than or equal (<=), and greater than or equal (>=) operators to compare values of the same data type. Results from less than and greater than expressions must always be either true or false. For example, 5 > 4 is always true and 5.0f >= 6.0f is always false. Table 5-2 lists these four less than and greater than expressions with examples of each.

	Operator	Conditional Expression
Equals	= =	4 = = 4 (true) 4 = = 3 (false)
Not equals	!=	4 != 3 (true) 3 != 3 (false)

Table 5-1 Equals and Not Equals Operators

	Operator	Conditional Expression
Less than	<	5 < 6 (true) 5 < 5 (false)
Greater than	>	4 > 3 (true) 4 > 5 (false)
Less than or equal	<=	4 <= 4 (true) 4 <= 3 (false)
Greater than or equal	>=	4 >= 4 (true) 4 >= 5 (false)

Table 5-2 Less Than and Greater Than Operators

AND and OR Operators

The logical AND and logical OR operators allow you to create composite conditional expressions. The logical AND operator is denoted with a double ampersand, &&. The logical OR operator uses the double pipe, ||, notation. With the logical AND, both conditions on each side of the operator must be true for the final outcome to be true. With the logical OR, at least one condition on either side of the operator must be true for the entire expression to be true. Table 5-3 presents examples for each type of operator.

Let's now look at how comparison operators work with conditional structures to implement decision logic.

<table>
<tr><th></th><th>Operator</th><th>Conditional Expression</th></tr>
<tr><td>Logical AND</td><td>&&</td><td>4= =4 && 4 >=3 (true)
4 = = 3 && 2 = = 2 (false)</td></tr>
<tr><td>Logical OR</td><td>| |</td><td>3 >= 9 | | 4 = = 4 (true)
5 = = 3 | | 3 < 2 (false)</td></tr>
</table>

Table 5-3 Logical AND and Logical OR Operators

Conditional Structures

Conditional structures allow you to select and execute different branches of code through the use of conditional expressions. Even the most complex decision-making systems and algorithms rely on these simple but essential structures. Whenever a conditional expression in a conditional structure is true, the code block that follows is executed and then the program exits the conditional series. The three types of conditional structures are

- If-else statements
- Conditional operators
- Switches

If-Else Statements

The if-else statement is the most commonly used conditional structure. The if-else statement is really a series of conditional expressions that are grouped together. After finding the first true conditional expression in the series, the block of code that follows is executed. Once the code block has executed, the program immediately exits the conditional series so no other expressions from the series are evaluated. This conditional series may use *if*, *else if*, and *else* structures. Together this series resembles the structure in this sample:

```
if (conditional_expression)
{
    // Execute this code block if the expression immediately above is true.
}
else if (conditional_expression)
{
    // Execute this code block if the expression immediately above is true.
}
else
{
    // This code block is executed when all previous conditions are not true.
}
```

To understand this better, let's examine the three possible branch types in an if-else series:

- **if** *if* statements contain the first conditional expression within the if-else statement. Only one *if* statement can exist in a series, and it is mandatory for any series or on its own. When the *if* statement is true, the code block underneath is executed.
- **else if** *else if* statements are optional and must follow the opening *if* statement. The *else if* statement presents another conditional expression and an alternative block of code

for execution if the expression is true. Multiple *else if* statements can exist within an if-else series.

- **else** An *else* statement is the default selection when no previous condition in the if-else series is true. Only one *else* condition is permitted, and it must be at the end of the conditional series.

Example 5-1 If-Else Statements

To demonstrate decision-making logic with if-else statements, this example selects and displays warning messages based on the tornado classification. When reading through the code, note how indentation helps to visually identify each conditional block.

```
using System;
namespace Starter {
    class Program {
        // Define constants to store tornado classifications.
        const int INACTIVE = -1;
        const int F0 = 0, F1 = 1, F2 = 2, F3 = 3;

        public static void Main() {
            int strength = INACTIVE;
            ShowWarning(strength);  // Call ShowWarning() method.
            strength     = F3;
            ShowWarning(strength);  // Call ShowWarning() method.
            Console.ReadLine();
        }

        // Show warning based on tornado strength.
        public static void ShowWarning(int strength) {
            if (strength == F3) {
                Console.WriteLine("F3+: Severe damage warning.");
            }
            else if (strength == F2) {
                Console.WriteLine("F2: Significant damage warning.");
            }
            else if (strength == F1) {
                Console.WriteLine("F1: Moderate damage warning.");
            }
            else {
                Console.WriteLine("Inactive: No damage expected.");
            }
        }
    }
}
```

Results are displayed from the selected condition whenever *ShowWarning()* is called. During the first call to *ShowWarning()*, the default condition is selected, and on the next call to *ShowWarning()*, only the branch for F3 is selected:

```
Inactive: No damage expected.
F3+: Severe damage warning.
```

Try This 5-1 Comparison Operator and If-Else Statement Practice

To get a better understanding of how the if-else statement works with comparison operators, try this experiment.

1. Starting with Example 5-1, set a breakpoint by clicking in the gray margin beside the first call to *ShowWarning()*.
2. Run the program. When it is halted, step into *ShowWarning()* by pressing F11.
3. Step over the code in *ShowWarning()* using F10 during the first pass through. Notice how all conditions in the if-else statement are evaluated but their nested code blocks are not entered since none of the conditions are true. Also notice how the default *else* block is entered since none of the previous conditions were selected.
4. Run the program to completion.
5. Add a new tornado strength category constant declaration at the top of the class:

   ```
   const int F4 = 4;
   ```

6. Just before the last *Console.ReadLine()* instruction, add this code:

   ```
   strength      = F4;
   ShowWarning(strength);
   ```

7. Modify one of the comparison operators in one of the conditional blocks so the following output displays when running the program:

   ```
   Inactive: No damage expected.
   F3+: Severe damage warning.
   F3+: Severe damage warning.
   ```

Example 5-2 Applying Logical AND and Logical OR Expressions

This example demonstrates how conditional expressions can be combined with logical OR and logical AND operators. In this case, the *Report()* method receives *windspeed* and *warningMsg* variables as parameters. Both parameters are used within conditional expressions to determine which warning message to show.

```
using System;

namespace Starter {
    class Program {
        public static void Main() {
            const bool SHOW_WARNING = true;
            int windSpeed = 74; // Miles per hour.
            Report(windSpeed, SHOW_WARNING);

            windSpeed      = 35; // Miles per hour.
            Report(windSpeed, SHOW_WARNING);

            windSpeed      = 74; // Miles per hour.
            Report(windSpeed, !SHOW_WARNING);
            Console.ReadLine();
        }

         static public void Report(int windSpeed, bool showWarning) {
            Console.Write("Wind speed = " + windSpeed + " mph.  ");

            if (windSpeed < 40 || !showWarning)
                Console.WriteLine("No wind warnings at this time.");

            else if (windSpeed >= 40 && windSpeed <= 112)
                Console.WriteLine("Warning: possible wind damage!");
        }
    }
}
```

In the third call to *Report()*, notice that the wind speed is just as strong as when it was called the first time, yet, as shown next, no wind warning is displayed. The warning does not display because the Boolean parameter *showWarning* is false and this is recognized in the first logical OR.

```
Wind speed = 74 mph.  Warning: possible wind damage!
Wind speed = 35 mph.  No wind warnings at this time.
Wind speed = 74 mph.  No wind warnings at this time.
```

Conditional (Ternary) Operators

Conditional operators can be used to return different values based on the outcome of a simple conditional expression. Conditional operators are sometimes called *ternary* operators. The ternary operator offers a shorthand alternative to writing an if-else block. To implement the conditional operator, place a question mark, ?, before the assignment value used when a conditional expression is true. This assignment statement is followed by a colon, :, along with the assignment value to be used when the conditional expression is false. In the following case, *message* is assigned the value "Wind Alert!" when *windSpeed* exceeds the minimum; otherwise, *message* is assigned the value "Safe!":

```
// Assign "Wind Alert!" if wind speed is greater than minimum. Otherwise
// assign "Safe!".
string message = windSpeed >= TORNADO_MIN ? "Wind Alert!" : "Safe!";
```

CAUTION

Conditional operators offer convenient shorthand syntax. However, this condensed format is sometimes difficult to read and step through while debugging. If you have trouble debugging a conditional operator, you might try breaking up the instructions and using an if-else statement to achieve the same result.

Example 5-3 Conditional (Ternary) Operators

This example shows the full implementation of a conditional operator to assign a tornado alert message if wind speeds are greater than or equal to 73 miles per hour:

```
using System;
namespace Starter {
    class Program {
        static void Main() {
            const int TORNADO_MIN = 73;     // Miles per hour.
            int windSpeed         = 35;
            string warningMessage =
                   windSpeed >= TORNADO_MIN // Conditional expression
                   // Use 1st option if expression is true otherwise use 2nd.
                   ? "Tornado alert!":"Tornado conditions not present.";
            Console.WriteLine( warningMessage);
            Console.ReadLine();
        }
    }
}
```

The output shows the value that is assigned when the conditional expression is false:

```
Tornado conditions not present.
```

Switches

A *switch* is another conditional structure that provides a selection of *case* values to determine which code block to execute. The *switch* structure begins with a header where one parameter is passed in. The parameter value is then sequentially compared with *case* values of the same data type inside the *switch*. If a *case* value matches the parameter value from the *switch* header, the program enters that code block. When encountering the *break* statement, the program exits the *switch* structure. You may also include a *default* condition at the end of the *switch* structure to select instructions when no other cases match.

The following example shows the *switch* header with a parameter named *tornadoRating*. This parameter value is matched against *case* values in the list. For this example there is only one *case*, which has a value of F1. The *default case* is selected when no other cases match the parameter.

```
const int F1 = 1, F2 = 2, F5 = 5;
int   tornadoRating = F2;

switch (tornadoRating)           // Switch header.
{
    case F1:                     // Check for matching value.
        minimumSpeed = 73;       // Execute this block if case match.
        ShowData(minimumSpeed);
        break;                   // Exit switch.
    default:                     // Default code if no case match.
        Console.WriteLine("Information not available.");
        Console.WriteLine();
        break;                   // Exit switch.
}                                // End switch.
```

Example 5-4 Switches

This full example uses a simple *switch* to assign and display statistics about tornadoes. Notice how the cases are indented and code for each *case* is indented as well. The code for each *case* is terminated with a *break* statement.

```
using System;

namespace Starter {
    class Program {
```

```
        const int F1 = 1, F2 = 2, F5 = 5;

        public static void Main()  {
            Console.WriteLine("* Statistics for F2 tornado*");
            ShowFrequency(F2);
            Console.WriteLine("* Statistics for F5 tornado*");
            ShowFrequency(F5);
            Console.ReadLine();
        }

        static void ShowFrequency(int tornadoRating) {
            int minimumSpeed = 0;           // Miles per hour.

            switch (tornadoRating) {        // Start switch.
                case F1:                    // Check for matching value.
                    minimumSpeed = 73;      // Execute this block if match.
                    ShowData(minimumSpeed);
                    break;                  // Exit switch.
                case F2:                    // Check for matching value.
                    minimumSpeed = 112;     // Execute this block if match.
                    ShowData(minimumSpeed);
                    break;                  // Exit switch.
                default:                    // Default code if no case match.
                    Console.WriteLine("Information not available.");
                    Console.WriteLine();
                    break;                  // Exit switch.
            }                               // End switch.
        }

        static void ShowData(int minimumSpeed) {
            Console.WriteLine("Minimum wind speed: " + minimumSpeed );
            Console.WriteLine();
        }
    }
}
```

When observing the output, you can see that the default option is selected for the F5 tornado since statistics are not available for this option:

```
* Statistics for F2 tornado*
Minimum wind speed: 112

* Statistics for F5 tornado*
Information not available.
```

Loops

As mentioned previously, loops are structures that repeatedly execute blocks of code while a condition remains true. The loop's ability to execute thousands or even millions of instructions extremely quickly provides powerful flexibility for processing data, creating animations, and performing repetitive tasks where automation is needed. The four most common types of C# loops are presented in this chapter:

- *for* loops
- *while* loops
- *do while* loops
- *foreach* loops

For Loops

For loops are one of the more common types of loops. These loops start with a *header,* which contains three instructions:

- The first instruction sets the initial value for a counter. To restrict the counter's scope to the loop only, the counter is usually declared and initialized in this first instruction of the header. The first instruction is executed only one time, when the program enters the loop.
- The second instruction of the loop header is a conditional expression that is evaluated for every iteration of the loop—if true, the instructions within the code block of the loop are executed.
- The third instruction of the *for* loop modifies the counter variable, usually with an increment or decrement. Starting at the second loop iteration, the third instruction is executed before the conditional expression is evaluated to determine whether or not to execute the code block again.

TIP

Often, the counter in a *for* loop is given the name *i*, for index. This practice may at first appear to contradict the practice of always using descriptive variable names. However, the variable name *i* is a commonly accepted shorthand name. If nested loops use counters too, they are often assigned consecutive letters of the alphabet as names, such as *j* and *k*.

Code to be executed by the *for* loop is nested and left-aligned between opening and closing curly braces:

```
string[] letters = new string[] { "a", "b", "c", "d" };
for (int i = 0; i < letters.Length; i++)
{
    Console.WriteLine(letters[i]);
}
```

Example 5-5 For Loops

This example shows how a *for* loop can iterate through all elements of an array and print them to the console:

```
using System;

namespace Starter {
    class Program {
        public static void Main() {
            string[] letters = new string[] { "a", "b", "c", "d" };
            for (int i = 0; i < letters.Length; i++) {
                Console.WriteLine("Element[" + i + "] = " + letters[i]);
            }
            Console.ReadLine();
        }
    }
}
```

When running the program, the elements of the array are obtained and printed while using the counter as a reference for the array:

```
Element[0] = a
Element[1] = b
Element[2] = c
Element[3] = d
```

Example 5-6 Nested For Loops

This example shows how helpful loops can be for data processing. In this case, the code calculates daily interest on a bank balance for three weeks. The week is tracked with the outer loop, and the day of the week is tracked with the inner loop.

NOTE

This example uses *ToString("N2")* to round the number output to two decimal places. More on rounding will be discussed in Chapter 6.

```
using System;

namespace Starter {
    class Program {
        public static void Main() {
            const int       NUM_WEEKS=3,      NUM_DAYS=7;
            const decimal   DAILY_INTEREST = 0.000194m;
            decimal         balance        = 23.00m;

            // Outer loop - Weeks
            for (int week = 0; week < NUM_WEEKS; week++) {
                Console.WriteLine("Daily Balance During Week " + (week + 1));

                // Inner loop - Days
                for(int day=0; day < NUM_DAYS; day++) {
                    balance += balance * DAILY_INTEREST;
                    // N2 rounds the output to two decimal places.
                    Console.Write(balance.ToString("N2") + "   ");
                }
                Console.WriteLine();Console.WriteLine();
            }
            Console.ReadLine();
        }
    }
}
```

The output shows the cumulative savings that are calculated within the loops:

```
Daily Balance During Week 1
23.00   23.01   23.01   23.02   23.02   23.03   23.03

Daily Balance During Week 2
23.04   23.04   23.04   23.05   23.05   23.06   23.06

Daily Balance During Week 3
23.07   23.07   23.08   23.08   23.08   23.09   23.09
```

Try This 5-2 Nested Loops

This exercise offers you practice with *for* loops and with nesting.

1. Write a program that uses three *for* loops with counters named *i*, *j*, and *k*. The *for* loop with the counter named *j* is nested inside the *for* loop with the counter named *i*. The *for* loop with the counter named *k* is nested inside the *for* loop with the counter named *j*.
2. Design your program to dynamically generate the following output:

```
i=0    j=0    k=0
i=0    j=0    k=1
i=0    j=1    k=0
i=0    j=1    k=1
i=1    j=0    k=0
i=1    j=0    k=1
i=1    j=1    k=0
i=1    j=1    k=1
```

While Loops

A *while* loop repeats instructions in its block as long as a specific condition is true. The keyword *while* starts the header. A conditional expression is inside the header. As long as the conditional expression is true, code within the loop block is executed. Instructions within the loop block are repeated until the conditional expression is false.

```
while (balance > 0) {
    balance *= MONTH_INTEREST;    // Add interest
    balance -= MONTHLY_FEE;       // Deduct fee
    Console.WriteLine("End of Month Balance = " + balance);
}
```

Example 5-7 While Loops

This example shows how a practical application of the *while* loop could calculate a bank balance until the total balance falls below zero:

```
using System;

namespace Starter{
```

```
    class Program{
        public static void Main() {
            decimal       balance         = 50.0m;
            const decimal MONTH_INTEREST = 1.0058m;
            const decimal MONTHLY_FEE     = 10.50m;
                  int     month           = 1;

            while (balance > 0) {
                balance *= MONTH_INTEREST;  // Add interest
                balance -= MONTHLY_FEE;     // Deduct fee
                Console.WriteLine("End of Month " + month++
                                 + ": Balance = " + balance.
ToString("N2"));
            }
            Console.ReadLine();
        }
    }
}
```

No funds are deposited and the balance is initially low. Over time, the service charges outweigh the interest earned and the account balance falls below zero:

```
End of Month 1: Balance = 39.79
End of Month 2: Balance = 29.52
End of Month 3: Balance = 19.19
End of Month 4: Balance = 8.80
End of Month 5: Balance = -1.65
```

Do While Loops

Do while loops are similar to *while* loops. However, the *do while* loop is always executed at least once, because the conditional expression is evaluated at the end. The keyword *do* starts this loop. The loop ends with the *while* keyword and a conditional expression in parentheses.

```
do
{
    balance *= MONTH_INTEREST;  // Add interest
    balance -= MONTHLY_FEE;     // Deduct fee
    Console.WriteLine("End of Month Balance = " + balance);
} while (balance > 0);
```

Example 5-8 Do While Loops

This example is slightly different from Example 5-7 because it allows the program to execute the code within the *do while* loop block at least once even though the balance is zero:

```
using System;

namespace Starter{
    class Program{
        public static void Main() {
            decimal       balance          = 0.0m;
            const decimal MONTH_INTEREST = 1.0058m;
            const decimal MONTHLY_FEE     = 10.50m;
                  int     month            = 1;
            do
            {
                balance *= MONTH_INTEREST;  // Add interest
                balance -= MONTHLY_FEE;     // Deduct fee
                Console.WriteLine("End of Month " + month++
                                + ": Balance = " + balance.ToString("N2"));
            } while (balance > 0);
            Console.ReadLine();
        }
    }
}
```

Even with a zero balance, the loop executes once to deduct service charges for the first month before it terminates:

```
End of Month 1: Balance = -10.50
```

Foreach Loops

A *foreach* loop allows you to iterate through a collection of similarly typed objects. The keyword *foreach* starts the loop header. A declaration within the header creates a temporary variable to store an item from the collection. The temporary variable is followed by the keyword *in* and the collection reference.

```
string[] names = {"Jane.", "Brad.", "Kara." };
foreach (string name in names){
    Console.WriteLine(name);
}
```

Example 5-9 Foreach Loops

Since an array is actually a collection of similarly typed objects, you can use a *foreach* loop to iterate through the values stored within it. This example shows how to use a *foreach* loop to iterate through an array of names:

```
using System;

namespace Starter {
    class Program {
        public static void Main() {
            string[] names = {"Jane.", "Brad.", "Kara." }; // Define array.
            foreach (string name in names) {      // Iterate through array.
                Console.WriteLine(name);
            }
            Console.ReadLine();
        }
    }
}
```

As expected when running the program, each name in the array is displayed on a separate line:

```
Jane.
Brad.
Kara.
```

Comparing Loop Types

With multiple loop types to choose from, let's consider the advantages of each:

- *for* loops allow convenient iteration through collections that have enumerable indexes, such as arrays.
- *while* loops enable repeated execution of code blocks when nonnumeric or complex conditions must be checked before iterating.
- *do while* loops share the same advantages of the *while* loop, but *do while* loops ensure that the loop iterates at least once.
- *foreach* loops can iterate through any type of collection.

Break Statements

Break statements force the program to exit the current loop when they are encountered. All C# loop types allow *break* statements.

Example 5-10 Break Statements

In this example, a menu prompts the program user to press 1 to keep running the program or press 2 to quit. The menu options and instructions are driven from a loop. When the user enters 2, the *break* statement forces the program to exit the loop.

```
using System;

namespace Starter {
    class Program {
        public static void Main() {
            bool readInput = true;

            while (readInput) {    // Iterate while readInput is true.
                ShowMenu();
                string option = Console.ReadLine(); // Get the user input.

                if (option == "2") // Enter block when quit option is selected.
                    break;         // Exit from the loop.
                else {             // Otherwise show status and loop again.
                    Console.WriteLine("You have chosen to keep running.");
                    Console.WriteLine("");
                }
            }                      // Loop end.
            Console.WriteLine("The program has been terminated.");
            Console.ReadLine();
        }

        public static void ShowMenu() {
            // Show the user menu.
            Console.WriteLine("** Menu **");
            Console.WriteLine("1. Keep running this program. ");
            Console.WriteLine("2. Quit.");
        }
    }
}
```

Here is some sample output. The user chooses to keep running the program during the first iteration. During the second iteration, the user chooses 2 to exit.

```
** Menu **
1. Keep running this program.
2. Quit.
1
You have chosen to keep running.
```

```
** Menu **
1. Keep running this program.
2. Quit.
2
The program has been terminated.
```

Continue Statement

A *continue* statement allows you to bypass all remaining instructions in a loop block to return to the top of the loop.

Example 5-11 Continue Statements

This example emulates a simplified game of 21 where the player can continually draw random playing cards, which have values between 1 and 11. The goal of the game is to get a sum of cards as close to 21 as possible without going over. Every time the program iterates through the loop, a random playing card value is generated and printed. If the sum of the card values drawn is less than or equal to 14, the *continue* statement forces the program to skip the remaining instructions within the loop to return to the top. If the sum of card values is 21, a message is printed to indicate that the player has won, and then the score is printed and the program breaks out of the loop. If the card value sum exceeds 21, a message is printed to indicate that the player has lost, and then the score is printed and the program breaks out of the loop.

```
using System;

namespace ConsoleApplication1 {
    class Program {
        static Random rnd = new Random();
        const int CARD_MIN = 1, CARD_MAX = 11;

        const int HOLD_LIMIT = 14;
        const int TWENTY_ONE = 21;

        static void Main() {
            int total = 0;
            while(total < TWENTY_ONE) {                 // Loop while total < 21.
                // Generate new random card.
                int newCard = rnd.Next(CARD_MIN,        // Inclusive lower bound.
                                       CARD_MAX+1       // Exclusive upper bound.
                Console.WriteLine("Card number: " + newCard);
                total += newCard;

                // Keep getting cards as long as total is less than 14.
                if (total < HOLD_LIMIT)
```

```
                    continue; // Skip other instructions and go to top of loop.

                if (total == TWENTY_ONE)     // Total equals 21 so user wins.
                    Console.Write("You win! ");

                else if (total > TWENTY_ONE) // Total is over 21 so user loses.
                    Console.Write("You lose! ");

                Console.WriteLine("Your score is " + total + ".");
                break;
            }
            Console.ReadLine();
        }
    }
}
```

This random set of output indicates that the loop encountered the *continue* statement twice before exiting during the third iteration:

```
Card number: 10
Card number: 7
Your score is 17.
```

Chapter 5 Self Test

The following questions are intended to help reinforce your comprehension of the concepts covered in this chapter. The answers can be found in the accompanying online Appendix B, "Answers to the Self Tests."

1. Given the following declarations,

```
const int MIN_AGE            = 5;
const int MAX_AGE            = 7;
const bool OVERRIDE_REQUEST = true;
int                   age = 6;
```

indicate if the following conditional expressions are true or false:

A. ____ !OVERRIDE_REQUEST || age >= MIN_AGE && age <= MAX_AGE

B. ____ OVERRIDE_REQUEST || age >= MIN_AGE && age <= MAX_AGE

C. ____ !OVERRIDE_REQUEST && age >= MIN_AGE && age <= MIN_AGE

D. ____ !OVERRIDE_REQUEST || age < MIN_AGE || age > MAX_AGE

2. Add a conditional block to the *ShowWarning()* method in Example 5-1 to output a "Devastating damage warning." message when the tornado strength equals F4. You will need to create a constant for this extra strength classification. Test this new method by assigning F4 to the *strength* variable inside the *Main()* method and then calling *ShowWarning()*.
3. Write a small program that declares a number variable with a suitable data type to store a temperature in Celsius. Assign the value of 19.3 to this variable. Then, convert this value to Fahrenheit and store the result in a different variable. Note that Fahrenheit = (Celsius * 9/5) + 32. Print both the original Celsius and Fahrenheit values in the window.
   - If the Fahrenheit value is less than or equal to 32, print "I am cold."
   - If the Fahrenheit value is greater than 32 and less than 65, print "It's chilly out."
   - If the Fahrenheit value is greater than or equal to 65 and less than 80, print "This feels good."
   - If the Fahrenheit value is greater than or equal to 80, then print "It is hot out."
4. Modify Example 5-4 to include a case statement that shows the wind speed that can lead to F3 tornadoes. (F3 tornadoes can occur when speeds reach 207 miles per hour.) Test the new case by calling the *ShowData()* method with F3 as the rating.
5. Write a small program to input a string value from a program user. To input the value, you can use this instruction:

   ```
   string input = Console.ReadLine();
   ```

   Use a *switch* to determine if the user types *a* when prompted. If the user types *a,* the program outputs "You pressed a." If the user types *b,* the program outputs "You pressed b." If the user types anything else, the program outputs "You did not press a or b."
6. Write a program that declares and initializes a bank balance of $10,000. Inside a *for* loop, calculate the interest on the current balance and add it to the current balance. The interest rate is 7 percent per year. Output the updated balance with interest to the window. Perform the operations in the loop 25 times to determine what the cumulative balance will be after 25 years.
7. Write the same program as in question 6, but this time use a *while* loop.
8. Write the same program as in question 6, but this time use a *do while* loop.
9. Write a small program that creates an array for storing float values. Then store 13.3f, 14.2f, and 5.2f in it. Next, using a *foreach* loop, iterate through the array to print values stored in the array to the window.

Chapter 6

String Manipulation

Key Skills & Concepts

- Numeric Format Specifiers
- Parsing Strings
- Editing Strings
- Escape Sequences
- Regular Expressions
- Converting Strings to Other Formats

An important part of data-driven development involves transforming text inputs and outputs into professional-looking and meaningful data. With security in mind, it is also important to ensure the text handled by your application is in the expected format. While string handling may seem trivial, being able to parse and modify string inputs and outputs is a core skill of any data-driven developer. To help with this effort, the C# language provides a rich library for managing strings of text. This chapter shows some of C#'s most common and essential string manipulation routines.

Numeric Format Specifiers

C# offers many convenient options to display numeric data in a user-friendly format. To enable numeric formatting, C# types such as float, decimal, integer, and double provide a *ToString()* method with options for controlling how the numeric data is displayed as text. The *ToString()* method is provided by all objects—numeric data types just provide some useful overloads.

Raw Text

With no parameters, the *ToString()* method converts the number to raw text:

```
double    num = 123456.789d;
Console.WriteLine(num.ToString());    // Outputs 123456.789
```

Rounding

Passing a string parameter with a decimal point followed by zeros as placeholders in the *ToString()* method rounds the number to the same total of digits as placeholders. Only passing a "0" as a parameter in the *ToString()* method rounds the number so the closest integer value is displayed:

```
double    num = 123456.789d;
Console.WriteLine(num.ToString(".00"));   // Outputs 123456.79
Console.WriteLine(num.ToString(".0"));    // Outputs 123456.8
Console.WriteLine(num.ToString("0"));     // Outputs 123457
```

Rounding with a Thousands Separator

The letter "N" followed by a digit in the *ToString()* method outputs the number with a thousands separator and a decimal place rounding to *n* digits:

```
double    num = 123456.789d;
Console.WriteLine(num.ToString("N2"));    // Outputs 123,456.79
```

Displaying Local Currency

To output a number in the local currency format, pass the letter "C" to the *ToString()* method:

```
double    num = 123456.789d;
Console.WriteLine(num.ToString("C"));     // Outputs $123,456.79
```

Parsing Strings

Parsing a string enables you to extract data about different parts of the string. C# provides lots of methods to help discover important information within a string.

Length

The string object's *Length* property returns the character count of the string:

```
string stringVarName = "some text";
int stringLength     = stringVarName.Length; // assigns 9
```

Example 6-1 String Length

The string type can be thought of as an array of characters—each character is a value of type char and can be referenced by an index. With the help of the string object's *Length* property, this code example uses a loop to reference and print each character in a string one character at a time:

```
using System;
namespace Starter {
    class Program {
        public static void Main() {
            int         letterCount = 0;
            const string FULL_NAME = "Maurine Shambarger";
            Console.Write("Length of original string: ");
            Console.WriteLine(FULL_NAME.Length);

            // Output each character of the string one at a time.
            for(int i=0; i<FULL_NAME.Length; i++) {
                char letter = FULL_NAME[i];
                Console.Write(letter);
                letterCount += 1;
            }
            Console.WriteLine();
            Console.WriteLine("The letter count is: " + letterCount);
            Console.ReadLine();
        }
    }
}
```

The output displays the individual characters of the string and the total number of characters in the string:

```
Length of original string: 18
Maurine Shambarger
The letter count is: 18
```

IndexOf()

To find the starting position of a specific set of characters, the *IndexOf()* method returns the position index of the first occurrence of a substring within a string object. When an occurrence of the substring is not found, the *IndexOf()* method returns –1. The two overloads listed next offer you flexibility when searching strings for character combinations. The first *IndexOf()* method listed receives the search string value as a parameter. The second *IndexOf()* method receives the search string and starting position of the search.

```
int IndexOf(string value);
int IndexOf(string value, int startIndex);
```

In this example, *IndexOf()* locates the position of each comma in a string:

```
string location = "Albany,Georgia,United States";
int first       = location.IndexOf(",");                 // assigns 6
int second      = location.IndexOf(",", first + 1);      // assigns 14
```

LastIndexOf()

The *LastIndexOf()* method returns the position of the last occurrence of a search string. When the desired substring is not found, *LastIndexOf()* returns –1.

```
int LastIndexOf(string value);
```

In this example, the position of the last comma is returned:

```
string location = "Albany,Georgia,United States";
int    second   = location.LastIndexOf(",");             // assigns 14
```

Substring

When parsing content, you may want to extract only a section of a string. The *Substring()* method can extract a section of a string when provided with the starting position and length for the substring:

```
string Substring(int characterStartPosition, int substringLength);
```

In the following example, the *Substring()* method extracts the city name from a string with a format that always starts the city name after a colon and a space. The city name is also always followed by a comma. The *IndexOf()* method locates the starting and ending positions of the city data so it can be read with the *Substring()* method.

```
string      location = "Location: Albany,Georgia,United States";
const string SEARCH = ": ";
int start    = location.IndexOf(SEARCH);                 // assigns 8
int end      = location.IndexOf(",");                    // assigns 16
string city = location.Substring(start + SEARCH.Length,  // assigns 'Albany'
                               end - start - SEARCH.Length);
```

Split()

When managing data contained in character-delimited strings, you have the option to create an array with string content. The *Split()* method stores parts of a string that are separated by a common character into an array. The character that is used as a separator is called a *delimiter*.

```
string[] stringArray = stringObject.Split(char charValue);
```

The *Split()* method uses a comma delimiter as the parameter to separate location components into a string array:

```
string storeLocation = "Retro Fitness,Secaucus,New Jersey";
string[] location    = storeLocation.Split(',');
Console.WriteLine(location[0]); // Outputs 'Retro Fitness'
```

Try This 6-1 String Formatting and Parsing Exercise

This exercise offers practice with format specifiers and different parsing methods.

1. Write a program that declares a string variable with the following text:

   `"Name: Spencer Potter  Balance: 3040.50".`

2. Find a way to dynamically extract the first name, last name, and dollar values separately.
3. Output the data in the manner shown next. Use a format specifier to output the dollar value.

```
First Name: Spencer
Last Name: Potter
Balance: $3,040.00
```

Join()

In contrast with the *Split()* method, the *Join()* method combines all elements of an array into a delimited string:

```
string Join(string separator, params object[] values);
```

In this example, information about a song within a comma-delimited string is converted into an array:

```
string[]      songInfo = {"Radio Nowhere", "Magic Lyrics",
                          "Bruce Springsteen", "3:19"};
// Creates "Radio Nowhere,Magic Lyrics,Bruce Springsteen,3:19"
string delimitedString = string.Join(",", songInfo);
```

StartsWith()

The string class provides a *StartsWith()* method to determine if a string begins with a specific set of characters. The *StartsWith()* method finds any string that meets this criteria and returns a *true* value whenever a match is found:

```
bool StartsWith(string value);
```

For example, you might want to view all last names in a string array that begin with the letters “Agl”:

```
string[] lastNames = {"Aglukkaq", "Jantzen"};
foreach(string lastName in lastNames)
    if(lastName.StartsWith("Agl"))
        Console.WriteLine(lastName); // Outputs "Aglukkaq"
```

Contains()

The *Contains()* method of the string class returns a Boolean value to confirm the existence of a specific set of characters within a string:

```
bool Contains(string value);
```

In this example, *Contains()* helps to search for last names that have “Ja” in them:

```
string[] lastNames = {"Aglukkaq", "Jantzen"};
foreach(string lastName in lastNames)
    if(lastName.Contains("Ja"))
        Console.WriteLine(lastName); // Outputs "Jantzen"
```

Editing Strings

When formatting data for storage or presentation, you will want to edit your strings. As you would expect, C# provides methods to help. Strings can be trimmed and joined. Their letter cases can be adjusted. Portions of a string can be replaced, inserted, and removed.

Trim()

When handling string inputs from unknown sources, you may need to remove leading or trailing spaces. String values with empty spaces preceding or trailing the content are not equivalent to strings without the padding. In other words:

```
" ABC " != "ABC"
```

Chances are you don't want to store the extra padding anyway. The *Trim()* method conveniently removes empty spaces positioned at either side of a character string:

```
string name = "  Marnie Laberge ";
Console.WriteLine(name.Length);          // Outputs 17
Console.WriteLine(name.Trim().Length);   // Outputs 14
```

Concatenation

Sometimes you may need to combine strings. The process of joining strings is called string concatenation. A simple way to append strings is using the + operator to add a string to the right of an existing string. In this code example, a first name and last name are concatenated to create a full name:

```
string firstName = "Leona";
string lastName  = "Aglukkaq";
string fullName  = firstName + " " + lastName;
Console.WriteLine(fullName);          // Outputs "Leona Aglukkaq"
```

Adjusting Letter Case

C# string comparisons are case sensitive. For example,

```
"ABC" != "abc"
```

In addition to requiring case-sensitive string comparisons for processes such as password validation, you may face situations where alphabetical characters of varying case must be stored or displayed in a specific letter case. To handle case conversions, C# string objects provide *ToUpper()* and *ToLower()* methods to transform your alphabetical characters. *ToUpper()* converts a string of alphabetical characters to uppercase, and *ToLower()* converts a string of alphabetical characters to lowercase:

```
const string ALPHABET = "AbCdEfGhIjKlMnOpQrStUvWxYz";
Console.WriteLine(ALPHABET.ToUpper()); // Outputs ABCDEFGHIJKLMNOPQRSTUVWXYZ
Console.WriteLine(ALPHABET.ToLower()); // Outputs abcdefghijklmnopqrstuvwxyz
```

Replace()

To help with string formatting and editing, string objects provide a *Replace()* method to swap all instances of one substring with another:

```
string Replace(string oldValue, string newValue);
```

This example uses *Replace()* to swap all instances of New Jersey with NJ:

```
string location = "Retro Fitness,Secaucus,New Jersey";
// Assigns 'Retro Fitness,Secaucus,NJ'
location = location.Replace("New Jersey", "NJ");
```

Insert()

When formatting string inputs and outputs, you may need to insert additional data in the middle of the string. String objects provide an *Insert()* method for inserting a group of characters into an existing string at a specific position:

```
string Insert(int startIndex, string value);
```

Here the day of the week is added to a town event announcement:

```
string townEvent = "Town Hall, November 12, 10:04 PM";
int      position = townEvent.IndexOf(",");
// Assigns 'Town Hall, Saturday November 12, 10:04 PM'
townEvent         = townEvent.Insert(position + 1, " Saturday");
```

Remove()

To remove ranges of characters from your string, you can use the *Remove()* method:

```
string Remove(int startIndex, int count);
```

In this example, *Remove()* extracts the sentence from the selection:

```
string answer = "e) All of the above.";
// Assigns 'All of the above.'
answer = answer.Remove(0, 3);
```

Escape Sequences

Escape sequences are character combinations that represent actions, nonprinted characters, and special characters such as single quotes, double quotes, file paths, newline entries, carriage returns, tabs, backspaces, and more. Escape sequences start with a backslash. Table 6-1 lists the escape sequences that are available in C#.

Use of the backslashes in string combinations other than escape sequences can cause errors. For example, this file path declaration will cause an error:

```
string filePath = "C:\CSharp\log.txt";    // Causes an error.
```

Since the escape sequence \\ represents an escaped backslash, you can use the following string declaration to define the file path:

```
string filePath = "C:\\CSharp\\log.txt"; // Escape sequence equivalent
```

Escape Sequence	Description
\a	Bell (alert)
\b	Backspace
\f	Form feed
\n	Newline
\r	Carriage return
\t	Horizontal tab
\v	Vertical tab
\'	Single quotation mark
\"	Double quotation mark
\\	Backslash
\?	Literal question mark
\ 000	ASCII character in octal notation
\x hh	ASCII character in hexadecimal notation
\x hhhh	Unicode character in hexadecimal notation for wide character constant or wide character string literal

Table 6-1 Recognized C# Escape Sequences

Verbatim String Literals

Verbatim string literal declarations prevent escape sequence processing. To define a verbatim string literal, begin the string declaration with the @ symbol. Using the file path definition example from the previous section, you could keep all of the text in the original format if you prefix the string with the @ symbol:

```
string filePath = @"C:\CSharp\log.txt";  // Verbatim string literal.
```

Regular Expressions

A regular expression is a sequence of characters that is used for pattern matching in strings. Regular expressions are often used to validate text inputs to ensure that the data conforms to the expected format. Most modern programming languages enable regular expressions since they offer such concise and efficient pattern searching. The C# regular expression library is defined in the *System.Text.RegularExpressions* namespace. Parsing and validation is enabled from this library with the *Regex* class. When initializing a *Regex* object to validate a string, the regular expression pattern is passed as a parameter:

```
Regex regex = new Regex(string regularExpression);
```

The *Regex* object provides an *IsMatch()* method to validate strings:

```
bool match = regex.IsMatch(string input);
```

Introductory Expressions

Regular expressions can be intimidating if you have never worked with them before, so let's ease into this topic by only examining three regular expression operators.

Starts With

The regular expression operator ^ ensures that a string begins with the character set on its right. A regular expression of "^Chapter" validates the string value of "Chapter 10":

```
const string PATTERN = @"^Chapter";
const string INPUT   = "Chapter 10";
Regex reg            = new Regex(PATTERN);
bool result          = reg.IsMatch(INPUT); // (true).
```

This same regular expression generates a false result with a string value of "Preface":

```
const string PATTERN = @"^Chapter";
const string INPUT   = "Preface";
Regex reg            = new Regex(PATTERN);
bool result          = reg.IsMatch(INPUT); // (false).
```

Ends With

A regular expression with the operator $ ensures that a string ends with a specific character set. The pattern Brazil$ validates strings that end with "Brazil" such as "San Paulo, Brazil":

```
const string PATTERN = @"Brazil$";
const string INPUT   = "San Paulo, Brazil";
Regex reg            = new Regex(PATTERN);
bool result          = reg.IsMatch(INPUT); // (true).
```

On the other hand, this regular expression does not validate a string that ends with "Peru":

```
const string PATTERN = @"Brazil$";
const string INPUT   = " Lima, Peru";
Regex reg            = new Regex(PATTERN);
bool result          = reg.IsMatch(INPUT); // (false).
```

Or

The pipe symbol | represents an OR operator in a regular expression. When using | for validation, at least one character set on either side of this operator is required for a match. A regular expression pattern of "Apples|Pears|Lemons" validates any string that contains "Apples" or "Pears" or "Lemons". In this case, the regular expression "Apples|Pears|Lemons" validates the string "Red Apples":

```
const string PATTERN = @"Apples|Pears|Lemons";
const string INPUT   = "Red Apples";
Regex reg            = new Regex(PATTERN);
bool result          = reg.IsMatch(INPUT); // (true).
```

The string "Grapes" fails to validate with this regular expression:

```
const string PATTERN = @"Apples|Pears|Lemons";
const string INPUT   = "Grapes";
Regex reg            = new Regex(PATTERN);
bool result          = reg.IsMatch(INPUT); // (false).
```

Example 6-2 Introductory Regular Expressions

This example combines regular expression operators to make a more complex expression. In this case, the pattern "^Apples|Pears|Lemons$" only validates "Apples", "Pears", or "Lemons" and nothing else:

```
using System;
using System.Text.RegularExpressions;

namespace Starter {
    class Program {
        public static void Main() {
            const string PATTERN = @"^Apples|Pears|Lemons$";
            ShowValidStatus(PATTERN, "Red Apples");
            ShowValidStatus(PATTERN, "Lemons and Grapes");
            ShowValidStatus(PATTERN, "Apples");
            ShowValidStatus(PATTERN, "Pears");
            ShowValidStatus(PATTERN, "Lemons");
            Console.ReadLine();
        }

        public static bool ShowValidStatus(string pattern, string input) {
            Regex reg    = new Regex(pattern);
            bool  result = reg.IsMatch(input);

            if (result)
```

```
                Console.WriteLine("PASS: "
                                + pattern + " validates " + input);
            else
                Console.WriteLine("FAIL: "
                                + pattern + " invalidates " + input);
            return result;
        }
    }
}
```

The following output proves that "Red Apples" and "Lemons and Grapes" fail, while strings that start and end with either "Apples", "Pears", or "Lemons" validate:

```
FAIL: ^Apples|Pears|Lemons$ invalidates Red Apples
FAIL: ^Apples|Pears|Lemons$ invalidates Lemons and Grapes
PASS: ^Apples|Pears|Lemons$ validates Apples
PASS: ^Apples|Pears|Lemons$ validates Pears
PASS: ^Apples|Pears|Lemons$ validates Lemons
```

More Regular Expression Operators

Many other regular operators exist to offer flexibility to design validation patterns. Table 6-2 provides a summary of common regular expression operator descriptions with examples.

TIP

For many aspiring programmers, regular expressions appear daunting at first glance. Do not be discouraged, though, because they really are not difficult if you break each pattern into simple components. Try the self-study questions at the end of this chapter to get practice with them. You will find they are actually easier to use once you get past the initial learning curve. With practice, you will find ways to divide challenging regular expression patterns into simple sections.

Example 6-3 Regular Expressions for Simple Patterns

This example shows how to set up the *Regex* object for validation with sets of characters. You can use this example to test all regular expressions and corresponding example inputs listed in Table 6-2.

```
using System;
using System.Text.RegularExpressions;

namespace Starter {
    class Program {
        public static void Main() {
            const string PATTERN = @"ba*";
```

```
            const string INPUT    = "b";
            Regex reg             = new Regex(PATTERN);

            if(reg.IsMatch(INPUT))
               Console.WriteLine("PASS:  " + PATTERN + " validates " + INPUT);
            else
               Console.WriteLine("FAIL:  "
                            + PATTERN + " invalidates " + INPUT);
            Console.ReadLine();
        }
    }
}
```

For the case presented in code, the input string in the preceding example conforms to the regular expression rules, so a successful validation message is displayed:

```
PASS:  ba* validates b
```

Description	Expression	Position	Example	Valid	Invalid
0 or more	*	After	ba*	b, bab, ba	a
1 or more	+	After	ba+	ba, bab	a, b
0 to 1	?	After	ab?	abb, a, abbb	b
Occurrences	{n}	After	ab{2}	abbb, cabb, dabbb	ab, bb
Minimum occurrences	{n,}	After	de{2,}g	deeg, deeeg, adeeg	deg, deeefg
Minimum and maximum occurrences	{n,m}	After	def{1,3}	defg, defffh	deeefg
Any single character	.		.	a,b,1,3,d,de	
Starts with	^	Before	^abc ^a*c	abc123, abc ac, c	aabcd, babc, a oaooc
Does not contain	[^]	Current	[^c]	ch, a, hc	c
Groups characters	()	Current	^(de)	def, delete	adelade

Table 6-2 Regular Expression Summary

Description	Expression	Position	Example	Valid	Invalid
Escapes characters from special meaning	\	Before	*\.* \.	*.* *.txt, Myfile.txt	*.txt a*
Ends with pattern	$	After	(\.txt)$ \.*t$	Myfile.txt ab.abt, ab.absafdasft	Myfiletxt, Myfile.txtt ab.absafdasf
Any digit	[0123456789] Or [0–9] Or \d	Current	[0123456789]a$ Or [0–9]a$ Or \da$	123a, 1a, 3a	aa, .a
Lowercase letters	[a–z]	Current	[a–z] ^[a–z]{2}$	xyz, Xyz ab, yz	XYZ, 123 xyz, a2
Uppercase letters	[A–Z]	Current	^[A–Z]{1,}[0–9]+	A1, AA22	3AA22, a1
Lower- and uppercase letters	[a–zA–Z]	Current	[a–zA–Z]{2}[0–9]{1}$	aB9, 9aB9	9a9B9
Letters or numbers	[a–zA–Z_0–9]	Current	^[a–zA–Z_0–9]+$	iu98	iu.98
Any word character	\w (words, numbers, punctuation)	Current	\w	24?, Wow!, Thanks., <not>	*,–, \",', &
No letters or numbers	[^a–zA–Z_0–9]	Current	^[^a–zA–Z_0–9]+$	.	a
Any non-word character	\W	Current	^\W+$	*,-, \",', &	24?, Wow!, Thanks., <not>
Whitespace character	\s	Current	a\sb	a b, ka b	kab
Non-whitespace character	\S	Current	a\Sb	akb, a.b	a b
Decimal digit	\d	Current	\d{3}	123	a23
Non-decimal digit	\D	Current	^\D$	A	3
Or	|	Current	^(apples|pears)$	apples, pears	grapes

Table 6-2 Regular Expression Summary

Try This 6-2 Regular Expression Exercise

Here is a chance to try writing regular expressions.

1. Start with the code solution from Example 6-3.
2. Create a regular expression to validate full names such as Jane Chen, Ron Terencio, or Raj Bains. Assume that each first name and last name must begin with a capital letter and that all other characters in the name must be lowercase letters. Each full name only has a first name and a last name. There are no hyphens. First and last names are separated with one space.

Example 6-4 Complex Regular Expressions

This example demonstrates how to build a complex regular expression for validating different phone number formats. The regular expression

```
^(\([0-9]{3}\)\s?|[0-9]{3}[-\.\s]?)[0-9]{3}[-\.\s]?[0-9]{4}$
```

validates

```
(201) 867-5309, 201-867-5309, 201.867.5309, 2018675309 and (201)867-5309
```

Aside from the pattern and input definitions, the code in the following example is identical to the preceding example:

```
using System;
using System.Text.RegularExpressions;

namespace Starter {
   class Program {
      public static void Main() {
         const string PATTERN =
         @"^(\([0-9]{3}\)\s?" +   // (999) + optional white single space
         @"|" +                   // OR
         @"[0-9]{3}[-\.\s]?)" +   // 999 + optional hyphen, dot, or blank

                                  // Followed by
         @"[0-9]{3}" +            // 999
         @"[-\.\s]?" +            // optional hyphen, dot, or blank space
         @"[0-9]{4}$";            // 9999

         // These phone numbers are validated with the pattern above:
```

```
            // (201) 867-5309, 201.867.5309, 2018675309, (201)867-5309

            const string INPUT              = "(201) 867-5309";
            Regex reg                       = new Regex(PATTERN);
            Console.WriteLine("Pattern: " + PATTERN);

            if(reg.IsMatch(INPUT))
               Console.WriteLine("PASS:  " + INPUT);
            else
               Console.WriteLine("FAIL:  " + INPUT);
            Console.ReadLine();
        }
    }
}
```

When running this example, the output confirms that the phone number is validated with the regular expression:

```
Pattern: ^(\([0-9]{3}\)\s?|[0-9]{3}[-\.\s]?)[0-9]{3}[-\.\s]?[0-9]{4}$
PASS:   (201) 867-5309
```

There are lots of free tools online to help automate the process of building complex regular expressions. You might find one you like, but often you will still need to understand how regular expressions work before you can use them effectively. Common patterns such as phone numbers and e-mail addresses are usually easy to find through quick searches on the Web, too. If you seek help online, just make sure your tool or pattern is C# compliant, since other languages will implement regular expressions in a very similar but slightly different manner. If you are really stuck while trying to figure out how to validate strings, you might find other ways to parse a string without a regular expression to get the job done. On the other hand, regular expressions are extremely helpful for automating the process of validation, especially in web development, so the extra effort of figuring out how to use them often is worthwhile.

Converting Strings to Other Formats

When working with forms and other data sources, you may be confronted with a need to convert string data into numeric, date, or Boolean formats. There are two common ways to convert strings to other data types:

- The *Convert* class offers easy-to-use methods for converting strings to simple data types.
- The *TryParse()* method also enables conversion of string values to other data formats. *TryParse()* also provides additional error checking to prevent a conversion to an invalid data type.

Convert

Referencing the *Convert* class allows you to access methods that transform string arguments to other data types. Here are seven quick examples to demonstrate how to convert strings to decimal, float, double, int, long, *DateTime,* and bool formats:

```
decimal  decimalValue  = Convert.ToDecimal("10.5");
float    floatValue    = Convert.ToSingle("10.5");
double   doubleValue   = Convert.ToDouble("10.5");
int      intValue      = Convert.ToInt32("64000");
long     longValue     = Convert.ToInt64("123234243242343");
DateTime dateTimeValue = Convert.ToDateTime("2014/12/31");
bool     boolValue     = Convert.ToBoolean("true");
```

TryParse()

All simple C# data type objects expose a *TryParse()* method to transform strings to other data types. *TryParse()* handles string conversions more gracefully than the *Convert* class since *TryParse()* also determines if a conversion is possible. When the conversion is not possible, *TryParse()* returns false and the program continues to execute on the next line without any run-time error. For example, with the *Convert* class, this instruction causes a run-time error:

```
Convert.ToInt32("hello");
```

The *TryParse()* method, however, attempts a string conversion and returns a Boolean value of false when unsuccessful:

```
int            intValue;
bool success = int.TryParse("hello", out intValue);
```

The value generated from the conversion is stored in the *out* parameter. Here are seven quick examples to demonstrate how to use *TryParse()* to convert strings to decimal, float, double, int, long, *DateTime,* and Boolean formats:

```
bool success;

decimal   decimalValue;
success = decimal.TryParse("10.5", out decimalValue);

float       floatValue;
success = float.TryParse("10.5", out floatValue);
```

```
double      doubleValue;
success = double.TryParse("10.5", out doubleValue);

int           intValue;
success = int.TryParse("64000", out intValue);

long          longValue;
success = long.TryParse("123234243242343", out longValue);

DateTime dateTimeValue;
success = DateTime.TryParse("2014/12/31", out dateTimeValue);

// ToBoolean() does not require the uninitialized parameter.
// Instead it returns the Boolean value if successful.
success = Convert.ToBoolean("true");
```

NOTE

Additional techniques for converting strings into *DateTime* formats will be presented in Chapter 7.

Chapter 6 Self Test

The following questions are intended to help reinforce your comprehension of the concepts covered in this chapter. The answers can be found in the accompanying online Appendix B, "Answers to the Self Tests."

1. In a new program, store your name in a string variable named *fullName*. Then, store the last character of this string in a char variable. You may reference the last character of the string with the index value of *fullName.Length* – 1. Finally, display the value that is stored in the char variable.
2. Write a program that declares a string variable that stores the value of "Jeffrey steinberg". Assuming you don't know what the last name is, devise a way to find the start of the last name and update the original string to ensure that the first character of the last name is capitalized. Output the value of your updated string.
3. An Internet company called retrofitness.com issues e-mail addresses to all employees. The application that adds new employees to the database validates all data before entering it in the database. Write a regular expression that permits the entry of a valid @retrofitness.com e-mail address where the address prefix may contain alphabetical, underscore, hyphen, and dot characters. Note also that the first character in the e-mail address must be an alphabetical character.

4. Write a regular expression that only permits an entry of either "Cable" or "DSL".
5. Write a regular expression to ensure that an age string is valid for all numbers between "1" and "110".
6. Write an expression that only validates phrases with two or more occurrences of the word substring "go". Each occurrence of "go" is case insensitive. Sample valid strings include "Go dogs go" and "Ogopogo".
7. Write an expression to ensure that monetary amounts always begin with a "$" sign, that at least one digit exists on the left side of the decimal point, and that there are always two digits on the right side of the decimal point.
8. Write a program that prompts a user to enter percentage data. If incorrect data is provided, the user is prompted again. Initially, the input is read into a string with the following instruction:

```
string input = Console.ReadLine();
```

When the correct input is provided, the program displays the data rounded to two decimal places. The text from the program and user input could appear similar to the following:

```
Input percentage earned: abc
This value is incorrect. Please try again.
Input percentage earned:
This value is incorrect. Please try again.
Input percentage earned: 12.32aa
This value is incorrect. Please try again.
Input percentage earned: 12.478
You entered 12.48%
```

Chapter 7

Date and Time Handling

Key Skills & Concepts

- TimeSpan Syntax
- TimeSpan Calculations
- DateTime Syntax
- Formatting DateTime Output
- DateTime Calculations

Date and time conversions are not overly difficult, and they appear innocent at a glance, but user demand for a wide variety of different formats can at times be challenging. This chapter presents popular C# structures and methods for working with date and time values. In addition to discussing formatting options, properties and methods for calculating and comparing date and time units are covered here. When considering all of the adjustments needed to transition between mornings, afternoons, months of varied lengths, years, and leap years, you are going to want to take advantage of the C# library to manage time intervals, dates, and times. Having awareness of how the C# library helps to parse or calculate dates and time values is important, since these routines can be challenging.

The two primary C# types you need for manipulating dates and times are the *TimeSpan* type and the *DateTime* type. Both C# types are available through the *System* namespace.

TimeSpan Syntax

The *TimeSpan* type stores and manages time interval components for blocks of time ranging from ticks to milliseconds to days. While *TimeSpan* objects do not store or manage dates, they are especially helpful when calculating time intervals between dates. To initialize a *TimeSpan* object, you may assign a combination of units that range from milliseconds to days:

```
TimeSpan ts = new TimeSpan(int hours, int minutes, int seconds);
TimeSpan ts = new TimeSpan(int days, int hours, int minutes, int seconds);
TimeSpan ts = new TimeSpan(int days, int hours, int minutes, int seconds,
                           int milliseconds);
```

Return Type	Property Name	Description
int	Ticks	Gets the total ticks. (There are 10,000 ticks in a millisecond.)
int	Milliseconds	Gets the milliseconds component of this time interval.
int	Seconds	Gets the seconds component of this time interval.
int	Minutes	Gets the minutes component of this time interval.
int	Hours	Gets the hours component of this time interval.
int	Days	Gets the days component of this time interval.
double	TotalMilliseconds	Gets the total time interval in milliseconds.
double	TotalSeconds	Gets the total time interval in seconds.
double	TotalMinutes	Gets the total time interval in minutes.
double	TotalHours	Gets the total time interval in hours.
double	TotalDays	Gets the total time interval in days.

Table 7-1 TimeSpan Properties

TimeSpan Properties

The *TimeSpan* type provides properties to offer information about the time interval it stores. The *TimeSpan* type's properties and their roles are summarized in Table 7-1.

NOTE

We will not use the *Ticks* property in this book. While ticks are not usually used in data-driven programming, they can be helpful for tracking time in programs that animate objects.

Example 7-1 TimeSpan Syntax and Properties

This example shows how the *TimeSpan* properties are used to extract information about a time interval. First, the total time is broken down into day, hour, minute, and second components. Then, the total duration of the *TimeSpan* object is displayed as different units, including total days, total hours, total minutes, and total seconds.

```
using System;
namespace Starter {
    class Program {
        public static void Main() {
            // Store daily work time.
            const int DAY=0, HRS=9, MIN=34, SEC=38;
```

```
            TimeSpan ts = new TimeSpan(DAY, HRS, MIN, SEC);
            Console.WriteLine(ts.Days + " days "
                            + ts.Hours + " hours "
                            + ts.Minutes + " minutes "
                            + ts.Seconds + " seconds ");

            Console.WriteLine("TimeSpan in Days:          " + ts.TotalDays
                                                              .ToString("N2"));
            Console.WriteLine("TimeSpan in Hours:         " + ts.TotalHours
                                                              .ToString("N2"));
            Console.WriteLine("TimeSpan in Minutes:       " + ts.TotalMinutes
                                                              .ToString("N2"));
            Console.WriteLine("TimeSpan in Seconds:       " + ts.TotalSeconds);
            Console.ReadLine();
        }
    }
}
```

The output shows the different values for this time interval:

```
0 days 9 hours 34 minutes 38 seconds 0 milliseconds
TimeSpan in Days:         0.40
TimeSpan in Hours:        9.58
TimeSpan in Minutes:      574.63
TimeSpan in Seconds:      34478
```

TimeSpan Calculations

The *TimeSpan* type also provides many options to perform calculations with time intervals. Here we will look at simple but popular methods for adding, subtracting, and comparing time intervals.

TimeSpan Addition

The *TimeSpan* type's *Add()* method adds one *TimeSpan* object to another and returns a *TimeSpan* object:

```
TimeSpan Add(TimeSpan ts);
```

In the following code example, a *TimeSpan* object that stores 1 day and 13 hours is added to itself. As expected, the value returned is twice as large as the original.

```
const int DAY=1, HRS=13, MIN=0, SEC=0;
TimeSpan ts = new TimeSpan(DAY, HRS, MIN, SEC);      // 1 day 13 hours
ts = ts.Add(ts);                                     // 3 days 2 hours
Console.WriteLine(ts.Days + " days " + ts.Hours + " hours ");
```

TimeSpan Subtraction

The *Subtract()* method of the *TimeSpan* type calculates the difference between *TimeSpan* values and returns the difference in *TimeSpan* format:

```
TimeSpan Subtract(TimeSpan ts)
```

In the following code example, a *TimeSpan* object storing1 day is subtracted from a *TimeSpan* object storing 1 day and 13 hours, resulting in a difference of 13 hours:

```
const int DAY=1, HRS_A=13, HRS_B=0, MIN=0, SEC=0;
TimeSpan tsA = new TimeSpan(DAY, HRS_A, MIN, SEC);  // 1 day 13 hours
TimeSpan tsB = new TimeSpan(DAY, HRS_B, MIN, SEC);  // 1 day 0  hours
TimeSpan tsC = tsA.Subtract(tsB);                   // 13 hours
Console.WriteLine(tsC.Days + " days " + tsC.Hours + " hours ");
```

TimeSpan Comparison

The *CompareTo()* method compares one *TimeSpan* object with a *TimeSpan* parameter value:

```
int CompareTo(TimeSpan ts)
```

This method returns

- –1 if the original *TimeSpan* value is less than the parameter value.
- 0 if the original *TimeSpan* value is equal to the parameter value.
- 1 if the original *TimeSpan* value is greater than the parameter value.

In the following example, a *TimeSpan* object storing 1 day and 13 hours is compared with a *TimeSpan* object storing 1 day. Since the first object is greater, the *CompareTo()* result is 1.

```
const int DAY=1, HRS_A=13, HRS_B=0, MIN=0, SEC=0;
TimeSpan tsA = new TimeSpan(DAY, HRS_A, MIN, SEC);  // 1 day 13 hours
TimeSpan tsB = new TimeSpan(DAY, HRS_B, MIN, SEC);  // 1 day 0  hours
int tsC      = tsA.CompareTo(tsB);                  // Returns 1
Console.WriteLine(tsC);
```

Try This 7-1 TimeSpan Practice

This exercise offers practice in setting up, subtracting, and comparing *TimeSpan* objects. Consider a case where a programmer spends 9 hours and 12 minutes at the office one day. The programmer spends 4 hours and 50 minutes testing. The rest of the time is spent coding.

1. Write a program that uses *TimeSpan* objects to calculate the time this programmer spends coding.
2. Using *TimeSpan* properties, show the time spent coding in hours and minutes.
3. In the same program, use the *CompareTo()* method to determine if more time is spent testing or coding during this day.

DateTime Syntax

The C# *DateTime* type stores, formats, and manages date and time values for specific points in time. Three common initializers (constructors) of the *DateTime* structure include

```
DateTime(int year, int month, int day);
DateTime(int year, int month, int day, int hour, int minute, int second);
DateTime(int year, int month, int day, int hour, int minute, int second,
        int millisecond);
```

NOTE

If needed, other options exist to store the time zone and calendar type when initializing a *DateTime* value.

System Time

Often, you may need to record the current time of a transaction or you may need to perform comparisons between the current time and future times or dates. The *DateTime.Now* property returns the current system date and time:

```
DateTime dtNow = DateTime.Now;
```

DateTime Properties

The *DateTime* type provides several properties to retrieve information about each component of the date and time value stored. These *DateTime* properties are summarized in Table 7-2.

Return Type	Property Name	Description
int	Millisecond	Gets milliseconds.
int	Second	Gets seconds.
int	Minute	Gets minutes.
int	Hour	Gets hours.
int	Day	Gets days.
{ Sunday, Monday, Tuesday, Wednesday, Thursday, Friday, Saturday }	DayOfWeek	Gets day of week.
int	DayOfYear	Gets day of year.
int	Month	Gets month.
int	Year	Gets year.
DateTime	Date	Gets or sets the date component of this instance but assigns the time 12:00:00 AM.

Table 7-2 DateTime Properties

Example 7-2 DateTime Syntax and Properties

Here is a full example that demonstrates how to initialize a *DateTime* object and show its different property values:

```
using System;
namespace Starter {
    class Program {
        public static void Main() {
            const int YR=1791, MTH=12, DAY=26, HRS=9, MIN=57, SEC=46;
            DateTime birthday = new DateTime(YR, MTH, DAY, HRS, MIN, SEC);
            ShowDateTime(birthday);
            Console.ReadLine();
        }

        public static void ShowDateTime(DateTime dt) {
            Console.Write("Year: "                 + dt.Year);
            Console.Write("    Month: "            + dt.Month);
            Console.WriteLine("    Day: "          + dt.Day);
            Console.Write("DayOfWeek: "            + dt.DayOfWeek);
            Console.WriteLine("    DayOfYear: "    + dt.DayOfYear);
            Console.Write("Hours: "                + dt.Hour);
```

```
            Console.Write("    Minutes: "       + dt.Minute);
            Console.WriteLine("    Seconds: "   + dt.Second);
        }
    }
}
```

The output shows details about the birthdate and time of Charles Babbage, who invented the first computer:

```
Year: 1791   Month: 12   Day: 26
DayOfWeek: Monday   DayOfYear: 360
Hours: 9   Minutes: 57   Seconds: 46
```

\

Formatting DateTime Output

To output *DateTime* values as formatted text, the *ToString()* method receives format specifiers as parameters to customize the output. Common *DateTime* format specifiers are summarized in Table 7-3.

Example 7-3 DateTime Format Specifiers

This example shows the implementation of three *DateTime* format specifiers from Table 7-3 to display the full weekday name, the full month name and day number, and the short time, which lists hours, minutes, and AM or PM:

```
using System;
namespace Starter {
    class Program {
        public static void Main() {
            DateTime dt = DateTime.Now;
            Console.Write(dt.ToString("dddd" + " "));    // Full day.
            Console.Write(dt.ToString("m")   + ", "      // Month and day.
                      +  dt.ToString("t"));              // Short time.
            Console.ReadLine();
        }
    }
}
```

Components of the *DateTime* value are displayed in the expected format:

```
Friday April 11, 3:03 PM
```

Format Specifier	Description	Example
ss	Seconds	32
mm	Minute	20
hh	Two-digit hour	02
HH	Two-digit 24 hour	14
tt	AM/PM	PM
t	Short time	2:20 PM
T	Time	2:20:32 PM
dd	Two-digit day	19
ddd	Short day	Wed
dddd	Full day	Wednesday
MM	Two-digit month	03
MMM	Short month	Mar
MMMM	Month name	March
yy	Two-digit year	86
yyyy	Four-digit year	1986
s	Sortable date/time	1986-11-19T14:20:32
u	Universal sortable date/time	1986-11-19 14:20:32Z
U	Universal full date/time	Wednesday, March 19, 1986 9:20:32 PM
o	Round-trip date/time	1986-03-19T14:20:32.4085556-07:00
r	RFC 1123 date	Wed, 19 Mar 1986 14:20:32 GMT
D	Long date format	Wednesday, March 19, 1986
f	Long date/short time	Wednesday, March 19, 1986 2:20 PM
F	Long date/time	Wednesday, March 19, 1986 2:20:32 PM
g	General date/short time	3/19/1986 2:20 PM
G	General date/time	3/19/1986 2:20:32 PM
m	Month and day	March 19
:	Separator (e.g., hh:mm:ss)	02:20:32
/	Slash (e.g., MM/dd/yyyy)	03/19/1986

Table 7-3 DateTime Format Specifiers

DateTime Calculations

Date and time calculations can be difficult, especially when you consider transitions between hours, mornings and afternoons, days, months, and leap years. To help manage this wide variety of possibilities, the *DateTime* type offers several methods for adding, subtracting, and comparing dates and times.

Adding Units of Time

Several methods exist for adding units of time to a *DateTime* instance, as summarized in Table 7-4.

Example 7-4 DateTime Addition

This example demonstrates implementation of the *DateTime* addition methods listed in Table 7-4. First, the birthday of Charles Babbage is assigned to a *DateTime* object and this value is then printed. Then, units of 14 are added to each component of the *DateTime* value. The resulting *DateTime* value after the addition is then printed. These same methods are then used to decrement units of 14 from each component from the original *DateTime* value. The value generated from the latest calculation is then printed.

```
using System;

namespace Starter {
    class Program {
```

Return Type	Method Name	Description
DateTime	AddMilliseconds(double value)	Adds milliseconds to DateTime value.
DateTime	AddSeconds(double value)	Adds seconds to DateTime value.
DateTime	AddMinutes(double value)	Adds minutes to DateTime value.
DateTime	AddHours(double value)	Adds hours to DateTime value.
DateTime	AddDays(double value)	Adds days to DateTime value.
DateTime	AddMonths(int months)	Adds months to DateTime value.
DateTime	AddYears(int years)	Adds years to DateTime value.
DateTime	Add(Timespan value)	Adds time specified in days, hours, minutes, seconds, or milliseconds to DateTime value.

Table 7-4 DateTime Addition Methods

```
        public static void Main() {
            const int YR=1791, MTH=12, DAY=26, HRS=9, MIN=57, SEC=46;
            DateTime cBabbage = new DateTime(YR, MTH, DAY, HRS, MIN, SEC);
            Console.WriteLine("Original DateTime: " + cBabbage.ToString("G"));
            Sum(cBabbage,  14);
            Sum(cBabbage, -14);
            Console.ReadLine();
        }
        static DateTime Sum(DateTime dt, double operand) {
            dt = dt.AddSeconds(operand);
            dt = dt.AddMinutes(operand);
            dt = dt.AddHours(operand);
            dt = dt.AddDays(operand);
            dt = dt.AddMonths((int)operand);
            dt = dt.AddYears((int)operand);
            Console.Write(operand + " added to each unit: ");
            Console.WriteLine( dt.ToString("G"));
            return dt;
        }
    }
}
```

The output shows the original date and the final dates after incrementing and decrementing each component in the object. Notice how easy it is to make the date and time adjustment without having to worry about overlap between mornings and afternoons or even year changes.

```
Original DateTime: 12/26/1791 9:57:46 AM
14 added to each unit: 3/10/1807 12:12:00 AM
-14 added to each unit: 10/11/1776 7:43:32 PM
```

Try This 7-2 DateTime Practice

In this exercise you will have a chance to practice using the *DateTime* object properties and addition methods. Write a program that does the following:

1. Initializes a *DateTime* variable that stores the current date.
2. Determines when the next Monday after the current day is.

3. Outputs the dates of six weekly meetings starting at 4:00 PM beginning next Monday. Use format specifiers with the *DateTime* object to output the series of dates in a format like the following:

```
*** Meeting Dates and Times ***
Monday, January 5, 4:00 PM
Monday, January 12, 4:00 PM
Monday, January 19, 4:00 PM
Monday, January 26, 4:00 PM
Monday, February 2, 4:00 PM
Monday, February 9, 4:00 PM
```

DateTime Subtraction

To calculate the difference between two dates, you can use the *Subtract()* method of the *DateTime* type. This method receives a *DateTime* object as a parameter and returns a *TimeSpan* object that stores the interval between dates and times:

```
TimeSpan Subtract(DateTime value)
```

Example 7-5 DateTime Subtraction

This example subtracts Pablo Picasso's birthdate from Bill Gates's birhdate to determine the number of days between their births:

```
using System;
using System;
namespace Starter {
    class Program {
        public static void Main() {
            DateTime pPicasso = new DateTime(1881, 10, 25, 23, 15, 0);
            DateTime bGates   = new DateTime(1955, 10, 28, 22, 0, 0);
            TimeSpan ts       = bGates.Subtract(pPicasso);
            Console.WriteLine("Pablo Picasso Birthday: "
                            + pPicasso.ToString("G"));
            Console.WriteLine("Bill Gates Birthday: "
                            + bGates.ToString("G"));
            Console.WriteLine("Bill Gates was born "
                            + ts.TotalDays.ToString("N0")
                            + " days after Pablo Picasso.");
            Console.ReadLine();
```

```
        }
    }
}
```

Very quickly we are able to determine that Bill Gates was born 27,030 days after Pablo Picasso:

```
Pablo Picasso Birthday: 10/25/1881 11:15:00 PM
Bill Gates Birthday: 10/28/1955 10:00:00 PM
Bill Gates was born 27,030 days after Pablo Picasso.
```

DateTime Comparison

The *CompareTo()* method of the *DateTime* type allows you to determine if one date and time combination is older than, newer than, or the same as another:

```
int CompareTo(DateTime value)
```

When used with *DateTime*, the *CompareTo()* method returns

- –1 if the value is earlier.
- 0 if the value is equal.
- 1 if the value is greater.

Example 7-6 DateTime Comparison

This example uses *CompareTo()* to evaluate the birthdates of Cubist artists Pablo Picasso and Marie Laurencin to determine who is older:

```
using System;
namespace Starter {
    class Program {
        public static void Main() {
            DateTime picasso    = new DateTime(1881, 10, 25);
            DateTime laurencin = new DateTime(1883, 10, 31);
            int comparison      = picasso.CompareTo(laurencin);

            Console.Write("Pablo Picasso is ");
            if (comparison > 0)
                Console.Write("younger than ");
            else if (comparison < 0)
                Console.Write("older than ");
```

```
            else
                Console.Write("the same age as ");
            Console.WriteLine("Marie Laurencin.");

            Console.ReadLine();
        }
    }
}
```

As expected, Pablo Picasso is older than Marie Laurencin, who was born two years later:

```
Pablo Picasso is older than Marie Laurencin.
```

Chapter 7 Self Test

The following questions are intended to help reinforce your comprehension of the concepts covered in this chapter. The answers can be found in the accompanying online Appendix B, "Answers to the Self Tests."

1. Write a program that uses *DateTime* format specifiers to display a date and time with the following format:

   ```
   Wednesday March 19, 10:18 PM
   ```

2. Write a program that calculates the total number of seconds that you have been alive.
3. Write a program that calculates the total number of days for each year during the last four years. Use this information to determine which year was a leap year. Print out the year number and the total days that year.

Part II

Object-Oriented Programming

Chapter 8

Encapsulation Through Object-Oriented Programming

Key Skills & Concepts

- Encapsulation
- Classes
- Static Structures
- Structs
- Namespaces
- Partial Classes

With C# and most modern programming languages, object-oriented design is such a prevalent methodology, it affects all aspects of your program. Robust software development relies on a solid understanding of object-oriented techniques.

Previous chapters have introduced C# structures that support object-oriented programming (OOP), but we have not yet taken an in-depth look at how to use this development style for encapsulation. *Encapsulation* refers to the grouping of related logic and data members within a unit while hiding their implementation details. Encapsulation is helpful because it allows us to write code that is compartmentalized, easy-to-read, reuseable, and testable as a stand-alone component. Well-designed encapsulated units work nicely with each other while also managing their own internal logic independently of others.

Encapsulation

Encapsulation is enabled through well-designed classes and structs. Classes and structs are really blueprints that define a series of related methods and data structures. The methods and data structures defined inside are referred to as *members*. This blueprint is then used to generate objects. Object instances are implementations of a class or struct, and each instance stores a separate data set.

Accessibility

Varying levels of access can be assigned to the data members and methods of a class or struct to either hide internal logic and data or to grant access to specific structures. Three common levels of access are *private, protected,* and *public.*

Private

Data structures and methods with private access can only be used inside the class or struct. The default access level for class members is private when none is specified.

Protected

Data members and methods that are protected can be accessed either from inside the class or from child classes that inherit from the parent class. Structs cannot inherit from other structs, so they do not have a protected access level for data members or methods.

NOTE

Inheritance will be discussed in more detail in Chapter 9.

Public

Declaring a variable, data structure, or method with public access allows users of this object to reference this member. In the following class declaration, the variables stored at the class level are private, so they are not directly accessible outside this class. However, the public *DisplayLocation()* method can be accessed by the object of the class to show the data that is stored within the object.

```
class Location {
    // Private data members which the object cannot access.
    private int    streetNumber;
    private string streetName;

    // Overloaded constructor that initializes the object.
    public Location(int streetNumber, string streetName) {
        this.streetName   = streetName;
        this.streetNumber = streetNumber;
    }

    // Publicly accessible method which the object can access.
    public void DisplayLocation() {
        Console.Write(streetNumber + " ");
        Console.WriteLine(streetName);
    }
}
```

Classes

Classes are blueprints that define methods and data sets. Their ability to group, encapsulate, and regulate access to members makes them a fundamental building block of well-designed software. Classes are a reference type, since they store address references to the data.

Objects

In this section, to stay focused on classes, we will refer to objects as objects of classes rather than as objects of structs. An object is an *instance* of the class or struct. If a class is a blueprint, then an object instance is the building that has been constructed using the blueprint. Classes can have multiple object instances. You declare an object of the class type with the class name. You can then initialize an object with the *new* keyword followed by a reference to the constructor. The constructor is a special method that initializes the instance of the class. The following is a sample of an instruction (from the upcoming Example 8-1) that declares and initializes an object named *empireStateBldg,* which is an object of the *Location* class:

```
// Declare object and initialize it with the Location() constructor.
Location empireStateBldg = new Location(350, " 5th Avenue");
```

Objects promote encapsulation because a specific data set is referenced with every instance. Private data members and methods are accessible to the object but not to consumers of the object. However, public methods and data members are accessible to both the object and users of the object. At the same time, the internal logic of the object is hidden from the rest of the program. As you'll see a bit later, the *Location* class in Example 8-1 contains the following public *DisplayLocation()* method so that the *empireStateBldg* object is able to provide an external reference to it:

```
empireStateBldg.DisplayLocation();
```

Class Declarations

Classes are declared with the keyword *class* followed by the class name. Most C# developers assign PascalCase class names that are nouns or word combinations starting with a noun that describes the class. All code within the class is enclosed within opening and closing curly braces that follow the class header.

NOTE

By default, the class declaration is *internal,* so you do not need to specify its access level. A class with an internal access modifier means it is publicly accessible to other structures but only within the current namespace.

Here is a shell that could serve as a valid class declaration for the *Location* class:

```
class Location {
}
```

Classes are usually written in a separate code file that has the same name as the class. As an example, a class with a name such as *AccountManager* would usually be stored in a code file named AccountManager.cs. To keep the code examples in this book compact, though, several classes are often placed in one file. The generally accepted practice, however, involves placing each class in a separate file for larger programs.

Keyword This

The keyword *this* may be used to explicitly reference a member within the class-level scope from a method. The upcoming Example 8-1 shows the keyword *this* being used to reference the variables named *streetNumber* and *streetName* at the class level:

```
class Location {
    private int    streetNumber;
    private string streetName;

    public Location(int streetNumber, string streetName) {
        this.streetName   = streetName;
        this.streetNumber = streetNumber;
    }
}
```

Constructors

A constructor is the first method of a class that is called to initialize the object when an instance is created. The constructor is referenced after the *new* keyword during object creation. Constructors are distinguishable from other methods because constructors share the same name as the class and do not have a return type. The constructor is sort of like the construction crew building the object. The following is a class declaration for a *Location* class that includes a *Location* constructor:

```
class Location {
    private int    streetNumber;                           // Data members.
    private string streetName;

    public Location(int streetNumber, string streetName) {  // Constructor.
        this.streetName   = streetName;
        this.streetNumber = streetNumber;
    }
}
```

The constructor is referenced after the *new* keyword during object creation. For example, when creating an object of the Location class, if a Location constructor overload receives the street number and name, it can be used to initialize the street number and name when creating a new instance of the class:

```
Location empireStateBldg = new Location(350, "5th Avenue");
```

Default Constructors

Classes can implement a default constructor that has no parameters. When no constructor is present in the class, the default constructor is automatically provided, so you are not required to include it for this case:

```
class Location {
}
```

With this class declaration, an object of this *Location* class can be created without having to specify any parameters:

```
Location apolloTheater = new Location();
```

In a class, though, you can also add a default constructor that has no parameters if you wish to include any initialization logic.

Here is a sample that shows a *Location* class that implements logic in a default constructor:

```
class Location {
    private string city;

    public Location() {                  // Default constructor.
        this.city = "New York";
    }
}
```

Example 8-1 Object Creation

To see how the basic components of a class fit together, let's examine a complete program that declares and implements a class named *Location*. This class is used to create two separate objects. One object stores street address information for the Empire State Building and the other stores street address information for the Republic Plaza. In the code, the class-level data members are private, so they are accessible inside the object but not to users of the object. The first object is created with a constructor overload that receives the parameters *streetNumber* and *streetName*. Inside the constructor, these values are assigned to class-level variables of the same name. The second object is created with a default constructor. A public method named *SetLocation()* is used by the second object to pass *streetNumber* and *streetName* data to the class. The *DisplayLocation()* method is public, too, so both objects can reference it to display data stored in each instance.

```
using System;
namespace Starter {
    class Program{
        public static void Main() {
            // Object creation.
            Location empireStateBldg = new Location(350, "5th Avenue");
            Location republicPlaza   = new Location();

            // Call public method to store data in object.
            republicPlaza.SetLocation(9, "Raffles Place");

            // Use object to access a public method for display.
            empireStateBldg.DisplayLocation();
            republicPlaza.DisplayLocation();
            Console.ReadLine();
        }
    }

    // Class declaration.
    class Location {
        // Private data members.
        private int    streetNumber;
        private string streetName;

        // Default constructor.
        public Location() {
        }

        // Overloaded constructor.
        public Location(int streetNumber, string streetName) {
            this.streetName   = streetName;
            this.streetNumber = streetNumber;
        }

        // Publicly accessible methods.
        public void SetLocation(int streetNumber, string streetName) {
            this.streetName   = streetName;
            this.streetNumber = streetNumber;
        }
```

```
        public void DisplayLocation() {
            Console.Write(streetNumber + " ");
            Console.WriteLine(streetName);
        }
    }
}
```

Consumers of the *Location* object cannot reference the private data contained in it, so we cannot write

```
Console.WriteLine(republicPlaza.streetName); // Not permitted.
```

However, consumers of the *Location* object have access to the public members like the *DisplayLocation()* method, so we can write

```
republicPlaza.DisplayLocation();             // Permitted.
350  5th Avenue
9 Raffles Place
```

Try This 8-1 Class Creation, Constructor, and Accessor Exercise

This exercise offers practice in class creation and implementation with different access levels. Here are the steps to try:

1. In a new console project, create a new class called *City*.
2. Set up the *City* constructor to initialize the *City* object with *name* and *population* parameter values that are then stored in private variables of the *City* class.
3. Create a public method called *GetCity()* that returns the name of the city from the *City* class.
4. Also, create a public method called *GetPopulation()* that returns the population value that is stored in the *City* class.
5. In the *Main()* method, create an instance of *City* and display the city name and population using values returned by the respective *City* methods.

Properties

C# properties store, read, and write data values at the class or struct level. This section discusses properties within the context of a class. Properties are like class-level variables, but a property value's access level can be managed with more flexibility and in fewer lines of code. Property names are usually PascalCased, so this is the convention used in the book.

Get and Set Accessors

A property value is read with a *get* accessor and written with a *set* accessor. These get and set accessors function like methods. Many languages don't have properties, so instead, it is common to create methods for writing to and reading from class-level variables to encapsulate class data as much as possible. The favored approach for C# developers, though, is to use properties rather than class-level variables to improve code readability and efficiency.

When declaring a property, both get and set accessors can be defined simultaneously with the same access level defined on the left. In the following example, the get and set accessors are private by default because the property is declared as private:

```
private string FirstName { get; set; }
```

It is possible, though, to declare a property that has a get accessor with a different access level than a set accessor. However, the set and get accessors cannot be more accessible than the property itself. In this example, the *Birthday* property has a public get accessor and a private set accessor:

```
public  DateTime Birthday { get; private set; }        // Correct.
```

This next example is an invalid property declaration because the get accessor is more accessible than the property:

```
private DateTime Birthday { public get; private set; } // Incorrect.
```

The auto-implemented properties with get and set accessors allow us to avoid having to write the standard boilerplate code. However, both accessors can contain extra logic. Return statements may be nested under get accessors to generate the return value of a property. A *value* keyword may be used within a set accessor's instruction set to assign data to the property:

```
private string buildingName;

public string BuildingName {
    get { return buildingName;  }
    set { buildingName = value; }
}
```

More than one line of code can be included in an accessor as well. Here is an example of a get accessor in a *FullName* property that uses multiple instructions to generate and return the value:

```
private string FirstName { get; set; }
private string LastName  { get; set; }
public  string FullName  { get { string fullName = FirstName + " " + LastName;
                                 return fullName; }}
```

Example 8-2 Properties

This example demonstrates how to create a *Person* class with a *Birthday* property that has a different level of access for the set and get accessors. The *FirstName* and *LastName* properties in the example are only available for reads and writes privately, but a public *FullName* property makes the full name available to the object.

```
using System;
namespace Starter {
    class Program {
        public static void Main() {
            DateTime birthday = new DateTime(1511, 6, 18);

            // Declare and initialize a Person object.
            Person      person = new Person("Bartolomeo", "Ammannati",
                                           birthday);
            Console.Write(person.FullName + " " );
            Console.WriteLine(birthday.ToString("yyyy/MM/dd"));
            Console.ReadLine(); // user must press 'Exit' to quit.
        }
    }

    class Person {
        // This property is available to the object for reads but not for writes.
        public DateTime Birthday  { get; private set; }

        // These properties are not readable or writable outside the class.
        private string FirstName  { get; set; }
        private string LastName   { get; set; }

        // This property has read-only access and is publicly accessible.
        public  string FullName   { get {return FirstName + " " + LastName; }}
```

```
        public Person(string firstName, string lastName, DateTime birthday) {
            FirstName = firstName;
            LastName  = lastName;
            Birthday  = birthday;
        }
    }
}
```

When running this program, the object can be used to display the data that is stored inside the class properties:

```
Bartolomeo Ammannati 1511/06/18
```

Destructors

The destructor is a method that is called every time an object instance is destroyed to de-allocate memory used by the object. By default, the destructor already exists, so you don't have to include it in your class. The destructor has no parameters, and only one destructor per class is allowed. You can include a destructor in your class if you want to implement a custom routine whenever your class instances are destroyed. A manually declared destructor can be useful in a situation such as when a series of tasks must be completed during an accidental application shutdown. Manually declared constructors are preceded with a tilde and the name of the class:

```
~ClassName() {                    // destructor
    Console.WriteLine("removing class instance.");
}
```

There is no way to directly call a destructor. When a class instance is set to null, the object is effectively de-referenced but the object remains in memory. To clear the memory, a garbage collector runs on another system thread that is managed by the .NET Framework. The garbage collector decides when to clear unused resources from memory. You can call the command *GC.Collect()* to force the garbage collector to clear the memory used by your object before the application shuts down.

CAUTION

Usually, you should avoid invoking the garbage collector from your code, since this can cause performance issues.

Example 8-3 Destructors

Even though you normally would not call *GC.Collect()*, this example implements a manually created destructor for a class to demonstrate how it works. When you run the application, you will notice that the destructor does not get called immediately when the object is set to null.

```
using System;
namespace Starter {
    class Program {
        public static void Main() {
            // Declare and initialize person objects.
            Person personA = new Person("Stephen", "Sauvestre");
            Person personB = new Person("Jorn", "Utzon");
            personB        = null;

            /* Uncomment the line below to observe the effect of
               forced garbage collection when 'Enter' is pressed. */
            // GC.Collect();
            Console.ReadLine();        // Wait for user input before shut down.
        }
    }

    class Person {
        protected string FirstName = "";
        protected string LastName  = "";
        public Person(string firstName, string lastName) {   // Constructor
            FirstName = firstName;
            LastName  = lastName;
        }

        ~Person() {                                            // Destructor
            Console.WriteLine(FirstName + " " + LastName);
            Console.WriteLine("*Removing instance.*");
        }
    }
}
```

When you launch the application, there will be no output. However, after you press ENTER to stop the application, if you watch closely, you might be able to view the following output printed from the destructor before the application closes:

```
Jorn Utzon
*Removing instance.*
Stephen Sauvestre
*Removing instance.*
```

Next, after stopping the program, uncomment the instruction, *GC.Collect()*, and run the application again. Before you press ENTER to quit the application, *firstName* and *lastName* values for *personB* are printed from the destructor since the garbage collector is directly invoked immediately after *personB* is set to null:

```
Jorn Utzon
*Removing instance.*
```

Then, press ENTER to stop the application from running. If you look closely, you might see the following output while the application shuts down:

```
Stephen Sauvestre
*Removing instance.*
```

Static Structures

Before this chapter, all classes, methods, and class-level variables have been declared as *static*. A static modifier for a class, method, or data member implies that it is accessed without an object instance. Static structures are accessible to the entire application, so they are said to be *shared*. Shared structures offer convenience due to their accessibility anywhere in a program without any instantiation. Static structures are helpful, but use them with care because they are not user session specific and are not as well encapsulated as features that are available with instantiation.

You might find static structures helpful for building constructs that are used universally throughout the application, such as for displaying generic error messages or for storing constant values that are used in multiple classes of a program.

Declaring Static Structures

Static structures are declared with the *static* keyword.

Static Data Members

Static data members can exist in instantiated and static classes. When declaring static variables or properties, the keyword *static* follows the access modifier, if there is one, and precedes the variable or property type:

```
static class Location {
    private static int    streetNumber;
    private static string streetName;
        public static string BranchLocation { get {
            return streetNumber + " " + streetName;
```

```
        }
    }
}
```

No object is needed to reference a static data member. You just need to reference the class name and data member. For the example, you can reference the data member outside the class with this instruction:

```
Location.BranchLocation;
```

Static Methods

Static methods can exist in instantiated or static classes. In method header declarations, the static modifier precedes the return type and follows the access modifier if one is declared:

```
static class Location {
    public  static int    StreetNumber { get; private set; }
    public  static string StreetName   { get; private set; }
    public static void SetLocation(int streetNumber, string streetName) {
        StreetName   = streetName;
        StreetNumber = streetNumber;
    }
}
```

Non-static fields of a class cannot be accessed from a static method without an object reference, so the following example is invalid:

```
decimal monthlyFee = 15.00m;
static decimal UpdateBalance(decimal balance) {
    return balance - monthlyFee; // Not allowed.
}
```

It is also not possible to call non-static methods from a static method without an object reference, so this example is also invalid:

```
decimal UpdateBalance(decimal balance) {
    const decimal MONTHLY_FEE = 15.00m;
    return balance - MONTHLY_FEE;
}
static void ShowBalance(decimal balance) {
    Console.Write("The month end balance is: ");
    Console.WriteLine(UpdateBalance(balance));    // Not allowed.
}
```

Static Classes

Whenever a class is static, it cannot be instantiated. Since it is not possible to create objects with static classes, static classes cannot have instance constructors. To declare a static class, the static modifier is placed before the *class* keyword in the class declaration:

```
static class Location {
}
```

Example 8-4 Static vs. Non-static Structures

This example highlights differences in the way that static classes, methods, properties, and variables are referenced. To enable the comparison, a static class, an instantiated class with a static variable and method, and an instantiated class with no static members are implemented.

When examining the code, note that all static method references must be prefixed with the class name, but the non-static method in the instantiated class must be referenced with an object:

```
using System;

namespace Starter {
    class Program {
        public static void Main() {
            // Use static class.
            StaticClass.ShowName("Pisano");

            // Use static method in a non-static class.
            StaticMethods.ShowName("Pisano");

            // Use non-static method in an instantiated class.
            InstantiatedClass instantiatedClass = new InstantiatedClass("Pisano");
            instantiatedClass.ShowName();

            Console.ReadLine();
        }
    }

    static class StaticClass {
        private static string first = "Bonanno";
        public static void ShowName(string last) {
            Console.WriteLine("Full Name: " + first + " " + last);
        }
    }

    class StaticMethods {
```

```
        private static string first = "Bonanno";
        public static void ShowName(string last) {
            Console.WriteLine( "Full Name: " + first + " " + last);
        }
    }

    class InstantiatedClass {
        private string first = "Bonanno";
        private string Last { get;set; }
        public InstantiatedClass(string last) {
            Last  = last;
        }

        public void ShowName() {
            Console.WriteLine("Full Name: " + first + " " + Last);
        }
    }
}
```

The output shows the same results with the different forms of reference:

```
Full Name: Bonanno Pisano
Full Name: Bonanno Pisano
Full Name: Bonanno Pisano
```

Try This 8-2 Examining Static Structures

This exercise offers you a chance to experiment with static structures. Since static structures are used throughout this exercise, it is important to recognize that no class instances are used during the exercise.

1. Starting with the code in Example 8-4, add a non-static variable at the class level of *StaticClass* and try to compile the program. Explain in your own words why you receive a compile error.
2. Starting with the code in Example 8-4, add the following class-level variable declaration to the *StaticMethods* class:

   ```
   string lastName = "Pisano";
   ```

   Next, in the *StaticMethods* class, replace the instruction

   ```
   Console.WriteLine( "Full Name: " + first + " " + last);
   ```

with

```
Console.WriteLine( "Full Name: " + first + " " + lastName);
```

When you try to run the program, explain in your own words why you receive an error.

3. Which instruction inside the *Main()* method of Example 8-4 supports the statement that a static class does not require instantiation?
4. Starting with Example 8-4, add the following class:

```
static class FirstNameClass{
    private static string first = "Bonanno";
    public static string First { get { return first; } }
}
```

5. Next, replace all references to the *first* name variable inside each of the three *WriteLine()* instructions with a reference to the *First* property of the *FirstNameClass.* Test your program to ensure the modification works correctly.

Example 8-5 A Practical Application of Static Modifiers

This example offers a more practical view of how static modifiers might be used to manage routines that are common to all classes of the application. For this case, the static class *App* hosts methods for displaying error messages and for showing the company title.

```
using System;

namespace Starter {
    class Program {
        public static void Main() {
            do {
                App.ShowCompanyTitle();      // Show title with static class.
                Console.WriteLine("1. Keep shopping");
                Console.WriteLine("2. Quit ");
                string input = Console.ReadLine().Trim();

                if (input != "1" && input != "2")
                    App.ShowInputError();    // Show error with static class.
                else if (input == "1")
                    Console.WriteLine("...shopping.");
                else {
                    Console.WriteLine("Thank you for shopping with us.");
                    break;
                }
```

```
                Console.WriteLine();
            } while (true);
            Console.ReadLine();
        }
    }

    static class App {
        public static void ShowCompanyTitle() {
            Console.WriteLine("** Hamley's Toys London England **");
        }
        public static void ShowInputError() {
            Console.WriteLine("Input error. Please try again.");
        }
    }
}
```

The display shows a menu that allows a user to enter their selection. When a user makes a selection and presses ENTER, the application responds accordingly. The methods used to display the menu title and error message are static, so they can be called from anywhere in the program without requiring an instance of their class:

```
** Hamley's Toys London England **
1. Keep shopping
2. Quit
1
...shopping.

** Hamley's Toys London England **
1. Keep shopping
2. Quit
ABC
Input error. Please try again.

** Hamley's Toys London England **
1. Keep shopping
2. Quit
2
Thank you for shopping with us.
```

Structs

As mentioned at the start of the chapter, a struct is a blueprint that encapsulates data members and methods. The struct is used to create objects to implement the logic with separate instances of data. In this way, structs are a lot like classes. Structs even look the same as classes at a glance. While there are many similarities between classes and structs,

Classes	Structs
Define reference types.	Define value types.
Are more suitable for large, complex data sets where values change after being initialized.	Are more suitable for smaller data sets that remain unchanged after they are initialized.
Allow you to customize the default constructors.	Do not allow you to manually include or customize the default constructor.
Allow destructors	Do not permit destructors.
Can inherit from other classes.	Cannot inherit from other structs, so a struct cannot have members with a protected access level.
Can be static.	Cannot be declared as static but can have static members.
Properties can be modified, so set and get accessors can coexist for the same property.	Properties are immutable (unchangeable), so set and get accessors cannot coexist for the same property.

Table 8-1 Comparing Classes and Structs

there are some subtle yet important differences. Usually, C# developers will favor use of classes over structs, but understanding how they work can be useful. One of the most important differences between a class and a struct is that a struct is a value type. Structs are more suitable for managing complex data sets that are not large.

Structs can have variables, properties, methods, and constructors. The members of the struct can be static too, but the struct declaration cannot be static. Structs can have constructors but not a default constructor. Structs cannot inherit from other structs. The differences between classes and structs may seem a little overwhelming, so Table 8-1 summarizes these differences.

Example 8-6 Structs

This example demonstrates the creation of a struct that implements a variable, a property, two methods, and a constructor for managing bank account information:

```
using System;
namespace Starter {
    struct BankAccount {
        // Struct properties are immutable so we don't create set methods.
        private string name;
        public  string Name    { get { return name; } }
```

```
        private float  balance;
        public  float  Balance { get { return balance; } }

        // struct constructor
        public BankAccount(string name, float balance) {
           this.name    = name;
           this.balance = balance;
           this.AddMonthlyInterest();
        }

        // private struct method
        void AddMonthlyInterest() {
            const float INTEREST_RATE = 0.056f;
            const float NUM_MONTHS    = 12.0f;
            balance *= (1.0f + INTEREST_RATE / NUM_MONTHS);
        }

        public void ShowDetail(string title) {
            Console.WriteLine("** " + title + " **");
            Console.WriteLine("Name:    " + Name);
            Console.WriteLine("Balance: " + Balance.ToString("C") + "\n");
        }
    }
    class Program {
        public static void Main() {
            // Initialize account.
            const string NAME       = "Cross Rail - Canary Wharf";
            const float  BALANCE    = 25900000000f;
            BankAccount  account    = new BankAccount(NAME, BALANCE);

            account.ShowDetail("Account after interest");
            Console.ReadLine();
        }
    }
}
```

The output from running this example is

```
** Account after interest **
Name:    Cross Rail - Canary Wharf
Balance: $26,020,870,000.00
```

Namespaces

Namespaces are logical groupings of classes. Namespace class groupings are also called *code libraries.* By convention, when creating your own namespace, all classes of a namespace are stored in separate files within a namespace folder of the code project. Each file has the same name as the class, and the folder has the same name as the namespace. All public classes of a namespace can be referenced in a separate class when the namespace is included with a *using* instruction at the top of the separate class file.

Namespaces prevent conflicts, also called *namespace collisions,* that occur when separate classes from different libraries have the same name. Example 8-7 shows how a namespace reference before the class name enables a fully qualified and distinct reference.

Example 8-7 Namespaces

This example uses namespaces for organizing classes and preventing naming conflicts. This demonstration uses a *Cost* class from a *Facility* namespace along with *Department* and *Cost* classes from a *Team* namespace. Since two *Cost* classes exist, each reference to *Cost* must also include the appropriate namespace as a prefix to correctly identify it.

All classes within the two namespaces are required to generate a report on organizational costs at Acme Corporation. Figure 8-1 provides a graphical summary of the class structure within the *Facility* and *Team* namespaces.

This example also demonstrates how to organize code files and folders properly in a C# project where namespaces are identified with a folder and classes are written in separate files that share the class name.

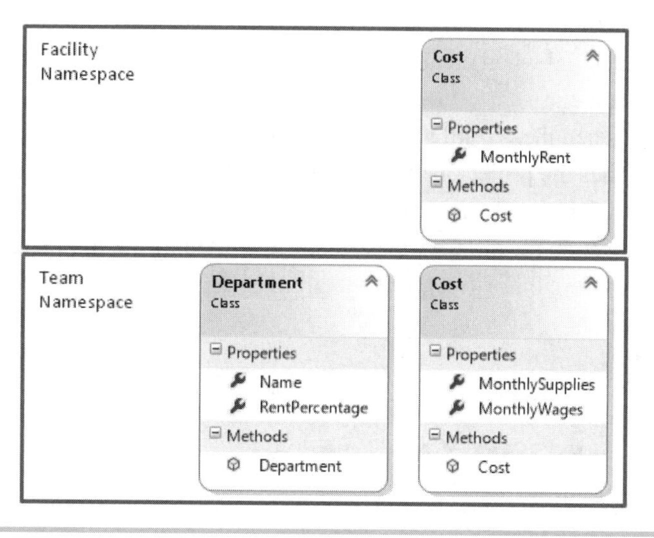

Figure 8-1 Namespaces and classes required for budget analysis

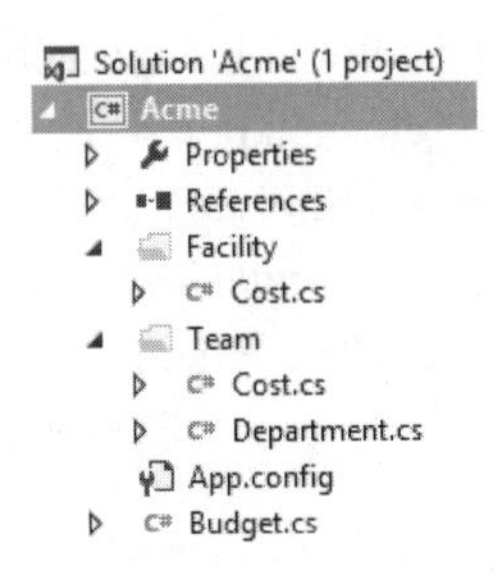

Figure 8-2 Project folders and files

To build this example, create a new console application. You will need to add *Facility* and *Team* namespace folders to the project along with the class files belonging to each namespace (see Figure 8-2).

To add the Facility folder, in the Solution Explorer, right-click the project name and choose Add | New Folder. Assign the name Facility to the new folder. Next, to add a code file named Cost.cs, right-click the Facility folder and choose Add | New Item. From the Installed Templates panel on the left of the Add New Item dialog that appears, choose Visual C#. Then, select the Class icon from the templates listed in the dialog in the middle. Assign the name Cost.cs, and click Add to have this new empty class file added to the Facility folder. Using similar steps, create a Team namespace folder with Cost.cs and Department.cs files in it. As the last change to the project structure, rename the Project.cs file that is generated when creating a console application to Budget.cs, since this file will contain a budget class.

Note that when the wizard generates the classes, the generated namespace assigned to the class includes the project name followed by a dot and then the folder name. The project name is optional, but will enable fully qualified classes within a multi-project solution.

Here is the code for the *Cost* class that is declared inside the *Facility* namespace. To declare this version of *Cost,* replace all existing code inside Facility/Cost.cs shell with this revision:

```
using System;

namespace Acme.Facility {
    class Cost {
        public decimal MonthlyRent { get; set; }

        public Cost(decimal monthlyRent) {
            MonthlyRent = monthlyRent;
```

```
        }
    }
}
```

This next *Cost* class declaration must be added to the *Team* namespace in the Team/Cost.cs file:

```
using System;

namespace Acme.Team {
    class Cost {
        public decimal MonthlyWages    { get; set; }
        public decimal MonthlySupplies { get; set; }

        public Cost(decimal monthlyWages, decimal supplies) {
            MonthlyWages    = monthlyWages;
            MonthlySupplies = supplies;
        }
    }
}
```

Now, replace the code inside Team/Department.cs with this code to declare a class that stores the department name and monthly building charges:

```
using System;

namespace Acme.Team {
    class Department {
        public string Name { get; set; }
        public float  RentPercentage { get; private set; }

        public Department(string name, float rentPercentage) {
            Name           = name;
            RentPercentage = rentPercentage;
        }
    }
}
```

The *Budget* class uses both code libraries from the *Facility* and *Team* namespaces to generate a department cost report. Because of this, *using* statements are required to reference both namespaces at the top of the file. To properly reference the *Budget* class within the project, if you haven't already renamed Program.cs to Budget.cs, do so now and then replace all code inside it with the following *Budget* class code:

```
using System;
using Acme.Facility;  // Reference the Facility namespace
using Acme.Team;      // Reference the Team namespace
```

```
namespace Acme {
    class Budget {
        static void Main() {
            const decimal MONTHLY_RENT  = 100000m;
            const decimal MONTHLY_WAGES = 24000m;
            const decimal SUPPLIES      = 3000m;
            const float   RENT_RATIO    = 25.0f;

            // Declare and initialize a Facility.Cost object.
            Facility.Cost facilityMonthlyCost = new Facility.Cost(MONTHLY_RENT);

            // Declare and initialize a Department object.
            Department  dept              = new Department("Sales", RENT_RATIO);

            // Declare and initialize a Team.Cost object.
            Team.Cost  deptMonthlyCost    = new  Team.Cost(MONTHLY_WAGES, SUPPLIES);

            ShowMonthlyCosts(facilityMonthlyCost, dept, deptMonthlyCost);
            Console.ReadLine();
        }

        static void ShowMonthlyCosts(Facility.Cost facilityCost,
                                     Department    dept,
                                     Team.Cost     departmentCost) {
            Console.WriteLine("Department Monthly Charges: " + dept.Name);
            decimal monthlyCharge = ((decimal)dept.RentPercentage/100m)
                                  * facilityCost.MonthlyRent;
            Console.WriteLine("building charges: " + monthlyCharge.ToString("C"));
            Console.WriteLine("           wages: "
                              + departmentCost.MonthlyWages.ToString("C"));
            Console.WriteLine("        supplies:  "
                              + departmentCost.MonthlySupplies.ToString("C"));
        }
    }
}
```

When running the program, the budget report is generated from the *Budget* class. For this case, the monthly costs for the sales department of the Acme Corporation are displayed:

```
Department Monthly Charges: Sales
building charges: $25,000.00
           wages: $24,000.00
        supplies:  $3,000.00
```

Partial Classes

By design, a default C# class must be declared in one file. A partial class, however, allows you to define your classes in more than one file. Partial classes simplify code organization of large classes. Many of the auto-generated code files in Windows Forms and Web Forms projects use partial classes to expose essential structures of a form to developers while hiding more complex detail in others.

Partial classes are declared with the *partial* keyword just before the *class* keyword in the class declaration. In a file named ClassName1.cs, the class declaration could look like the following:

```
public partial class ClassName { }
```

In another file, named ClassName2.cs, you could have the same class declaration to continue with the definition of the *ClassName* class:

```
public partial class ClassName { }
```

Example 8-8 Partial Classes

This example uses a partial class to separate the constructor and properties from the methods for a *Castle* class. Two objects of the class are created for storing information about Irish castles. To build this application, create a new console application that has a file and folder structure similar to the one shown in Figure 8-3.

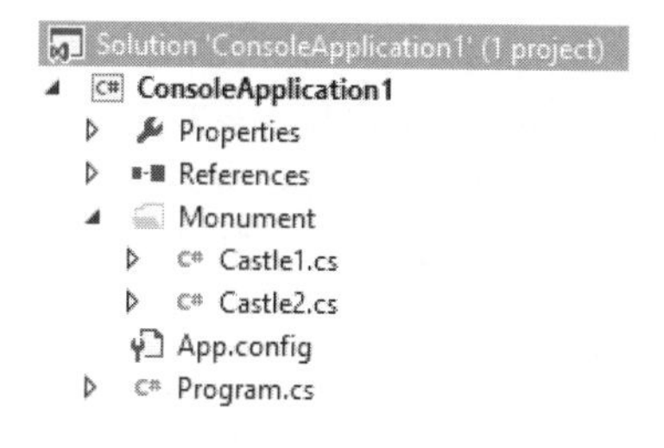

Figure 8-3 Partial class setup

In Castle1.cs, add this code to declare the portion of the *Castle* class that defines the properties and constructor of the class:

```
using System;

namespace ConsoleApplication1.Monument {
    public partial class Castle {
        int    Year { get; set; }  // Private properties
        string Name { get; set; }

        // Constructor
        public Castle(string name, int constructed) {
            Year = constructed;
            Name = name;
        }
    }
}
```

In Castle2.cs, add this code to declare the portion of the *Castle* class that contains the methods:

```
using System;

namespace ConsoleApplication1.Monument {
    public partial class Castle {
        public void DiplayDetail() {    // Output
            Console.WriteLine("*** " + Name + " Castle ***");
            Console.WriteLine("Build Date: " + Year);
            Console.WriteLine();
        }
    }
}
```

Next, replace the code inside Program.cs with the following code. This code includes a namespace reference to the *Castle* class. Inside *Main()*, two instances of the *Castle* class are declared and initialized. Notice that the *Castle* objects implement members from both partial classes without error.

```
using System;
using ConsoleApplication1.Monument;

namespace ConsoleApplication1 {
    class Program {
        static void Main() {
            Castle castleA = new Castle("Ballymoon", 1300);
```

```
            Castle castleB = new Castle("Leighlinbridge", 1547);
            castleA.DiplayDetail();
            castleB.DiplayDetail();
            Console.ReadLine();
        }
    }
}
```

When running the program, the output confirms that both partial classes successfully work together to manage and display details about each *Castle* object:

```
*** Ballymoon Castle ***
Build Date: 1300

*** Leighlinbridge Castle ***
Build Date: 1547
```

Chapter 8 Self Test

The following questions are intended to help reinforce your comprehension of the concepts covered in this chapter. The answers can be found in the accompanying online Appendix B, "Answers to the Self Tests."

1. Use these words—public, parameters, classes, objects, default, methods—to complete the following statements:

   ______ are implementations of _____.
   ______ constructors have no ______.
   Classes by default are ______.
   ______ by default are private.

2. Using the original code in Example 8-1, add a new constructor inside the *Location* class. This new constructor should receive the street name and number and the city name as parameters. The city name must be stored in a class variable that is private so that it is not externally available. In your new constructor, initialize the values for the *streetNumber, streetName,* and *city* variables at the class level. Add to the *Location* class a public method called *GetCity()* which returns the *city* value. Then, create an *addressC* object that invokes the new constructor with the address of 1 Main Street, San Jose as parameters. With the new object, display the street address and city name using the methods of this new *Location* object.

3. Starting with the code in Example 8-2, add a read-only property called *Age* that is publicly accessible to return the total years passed since a person's birth. You may calculate age with code similar to the following:

```
// Generates yyyy.mmdd
string now = DateTime.Now.ToString("yyyy.MMdd");
// Generates 1511.0618 for Bartolomeo Ammannati
string dob = person.Birthday.ToString("yyyy.MMdd");
// Calculate age. For example;
// (int)(2013.1009 - 2012.0618) = 1
// (int)(2013.1009 - 2012.1118) = 0
int age = (int)(Convert.ToSingle(now) - Convert.ToSingle(dob));
```

4. Using the code from Example 8-7, compare the declarations for the *Department* and both *Cost* objects inside the *Budget* class. Which declarations are fully qualified and which declarations are not? Why are the fully qualified declarations required?

5. Inside the Budget.cs file in Example 8-7, which two lines of code are required to reference the *Team* and *Facility* namespaces?

6. Starting with Example 8-8, add a third partial *Castle* class that declares a property called *Architect.* The property implements a public get accessor and a private set accessor. Next, add a constructor overload to Castle1.cs to receive the castle name, year of construction, and architect name as parameters. Then, in Castle2.cs, add an extra instruction to output the architect name from the *DisplayDetail()* method. In Program.cs, replace the object declarations with new ones that use the new constructor overload:

```
Castle castleA = new Castle("Ballymoon", 1300, "Roger Bigod");
Castle castleB = new Castle("Leighlinbridge", 1547,
                            "Edward Bellingham");
```

Your new output should be

```
*** Ballymoon Castle ***
Build Date: 1300
Architect:  Roger Bigod

*** Leighlinbridge Castle ***
Build Date: 1547
Architect:  Edward Bellingham
```

Chapter 9

Inheritance

Key Skills & Concepts

- Inheritance Introduction
- Virtual Inheritance
- Abstract Inheritance
- Virtual and Abstract Comparison
- Polymorphism
- Sealed Modifiers

For efficiency, as coders we always want to avoid writing duplicate code. Use of inheritance can help us to escape this pitfall when many similar but unique classes are needed. *Inheritance* is the practice of creating a hierarchy of descendant classes that are derived from the same root. When this is done properly, all of the shared code exists in a parent class and each child class implements their own unique features. This practice is very efficient since you can write your code once and use it in many derived classes.

Inheritance Introduction

With *inheritance* a hierarchy of descendant classes is derived from the same root. The root is the top class in the hierarchy. Well-designed parent classes, also known as *base* classes, contain data members and methods that are shared by descendant classes. Each descendant class can include customized data members and methods of their own. With a proper hierarchy of classes, we can create unique classes that use shared code that is higher up in the family and only written once.

To illustrate how inheritance may be used, consider a bank *Account* class. Figure 9-1 shows a graphical view of a possible bank *Account* hierarchy. *Checking* and *Savings* account classes for this example are derived from the *Account* class to share the common *Account* features while implementing custom features of their own.

In Figure 9-1, the *BankBalance* property and *ShowBalance()* method are implemented in the parent *Account* class, but these features are also available for use in the child classes. The *Checking* class implements a unique *DeductServiceCharge()* method that applies checking charges. The *Savings* class implements a unique *AddMonthlyInterest()* method that adjusts the bank balance according to the savings plan at the bank.

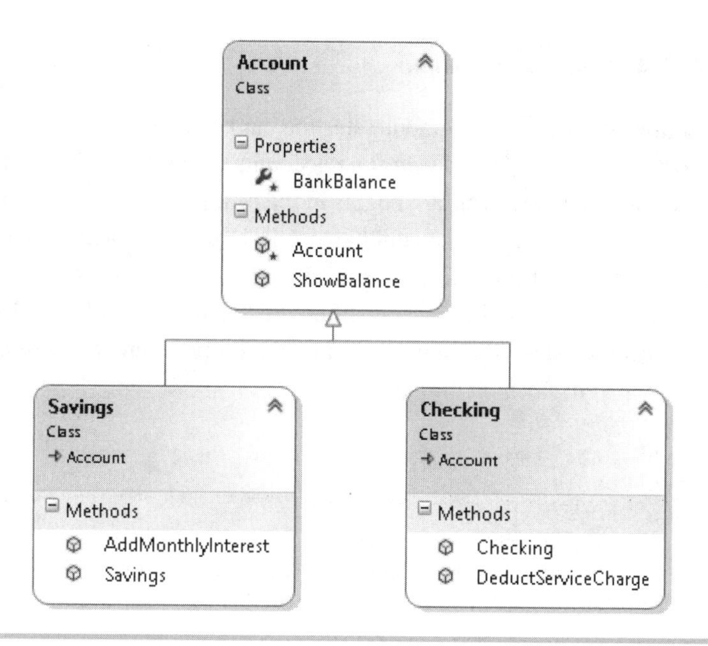

Figure 9-1 Bank *Account* class hierarchy

Declaring a Child Class

When declaring a child class that inherits from another class, the child class name in the declaration is followed by a colon and the parent class name. Here are the empty class declarations for the hierarchy shown in Figure 9-1:

```
class Account {              // Base class.
}
class Savings : Account   { // Child of Account.
}
class Checking : Account { // Child of Account.
}
```

Protected Members

As discussed in Chapter 8, the protected access modifier enables use of parent data members and methods in derived classes. Protected variables, properties, and methods are not accessible externally with the object. The *BankBalance* property of the *Account* class in Figure 9-1 is declared with a protected access level so that it can be used in the current and child classes:

```
protected decimal BankBalance{ set; get; }
```

Since *BankBalance* is protected, the property remains inaccessible for non-derived classes.

Example 9-1 Inheritance Introduction

This example of inheritance demonstrates the bank account hierarchy that is described by Figure 9-1, where *Savings* and *Checking* accounts are children classes that derive from the *Account* class. When the program begins in the *Main()* method, an instance of the *Savings* class is created. The *Savings* account balance is adjusted for accumulated interest and the balance is displayed. Then a *Checking* account class object is created, a service charge is deducted from the *Checking* account, and the balance is displayed. Both *Savings* and *Checking* accounts share the same *BankBalance* property and *ShowBalance()* method that exist in their parent *Account* class.

```
using System;
namespace Starter {
    class Program {
        public static void Main() {
            const decimal OPENING_BALANCE   = 55m;
            const decimal MONTHLY_INTEREST = 0.0033m;

            // Create and use Savings object.
            Savings savings = new Savings(OPENING_BALANCE);
            savings.AddMonthlyInterest(MONTHLY_INTEREST);
            savings.ShowBalance();

            // Create and use Checking object.
            Checking checking = new Checking(OPENING_BALANCE);
            checking.DeductServiceCharge();
            checking.ShowBalance();

            Console.ReadLine();
        }
    }
    class Account {                 // Base class - Account
        protected decimal BankBalance{ set; get; }

        protected Account() {
            Console.WriteLine();
            Console.WriteLine("Inside the Account constructor.");
        }

        public void ShowBalance() {
```

```
            Console.WriteLine("The balance is " +
                              BankBalance.ToString("C"));
        }
    }
    class Savings : Account {    // Derived class - Savings
        public Savings(decimal balance) {
            Console.WriteLine("Inside the Savings constructor.");
            BankBalance = balance;
        }
        // Custom child method.
        public void AddMonthlyInterest(decimal interest) {
            BankBalance *= (1.0m + interest);
        }
    }
    class Checking : Account {  // Derived class - Checking
        public Checking(decimal balance) {
            Console.WriteLine("Inside the Checking constructor.");
            BankBalance = balance;
        }
        // Custom child method.
        public void DeductServiceCharge() {
            const decimal CHECKING_FEE = 1.50m;
            BankBalance -= CHECKING_FEE;
        }
    }
}
```

When running this program, output is displayed from the base class constructor before each child class constructor executes. This result helps to show that the base class constructor executes first before the child. While the bank balance for each account is initially $55.00, it is clear from the output that the *Savings* account balance increases with interest while the *Checking* account balance decreases after the service charge:

```
Inside the Account constructor.
Inside the Savings constructor.
The balance is $55.18

Inside the Account constructor.
Inside the Checking constructor.
The balance is $53.50
```

Try This 9-1 Inheritance Exercise

This exercise offers practice with simple derivation, use of protected access modifiers, and execution of constructors within the family hierarchy.

1. Starting with the solution from Example 9-1, add a new class called *JointSavings* that inherits from the *Savings* class. This *JointSavings* class must implement two properties that store the two first names of the people who share the account. To help set this up, when the *JointSavings* object is initialized, add this constructor in your new class:

```
public JointSavings(string firstNameA, string firstNameB,
                    decimal balance) {
}
```

2. Modify the new *JointSavings* constructor so it stores the account balance with the protected *BankBalance* property of the base class. As well, add code to the new constructor to store the first name properties within the *JointSavings* class.
3. When the *JointSavings* constructor is invoked, since *JointSavings* inherits from *Savings,* the default parameterless *Savings* constructor will also be invoked. Since another constructor already exists in the *Savings* class, the default constructor must also be explicitly declared inside the *Savings* class. Add the following default constructor for *Savings()* with the *WriteLine()* instruction to show when it is called:

```
public Savings() {
    Console.WriteLine("Inside the default Savings constructor.");
}
```

4. To reuse the parent code, your *JointSavings* class must use the *AddMonthlyInterest()* method of the *Savings* class and the *ShowBalance()* method of the *Account* class. Since the *JointSavings* account stores first names of the owners, add a new method to the *JointSavings* account to display the owner names.
5. Finally, add code to the *Main()* method to declare a *JointSavings* object and use it in a way that generates the following output:

```
Inside the Account constructor.
Inside the Savings constructor.
The balance is $55.18

Inside the Account constructor.
Inside the Checking constructor.
The balance is $53.50
```

```
Inside the Account constructor.
Inside the default Savings constructor.
Inside the JointSavings constructor.
The account owners are: George and Jane.
The balance is $55.18
```

Inherited Constructor Overloading

When creating derived objects, the parameterless constructor of the base class is called by default. However, you might want to invoke a base class constructor with a different parameter set. You might even want to pass to the base class constructor a parameter set that is different from the one used in the derived class. When passing arguments to the parent class parameter list, the arguments are appended to the child constructor header with a colon followed by the keyword *base* and the parameter list. In the following example, the *Organization* constructor with two parameters is invoked from the constructor of the child class named *Charity*:

```
// Base class.
class Organization {
    public Organization(string name, string taxCode) {
    }
}

// Child class.
class Charity : Organization {
    public Charity(string name, string taxCode) : base(name, taxCode) { }
}
```

Example 9-2 Passing Parameters to Parent Constructors

This example shows different ways to pass parameters to the constructor of a base class named *Organization* from a child class named *Charity*. The base class constructor receives two parameters:

```
public Organization(string name, string taxCode) {}
```

One of the two *Charity* constructors passes a constant and a constructor parameter value to the base class constructor:

```
const string TAXATION_CODE = "Unassigned";
public Charity(string name) : base(name, TAXATION_CODE) {}
```

The other *Charity* constructor passes both of its parameter values to the base class constructor:

```
public Charity(string name, string taxCode) : base(name, taxCode) {}
```

The two different *Charity* constructors offer two different ways to initialize *Charity* objects:

```
Charity unicef          = new Charity("Unicef"); // Charity 1

const string TAX_CODE = "TAX-FREE GIVING";      // Charity 2
Charity unitedWay       = new Charity("United Way", TAX_CODE);
```

Here is the full example:

```
using System;
namespace Starter {
    class Program {
        public static void Main() {
            Charity unicef          = new Charity("Unicef"); // Charity 1

            const string TAX_CODE = "TAX-FREE GIVING";      // Charity 2
            Charity unitedWay       = new Charity("United Way", TAX_CODE);
            Console.ReadLine();
        }
    }

    public class Organization {
      // These properties can't be accessed outside the base class.
       private string Name     { get; set; }
       private string TaxCode { get; set; }

        // Base class constructor.
        public Organization(string name, string taxCode) {
            Name     = name;
            TaxCode = taxCode;
            Console.WriteLine("* Base constructor *");
        }
        // This protected method can only be accessed from child classes.
        protected void ShowOrganizationInfo() {
            Console.WriteLine("Organization Name: " + Name);
            Console.WriteLine("Tax code: " + TaxCode);
            Console.WriteLine();
        }
    }
    public class Charity : Organization {
```

```
        const string TAXATION_CODE = "Unassigned";
        // Calls base constructor with 1 child constructor parameter
        // and 1 constant.
        public Charity(string name) : base(name, TAXATION_CODE) {
            Console.WriteLine("* Child Constructor A *");
            ShowOrganizationInfo();
        }
        // Calls base constructor with both child constructor parameters.
        public Charity(string name, string taxCode) : base(name, taxCode) {
            Console.WriteLine("* Child Constructor B *");
            ShowOrganizationInfo();
        }
    }
}
```

The output generated from this example shows how the base class constructor for the *Organization* class is executed before the child class constructor is executed:

```
* Base constructor *
* Child Constructor A *
Organization Name: Unicef
Tax code: Unassigned

* Base constructor *
* Child Constructor B *
Organization Name: United Way
Tax code: TAX-FREE GIVING
```

Virtual Inheritance

When base class methods, variables, and properties or other members are declared with a *virtual* modifier, they can be either implemented in the parent class or overridden in the child class. The *override* in the child implementation takes precedence and replaces the parent behavior. Virtual overrides also provide the option to call the base implementation with the *base* keyword.

Declaring Virtual Methods

Methods that can be implemented in the parent class and overridden in the child class are denoted with the *virtual* keyword in the parent class:

```
public virtual void ShowStartBalance() {}
```

Overriding Virtual Methods

When declaring an implementation of a virtual method alternative in the child class, the *override* keyword is required. As an option, the parent implementation of the same method can be called with the *base* keyword:

```
public override void ShowStartBalance() {
    base.ShowStartBalance();
}
```

Declaring Virtual Properties

A virtual property declaration in the parent class allows an implementation in the parent that can be overridden by the child. The *virtual* keyword is required in this declaration:

```
protected virtual decimal StartBalance { set; get; }
```

Overriding Virtual Properties

Virtual properties can be overridden by the child class as long as they are declared with the *override* keyword. You also have the option to reference the parent property with the *base* keyword:

```
protected override decimal StartBalance {
    set {  const decimal START_FEE = 10.40m;
           base.StartBalance      = value - START_FEE; }
}
```

CAUTION

You may omit the *override* keyword when defining a method, property, or data member in a child class. However, if you derive a new class from your child, you will not be able to implement a new override.

Example 9-3 Virtual Inheritance

This example shows the creation of a parent class named *Account* with two derived classes named *Checking* and *Savings.* This *Account* class includes a virtual declaration for the *ShowStartBalance()* method, which is overridden inside the child class named *Checking.* The *Account* declaration also includes a virtual declaration for a *set* accessor named *StartBalance.* The *StartBalance* property is overridden in the *Checking* class.

```
using System;
namespace Starter {
```

```
    class Program {
        public static void Main() {
            const decimal OPENING_BALANCE = 55m;
            Savings savings   = new Savings(OPENING_BALANCE);
            savings.ShowStartBalance();
            Checking checking = new Checking(OPENING_BALANCE);
            checking.ShowStartBalance();

            Console.ReadLine();
        }
    }
    class Account {              // Base class - Account
        protected virtual decimal StartBalance{ get; set; }
        protected string          AccountType { get; set; }

        protected Account() {
        }

        public virtual void ShowStartBalance() {
            Console.WriteLine( AccountType + " balance is {0}",
                               StartBalance.ToString("C"));
        }
    }
    class Savings : Account {   // Derived class - Savings
        public Savings(decimal balance) {
            const string ACCOUNT_TYPE = "Savings";
            AccountType  = ACCOUNT_TYPE;
            StartBalance = balance;
        }
    }
    class Checking : Account {  // Derived class - Checking
        protected override decimal StartBalance{
            set {
                const decimal START_FEE = 10.40m;
                base.StartBalance        = value - START_FEE; }
        }
        public Checking(decimal balance) {
            const string ACCOUNT_TYPE = "Checking";
            AccountType  = ACCOUNT_TYPE;
            StartBalance = balance;
        }
        public override void ShowStartBalance() {
            base.ShowStartBalance();
        }
    }
}
```

The output verifies that the child objects of the *Account* class are initialized with the same data but behave differently due to customization at the child level:

```
Savings balance is $55.00
Checking balance is $44.60
```

Abstract Inheritance

Abstraction is another approach that can be taken to implement inheritance to enforce code uniformity in derived classes. Methods and attributes that are declared as abstract cannot be implemented in the class where they are declared, but they must be implemented in the child. If a class has at least one abstract attribute or method declaration, the class must also be declared with the *abstract* keyword.

Declaring Abstract Classes

To declare one or more abstract methods or properties in your class, the class itself must be declared as abstract:

```
abstract class Parent { // Base class declaration.
}
class Child : Parent {  // Child class declaration.
}
```

NOTE

When declaring abstract classes, it is important to remember that you cannot directly create an instance of an abstract class. Also, you can include virtual methods and properties in your abstract classes.

Declaring Abstract Methods

Since abstract methods do not implement any code in the base class, you can usually declare the abstract method with one line of code. The method declaration inside the parent must include the *abstract* keyword:

```
protected abstract void AssignPromotions();
```

Overriding Abstract Methods

Abstract methods only contain executable code inside derived classes. In order to implement an abstract method in a derived class, you must include the *override* keyword in your implementation:

```
protected override void AssignPromotions() { }
```

Declaring Abstract Properties

Abstract property declarations have no implementation. They are denoted with the *abstract* keyword:

```
public abstract string DepartmentName { get; protected set; }
```

Overriding Abstract Properties

Once the abstract property is declared, the property can be implemented in the derived classes. Note the presence of the keyword *override*:

```
public override string DepartmentName { get; protected set; }
```

Example 9-4 Abstract Inheritance

This example examines a class hierarchy that is established with a *Fashion* class that is derived from a *Department* class. In the code, an abstract declaration for the *Department* class enables the declaration of an abstract property *DepartmentName* and an abstract method *AssignPromotions()*. The *Fashion* class then provides the required implementations of *DepartmentName* and *AssignPromotions()*.

```
using System;

namespace Starter {
    class Program {
        static void Main() {
            Fashion fashionDepartment = new Fashion();
            fashionDepartment.DisplayPromotions();
            Console.ReadLine();
        }
    }

    // Stores sale event data.
    class Promotion {
        public string      Name  { get; private set; }
        public DateTime    Start { get; private set; }
        public DateTime    End   { get; private set; }

        public Promotion(DateTime start, DateTime end, string name) {
            Start = start; End = end; Name = name;
        }
    }
```

```
    // Abstract class that stores and displays promotional information.
    abstract class Department {
        public abstract string  DepartmentName { get; protected set; }
        protected Promotion[]   sales;
        protected abstract void AssignPromotions();

        public virtual void DisplayPromotions() {
            Console.WriteLine("{0} Department Promotions: ",
                              DepartmentName);
            foreach(Promotion sale in sales) {
                Console.WriteLine("Name:  " + sale.Name);
                Console.WriteLine("Start: " + sale.Start.ToString("m"));
                Console.WriteLine("End:   " + sale.End.ToString("m"));
            }
        }
    }

    // Implementing class that sets department name and assigns promotions.
    class Fashion : Department {
        public override string DepartmentName { get; protected set; }
        public Fashion() {
            DepartmentName = "Fashion";
            AssignPromotions();
        }
        protected override void AssignPromotions() {
            DateTime  start     = new DateTime(2014, 9, 1);  // Sept.  1
            DateTime  end       = new DateTime(2014, 9, 15); // Sept. 15
            Promotion promotion = new Promotion(start, end,
                                                "Fall Sale");
            sales = new Promotion[] { promotion };
        }
    }
}
```

The output from the program is generated from the implementation of the *DisplayPromotions()* method of the abstract *Department* class:

```
Fashion Department Promotions:
Name:  Fall Sale
Start: September 1
End:   September 15
```

Virtual and Abstract Comparison

To help summarize differences between virtual and abstract declarations, Table 9-1 provides a side-by-side comparison.

	Virtual	Abstract
Classes	Cannot be declared with a virtual modifier.	Must be declared with an abstract modifier if any class members are declared with an abstract modifier. Cannot be instantiated. May contain virtual attributes and methods. Require the *abstract* keyword in the declaration.
Methods, Properties, and Class-Level Variables	Can be implemented in the declaring class. Can be overridden in derived classes as an option.	Cannot be implemented in the declaring class. Must be overridden with an implementation in child classes.

Table 9-1 Comparing Virtual and Abstract Declarations

Try This 9-2 Abstraction Exercise

This exercise offers practice to observe the differences between a class that is set up to enable virtual inheritance and a class that enforces abstract inheritance.

1. Try running the following program:

```
using System;
namespace Starter {
    class Program {
        public static void Main() {
            Person person = new Person("Brad", "May");
            person.SetTitle("Athlete");
            person.ShowPersonalData();

            Console.ReadLine();
        }
        class Person {
            public    string FirstName { get; private set; }
            public    string LastName  { get; private set; }
            protected string Title     { get; private set; }

            public Person(string firstName, string lastName) {
                FirstName = firstName;
                LastName  = lastName;
            }
            public virtual void SetTitle(string title) {
                Title = title;
            }
```

```
                public virtual void ShowPersonalData() {
                    Console.WriteLine("First name: " + FirstName);
                    Console.WriteLine("Last name:  " + LastName);
                    Console.WriteLine("Title:      " + Title);
                }
            }
        }
    }
```

The output is

```
First name: Brad
Last name:  May
Title:      Athlete
```

2. Modify the program by first making the *Person* class abstract. Notice that immediately after this change, the program no longer compiles because it is not possible to create an instance of an abstract class.
3. Remove the constructor from the *Person* class, since instantiation of an abstract class is not possible.
4. Make the *FirstName* and *LastName* properties abstract. As well, make the *ShowPersonalData()* method abstract.
5. Create a new child class called *Visitor* that inherits from the *Person* class.
6. In the *Visitor* class, implement *FirstName* and *LastName* properties and the *ShowPersonData()* method. Then, add a *Person* constructor that receives the first and last name as parameters and that stores their values in the corresponding properties.
7. Adjust your code to generate the same output as the original program.

Polymorphism

For times when you need to manage a collection of related objects but are uncertain about their specific type at design time, you can use polymorphism. *Polymorphism* is a technique that allows you to declare a variable of a specific class type that can be assigned an instance of any derived class. In other words, polymorphism lets you declare a generic object that can morph into something more specific later. In promoting shared parent code and custom child code, polymorphism treats a group of related derived types as a single collection with shared members.

Example 9-5 Polymorphism

This example shows an implementation of polymorphism that first declares an array of *Mammal* objects. Later, each element of the array is initialized with instances of a *Mammal, Lion,* or *Bear* class. Effectively, a general parent object is created that can be morphed into different mammal types. Once the elements are initialized with different types of mammals, a *foreach* loop iterates through the objects to display their mammal type.

```
using System;
namespace Starter {
    public class Program {
        public static void Main() {
            const int NUM_MAMMALS     = 3;
            // Declare array of Mammal Objects
            Mammal[] mammals          = new Mammal[NUM_MAMMALS];

            // Initialize array with different mammal types
            // using polymorphism.
            mammals[0]                = new Lion();
            mammals[1]                = new Bear();
            mammals[2]                = new Mammal();
            foreach (Mammal mammalGroup in mammals) {
                mammalGroup.DisplayMammalType();
            }
            Console.ReadLine();
        }
    }
    public class Mammal {         // Base class
        public virtual void DisplayMammalType() {
            Console.WriteLine("I am a Mammal!");
        }
    }
    public class Lion : Mammal { // Child class
        public override void DisplayMammalType() {
            Console.WriteLine("I am a Lion!");
        }
    }
    public class Bear : Mammal { // Child class
        public override void DisplayMammalType() {
            Console.WriteLine("I am a Bear!");
        }
    }
}
```

Overridden versions of *DisplayMammalType()* show the mammal type from the *Bear* and *Lion* classes. The third element's object type is shown with the virtual implementation of the *DisplayMammalType()* method in the *Mammal* class:

```
I am a Lion!
I am a Bear!
I am a Mammal!
```

Example 9-6 Practical Polymorphism

This example shows a more compelling scenario to use inheritance and polymorphism. In this case, a base class called *ShipOrder* manages data that is required for any shipping order. However, each courier applies a different algorithm to calculate changes, so these calculations are performed either in a *Fedex* class or in a *Purolator* class. Once the courier is selected, the variable is assigned an instance of the selected courier class.

```
using System;

namespace ConsoleApplication5 {
    class Program {
        static void Main() {
            ShipOrder cambridge, hampshire;
            cambridge = new FedEx(23.3f, "Lobster", "477 Cambridge St.");
            cambridge.ShowOrder();

            hampshire = new Purolator(54.54f, "Brie cheese", "92 Hampshire St.");
            hampshire.ShowOrder();
            Console.ReadLine();
        }
    }
    class ShipOrder {
        public float     WeightInPounds { get; private set; }
        public string    Description    { get; private set; }
        public string    Destination    { get; private set; }
        public DateTime  Created        { get; private set; }
        public decimal   Charge         { get; protected set; }
        public string    Carrier        { get; protected set; }

        public ShipOrder(float weight, string description,
                         string destination, string carrier) {
            Created        = DateTime.Now;
            WeightInPounds = weight;
            Description    = description;
            Destination    = destination;
            Carrier        = carrier;
        }
```

```
        public void ShowOrder() {
            Console.WriteLine("Order Date:   " + Created.ToString("m"));
            Console.WriteLine("Carrier:      " + Carrier);
            Console.WriteLine("Detail:       " + Description + " "
                             + WeightInPounds.ToString("N2") + " lbs");
            Console.WriteLine("Destination:  " + Destination);
            Console.WriteLine("Charge:       " + Charge.ToString("C") + "\n");
        }
    }
    class FedEx : ShipOrder {
        public FedEx(float weight, string description, string destination)
                  : base(weight, description, destination, "FedEx") {
            const decimal CHARGE_RATE = 0.53m;
            Charge = CHARGE_RATE * (decimal)weight;
        }
    }
    class Purolator : ShipOrder {
        public Purolator(float weight, string description, string destination)
                  : base(weight, description, destination, "Purolator") {
            const decimal CHARGE_RATE = 0.40m;
            const decimal BASE_FEE    = 12.50m;
            Charge = BASE_FEE + CHARGE_RATE * (decimal)weight;
        }
    }
}
```

The output from this example is displayed with the shared code in the base class, but different charges are applied in the child classes depending on which carrier is used:

```
Order Date:  August 21
Carrier:     FedEx
Detail:      Lobster 23.30 lbs
Destination: 477 Cambridge St.
Charge:      $12.35

Order Date:  August 21
Carrier:     Purolator
Detail:      Brie cheese 54.54 lbs
Destination: 92 Hampshire St.
Charge:      $34.32
```

Sealed Modifiers

To further customize inherited structures, *sealed* modifiers are available to set the last point of derivation for a class, method, property, or field.

Sealing Classes

Prefixing class declarations with a sealed modifier indicates that no classes can inherit from it. As an example, if we seal a *SalesRep* class

```
sealed public class SalesRep : Employee {
    public SalesRep() {
        Title = "Sales Representative";
    }
}
```

then it would not be possible to derive a new class from the *SalesRep* class:

```
public class RegionalRep : SalesRep { } // Not permitted.
```

Sealing Members

Prefixing a class member like a method with the keyword *seal* indicates that child classes cannot override this implementation. In this case, the *ShowTitle()* method is sealed:

```
public class Employee : Person {
    sealed public override void ShowTitle() {
        Console.WriteLine("Employee Title: " + Title);
    }
}
```

Since *ShowTitle()* is sealed in the *Employee* class, it is not possible to override this method in a child class:

```
public class SalesRep : Employee {
    public override void ShowTitle() { // Not permitted.
        Console.WriteLine("Employee Title: SalesRep");
    }
}
```

Example 9-7 Sealed Classes and Members

This example demonstrates how the sealed access modifier can be applied in a hierarchy downward from a *Person* to an *Employee* to a *SalesRep* class. A sealed modifier for the *Title* property and *ShowTitle()* method in the *Employee* class prevents child classes from overriding them. A sealed modifier for the *SalesRep* class prevents further derivations at a lower level in the class hierarchy.

```
using System;
namespace Starter {
```

```
    public class Program {
        public static void Main() {
            Employee employee = new Employee();
            employee.ShowTitle();

            SalesRep salesRep = new SalesRep();
            salesRep.ShowTitle();
            Console.ReadLine();
        }
    }
    public abstract class Person {
        public abstract string Title { get; protected set;  }
        public abstract void   ShowTitle();
    }
    public class Employee : Person {
        // Prevent further derivation of property.
        sealed public override string Title { get; protected set;}

        public Employee() {
            const string TITLE = "Unassigned";
                         Title = TITLE;
        }
        // Prevent further derivation of method.
        sealed public override void ShowTitle( ) {
            Console.WriteLine("Employee Title: " + Title);
        }
    }

    // Prevent further derivation of class.
    sealed public class SalesRep : Employee {
        public SalesRep() {
            Title = "Sales Representative";
        }
    }
}
```

The program runs without any issues to display data for the *Employee* and *SalesRep* objects:

```
Employee Title: Unassigned
Employee Title: Sales Representative
```

If you were to modify this example by trying to create a class that inherits from the *SalesRep* class, your project would not compile, because derivation from a sealed class is not allowed. If you tried to override the *Title* property or *ShowTitle()* method in the *SalesRep* class, your project also would not compile, since overrides are not allowed for sealed members.

Chapter 9 Self Test

The following questions are intended to help reinforce your comprehension of the concepts covered in this chapter. The answers can be found in the accompanying online Appendix B, "Answers to the Self Tests."

1. Indicate whether the following statements are true or false.

   A. ____ Code within a child constructor is executed before code in the parent constructor is executed.

   B. ____ A major advantage of inheritance is that shared code can be implemented in the parent class while custom code is implemented in the child class.

   C. ____ Virtual data members and methods do not permit implementation in the base class.

   D. ____ Abstract constructors can be overloaded in the base class.

   E. ____ It is not possible to create an object of an abstract class.

   F. ____ In a child class, while overriding a method, it is possible to override a public, protected, or private access specifier. For example, you can change a method that is protected in the parent to become public in the child.

   G. ____ Abstract methods and properties may be implemented in the class where they are declared.

   H. ____ An abstract class may contain an implementation of a property or method.

2. Modify the current base class constructor inside Example 9-2 by adding a third string parameter called *sector*. Then, create a new property called *Sector* in the base class to store the sector data when the base constructor is called. Next, modify both constructors in the *Charity* class to also receive a *sector* parameter. After making these changes, adjust your code as required to enable object creation with the following instructions:

```
Charity unicef    = new Charity("Unicef", "Child Advocacy");
Charity unitedWay = new Charity("United Way", TAX_CODE, "Community Support");
```

   Finally, change the *ShowOrganizationInfo()* method so the final output after all changes resembles the following:

```
* Base constructor *
* Child Constructor A *
Organization Name: Unicef
Sector:   Child Advocacy
Tax code: Unassigned
```

```
* Base constructor *
* Child Constructor B *
Organization Name: United Way
Sector:    Community Support
Tax code: TAX-FREE GIVING
```

3. Starting with Example 9-4, override *DisplayPromotions()* in the *Fashion* class to provide the same output as before except with the year included with the start and end dates. You may modify the parent implementation of *DisplayPromotions()* to output the data as needed. Why are you able to override *DisplayPromotions()* in the *Fashion* class?
4. Starting with Example 9-4, create a new class called *Womens* that inherits from *Fashion.* Inside the *Womens* class, override the *DisplayPromotions()* method. Code your new *DisplayPromotions()* method so that it efficiently generates the following output:

```
*** Women's ***
Fashion Department Promotions:
Name:  Fall Sale
Start: September 1
End:   September 15
```

5. Modify the *Mammal* class in Example 9-5 to make the *DisplayMammalType()* method declaration abstract. You will not be able to call *DisplayMammalType()* with a *Mammal* object, so you do not need to assign a *Mammal* object to the array in your revised program. Your revision should only assign *Lion* and *Bear* objects to elements of the array.
6. Using the original code in Example 9-7, add a class declaration called *RegionalSalesRep* to inherit from the *SalesRep* class. You will not be able to compile your program. What is the exact error message that you receive when you try to compile your program? Explain in your own words why the error message appears.

Chapter 10

Generic Types and Collections

Key Skills & Concepts

- Generic Types
- List Collections
- ArrayList Collections
- KeyValuePair Types
- Dictionary Collections
- Hashtable Collections

This chapter focuses mostly on ways to manage large groups of objects with *List, ArrayList, Dictionary,* and *Hashtable* collections. All collection types covered in this chapter are dynamically sized so items can be added or removed to and from them at run time. Each collection class offers useful methods and options to add, insert, remove, and find specific items within the collection.

Before we delve into collections, we will cover generic types. Coverage of generic types is necessary to understand how the *List* and *Dictionary* collections enforce uniform types that are defined when these collections are initialized. Generic structures are an important part of the C# library too, because they enable other structures such as LINQ syntax.

Generic Types

Generic classes and structs are type-safe templates that are defined without a specific data type. The big advantage generic templates offer is that they can be reused with different data types.

Declaring Generic Templates

A generic class or struct declaration is similar to a regular class or struct declaration. The generic declaration, however, includes at least one generic type argument within opening and closing angle brackets immediately after the class name.

NOTE

Type arguments in the generic template are often given the name *T*, followed by consecutive letters of the alphabet such as *U*, *V*, and *W* for additional arguments. For the sake of clarity, you can add more descriptive type arguments, such as *TKey* or *TValue*.

A class header for a declaration that includes one generic type could look like the following:

```
class QuizQuestion <T> {}
```

On a similar note, a class header for a class with two generic types could look like

```
class QuizQuestion <T,U> {}
```

A key point to remember is that *T* and *U* can be any type and the template doesn't care what type *T* or *U* is. The *QuizQuestion* declaration is for a class that operates on object(s) of type *T* or *U* regardless of the object types.

Generic Constructors

When a generic class or struct is defined, it can also be implemented to receive parameters of the generic type as an option:

```
public QuizQuestion(string question, T answer) {
}
```

Declaring and Initializing Objects of a Generic Class or Struct

To declare objects of a generic class or struct, provide the template name, the type arguments, and the name of the object. When initializing objects of generic classes or structs, you define the actual data type(s) to be implemented in angle brackets after the *new* keyword and constructor with parameters.

Here is an example of how to define an object of a generically typed *QuizQuestion* class. Start with the class and constructor declarations. The class declaration includes the type argument within angle brackets, and the *QuizQuestion* constructor receives a parameter of the generic type:

```
class QuizQuestion <T> {
    public QuizQuestion(string question, T answer) { // Constructor parameter
                                                      // implements generic type.
    }
}
```

When declaring an object of the generically typed *QuizQuestion* class, the data type in this case is set to an integer within the angle brackets. Since an integer is used in this object declaration, an integer value can be passed to the constructor when the object is initialized:

```
QuizQuestion<int> questionA
= new QuizQuestion<int> ("How many teeth do sharks use in a lifetime?", 30000);
```

Here is another valid declaration of a *QuizQuestion* object that defines the generic type with a string to store the answer in the string format:

```
QuizQuestion<string> questionB
= new QuizQuestion<string> ("What type of shark swims fastest?",
                            "The short fin mako shark.");
```

Generic Methods

In addition to receiving parameters of generic types, methods can be designed to return values of the generic type:

```
T GetAnswer() {}
```

Generic Properties

Properties can also be defined with the format of a generic type:

```
T Answer { get; private set; }
```

Generic Variables

Variables in a generic class or struct may be declared with the generic format. Generic variables can be declared at the class or struct level, in the method header, and inside methods:

```
T answerVariable;
```

Example 10-1 Generic Class Introduction

This example shows a generic *QuizQuestion* class that stores quiz questions and answers in varying data formats. The type argument, *T*, defines a generic data type used within the class. The first *QuizQuestion* object assigns an integer to the generic type. The second *QuizQuestion* object assigns a string to the generic type.

```
using System;
namespace Starter {
    class Program {
```

```
        public static void Main( ) {
            // Initialize question with an 'integer' type.
            QuizQuestion<int>    questionA = new QuizQuestion<int>
            ("How many teeth do sharks use in a lifetime?", 30000);
            questionA.ShowType();
            questionA.ShowQandA();

            // Initialize question with a 'string' type.
            QuizQuestion<string> questionB = new QuizQuestion<string>
            ("What type of shark swims fastest?",
             "The short fin mako shark.");
            questionB.ShowType();
            questionB.ShowQandA();

            Console.ReadLine();
        }
    }
    // Declare class with dynamically typed data members.
    class QuizQuestion<T> {
        public T Answer { get; private set; } // Generic property.
        private string Question { get; set; } // String property.

        public QuizQuestion(string question, T answer) { // Constructor.
            Question = question;
            Answer   = answer;
        }

        public void ShowType() {                     // Show data type.
            Console.Write("The instance type is: ");
            Console.WriteLine(typeof(T).ToString());
        }

        public void ShowQandA() {                    // Question & Answer
            Console.WriteLine("Question: " + Question);
            Console.WriteLine("Answer:   " + Answer.ToString() + "\n");
        }
    }
}
```

The output from this example shows answers of different data types, where the first answer is an integer type and the second answer is a string type:

```
The instance type is: System.Int32
Question: How many teeth do sharks use in a lifetime?
Answer:   30000

The instance type is: System.String
Question: What type of shark swims fastest?
Answer:   The short fin mako shark.
```

Example 10-2 Multiple Generic Type Parameters

This example shows how a *QuizQuestion* class could implement two generic types. The *QuizQuestion* class in this case manages a question and two multiple choice responses of varying data types. Most often, C# developers will declare the first type argument as *T*. The next generic type is represented with *U*.

```
using System;
namespace Starter {
    class Program {
        public static void Main( ) {
            // Declare question with an integer and string response.
            QuizQuestion<int, string> question = new QuizQuestion<int, string>
            ("Approximately how many shark species exist?", 350,
             "None of the above.");

            question.ShowTypes();
            question.ShowQuestion();
            Console.ReadLine();
        }
    }

    // Declare class that implements two generic types.
    class QuizQuestion<T, U> {
        string Question { set; get; }
        T ResponseA;
        U ResponseB;

        // Constructor.
        public QuizQuestion(string question, T a, U b) {
            Question  = question;
            ResponseA = a;
            ResponseB = b;
        }
        // Show data types.
        public void ShowTypes( ) {
            Console.WriteLine("(a) is a " + typeof(T).ToString());
            Console.WriteLine("(b) is a " + typeof(U).ToString());
        }

        public void ShowQuestion() {
            Console.WriteLine(Question);
            Console.WriteLine("a) " + ResponseA.ToString());
            Console.WriteLine("b) " + ResponseB.ToString());
        }
    }
}
```

When you run this, the output shows the answers implemented with an integer and string type:

```
(a) is a System.Int32
(b) is a System.String
Approximately how many shark species exist?
a) 350
b) None of the above.
```

Try This 10-1 Practice with Generic Types

This exercise offers you a chance to practice working with generic types. Here are the steps:

1. Modify Example 10-2 so that the *QuizQuestion* class accepts three type arguments and manages a question with three different types of responses.
2. Modify the *QuizQuestion* class and question declaration inside *Main()* so that the output from running the program becomes

```
(a) is a System.String
(b) is a System.String
(c) is a System.String
Circle the responses which are true.
a) Sharks are the only fish that have eyelids.
b) Starfish and jellyfish are not fish.
c) Somebody who studies fish is an ichthyologist.
```

Now that we have covered generic types, let's apply this knowledge to collections.

List Collections

List collections are dynamically allocated type-safe collections that implement generic types. They contain either objects of identical types or objects that inherit from the same base class. Fittingly, the *List* class is included in the *System.Collections.Generic* namespace. Where *T* is the data type stored in the list, this collection is declared with the syntax:

```
List<T> collection = new List<T>();
```

The *List* class implements the *IEnumerable* interface, which allows you to iterate through the collection. We will discuss interfaces in Chapter 12. Basically, though, the *IEnumerable* interface supports iteration through the collection.

List Methods

The *List* collection provides convenient methods for adding, retrieving, and removing data from the collection. Since the *List* class is a generic template, it doesn't care which type is being passed to it. It just offers a structure to manage items of the same type so you can add items, remove items, and iterate over them. There is nothing that a list does that ties it to the type of item that is being listed. Because of this, the methods provided in the *List* class are also generic. With this in mind, let's look at the methods in this series. The *Add()* method adds items of type *T*:

```
void Add(T item);
```

The *Insert()* method adds an object of type *T* to the *List* collection at a specific position set by the index:

```
Insert(int index, T item);
```

The *InsertRange()* method inserts a *List* collection into another *List* collection of the same type at a specific position set by the index:

```
void InsertRange(int index, IEnumerable<T> collection);
```

Remove() deletes an item from the *List* collection by value:

```
bool Remove(T item);
```

The *RemoveRange()* method deletes a fixed number of objects from a list starting at a specific indexed position:

```
void RemoveRange(int index, int count);
```

RemoveAt() deletes an object at a specific position from the list:

```
void RemoveAt(int index);
```

Clear() removes all items from the list:

```
void Clear();
```

Example 10-3 List Introduction

This example demonstrates some of the methods for adding and deleting names to and from a *List* collection. The list in this case is defined with a string type.

```
using System;
using System.Collections.Generic;

namespace Starter {
    public class Program {
        public static void Main( ) {
            List<string> collection = new List<string>();
            AddItems(collection);
            ShowItems(collection);
            RemoveItems(collection);
            ShowItems(collection);
            Console.ReadLine();
        }
        public static void AddItems(List<string> collection) {
            collection.Add("Al");          // Add 'Al'.
            collection.Add("Ed");          // Add 'Ed'.
            collection.Insert(1, "Bob"); // Place 'Bob' at 2nd position.

            List<string> subCollection = new List<string>();
            subCollection.Add("Cal");
            subCollection.Add("Dora");

            // Insert list with 'Cal' and 'Dora' at 3rd position after 'Bob'.
            collection.InsertRange(2, subCollection);
        }
        static void ShowItems(List<string> collection) {
            foreach (string letter in collection)
                Console.Write(letter + ", ");
            Console.WriteLine();
        }
        public static void RemoveItems(List<string> collection) {
            collection.Remove("Dora");     // Remove 'Dora' by value.
            collection.RemoveAt(0);        // Remove first item.
        }
    }
}
```

The items of the collection are displayed with a *foreach* loop once items have been added to the list and then after some have been removed:

```
Al, Bob, Cal, Dora, Ed,
Bob, Cal, Ed,
```

Try This 10-2 Practice with List Collections

This exercise offers a chance to practice working with *List* collections and methods of the *List* class.

1. Write a program that has a list of integers.
2. Add, display, insert, and remove the *List* items in a manner that generates the following output exactly:

```
Adding items:
1, 8
*** Inserting one item:
1, 2, 8
*** Inserting range of items:
1, 2, 3, 4, 5, 6, 7, 8
*** Removing range of two items:
1, 4, 5, 6, 7, 8
*** Removing item by object:
1, 4, 5, 6, 8
*** Removing item by index:
4, 5, 6, 8
The first item is 4
*** Clearing all items:
```

Example 10-4 Lists with Polymorphism

This example uses a *List* collection to store a family of bank account objects. Since the *List* type is defined with the *Account* base class, the list implements polymorphism because it also manages any descendant objects of the base class that are added or removed at run time. In this case, *Savings* and *Checking* objects are stored within the *List* collection that is initialized with the *Account* base class.

```
using System;
using System.Collections.Generic;

namespace Starter {
    public class Program {
        public static void Main( ) {
            // Build a List of Account family objects with polymorphism.
            List<Account> accounts  = new List<Account>();
            accounts.Add(new Checking());
            accounts.Add(new Savings());
```

```
            // Display the Account family object values.
            for(int i=0; i<accounts.Count; i++)
                accounts[i].DisplayDetail();
            Console.ReadLine();
        }
    }
    // Create the Account base class.
    public abstract class Account {
        public abstract void DisplayDetail();
    }
    // Create a child of the Account class.
    public class Checking : Account {
        public override void DisplayDetail() {
            Console.WriteLine("This is a Checking object.");
        }
    }
    // Create a child of the Account class.
    public class Savings : Account {
        public override void DisplayDetail() {
            Console.WriteLine("This is a Savings object.");
        }
    }
}
```

The output from this example is displayed by iterating through the list and referencing each object with a position index:

```
This is a Checking object.
This is a Savings object.
```

The objects for this example went into the list as *Checking* and *Savings* instances, but the objects taken out are of the type *Account*. As long as you access objects in the list through the methods and properties defined in the *Account* class, you're fine. You can cast each object to their implemented class, but the list and its users see only *Account* objects.

ArrayList Collections

The *ArrayList* class is similar to the *List* class in many ways. However, the *ArrayList* class can store multiple objects of unrelated data types. To enable the *ArrayList* class in your code, you must reference the *System.Collections* namespace. The *ArrayList* class implements the *IList* interface to manage non-generic objects, so objects of the collection can be of any data type. *IList* extends the *IEnumerable* interface, so *ArrayList* also enables iteration through its objects.

Since any type of object can be placed in an *ArrayList* collection, the *ArrayList* declaration does not have a generic type in its definition:

```
ArrayList errands   = new ArrayList();
```

Determining Object Types

Since *ArrayList* collections can store any type, you will often need to determine the data format of each object when retrieving items from the collection. When determining formats, all *ArrayList* collection items can be stored as objects of the *Object* class. The *Object* class supports all classes in C#. All object types also have a *GetType()* method that returns the object's data type. This data type can be compared with the return value of the *typeof* operator when a specific class type is passed as a parameter.

The following example shows iteration through an *ArrayList* called *errands.* If the object belongs to the *GroceryItem* class, it is casted to an object of the *GroceryItem* type. The *GroceryItem* object can then be used to access the methods and properties of its class.

```
foreach (Object obj in errands) {
    if (obj.GetType() == typeof(GroceryItem)) {
        GroceryItem groceryItem = (GroceryItem)obj;
        groceryItem.Display();
    }
}
```

ArrayList Methods

Like *List* collections, *ArrayList* collections offer many similar methods that enable easy addition, insertion, and removal of items. The *Add()* method can add objects of any type to the *ArrayList* collection even when objects of unrelated types also exist in the collection:

```
void Add(object item);
```

The *Insert()* method adds a new object of any type at the specified position index:

```
void Insert(int index, object item);
```

The *InsertRange()* method inserts any collection that implements the *ICollection* interface to an *ArrayList* collection at a specific index position. You can use *InsertRange()* to add collections like *List* collections or an array to an *ArrayList* collection:

```
void InsertRange(int index, ICollection collection);
```

The *Remove()* method removes any item from the *ArrayList* collection by value:

```
bool Remove(object item);
```

RemoveRange() can delete a set number of objects from the collection starting at a specified position index:

```
void RemoveRange(int index, int count);
```

RemoveAt() removes an item from the *ArrayList* collection at a specific position:

```
void RemoveAt(int index);
```

Clear() removes all items from the *ArrayList* collection:

```
void Clear();
```

Example 10-5 ArrayList Introduction

This example demonstrates how to implement an *ArrayList* collection to manage a daily list of errands. This list currently stores both string data and *GroceryItem* formats, but it could store objects of any data type.

```
using System;
using System.Collections;

namespace ConsoleApplication1 {
    class Program {
        static void Main() {
            ArrayList errands    = new ArrayList();     // Declare and initialize.
            errands.Add(new GroceryItem("Apples", 6));// Add 'Grocery' objects.
            errands.Add(new GroceryItem("Carrots", 3));
            string[] toDo        = { "Go to tailors.", "Put air in tire." };
            errands.InsertRange(2, toDo);               // Add string array starting
                                                        // at third position.
            GroceryItem bananas = new GroceryItem("Bananas", 5);
            errands.Insert(1, bananas);                 // Add item at 2nd position.
            ShowErrands(errands);                       // Show all items.
            errands.RemoveAt(0);                        // Remove first item.
            errands.Remove(bananas);                    // Remove item by value.
            ShowErrands(errands);                       // Show all items.
            Console.ReadLine();
        }
        static void ShowErrands(ArrayList errands) {
            Console.WriteLine("* ToDo List *");
            foreach (Object obj in errands) {
```

```
                // If the object is a 'GroceryItem' item cast it and call its
                // Display() method.
                if (obj.GetType() == typeof(GroceryItem)) {
                    GroceryItem groceryItem = (GroceryItem)obj;
                    groceryItem.Display();
                }
                else
                    Console.WriteLine(obj.ToString());
            }
            Console.WriteLine();
        }
    }
    class GroceryItem {
        public string  Description { get; set; }
        public int     Quantity    { get; set; }
        public GroceryItem(string description, int quantity) {
            Description = description;
            Quantity    = quantity;
        }
        public void Display() {
            Console.WriteLine(Description + ":  " + Quantity);
        }
    }
}
```

Two different versions of the errands list are shown in the output. The first version is displayed after all items are added. The second version is shown after two of the items have been removed from the collection. Methods used to display the output are selected according to the object type for each item in the collection. The *Description* and *Quantity* properties for *GroceryItem* objects are written to the console with the *Display()* method of the object. When the *ArrayList* item is just a string, it is written directly to the console.

```
* ToDo List *
Apples:  6
Bananas:  5
Carrots:  3
Go to tailors.
Put air in tire.

* ToDo List *
Carrots:  3
Go to tailors.
Put air in tire.
```

KeyValuePair Types

Now that you have an idea of how flexible different collection types are, let's examine the *KeyValuePair* type, which enables additional search options for large collections. The *KeyValuePair* type is a struct that stores a reference key and corresponding value.

The data type for the key and the value are defined when the *KeyValuePair* is initialized with *TKey* and *TValue* type parameters within angle brackets. The actual values of the *KeyValuePair* struct are passed as parameters to the *KeyValuePair* constructor:

```
KeyValuePair<TKey, TValue> kvp = new KeyValuePair<TKey, TValue>(key, value);
```

Once the *KeyValuePair* object is defined, you can reference the key with the *Key* property:

```
keyValuePair.Key
```

You can also reference the value of a *KeyValuePair* with the *Value* property:

```
keyValuePair.Value
```

Example 10-6 KeyValuePair Introduction

This example shows how to create a *KeyValuePair* item to reference Greek and Roman names of mythological figures. The struct includes a bibliography identifier named *BIBLIOGRAPHY_ID* for the key and a *Myth* object for the value:

```
const int BIBLIOGRAPHY_ID   = 1039;
Myth  kingOfIthaca          = new Myth("Odysseus", "Ulysses");
KeyValuePair<int, Myth> kvp = new KeyValuePair<int, Myth>
                                  (BIBLIOGRAPHY_ID, kingOfIthaca);
```

This example is not very practical, but it does offer a simple view of how to create and access properties of the *KeyValuePair* struct:

```
using System;
using System.Collections.Generic;

namespace Starter {
    class Program {
        public static void Main( ) {
            // Create a KeyValuePair item that stores a Myth object.
            const int BIBLIOGRAPHY_ID   = 1039;
```

```
            Myth  kingOfIthaca          = new Myth("Odysseus", "Ulysses");
            KeyValuePair<int, Myth> kvp = new KeyValuePair<int, Myth>
                                         (BIBLIOGRAPHY_ID, kingOfIthaca);
            // Display the 'key' and 'values' stored in the KeyValuePair.
            Console.WriteLine("Key   = {0}", kvp.Key);
            Console.WriteLine("Value = {0}", kvp.Value.GreekName);
            Console.WriteLine("Value = {0}", kvp.Value.RomanName);
            Console.ReadLine();
        }
    }
    public class Myth {
        public string GreekName { get; private set; }
        public string RomanName { get; private set; }

        public Myth(string greekName, string romanName) {
            GreekName = greekName;
            RomanName = romanName;
        }
    }
}
```

When you run the program, the output shows details about the *KeyValuePair*'s *Key* and *Value* properties:

```
Key   = 1039
Value = Odysseus
Value = Ulysses
```

Dictionary Collections

This section looks at *Dictionary* collections that take advantage of the enhanced searches offered by *KeyValuePair* objects. *Dictionary* collections are type-safe collections that enable storage, retrieval, and removal of *KeyValuePair* objects. The *Dictionary* class is available through the *System.Collections.Generic* namespace. When declaring and initializing a *Dictionary* object, arguments denoted by *TKey* and *TValue* define the key and value data types:

```
Dictionary<TKey, TValue> dictionary = new Dictionary<TKey, TValue>();
```

Here is the definition of a *Dictionary* object that manages driver's license certifications with a char type for the key and a string type for the value:

```
Dictionary<char, string> certifications = new Dictionary<char, string>();
```

Dictionary Methods

Dictionary collections offer several helpful methods for adding, updating, and deleting *KeyValuePair* items. The *Add()* method adds a *KeyValuePair* item to the collection. The first parameter includes a key of the type *TKey* and the second parameter includes a value of type *TValue*:

```
void Add(TKey key, TValue value);
```

The *ContainsKey()* method checks the *Dictionary* collection to determine if a key exists and returns a true or false value, depending on the search outcome. The *ContainsKey()* method uses the key of the search item as the parameter:

```
bool ContainsKey(TKey key);
```

TryGetValue() performs a search of the *Dictionary* based on the key passed to it. This method returns a true or false value, depending on the search results. If the key is found, the associated value is stored in the second parameter:

```
bool TryGetValue(TKey key, out TValue value);
```

The *Remove()* method deletes items from the *Dictionary* collection:

```
bool Remove(TKey key);
```

Clear() removes all items from the *Dictionary* collection:

```
void Clear();
```

Iterating Through Dictionary Items

After adding items to the dictionary, you can iterate through the collection of *KeyValuePair* objects. If you had

```
Dictionary<char, string> certifications  = new Dictionary<char, string>();
```

and you were to add items like

```
certifications.Add('P', "Passenger transport");
```

you could loop through all *KeyValuePair* objects as follows:

```
foreach(KeyValuePair<char, string> cert in certifications)
    Console.WriteLine("Key: " + cert.Key + "  Value: " + cert.Value);
```

Example 10-7 Dictionary Introduction

This example demonstrates the creation and management of a *Dictionary* that stores driver license certifications. The license certification type is referenced with a key of type char. The license value is a string that describes the license.

```
using System;
using System.Collections.Generic;

namespace Starter {
    class Program {
        public static void Main( ) {
            Dictionary<char, string> certifications
            = new Dictionary<char, string>();
            certifications.Add('P', "Passenger transport");
            certifications.Add('H', "Hazardous materials");
            certifications.Add('N', "Tank vehicles (Liquids in bulk)");
            certifications.Add('T', "Double/Triple trailers");
            ShowCertifications(certifications);

            // Search for certification by key and confirm.
            if (certifications.ContainsKey('P'))
                Console.WriteLine("Has certification 'P'.");

            // Check certification for a specific value and confirm.
            if (certifications.ContainsValue("Double/Triple trailers"))
                Console.WriteLine("Has certification 'T'.");

            // Remove certification 'T' by key.
            certifications.Remove('T');
            if (!certifications.ContainsValue("Double/Triple trailers"))
                Console.WriteLine("No longer has certification 'T'.");

            // Remove all certifications.
            certifications.Clear();
            if (certifications.Count == 0)
                Console.WriteLine("All certifications removed.");
            Console.ReadLine();
        }

        static void ShowCertifications(Dictionary<char, string> certifications) {
            foreach (KeyValuePair<char, string> cert in certifications)
                Console.WriteLine("Key: " + cert.Key + "  Value: " + cert.Value);
            Console.WriteLine();
        }
    }
}
```

The output is as follows:

```
Key: P  Value: Passenger transport
Key: H  Value: Hazardous materials
Key: N  Value: Tank vehicles (Liquids in bulk)
Key: T  Value: Double/Triple trailers

Has certification 'P'.
Has certification 'T'.
No longer has certification 'T'.
All certifications removed.
```

Hashtable Collections

The *Hashtable* class is similar to the *Dictionary* class, but a *Hashtable* collection can manage *KeyValuePair* objects of varying types. Consequently, the *Hashtable* constructor does not require data type declarations for the key or value:

```
Hashtable hashTable = new Hashtable();
```

The *Hashtable* class is available in the *System.Collections* namespace.

Hashtable Methods

The *Add()* method of the *Hashtable* class adds a dictionary item where keys of any value and type can be added to the collection:

```
void Add(object key, object value);
```

The *ContainsKey()* method checks for the existence of a *Hashtable* object by key:

```
bool ContainsKey(object key);
```

ContainsValue() checks for the existence of a *Hashtable* object with a specific value:

```
bool ContainsValue(object value);
```

The *Remove()* method deletes objects from the collection by key:

```
void Remove(object key);
```

Clear() removes all objects from the *Hashtable* collection:

```
void Clear();
```

Iterating Through Hashtable Items

When iterating through *Hashtable* items, the *DictionaryEntry* struct can be used to isolate each item in the collection. Then the *GetType()* method can be used to determine the data types of the *Key* and *Value* properties. Once the *Dictionary* object type is determined, the value can be converted to the required format with a cast:

```
foreach (DictionaryEntry item in hashTable) {
    if (item.Key.GetType() == typeof(string)) {      // Key is a string.
        if (item.Value.GetType() == typeof(float)) { // Value is a float.
            // Convert value to float with a cast.
            float grade = (float)item.Value;
        }
    }
}
```

Example 10-8 Hashtable Introduction

This example offers practice with using a *Hashtable* class to store and manage letter and number grades:

```
using System;
using System.Collections;
namespace Starter {
    class Program {
        public static void Main() {
            Hashtable grades = new Hashtable(); // Add letter and number grades.
            grades.Add("C#", "A");
            grades.Add("Java", 74.0f);
            grades.Add("ASP.NET", "A");
            DisplayAllValues(grades);

            if (grades.ContainsKey("C#"))       // Check for object by key.
                Console.WriteLine("A C# Course Exists");
            if (grades.ContainsValue(74.0f))    // Check for object by value.
                Console.WriteLine("A course has a grade that is 74.0f");
            grades.Remove("Java");              // Remove object by key.
            if (!grades.Contains("Java"))
                Console.WriteLine("The Java course no longer exists");
            grades.Clear();                     // Clear all grades.
            DisplayAllValues(grades);
            Console.ReadLine();
        }

        static void DisplayAllValues(Hashtable ht) {
            foreach (DictionaryEntry item in ht) {
                // Follow instructions if key is a string.
                if (item.Key.GetType() == typeof(string)) {
                    // If value is letter grade show it.
```

```
                    if (item.Value.GetType() == typeof(string))
                        ShowGrade((string)item.Key, (string)item.Value);
                    // If value is a float convert it to a letter grade.
                    else if(item.Value.GetType() == typeof(float)) {
                        float grade = (float)item.Value;
                        string letterGrade = "F";
                        if (grade >= 80.0f)
                            letterGrade = "A";
                        else if (grade >= 70.0f)
                            letterGrade = "B";
                        ShowGrade((string)item.Key, letterGrade);
                    }
                }
            }
            Console.WriteLine();
        }

        static void ShowGrade(string course, string grade) {
            Console.WriteLine("Course: " + course + "  Grade: " + grade);
        }
    }
}
```

Before the *Hashtable* collection contents are displayed, any number grades are converted to letter grades. After all items are displayed, additional output is used to test the *ContainsKey()*, *ContainsValue()*, and *Remove()* methods:

```
Course: C#  Grade: A
Course: ASP.NET  Grade: A
Course: Java  Grade: B

A C# Course Exists
A course has a grade that is 74.0f
The Java course no longer exists
```

Chapter 10 Self Test

The following questions are intended to help reinforce your comprehension of the concepts covered in this chapter. The answers can be found in the accompanying online Appendix B, "Answers to the Self Tests."

1. Answer the following questions true or false.

A. ____ The *Dictionary* class is available from the *System.Collections.Generic* namespace.

B. ____ One *ArrayList* collection can only store objects of the same type.

C. ____ One *List* collection can only store objects of the same type.

2. Match these terms—List, ArrayList, KeyValuePair, Dictionary, Hashtable—with the statements provided. Use each term only once:

   A. ____________ This collection type stores objects with the same type of key value pairs.

   B. ____________ This collection type does not require a key value pair and can store more than one type of object in a collection.

   C. ____________ Implements generic types.

   D. ____________ This collection type can store multiple key value pairs that do not have the same types.

   E. ____________ This collection type stores only one type of object in a collection of multiple objects.

3. Starting with Example 10-4, declare a new class called *JointSavings* that inherits from the *Savings* class. Create an object of the *JointSavings* class and add it to the list. Modify the code so your output appears as follows:

```
This is a Checking object.
This is a Savings object.
This is a JointSavings object.
```

4. Starting with Example 10-5, add the following new class called *BillableItem*:

```
class BillableItem {
    public string  Description { get; set; }
    public decimal Amount      { get; set; }
    public BillableItem(string description, decimal amount) {
        Description = description;
        Amount      = amount;
    }
    public void Display() {
        Console.WriteLine("Pay " + Description + " bill:  "
                          + Amount.ToString("C"));
    }
}
```

   Then inside the *Main()* method, create a new object called *BillableItem* and add it to the *ArrayList* collection. When iterating through all items in your collection, invoke the *Display()* method of the *BillableItem* object to also show the bill description and amount with the output.

5. Write a program to create a *KeyValuePair* item that stores an integer for the key and a string for the value. Then, initialize the *KeyValuePair* item with a reference of 1 for the key when storing "apple" for the value. Finally, output the key and value of your *KeyValuePair* item.
6. Create a *Dictionary* collection that stores information about books where the ISBN number is the key and the book title is the value. Store two books in the dictionary and then iterate through the collection to display the book titles. For sample data, try adding ISBN#978-0071809375, "JavaScript, Fourth Edition: A Beginner's Guide" and ISBN#978-0071817912, "jQuery: A Beginner's Guide".
7. Create a *Hashtable* collection that stores document information and add data shown here.

Invoice: 208	44.33
Invoice: 344	34.22
YRC	Packing List - Jan. 28

Iterate through the *Hashtable* collection to display both the key and value for each item in the collection.

Part III

Advanced Structures

Chapter 11

Delegates, Anonymous Functions, and Events

Key Skills & Concepts

- Delegates
- Anonymous Functions
- Events

This chapter discusses delegates and anonymous functions as well as how these concepts can be applied to understand events.

NOTE

The discussion of delegates and anonymous functions is also helpful preparation for understanding LINQ extension methods, which are covered in Chapters 16 and 17.

Events provide a mechanism for a class to publish notifications to other subscribing classes. Events may be used to relay changes in state within the class, to notify subscribing classes about actions that have taken place (such as mouse clicks and key presses), or to indicate that a file has finished loading, for instance.

Delegates enable us to pass a reference to a method to another class. In the case of events, we pass a reference to a callback method of a subscribing class to the publishing class. The publishing class will invoke the callback with the delegate when the event occurs.

With so many new concepts mentioned at once, it is understandable if you feel a little overwhelmed at this point, so this chapter will take the time to properly explain each topic that was introduced here.

Delegates

A delegate is a C# type that represents a reference to a method that can be passed between objects.

Delegate Syntax

A delegate declaration looks a lot like a method signature, but the delegate declaration starts with the *delegate* keyword:

```
public delegate void Writer(string output);
```

The return type and parameter type sequence of a method assigned to a delegate instance must also match the return type and parameter type sequence of the delegate:

```
public void Display(string output) {
    Console.WriteLine(output);
}
```

When a delegate and method have matching types, you can initialize the delegate instance by passing the target method as a parameter:

```
Output.Writer writer = new Output.Writer(output.Display);
```

Example 11-1 Simple Delegates

This code example declares a delegate named *Writer()* in the *Output* class. The *Writer()* delegate is then initialized with a reference to the *Display()* method of the *Program* class. The delegate object is then used to display some output in the window with the help of the method it currently references.

NOTE

This example really is not very practical but it does offer a simple view of how to declare, initialize, and implement a delegate to call different methods.

```
using System;

namespace Starter {
    public class Program {
        public static void Main() {
            // Declare delegate object and reference method of current class.
            Output.Writer writer = new Output.Writer(Display);
            writer("Hello");    // Invoke method with delegate.
            Console.ReadLine();
        }
        static void Display(string output) {
            Console.WriteLine(output);
        }
    }
    public class Output {
        public delegate void Writer(string output); // Declare delegate type.
    }
}
```

Running this program generates output that is printed through the delegate reference. No mention of the method or class name is required when invoking the method:

```
Hello
```

Try This 11-1 Practice with Delegates

The language and structure of delegates can be challenging to understand initially, so to help with learning, here is an exercise for creating and implementing a trivial delegate. While not very practical, to keep this exercise simple, you will create a delegate that calls a method to perform a conversion of pounds to kilograms.

1. Create a new console application.
2. Add this new class and delegate declaration after the auto-generated *Program* class:

```
public class Output {
    public delegate float Kilograms(float pounds);
}
```

3. Create an instance of the *Kilograms* delegate inside the *Program* class.
4. Pass a reference to a method to the delegate instance. The body of the method referenced needs to return the mass in kilograms based on this formula:

```
kg = pounds * 0.4535f;
```

5. Use the delegate instance to calculate the total mass in kilograms for a two-pound weight.
6. Output the result returned by the delegate method to the window.

Anonymous Functions

An anonymous function is an inline expression that you define with the help of a delegate. So instead of passing a named method reference to a delegate, you assign a code block to the delegate. This anonymous function can be defined or redefined at run time.

The anonymous function body is usually only a few lines at the most so their routines are typically short. The *return* statement of the anonymous function body is optional. Anonymous function headers can be declared two different ways:

- With a formal delegate declaration
- With the *Func<T, TResult>* delegate

Anonymous Functions with Delegates

One way to create an anonymous function is with a delegate. You can define the anonymous function return type and parameter types with the following delegate type declaration:

```
delegate float Average(int x, int y);
```

Lambda Syntax

After declaring the anonymous function parameter and return types, you assign or reassign the body of the function by using lambda syntax. The lambda operator => separates function parameters on the left from the expression on the right. Notice that the parameters (int x, int y) on the left match the signature of the delegate.

```
Average average = (int x, int y) =>{ float  z;
                                            z = (x + y) / 2.0f;
                                            return z; };
```

The parameter data types can be inferred from the object referenced within the anonymous function's scope. The *return* statement is optional. Because of this, the anonymous function body shown previously can be reduced to

```
Average average = (x, y) => (x + y) / 2.0f;
```

Once a body for the anonymous function is assigned, the function can be invoked with a calling statement that provides the required parameter values:

```
Console.WriteLine(average(9, 2).ToString("N1"));
```

Example 11-2 Anonymous Functions with Delegates

This example defines a delegate type that can reference a method that receives two integer parameters and returns a float. For this case, the method is used to reference an anonymous method that calculates the average of two integer parameters.

```
using System;
namespace Starter {
    class Program {
        // Declare delegate type.
        delegate float Average(int x, int y);
        public static void Main() {
            // Declare anonymous function reference.
            Average average;

            // Assign body of the anonymous function.
            average = (int x, int y) =>{ float  z;
                                                 z = (x + y)/2.0f;
                                                 return z; };
            // Invoke the anonymous function.
            Console.WriteLine(average(9,2).ToString("N1"));
```

```
                // Re-assign the body of the anonymous function.
                average = (x, y) => (x + y)/2.0f;

                // Invoke the anonymous function with the simplified body.
                Console.WriteLine(average(9, 2).ToString("N1"));

                Console.ReadLine();
            }
        }
    }
```

The results from invoking the anonymous function for each of the two bodies provide the same result:

```
5.5
5.5
```

Try This 11-2 Practice with Delegates and Anonymous Functions

This exercise offers a chance to practice working with delegates and anonymous functions.

1. Create a new console application.
2. At the class level, add the following code to declare a delegate:

   ```
   delegate void ShowOutput(string message);
   ```

3. Inside *Main()* declare an instance of the *ShowOutput()* delegate.
4. Assign a body to the delegate instance that prints the value stored in *message* to the window.
5. Invoke the anonymous function with your delegate instance so the output to the window is

   ```
   output("Hello world from anonymous function!");
   ```

Anonymous Functions with Func<T,TResult> Delegates

Instead of defining anonymous functions with a delegate declaration, you can declare anonymous functions using the *Func<T, TResult>* delegate to do the same thing but without the formal declaration. The *Func<T, TResult>* delegate is available through the *System* namespace. *T* represents the generic input parameter data type, and *TResult* represents the function's generic return type. The function parameter data types are defined on the left inside the angle brackets. The return type of the anonymous function is set in the last parameter on the right inside the angle brackets:

```
Func<int, int, float> average;
```

When the declaration is made, the anonymous method assignment can be made with lambda syntax:

```
average = (int x, int y) =>{ float  z;
                                    z = (x + y) / 2.0f;
                                    return z; };
```

Since the parameter types are inferred and the *return* statement is optional, the anonymous method assignment can be reduced to

```
average = (x, y) => (x + y)/2.0f;
```

Just like the original delegate declaration, in the end, you can invoke the anonymous function with a call to the *Func<T, TResult>* delegate:

```
Console.WriteLine(average(9, 2).ToString("N1"));
```

Example 11-3 Anonymous Function Declaration with System.Func<T, TResult> Delegates

This example presents a full view of an anonymous function declaration and implementation of a *Func<T, TResult>* delegate. The anonymous function is defined to receive two integer parameters and to return a float value. The anonymous function body is assigned and invoked. Then, a simplified version of the function body is created without declaring the parameter types or the inclusion of a *return* statement. This simpler version of the function body is assigned to the anonymous function delegate. Then the anonymous function is invoked once again to provide the same output.

```
using System;

namespace Starter {
    class Program {
        public static void Main() {
            // Declare an anonymous function with two integer parameters
            // and a float return type.
            Func<int, int, float> average;
```

```
                // Assign a body that calculates the average.
                average = (int x, int y) =>{ float  z;
                                                    z = (x + y) / 2.0f;
                                                    return z; };
                // Invoke the anonymous function.
                Console.WriteLine(average(9,2).ToString("N1"));

                // Simplified body to calculate average.
                average = (x, y) => (x + y) / 2.0f;

                // Invoke the anonymous function with the simplified body.
                Console.WriteLine(average(9, 2).ToString("N1"));
                Console.ReadLine();
            }
        }
    }
```

The output from invoking the same anonymous method with *Func<T, TResult>* delegate syntax is identical to the result that is generated in Example 11-2 when using regular delegate syntax:

```
5.5
5.5
```

Events

Events are simply notifications that a class can raise/publish—they can be anything, for any reason. Events are changes of state that occur due to either external actions such as a mouse click or internal actions such as the start of a file read, the end of a file read, an error, or really any critical part of the routine. A class that defines, raises, and issues notifications about an event is the event publisher. The class that requests notification of an event is an event subscriber. When an event is published, a subscribing class can implement a *callback* method to receive notification.

Event Declaration Syntax

To declare an event, you must first declare a delegate that represents a method that will be called when the event is raised. Then, you declare an event with the delegate type using the *event* keyword.

```
public delegate void Notify(string message);    // Declare delegate.
public event         Notify BeginOutput;        // Declare event.
```

Subscribing to an Event

The process of subscribing to an event is often called "hooking up" to an event. When hooking up an object of the publishing class to an event, the local callback method in the subscribing class is assigned to the event delegate with the += operator. It is important to note that the callback signature matches the delegate signature that was declared earlier.

```
public static void Main() {
    Publisher publisher  = new Publisher();
    publisher.BeginOutput += StartOutputCallback;
}
public static void StartOutputCallback(string message) {
    Console.WriteLine("StartOutputCallback - " + message);
}
```

Raising an Event

The publishing class raises the event at any time desired in its routine. If the delegate in the publishing class is pointing to any callback methods in subscribing classes, it calls them.

```
public delegate void Notify(string message);     // Declare delegate.
public event         Notify BeginOutput;         // Declare event.

public void Display(string message) {
    OnBeginOutput();                             // Raise event.
    Console.WriteLine(message);                  // Show output.

}
private void OnBeginOutput() {
    if (BeginOutput != null) // See if anyone has subscribed via BeginOutput +=
       // Notify callback method by invoking the delegate.
       BeginOutput("Starting output!");
}
```

Unsubscribing from an Event

The process of unsubscribing from event notification is called "unhooking" the event. To do this, the –= operator de-references the callback method from the event delegate:

```
publisher.BeginOutput -= StartOutputCallback;
```

Example 11-4 Events

This example shows a complete view of the steps needed for publishing and subscribing to an event. Basically, the *Publisher* class raises an event before outputting text to the console. The *Publisher* class also raises an event after outputting text in the console. Each time an event is raised, notification is sent to the *Subscriber* class.

In this case, the event publishing class named *Publisher* declares an event called *BeginOutput* that is raised immediately at the start of its *Display()* method. A subscribing class receives notification about the event through the *OnBeginOutput()* method in the host that calls the *StartOutputCallback()* method of the *Subscriber* class. *Publisher* also declares an event called *EndOutput* that is raised at the very end of its *Display()* method. The *Subscriber* class receives notification about the *EndOutput* event through the *EndOutputCallback()* method. The object of the *Publisher* class hooks up to the events and sets references to the callback methods in the *Subscriber* class after it is initialized.

```
using System;

namespace Starter {
    public class Subscriber {
        public static void Main() {
            Publisher publisher   = new Publisher();

            // Subscribe to events and set method reference.
            publisher.BeginOutput += StartOutputCallback;
            publisher.EndOutput   += EndOutputCallback;
            publisher.Display("I am a subscriber.");

            // De-reference callback methods.
            publisher.BeginOutput -= StartOutputCallback;
            publisher.EndOutput   -= EndOutputCallback;

            // Output text when not subscribed to the event.
            publisher.Display("\nI am not a subscriber.");
            Console.ReadLine();
        }
        public static void StartOutputCallback(string message) {
            Console.WriteLine("StartOutputCallback - " + message);
        }
        public static void EndOutputCallback(string message) {
            Console.WriteLine("EndOutputCallback   - " + message);
        }
    }
    public class Publisher{
        public delegate void Notify(string message);      // Declare delegate.
        public event         Notify BeginOutput;          // Declare event.
        public event         Notify EndOutput;            // Declare event.
```

```
        public void Display(string message) {
            OnBeginOutput();                          // Raise event.
            Console.WriteLine(message);               // Show output.
            OnEndOutput();                            // Raise event.
        }
        private void OnBeginOutput() {
            if (BeginOutput != null)
                BeginOutput("Starting output!");      // Notify callback method.
        }
        private void OnEndOutput() {
            if (EndOutput != null)
                EndOutput("Ending output!");          // Notify callback method.
        }
    }
}
```

When running the program, notifications from the *Publisher* class are received in the callback methods of the *Subscriber* class before and after events are raised from the *Display()* method. When the *Publisher* object no longer subscribes to these events, the callback methods in the *Subscriber* class are no longer notified:

```
StartOutputCallback - Starting output!
I am a subscriber.
EndOutputCallback   - Ending output!

I am not a subscriber.
```

Chapter 11 Self Test

The following questions are intended to help reinforce your comprehension of the concepts covered in this chapter. The answers can be found in the accompanying online Appendix B, "Answers to the Self Tests."

1. Using a regular delegate, declare, assign, and invoke a named method function to return the string value of a float value rounded to two decimal places. Test the delegate reference by invoking it with the value 3.1415f. Print out the value returned by the referenced method.
2. Using a regular delegate, declare, assign, and invoke an anonymous function to return the string value of a float value rounded to two decimal places. Test the delegate reference by invoking it with the value 3.1415f. Print out the value returned by the anonymous function.
3. Using the *Func<T, TResult>* delegate, declare, assign, and invoke an anonymous function to return the string value of a float value rounded to two decimal places. Test the delegate reference by invoking it with the value 3.1415f. Print out the value returned by the anonymous function.

4. How is the output different from the original output in Example 11-4 if you modify the solution so the object is only unsubscribed from the *EndOutput* event?

5. Create a new console application and add the following code:

```
using System;

namespace Starter {
    public class Program {
        public static void Main() {
            Input input       = new Input();
            input.GetUserInput();
            Console.ReadLine();
        }
    }
    public class Input {
        public void GetUserInput() {
            while (true) {
                Console.WriteLine(
                "Type any characters or 'q' to quit and press enter. ");
                string input = Console.ReadLine();

                if (input.Trim() != "q") {
                }
                else {
                    break;
                }
            }
        }
    }
}
```

Then, in the *Input* class, set up an event called *UserInput.* Raise the *Input* event whenever the user inputs text and presses ENTER. Have your *Input* object subscribe to the event. Whenever the event is raised, send the data that was input by the user to the callback method in the subscribing class. Design your program so the user input and program output could resemble the following:

```
Type any characters or 'q' to quit and press enter.
Hello
You typed: Hello
Type any characters or 'q' to quit and press enter.
World
You typed: World
Type any characters or 'q' to quit and press enter.
q
You typed 'q' to quit.
```

Chapter 12

Interfaces

Key Skills & Concepts

- Interface Syntax
- Interface Hierarchies
- Generic Interfaces
- Existing .NET Interfaces

Interfaces declare public data members and methods that must be implemented in a class or struct. Interfaces are similar to abstract classes since interfaces also do not permit a base implementation. So why bother going through the trouble of creating an interface to enforce implementation of public members? A class can implement multiple interfaces but can inherit only from one base class. The interface, of course, also helps to enforce good object-oriented design. Understanding interfaces will also help with your understanding of really important C# structures like collections and LINQ. You might even need to use interfaces to enforce consistent accessibility for a series of classes in your own projects.

Interface Syntax

The interface declaration is internal by default, but interfaces can explicitly be declared as public or internal. Access modifiers cannot be declared for interface members, since members of the interface are always public. While other conventions exist, most C# developers will assign PascalCase names that are prefixed with the capital letter *I*. Here is a typical interface declaration:

```
interface IPerson {
    string LastName { get; }      // Required property.
    string GetFullName();         // Required method.
}
```

To include an interface implementation in a class declaration, a colon and the interface name follow the class header:

```
class Employee : IPerson {}
```

Even though a class can inherit only from one other class, classes can implement multiple interfaces. When classes implement multiple interfaces, the list of interface names is separated by commas and appears to the right of the class header after a colon:

```
class Parcel : IMexico, IJapan
```

Example 12-1 Interface Introduction

This demonstration shows an interface that requires the implementing *Employee* class to include *LastName* and *FirstName* properties and a *GetFullName()* method:

```
using System;

namespace Starter {
    class Program {
        public static void Main( ) {
            Employee  employee   =  new Employee("Treele", "Grumbus");
            Console.Write("Full Name: ");
            Console.WriteLine(employee.GetFullName());
            Console.ReadLine();
        }
    }

    // Declare interface.
    interface IPerson {
        string LastName  { get; }    // Required properties.
        string FirstName { get; }
        string GetFullName();        // Required method.
    }

    // Declare a class that implements the IPerson interface.
    class Employee : IPerson {
        public string LastName  { get; private set; }   // Implement properties.
        public string FirstName { get; private set; }

        public string GetFullName( ) {                   // Implement method.
            return FirstName + " " + LastName;
        }
        public Employee(string lastName, string firstName) {
            LastName  = lastName;
            FirstName = firstName;
        }
    }
}
```

The output is predictable. The text displayed shows the full name that is returned from the *GetFullName()* method that is required by the *IPerson* interface:

```
Full Name: Grumbus Treele
```

Try This 12-1 Interface Exercise

This exercise offers practice working with interfaces and implementing interfaces in your classes.

1. Starting with Example 12-1, add the following member declarations to the *IPerson* interface:

```
DateTime HireDate { set; }
void ShowHireDate();
```

2. After changes to the interface declaration, fix the class implementation to comply with the interface.
3. Design the *ShowHireDate()* method so the program displays output similar to the following:

```
Full Name: Grumbus Treele
Hire Date: Wednesday, January 1
```

TIP

If an interface has been defined, using Visual Studio, it is possible to auto-generate a code shell of required members by right-clicking the interface name in the class declaration and choosing Implement Interface. Some editions of Visual Studio will also let you generate an interface from an existing class. Visual Studio Express for Windows Desktop, however, does not allow you to auto-generate an interface from a class.

Try This 12-2 Generating Code from the Interface

As just mentioned, you can use Visual Studio to generate a class from an interface. To practice using this feature:

1. Create a new console application.
2. Replace all auto-generated code inside Program.cs with the following:

```
using System;

namespace Starter {
    // Declare interface.
    interface IPerson {
```

```
            string LastName  { get; }   // Required properties.
            string FirstName { get; }
            string GetFullName();       // Required method.
        }

        // Declare a class that implements the IPerson interface.
        class Employee : IPerson {
        }
    }
```

3. Right-click the interface name *IPerson* reference that follows the *Employee* class declaration and choose Implement Interface | Implement Interface.
4. Examine the code that is generated. You will see a shell that includes all required interface members.

Explicit Interface Implementation

When a class implements two or more interfaces that have identical members, each specific member implementation must be accessed explicitly through the interface, and not the class.

TIP

Most of the time, developers use interfaces implicitly, as shown in the previous section of this chapter. However, explicit interfaces are discussed here in case you need one.

In this example, two separate interfaces require an implementation of an identical *Cost()* method:

```
interface IMexico {
    decimal Cost(decimal weight);
}
interface IJapan {
    decimal Cost(decimal weight);
}
```

If a class implements members that have the same name in each interface, you must prefix each member with the interface name and you cannot include the public access modifier:

```
class Parcel : IMexico, IJapan {
    decimal IJapan.Cost(decimal weight) {   // Explicitly implement IJapan.
        const decimal RATE = 2.54m;
        return weight * RATE;
```

```
    }
    decimal IMexico.Cost(decimal weight) {  // Explicitly implement IMexico.
        const decimal RATE = 1.84m;
        return weight * RATE;
    }
}
```

To explicitly reference an interface, you initialize an object with a class and then create an interface instance by casting the object with the interface:

```
Parcel  parcel   =  new Parcel();     // Declare Parcel object.
IJapan  toJapan  = (IJapan) parcel;  // Use IJapan interface.
decimal cost     = toJapan.Cost(5.45m);
```

Example 12-2 Explicit Interface Implementation

This example shows explicit use of interfaces by a *Parcel* class to manage delivery costs. The *Parcel* class implements both *IJapan* and *IMexico* interfaces, which both require implementations of the *Cost()* method:

```
using System;

namespace Starter {
    class Program {
        public static void Main() {
            Parcel  parcel   = new Parcel();     // Declare Parcel object.
            IJapan  toJapan  = (IJapan) parcel;  // Use IJapan interface.
            IMexico toMexico = (IMexico)parcel;  // Use IMexico interface.

            const decimal WEIGHT = 3.89m;        // Compare mail costs.
            Console.WriteLine("Mailing to Mexico costs " +
                              toMexico.Cost(WEIGHT).ToString("C"));
            Console.WriteLine("Mailing to Japan costs " +
                              toJapan.Cost(WEIGHT).ToString("C"));

            Console.ReadLine();
        }
    }

    // Declare two interfaces.  Each interface requires a Cost() method.
    interface IMexico {
        decimal Cost(decimal weight);
    }
    interface IJapan {
        decimal Cost(decimal weight);
    }
```

```
    // Declare a class that implements two interfaces with identical members.
    class Parcel : IMexico, IJapan {
        decimal IJapan.Cost(decimal weight) {    // Explicitly use IJapan.
            const decimal RATE = 2.54m;
            return weight * RATE;
        }
        decimal IMexico.Cost(decimal weight) {  // Explicitly use IMexico.
            const decimal RATE = 1.84m;
            return weight * RATE;
        }
    }
}
```

The output from running the program shows different costs depending on the interface instance:

```
Mailing to Mexico costs $7.16
Mailing to Japan costs $9.88
```

Implicit Interface Implementation

When no interface is specified for an object of a class that implements an interface, the interface use is implied. Example 12-1 demonstrates implicit use of an interface.

In addition, if a class implements more than one interface and the interfaces require identical members, a class can implement one member to satisfy each interface. In the implementing class, the member is not prefixed with the interface reference and the member must be public.

```
interface IMexico {
    decimal Cost(decimal weight);
}
interface IJapan {
    decimal Cost(decimal weight);
}

class Parcel : IMexico, IJapan {
    public decimal Cost(decimal weight) {
        const decimal RATE = 2.54m;
        return weight * RATE;
    }
}
```

Here the object's interface is then implied:

```
Parcel  parcel    =  new Parcel();
decimal cost      = parcel.Cost(3.50m);
```

Interface Hierarchies

An interface can extend another interface to create a hierarchy of interfaces. This ability to extend interfaces creates more flexibility for code sharing up the interface hierarchy. Classes or structs that implement a hierarchy of interfaces must implement all methods that are declared in the nested interface hierarchy. In this example, the *IEmployee* interface extends the *IPerson* interface:

```
interface IPerson {              // IPerson is at the top of the hierarchy.
    string FirstName { get; set; }
    string LastName  { get; set; }
}
interface IEmployee : IPerson {  // IEmployee extends IPerson.
    int EmployeeID { get; set; }
    void DisplayEmployeeData();
}
```

When a class implements an interface, it must implement all four members that are defined in the interface hierarchy:

```
class Staff : IEmployee {
    public string FirstName  { get; set; }
    public string LastName   { get; set; }
    public int    EmployeeID { get; set; }

     public void DisplayEmployeeData() {
        Console.WriteLine(EmployeeID + ": " + FirstName + " " + LastName);
    }
}
```

Example 12-3 Interface Hierarchies

This example shows how a class implements an *IEmployee* interface that extends an *IPerson* interface. The *IPerson* interface requires *FirstName* and *LastName* properties. The *IEmployee* interface requires an *EmployeeID* property and a *DisplayEmployeeData()* method. The class that implements the *IEmployee* interface must implement all of the members within the hierarchy.

```
using System;

namespace Starter {
    class Program {
        public static void Main() {
            Staff staff = new Staff(1, "Paolo", "Morselli");
            staff.DisplayEmployeeData();
            Console.ReadLine();
```

```
        }
    }

    interface IPerson {              // IPerson is at the top of the hierarchy.
        string FirstName { get; set; }
        string LastName  { get; set; }
    }
    interface IEmployee : IPerson {  // IEmployee extends IPerson.
        int EmployeeID { get; set; }
        void DisplayEmployeeData();
    }
    class Staff : IEmployee {        // This class implements IEmployee.
        public string FirstName  { get; set; }
        public string LastName   { get; set; }
        public int    EmployeeID { get; set; }

        public Staff(int id, string firstName, string lastName) {
            FirstName  = firstName;
            LastName   = lastName;
            EmployeeID = id;
        }
        public void DisplayEmployeeData() {
            Console.WriteLine(EmployeeID + ": " + FirstName + " " + LastName);
        }
    }
}
```

The output is simple but does involve all four members that are required by the interface:

```
1: Paolo Morselli
```

Generic Interfaces

A generic interface offers some interesting possibilities since it enforces implementations of properties and methods without specifying the data type. In this sample the *IInspection* interface requires an *InpectionDate* property and a generic *List* collection called *Items*:

```
interface IInspection<T> {
    DateTime InspectionDate { get; set; }
    List<T>  Items          { get; set;  }
}
```

Any class that implements the *IInspection* interface must include these interface members:

```
class Inspection<T> : IInspection<T> {
    public DateTime InspectionDate { get; set;}
    public List<T>  Items          { get; set; }
}
```

Example 12-4 Generic Interfaces

In this example, an *IInspection* interface ensures that the implementing class contains a generic list and a *Time* property. The implementing class implements these members to store and display carbon samples during air quality testing.

```
using System;
using System.Collections.Generic;

namespace Starter {
    class Program {
        public static void Main( ) {
            Inspection<float> airTest = new Inspection<float>();
            airTest.Items.Add(290.0f);
            airTest.Items.Add(287.0f);


            Console.WriteLine("Sample Date: " + airTest.Time.ToString("m")
                        + ", " + airTest.Time.ToString("T"));
            foreach (float sample in airTest.Items)
                Console.WriteLine(sample + " parts per million.");
            Console.ReadLine();
        }
    }
    interface IInspection<T> {
        DateTime Time   { get; set; }
        List<T>  Items  { get; set; }
    }
    class Inspection<T> : IInspection<T> {
        public DateTime Time    { get; set;}
        public List<T>  Items   { get; set; }

        public Inspection() {
            Time    = DateTime.Now;
            Items   = new List<T>();
        }
    }
}
```

The output shows the carbon level data that is stored in the list by the implementing *Inspection* class:

```
Sample Date: August 23, 12:25:06 PM
290 parts per million.
287 parts per million.
```

NOTE

When running Example 12-4 you may have noticed that the *IInspection* interface requires a *List* collection that is both publicly readable and writeable. However, a class with a publicly modifiable list may not be desirable. The next section discusses how to create a class that contains a list with read-only access.

Existing .NET Interfaces

In addition to creating your own interfaces, you will want to use many of the interfaces that are included with the .NET Framework. There are too many great interfaces to discuss in this book. However, for optimizing query performance, Chapter 14 discusses the *IEnumerable, IQueryable,* and *IList* collection interfaces. For now, to answer some basic questions like "How do I create a read-only collection?" and "How do I sort collections?" we will discuss the *IReadOnlyCollection* and *IComparable* interfaces.

IReadOnlyCollection

The *IReadOnlyCollection* interface from the *System.Collections.Generic* namespace represents a strongly typed read-only collection. Instances of this interface have access to an *AsReadOnly()* method that returns an unchangeable collection of elements:

```
private List<T> items = new List<T>();
public IReadOnlyCollection<T> GetIt() {
    return items.AsReadOnly();
}
```

Example 12-5 IReadOnlyCollection

The code in this example provides similar management for *Inspection* objects as Example 12-4. This example differs, though, because a custom interface hierarchy is not declared and the *Inspection* class provides read-only access to the *Items* collection through the *IReadOnlyCollection* interface:

```
using System;
using System.Collections.Generic;

namespace Starter {
    class Program {
        public static void Main( ) {
            Inspection<float> airTest = new Inspection<float>();
```

```
            airTest.Add(290.0f);
            airTest.Add(287.0f);

            Console.WriteLine("Sample Date: " + airTest.Time.ToString("f"));
            foreach (float sample in airTest.Items)
                Console.WriteLine(sample + " parts per million.");

            Console.ReadLine();
        }
    }

    class Inspection<T> {
        public DateTime Time { get; set;}                    // Properties
        public IReadOnlyCollection<T> Items {
            get { return items.AsReadOnly(); }
        }

        private List<T> items = new List<T>();               // Private data members

        public Inspection() {                                // Constructor
            Time = DateTime.Now;
        }

        public void Add(T item) {                            // Methods
            items.Add(item);
        }
    }
}
```

The output is identical to the output from Example 12-4.

IComparable

The *IComparable* interface is a public interface that exists in the *System* namespace. This interface allows us to choose the sorting property for complex classes and structs. When a class implements the generic *IComparable* interface, the class must include a *CompareTo()* method: The *List* collection object's *Sort()* method uses this *CompareTo()* method to arrange the elements in ascending order. *CompareTo()* performs comparison of one element to another and returns –1 when the object property is less, 0 when the same, and 1 when the property is more. In this case, the string object's *CompareTo()* method is used:

```
// Implement the generic IComparable<T> interface.
class Product : IComparable<Product> {
    public string  Name  { get; private set; }
    public decimal Price { get; private set; }
```

```
    // This method is required by the IComparable<T> interface.
    public int CompareTo(Product product) {
        return Name.CompareTo(product.Name);  // Sort by Name property.
    }
}
```

Example 12-6 IComparable

Here is a full example of a class that implements the *IComparable* interface to sort *Product* objects by their *Name* property:

```
using System;
using System.Collections.Generic;

namespace Starter {
    // Implement the generic IComparable<T> interface.
    class Product : IComparable<Product> {
        public string  Name  { get; private set; }
        public decimal Price { get; private set; }

        public Product(string produceName, decimal itemPrice) {
            Name  = produceName;
            Price = itemPrice;
        }

        // This method is required by the IComparable<T> interface.
        public int CompareTo(Product product) {
            return Name.CompareTo(product.Name);  // Sort by Name property.
        }
    }
    class Program {
        public static void Main( ) {
            List<Product> products = new List<Product>();
            products.Add(new Product("carrots", 0.48m));
            products.Add(new Product("apples", 0.98m));
            products.Add(new Product("bananas", 0.88m));
            products.Add(new Product("dates", 0.53m));

            ShowProducts("Before sorting:", products);
            products.Sort(); // Apply the Sort() method of the List class.
            ShowProducts("After sorting:", products);

            Console.ReadLine();
        }
        static void ShowProducts(string caption, List<Product> products) {
            Console.WriteLine(caption);
            foreach(Product product in products) {
```

```
                Console.Write("    Product:  " + product.Name + "    ");
                Console.WriteLine("Price:  " + product.Price.ToString("C"));
            }
            Console.WriteLine();
        }
    }
}
```

Once the sort is done, the *Product* object collection is arranged by name in ascending order:

```
Before sorting:
    Product:  carrots    Price:  $0.48
    Product:  apples    Price:  $0.98
    Product:  bananas    Price:  $0.88
    Product:  dates    Price:  $0.53

After sorting:
    Product:  apples    Price:  $0.98
    Product:  bananas    Price:  $0.88
    Product:  carrots    Price:  $0.48
    Product:  dates    Price:  $0.53
```

Chapter 12 Self Test

The following questions are intended to help reinforce your comprehension of the concepts covered in this chapter. The answers can be found in the accompanying online Appendix B, "Answers to the Self Tests."

1. Why is the following interface declaration invalid?

```
interface IPerson {
    public string LastName  { get; }
    public string FirstName { get; }
}
```

2. Create a brand-new console application and add the following *IAccount* interface and *Program* class declarations:

```
interface IAccount {
    decimal Balance    { get; set; }
    int     AccountID { get; }
    void    DeductMonthlyCharge();
    void    ShowBalance();
}
```

```
class Program {
    public static void Main( ) {
        Savings account = new Savings(123, 150.00m);
        account.ShowBalance();
        account.DeductMonthlyCharge();
        account.ShowBalance();
        Console.ReadLine();
    }
}
```

Design a *Savings* class to generate the following output:

```
Balance for account #123 = $150.00
Balance for account #123 = $135.00
```

3. Modify Example 12-1 to explicitly initialize an instance of the *IEmployee* interface.
4. Modify Example 12-3 to add the following property declaration to the *IPerson* interface:

```
DateTime Birthdate { get; }
```

Then add the following property to the *IEmployee* interface:

```
string   Email    { get; }
```

Adjust the program to generate the following output:

```
1: Paolo Morselli
Email: pmorselli@acme.com
Birthdate: Saturday, January 6, 1968
```

5. Without making any changes to the *IInspection* interface or the *Inspection* class, modify the code inside the *Main()* method of Example 12-5 to generate the following output:

```
Sample Date: May 1, 15:37:06 PM
No visible leaks from bathroom faucets.
No visible leaks from kitchen faucets.
No visible leaks from shower heads.
```

6. Modify Example 12-6 to sort *Product* objects by *Name* in descending order.
7. Modify Example 12-6 to sort *Product* objects by *Price* in ascending order.

Part IV

Data-Driven Development

Chapter 13

Database Setup

Key Skills & Concepts

- Accessing Database Resources for This Book
- Creating a Database Connection String
- Browsing Database Content with Visual Studio

As a C# developer, you most likely will want to work with database content in your code at some point early in your career. To help you prepare for data-driven C# development, this chapter focuses on the project setup and environment rather than code. Regardless of your level of experience in working with databases, whether you have lots or none, this chapter offers helpful information on how to use the tools in Visual Studio to access database content.

Accessing Database Resources for This Book

To support the focus of this book on data-driven content, this book uses a database named *FoodStore* in all chapters where examples require database content. For readers with little to no experience or those who just don't have Microsoft SQL Server installed, you can use the database that is contained in the FoodStore.mdf file, which is included in the FoodStoreDatabase directory with the download for this book. For experienced database developers who have Microsoft SQL Server installed, the SQL script is also included in a file named FoodStore.sql in the FoodStore directory within the code download for this book. Also, for experienced developers, the entity relationship diagram that shows all tables in this database is included in the appendix.

Creating a Database Connection String

To communicate with a database from your C# application, the database location, the name, and the authentication parameters are required. These database parameters are contained in a database connection string.

TIP

Determining connection string parameters is not an overly challenging task, but when the connection string is assembled incorrectly, this issue may be difficult to detect. For this reason, whenever possible, using the wizard in Visual Studio to generate the connection string will help you to ensure it is configured properly.

For all database demonstrations in this book, you may choose to use one of two database types:

- A Microsoft SQL Server Database File (also known as an .mdf file). Use of the FoodStore.mdf file is recommended for database beginners.
- A separate Microsoft SQL Server install. Use of a separate SQL Server install is only recommended for advanced database users who already have a free Express edition or a paid edition of Microsoft SQL Server installed.

Regardless of your selection from these two options, use of either data source type is perfectly acceptable for all code examples in this book.

Example 13-1 Creating a Connection String for Database Development Beginners

Steps in this example show how to add a reference to a database file. In this case, you are going to create a reference to the FoodStore.mdf database file. This example is recommended for database development beginners or advanced database users who do not have Microsoft SQL Server installed separately.

The FoodStore.mdf file is included with the code download for this book. Also in the same directory as this database file you will find a log file named FoodStore_log.ldf. The FoodStore.mdf file references the FoodStore_log.ldf file, so the two files need to be kept together at all times. These two files were exported from a Microsoft SQL Server database that was created with a script that is contained in the FoodStore.sql file. As a developer, you can consume these FoodStore.mdf and FoodStore.ldf files as a package. The result is that you can run your code as if you are working with a live database, but you don't need to install a separate database application.

To add a reference to the FoodStore.mdf file, first create a console application. Next, right-click the project name in the Solution Explorer, click Properties, and choose the Settings tab on the left. In the Settings panel that appears on the right, the following message may display as a hyperlink: "This project does not contain a default settings file. Click here to create one." If so, click the hyperlink. Under the Type column, choose the Connection String option in the drop-down menu. Under the Scope column, select Application if this choice isn't already selected (refer to Figure 13-1).

Next, click in the Value column to display an ellipsis (…) button. Click this button to launch the Connection Properties dialog. Click the Change button to select Microsoft SQL Server Database File, since you are reading from the FoodStore.mdf file. Then click OK after you have selected the file option. Next, click the Browse button to launch a dialog

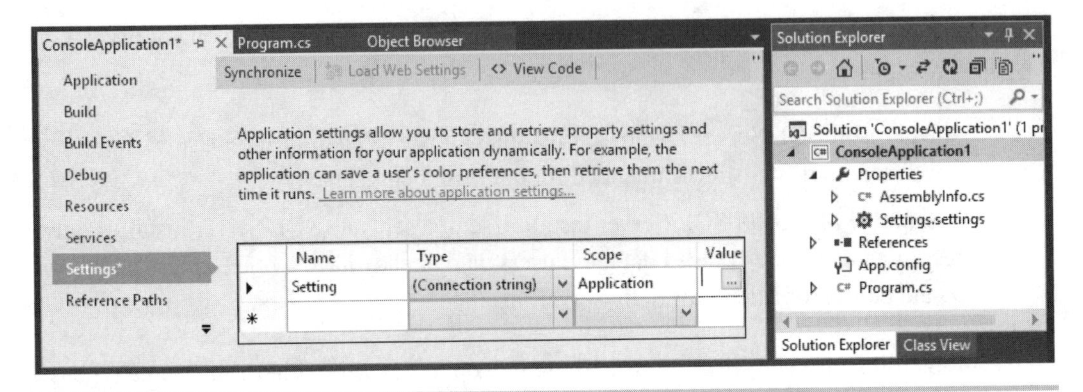

Figure 13-1 Setting the connection string from the project Settings panel

that lets you navigate to the FoodStore.mdf file. Select the file. Leave the default Use Windows Authentication option selected (see Figure 13-2).

Next, ensure your connection is valid by clicking the Test Connection button. A dialog should appear to report that the "Test Connection Succeeded." Click OK to exit the Connection Properties dialog.

Connection Properties
Enter information to connect to the selected data source or click "Change" to choose a different data source and/or provider.
Data source:
Microsoft SQL Server Database File (SqlClient)
Change...
Database file name (new or existing):
C:\FoodStore.mdf
Browse...
Log on to the server
Use Windows Authentication
Use SQL Server Authentication
User name:
Password:
Save my password
Advanced...
Test Connection
OK
Cancel

Figure 13-2 Connection Properties settings for a SQL Server Database File

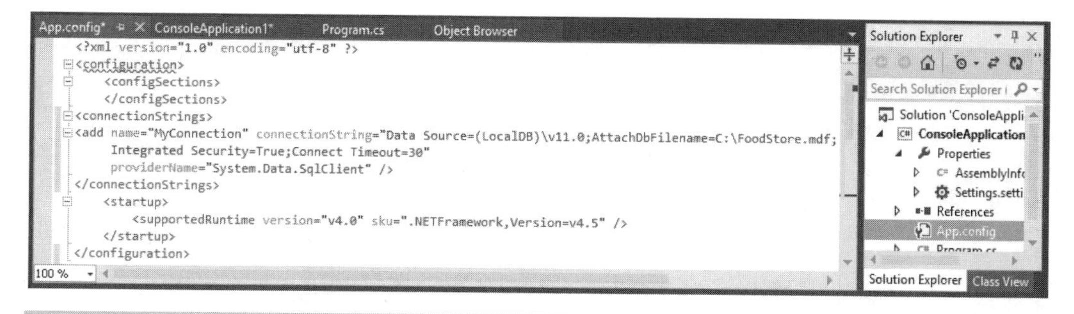

Figure 13-3 Adjusting connection string reference in App.config file

After these last steps, you will see a *connectionStrings* element in your App.config file like the one displayed in Figure 13-3. Change the *name* attribute to *MyConnection* and save the file by choosing File | Save App.config or pressing CTRL-S. We will use this named reference in future examples.

CAUTION

Remember to save your App.config file after changing the *name* attribute to *MyConnection*. Otherwise, the code examples within this book, which rely on this named connection, will fail.

The solution for this example is now complete. While the result may seem uneventful, keep the solution handy. You will use this solution in Example 13-3, and you will need this solution as well to complete the examples in Chapter 18.

Example 13-2 Generating a Connection String to SQL Server

This example explains how to create a database connection string to reference databases that are stored in Microsoft SQL Server.

NOTE

If you already completed Example 13-1, you may skip this example. This example is intended only for advanced database users who want to use their current installation of Microsoft SQL Server instead of a database file.

If you have Microsoft SQL Server installed, you can use it to host the database instead of using the database file. First, create a database named *FoodStore* and then run the script that is located in FoodStore.sql, which is provided with the download for this book. To begin this example, create a new console application. Then, right-click the project node in the Solution Explorer and choose Properties. In the project window, select the Settings tab. You may be shown a panel with the message "This project does not contain a default

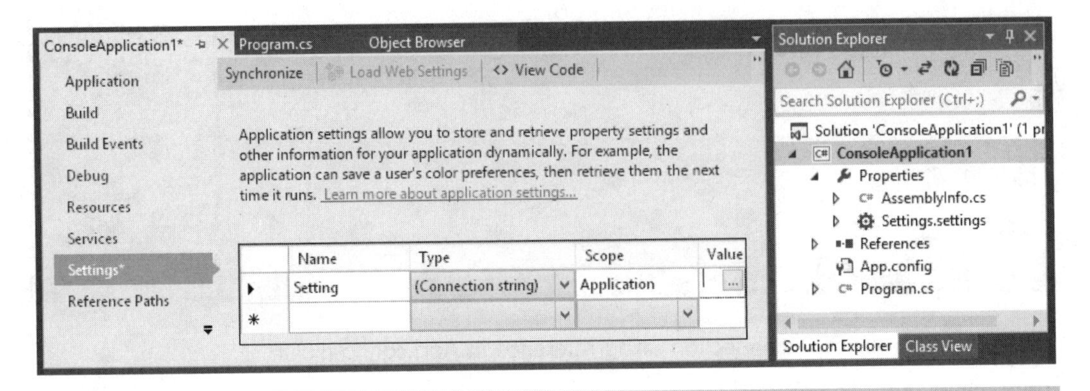

Figure 13-4 Setting the connection string from the project Settings panel

settings file. Click here to create one" in a hyperlink. If so, click the hyperlink. Now the Settings view will be visible, as shown in Figure 13-4.

In the Settings panel, select Connection String for the Type and choose Application for the Scope. Next, click in the Value column and click the ellipses (…) button at the right to launch the Connection Properties dialog shown in Figure 13-5.

In the Connection Properties dialog, the data source must be Microsoft SQL Server. If it isn't, click Change, select Microsoft SQL Server from the Change Data Source dialog, and click OK. Now you can enter the server name. If you do not know the server name, one quick way to obtain it is from the Connect To Server dialog that appears when SQL Server Management Console launches (see Figure 13-6).

Back in the Connection Properties dialog, enter the server name. Then select Windows Authentication, provided that you were logged in using Windows authentication when creating the *FoodStore* database. If instead you created the *FoodStore* database while using SQL Server Authentication mode, then you also need to enter your database login credentials. Once you have entered the correct server name and authentication data, select the database name from the drop-down list. If you did not enter the correct information, the database will not appear.

To ensure your connection information has been entered properly, click the Test Connection button at the bottom of the Connection Properties dialog. A pop-up message should indicate that your connection was successful, in which case you can click OK to close the Connection Properties dialog.

After successfully setting your data connection from the Connection Properties dialog, you will then find a *connectionStrings* element inside your App.config file. The *add* element will contain a connection string like the one shown in Figure 13-7. To prepare the connection string for use in future examples within this chapter, assign the value of *MyConnection* to the *name* attribute (refer to Figure 13-7).

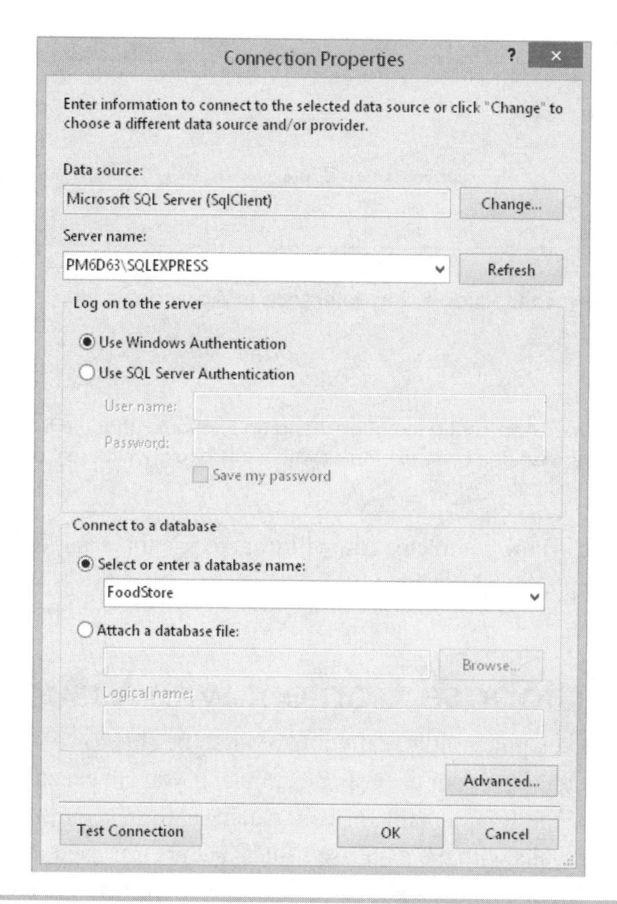

Figure 13-5 Connection Properties dialog for Microsoft SQL Server

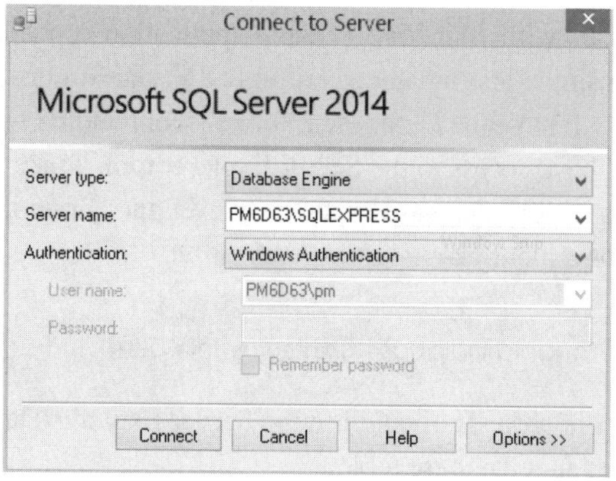

Connect to Server
Microsoft SQL Server 2014
Server type: Database Engine
Server name: PM6D63\SQLEXPRESS
Authentication: Windows Authentication
User name: PM6D63\pm
Password:
Remember password
Connect Cancel Help Options >>

Figure 13-6 Connect to Server dialog

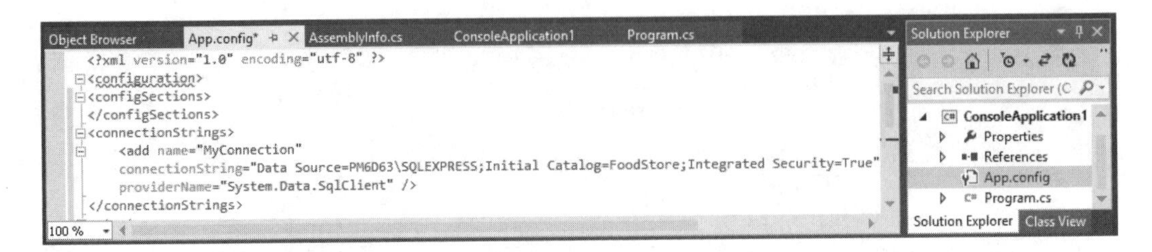

Figure 13-7 Adjusting connection string reference in App.config file

CAUTION

Remember to save your App.config file after changing the *name* attribute to *MyConnection*. Otherwise, the code examples within this book, which rely on this named connection, will fail.

Example 13-2 is now complete. You will want to use this solution later to start the examples that are presented in Chapter 18.

Browsing Database Content with Visual Studio

For data-driven development, it is really important to be able to view the actual database content without relying on your code. For example, if you are executing a query in C# to view data stored in the *Product* table of your database, for test purposes, you likely will want to compare results with the database values that are retrieved independently of your own application. If you are an experienced database developer, you could use SQL Server Management Studio to view the data directly. If, however, you are new to databases or to SQL Server, Visual Studio provides either a Server Explorer tool or a Database Explorer tool. Other than the differences in names, these tools basically look and work the same. Which tool is included with your Visual Studio application depends on your application edition. If you are using a less advanced edition of Visual Studio, such as an Express edition, you likely will have the Database Explorer tool bundled with your application. Otherwise, you will have access to the Server Explorer tool, which offers the same identical features. Regardless of your database experience level, the Server Explorer/Database Explorer offers a convenient way to view the data.

Example 13-3 Browsing Database Content with Visual Studio

This example shows how to set up and use the Server Explorer/Database Explorer to view data that is contained in a database table.

CAUTION

If you receive any errors while working with the Server Explorer/Database Explorer, you might need to download and install the latest release of Microsoft's SQL Server Data Tools.

To begin, start with the solution from Example 13-1 or Example 13-2. Once your project is created, you can open the Server Explorer from the View menu or open the Database Explorer from View | Other Windows | Database Explorer.

Right-click the Database Connections node that appears in the Server Explorer/Database Explorer panel. You will then see your existing database connection listed. If you do not see it, you can add it by choosing Add Connection. Then, follow the steps presented either in Example 13-1 or Example 13-2 starting where you select the data source type. Once the *FoodStore* database appears as a listing in the Server Explorer/Database Explorer, you can expand the *FoodStore* connection node, which contains folders for different types of database objects (see Figure 13-8). The directory of interest for this discussion is the Tables folder, which contains the database tables that store the actual data. Figure 13-8 shows data that is stored within the *Product* table in tabular format. To view table data, click the Tables folder, right-click the desired data table, and then select Show Table Data in the drop-down menu. When you do, the column names and corresponding rows of data will display on the right.

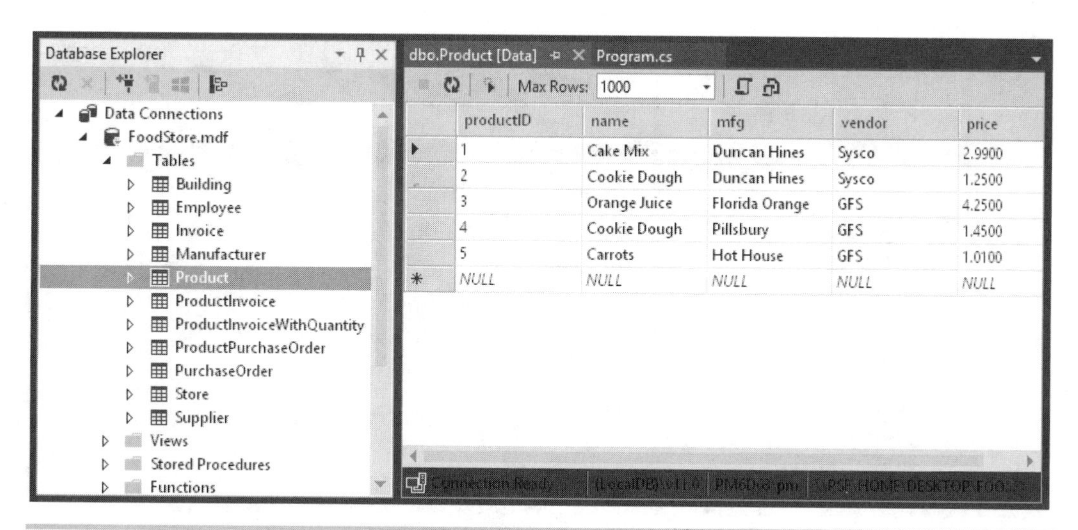

Figure 13-8 Examining database objects and content

Try This 13-1 Examining Table Data

This exercise ensures that you can connect to a database and view data. To practice, try these steps:

1. Complete either Example 13-1 if you are a database beginner or Example 13-2 if you are a database expert.
2. Complete Example 13-3 to explore the *FoodStore* database with the Server Explorer/Database Explorer.
3. Browse the data for the *Employee* table.

Examining Database Column Detail

If you wish to examine details about each column in the data table, right-click the column name in the Server Explorer/Database Explorer and choose Properties. The Properties window that appears displays information such as the column name, data type, size, and other items that might be of interest to an experienced database developer (refer to Figure 13-9).

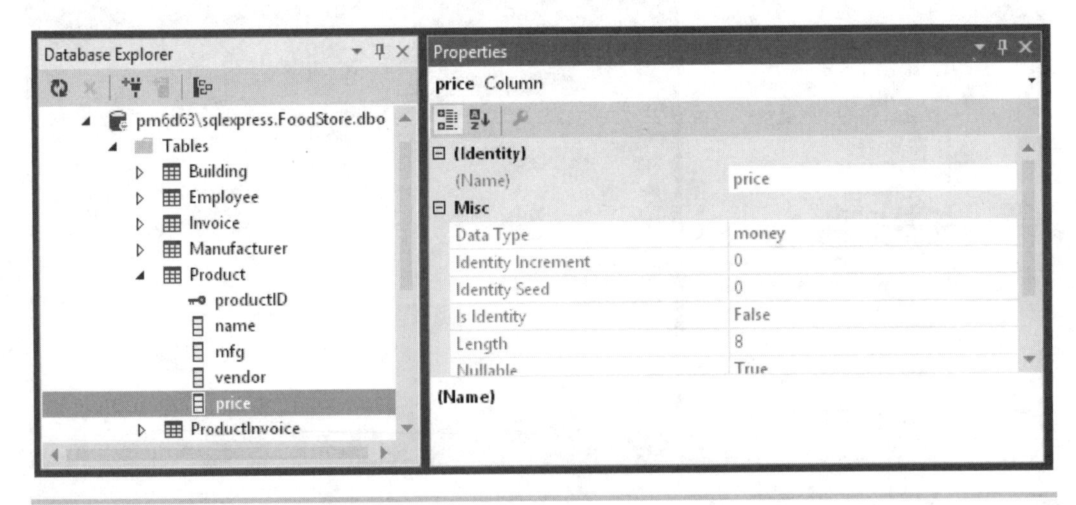

Figure 13-9 Examining data table column properties

NOTE

The data types reported by the Server Explorer/Database Explorer are data types that are provided by the database. These types may differ from existing C# types. For example, the Microsoft SQL Server varchar(*n*) type defines a string with a length of *n*. The varchar type is automatically mapped to a C# string type by Visual Studio when you are working with it in code.

Try This 13-2 Examining Database Column Detail

This exercise gives you a bit more practice using the Server Explorer/Database Explorer. This time, try using it to inspect the structure of the *Employee* table instead of the data. Open the *Employee* table with Server Explorer/Database Explorer and ensure that you can determine the data types of each column within the table.

Chapter 13 Self Test

The following questions are intended to help reinforce your comprehension of the concepts covered in this chapter. The answers can be found in the accompanying online Appendix B, "Answers to the Self Tests."

1. Using the Server Explorer/Database Explorer, list the data content that is stored in the *Supplier* table of the *FoodStore* database.
2. List the database properties of each column of the *Supplier* table that are presented in the Server Explorer/Database Explorer.

Chapter 14

The Entity Framework

Key Skills & Concepts

- The Entity Data Model
- Querying Database Objects with the Entity Data Model
- Updating the Entity Data Model
- LINQ to Entities Introduction

The Microsoft Entity Framework (EF) is a framework that automatically generates an object-oriented data access layer for your C# code to communicate with your database. Frameworks such as EF are called object-relational mapping frameworks, or ORM frameworks.

The Entity Data Model

At the core of the Entity Framework is the Microsoft ADO.NET Entity Data Model, known as the EDM. The EDM is an object-oriented code representation of your database objects. A wizard exists in Visual Studio to automate the process of adding an EDM to your code project. It is possible to add multiple Entity Data Models to your project when connections to more than one database are required. Throughout this book though, you will only need to add one EDM per project.

Adding an Entity Data Model to Your Code Project

The Entity Data Model is automatically created in your C# project if you specify that you want to include it. Once it is generated, the EDM contains classes that are mapped to the selected data objects in your database. This section describes how to add an Entity Data Model to your code project.

Example 14-1 Adding an ADO.NET Entity Data Model to Your Project

To begin, create a new console application. Next, in the Solution Explorer, right-click the project node and choose Add | New Item. In the Add New Item dialog, shown in Figure 14-1, expand the Visual C# Items folder, select Data, and then select ADO.NET Entity Data Model. Change the name of the *.edmx model, if desired, and click Add to launch the Entity Data Model wizard.

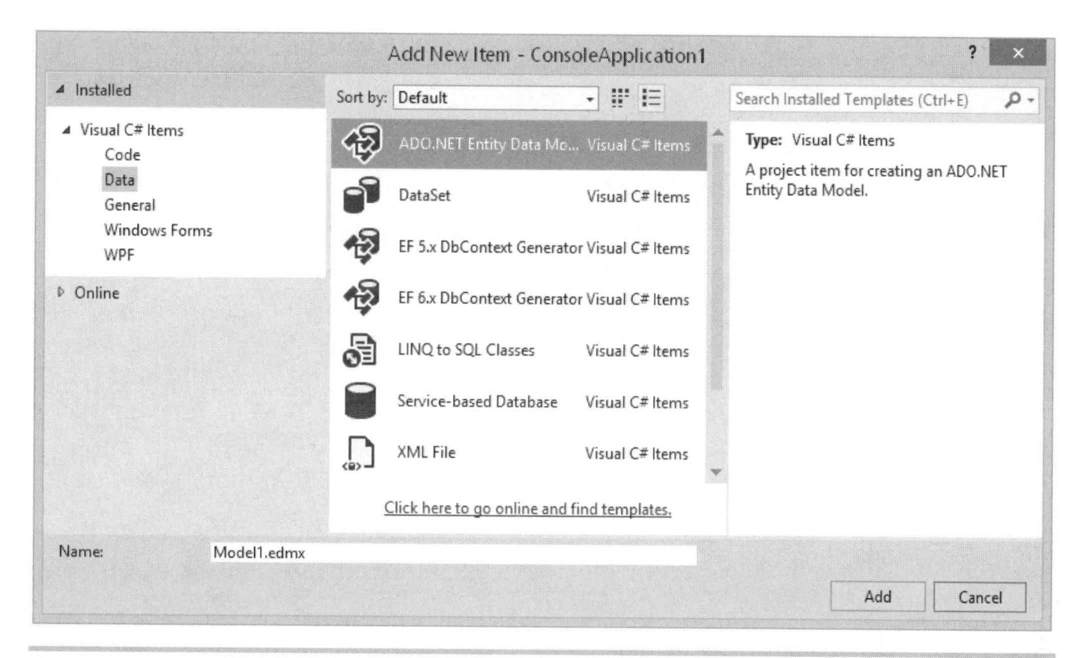

Figure 14-1 Adding an ADO.NET Entity Data Model to the project

In the Choose Model Contents screen that appears first in the wizard, select EF Designer From Database and click Next. Then, to build the database connection string, click the New Connection button. Provide all required information in the Connection Properties dialog, as displayed in Figure 14-2, and click Test Connection to ensure that your inputs are correct. In Chapter 13, Example 13-1 provides a detailed description of how to complete this dialog for database beginners, and Example 13-2 provides a detailed description of how to complete this dialog if you have the *FoodStore* database hosted in Microsoft SQL Server. Either example is suitable.

After you click OK to accept your database connection properties, the Choose Your Data Connection screen reappears, but this time it shows the newly generated connection string. Ensure that Save Entity Connection Settings In App.Config is checked so that your Entity Data Model can reference the database connection there (see Figure 14-3).

Click the Next button once you are ready to use this new connection. The Choose Your Database Objects And Settings screen appears (see Figure 14-4). This screen allows you to select the tables, views, and stored procedures that you want to have referenced in your EDM. For this example, select all tables and stored procedures.

CAUTION

When adding a table to the Entity Data Model, it will not appear in the conceptual view unless it has a primary key, which is a unique identifier for each row of a table.

Connection Properties

Enter information to connect to the selected data source or click "Change" to choose a different data source and/or provider.

Data source:

Microsoft SQL Server Database File (SqlClient) | Change...

Database file name (new or existing):

C:\FoodStore.mdf | Browse...

Log on to the server

Use Windows Authentication

Use SQL Server Authentication

User name:

Password:

Save my password

Advanced...

Test Connection | OK | Cancel

Figure 14-2 Connection Properties dialog

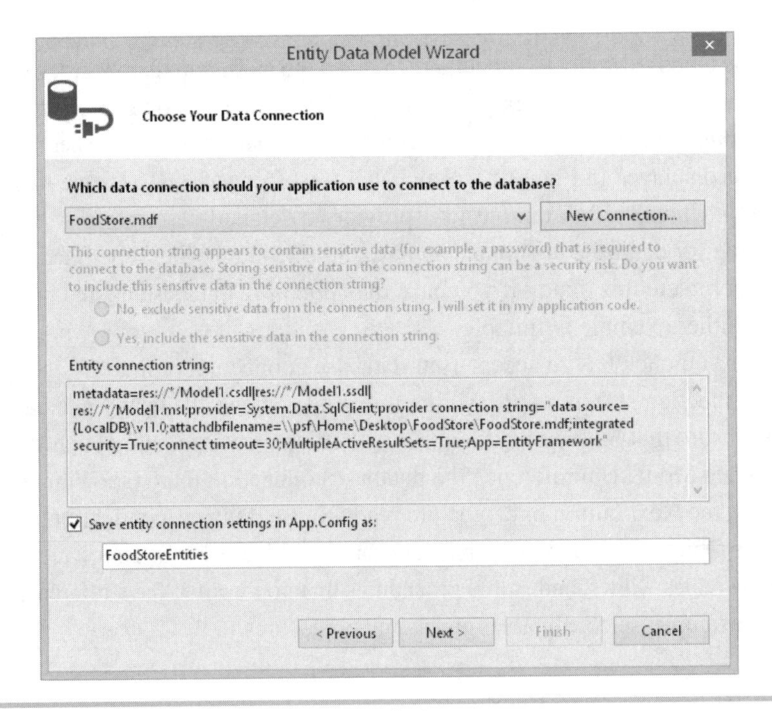

Figure 14-3 Choose Your Data Connection dialog

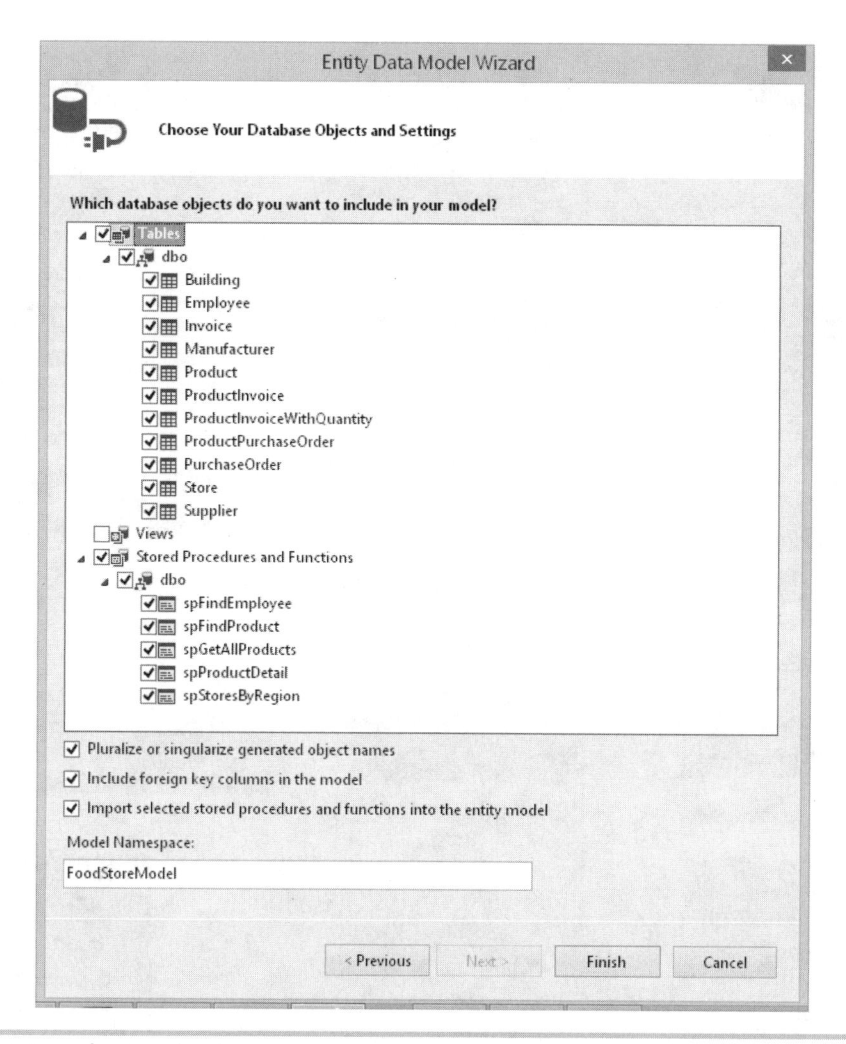

Figure 14-4 Selecting database objects

By default, the Pluralize Or Singularize Generated Object Names check box is selected. For this example, keep it checked, since pluralizing is the more common alternative when naming EDM objects. Then, click Finish to generate the .NET classes for your data model.

Once the wizard finishes building classes for your .NET data model, a conceptual view of your data model will appear in your code project, like the one shown in Figure 14-5.

In addition to having a conceptual view, when the Entity Data Model is generated, you will see the EDM referenced in your project. Figure 14-6 shows the Model1.edmx reference from the Solution Explorer. Expanding the *.edmx node exposes the C# files that contain the code that represents the database objects.

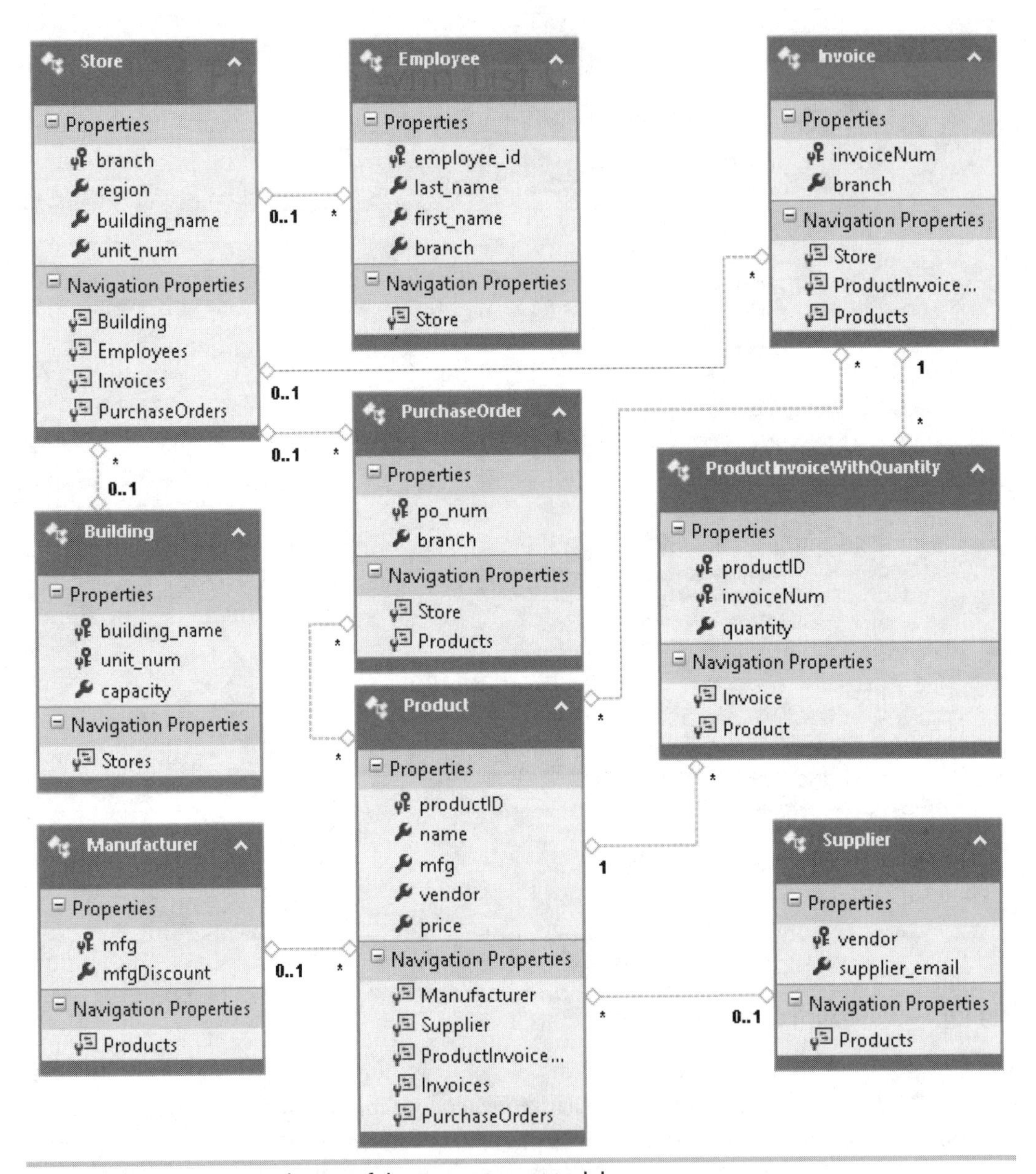

Figure 14-5 Conceptual view of the Entity Data Model

Once you add an EDM to your project, if you are using the database file, the .mdf file will also appear in the Solution Explorer as listed in Figure 14-6. If you are using the database file to save changes while adding, updating, or deleting data, you will have to set the Copy To Output Directory property of the FoodStore.mdf file to "Copy if newer". Otherwise, changes to the data will be overwritten in the original database file when the application runs again.

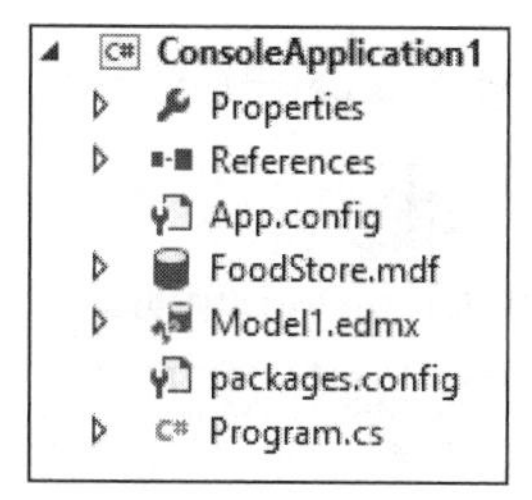

Figure 14-6 Entity Data Model project reference

You can find the Copy To Output Directory setting in the drop-down menu that appears when right-clicking the .mdf file in the Solution Explorer (refer to Figure 14-7).

CAUTION

When the Copy To Output Directory property is set to "Copy if newer", this effectively creates a copy of the latest version of the database file. The database file copy is created inside the Debug\bin folder of your project when the application runs. The same database file that is created in the Debug\bin folder is used as the data source every time the application runs until the database file that is referenced in the Solution Explorer is replaced. As a result, when you set up the Server Explorer/Database Explorer tool to view changes to your data, you will have to reference the database file that is referenced inside your Debug\bin folder.

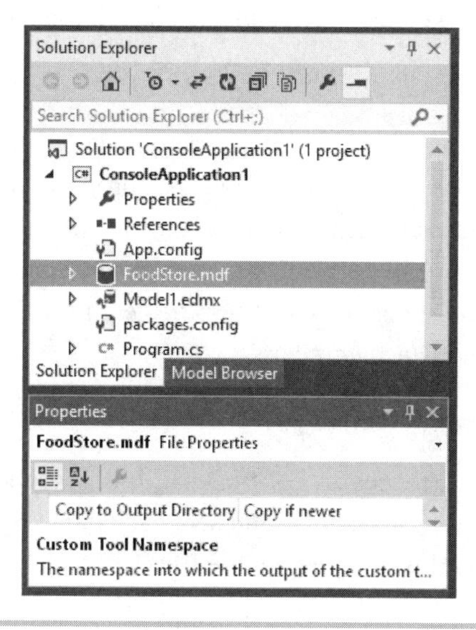

Figure 14-7 Copy To Output Directory setting

Querying Database Objects with the Entity Data Model

When adding an Entity Data Model to your project, several classes are generated to support database management from your code project.

DbContext

Every Entity Data Model provides a *DbContext* class, also known as a database context, to reference the database. A *DbContext* instance manages execution of commands against the database with the EDM. The default name assigned to the *DbContext* class instance is the database name followed by the word *Entities*. For example, when creating an Entity Data Model for a database named *FoodStore,* the ADO.NET Entity Framework automatically generates a *FoodStoreEntities* class to reference the database:

```
FoodStoreEntities context = new FoodStoreEntities();
```

Entities

Entities are classes that are generated when the EDM is created and represent the database tables. A database table is a structure that stores rows of data in a predefined set of columns. The properties of the entity class represent columns of the associated table. The entity name and properties that are generated correspond to the table name and column names in the database. Each row of the table can be referenced with an object of the corresponding entity class.

DbSet

DbSet is a generic class that manages create, read, update, and delete operations for entity collections. The *DbSet* class is only accessible as a property through an instance of the *DbContext* class. *DbSet* is available through the *System.Data.Entity* namespace. By default, the EDM pluralizes the name of each entity reference when creating the associated *DbSet* name. For example, an EDM that includes a *Product* entity will also define a *DbSet* property named *Products* inside the *DbContext* class:

```
var products = context.Products;
```

When your project references an Entity Data Model for the *FoodStore* database, you effectively have a series of classes that represent each database table, view, and stored procedure that is generated when creating the EDM.

Querying Entities

Now that we have covered some of the main structures and code components of the Entity Data Model, we can observe how they work together to simplify basic database queries.

Example 14-2 Querying an Entity

Try testing your EDM by selecting data from all rows from the *Product* table through the Entity Framework. To build this project, start with the solution for Example 14-1. Then replace all code inside the *Main()* method of Program.cs with the following code. This code first defines a *DbContext* object that references the *FoodStore* database. A product list is then implicitly defined with the *var* keyword. The compiler knows to create a list of products because the variable is assigned the *Products DbSet* that is retrieved with the *DbContext* object. The properties associated with each *Product* entity object take the names and types from the columns of the *Product* table. These properties were actually set up for the *Product* entity when the EDM was generated. When the data is needed, the Entity Framework generates SQL and sends it to the database to get the data. This code effectively retrieves all rows from the *Product* table and returns it to the application, which then displays the data.

```
using System;
using System.Collections.Generic;
using System.Linq;

namespace ConsoleApplication1 {
    class Program {
        static void Main() {
            // Declare the DbContext.
            FoodStoreEntities    context = new FoodStoreEntities();

            // Get all Product objects in the DbSet named Products.
            var products = context.Products;

            // Display details for each Product object in Products DbSet.
            foreach (Product productObject in products) {
                Console.Write(productObject.productID.ToString() + ": ");
                Console.Write(productObject.name    + " - ");
                Console.Write(productObject.vendor + " - ");
                decimal price    = (decimal)productObject.price;
                string priceStr = price.ToString("C");
                Console.WriteLine(priceStr);
            }
            Console.ReadLine();
        }
    }
}
```

When you run the code, the output displays attribute values for all objects within the *Products* list:

```
1: Cake Mix - Sysco - $2.99
2: Cookie Dough - Sysco - $1.25
3: Orange Juice - GFS - $4.25
4: Cookie Dough - GFS - $1.45
5: Carrots - GFS - $1.01
```

As you can see, it is pretty easy to query data with the help of an EDM.

Try This 14-1 Querying Entities with the Entity Data Model

Here is an opportunity to experiment with the Entity Data Model.

1. Starting with the solution for Example 14-2, modify the query so you can retrieve all rows of the *Employee* table.
2. Change the code inside the *foreach* loop to display values for the *employee_id*, *last_name*, and *first_name* properties.
3. Run the project to test your code.
4. Check to ensure the data retrieved by your code is correct. You can do this independently of your code by browsing the *Employee* table with the Server Explorer/ Database Explorer (see Example 13-3 in Chapter 13).

Example 14-3 Querying Stored Procedures with the Entity Data Model

When using the Entity Framework, the steps required to run a stored procedure are similar to those required to query a table. This example shows how to use the Entity Data Model to execute the stored procedure named *spProductDetail* and display results.

NOTE

This discussion of stored procedures has been included for experienced database developers. However, if you are new to database development, you may skip this example since it will not impact your understanding of any other section in the book.

The stored procedure was entered in the *FoodStore* database with this script:

```
CREATE PROCEDURE spProductDetail (@name VARCHAR(25), @vendor
    VARCHAR(25))
    AS SELECT * FROM Product WHERE @name = name
    AND @vendor = vendor;
    GO
```

Next, using the solution for Example 14-1, replace the existing code inside the *Main()* method of the Program.cs file with the following code. You will notice, much like querying an entity, the *DbContext* object is used to reference the stored procedure by name. When you reference the stored procedure, though, you pass in the required parameters at the same time. Accessing properties of the rows returned is just like referencing columns of the result set.

```
// Reference the database.
FoodStoreEntities dbContext = new FoodStoreEntities();

// Execute the stored procedure with two parameter values.
var productDetail = dbContext.spProductDetail("Cookie Dough", "GFS");

// Display data retrieved from the stored procedure.
foreach (var row in productDetail) {
    float price = (float)row.price;
    Console.Write(row.name + " $" + price.ToString("N2") + " ");
    Console.WriteLine(row.vendor);
}
Console.ReadLine();
```

When you run your application, the data retrieved verifies that *spProductDetail* was successfully executed with the parameter values of *Cookie Dough* and *GFS*:

```
Cookie Dough $1.45 GFS
```

Updating the Entity Data Model

When simultaneously developing a database and a C# code project, you will somehow need to update your Entity Data Model in your C# project to reflect the changes. If you add new tables or other data objects to your database without changing the structure of existing database objects, you can update your EDM from the Model Browser. You can do this by right-clicking either the conceptual view or the Model Browser and then choosing Update Model From Database to launch the Update Wizard dialog. The Update Wizard dialog displays any objects that have not been added to the EDM yet. From there, select the new objects you want in your EDM (see Figure 14-8) and then click Finish to add them.

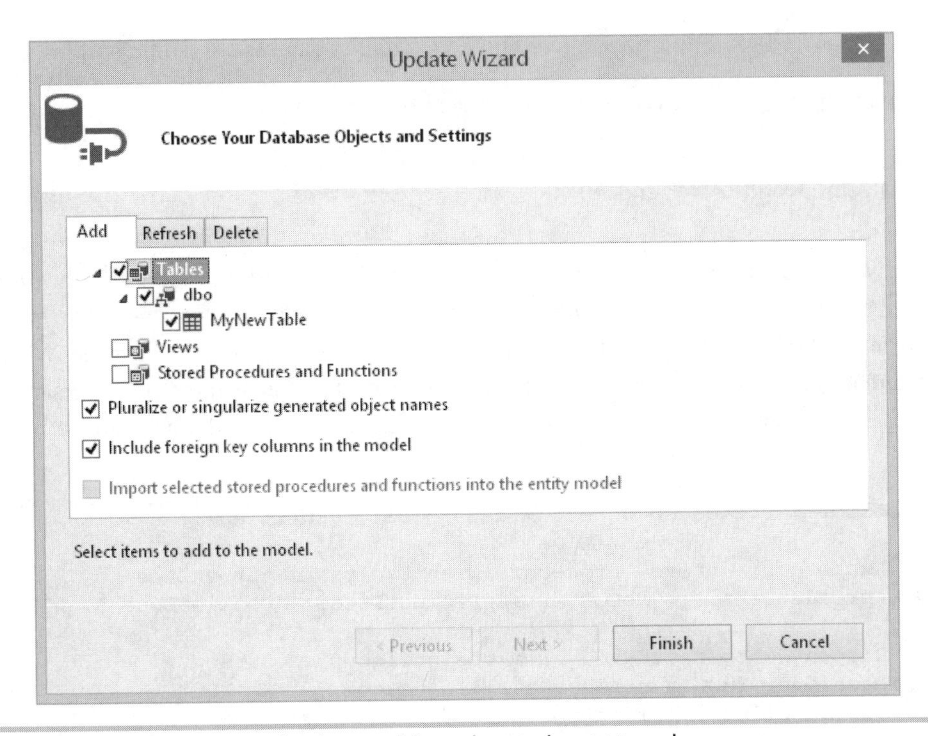

Figure 14-8 Adding a new database table in the Update Wizard

TIP

Changes in database structure where deletions occur or relationships change may not be updated as easily. Because deprecated entity associations or columns might exist in your EDM after a database change, consider deleting the existing EDM and adding a new version of the EDM. To keep things simple, I recommend a complete replacement of the EDM in most cases, as described next.

Replacing the Entity Data Model

If you make significant changes to the entities in your database, one of the easiest ways to update your EDM involves deleting the existing EDM and re-adding it. When replacing an EDM, if you do not properly remove existing connection information from your config file, you could end up with a new database context that has a different name than the original. For example, if the original database context is named *FoodStoreEntities* and it remains referenced in your project, when adding a new EDM, the new database context will be named *FoodStoreEntities1*. In such a case, existing C# code references to *FoodStoreEntities* will then throw errors because the original class no longer exists.

```
  <connectionStrings>
  <add name="FoodStoreEntities" connectionString="..." providerName="System.Data.EntityClient" />
  </connectionStrings>
</configuration>
```

Figure 14-9 Reference to FoodStoreEntities in the App.config file

To avoid having an EDM added that uses a different name than the one currently referenced in your code, take these two steps:

1. Before adding the new EDM, delete the connection string that is defined inside the *connectionStrings* element in the config file for your project.
2. Save the config file.

Figure 14-9 shows a connection string named *FoodStoreEntities* within the *add* element. This *add* element must be removed and the config file must be saved before deleting and re-adding the new EDM to your code project.

LINQ to Entities Introduction

LINQ to Entities allows you to write advanced database queries that execute through the Entity Framework. Language-Integrated Query (LINQ) is a branch of C# for writing commands to add, update, query, and delete objects. You can use LINQ to query collections and lists of almost any type, but it is especially essential for executing database queries when using an Entity Data Model. Two types of LINQ syntax exist:

- Query syntax (refer to Chapter 15)
- Lambda (method-based) syntax (refer to Chapter 16)

When you execute database instructions written with LINQ from your application, the final query is transformed into a command tree. The Entity Framework then transforms the command tree into SQL that is sent to the database server. The interface that you use to define your query determines when the query is executed.

Lazy Loading and Deferred Execution

Queries can be defined such that they do not execute until results are needed in the application. Queries that are defined in such a manner are said to be *lazy loaded*. Lazy loading allows you to build your query incrementally before the command is sent to the database server. Information about each lazy-loaded query is stored in a separate instance of the *ObjectQuery* class. Once you try to access values in the result set later, the first instruction that attempts to access the data will trigger the process that generates and sends SQL to the database server for execution. This delay in sending the database command is called *deferred execution.*

Queries that are defined with the *IEnumerable* interface and the *IQueryable* interface (which inherits from *IEnumerable*) are lazy loaded. The *IEnumerable* interface is from the *System.Collections.Generic* namespace, and the *IQueryable* interface is available from the *System.Linq* namespace. Queries that are defined with an implicit type *var* are using the *IQueryable* interface, so these queries are also lazy loaded. The following three declarations define lazy-loaded collections of *Product* objects. When *var* is used, the implicit type for *results* is a collection of *Product* objects since the compiler knows that a *DbSet<Product>* type is assigned to it:

```
var results = context.Products;
IEnumerable<Product> results = context.Products;
IQueryable<Product>  results = context.Products;
```

The query declared in Example 14-2 is lazy loaded because it is not executed until the data is needed in the *foreach* loop:

```
// Declare the DbContext.
FoodStoreEntities    context = new FoodStoreEntities();

// The query is defined but is not executed yet.
var products = context.Products;

// The data is needed in the loop so SQL is generated and sent to database.
foreach (Product productObject in products) {
}
```

Immediate (Eager) Data Loading

Sometimes you may need to preload extremely large objects to avoid sudden performance hits when data is required. One way to enforce immediate execution of a query is through the *IList* interface. The *IList* interface inherits from the *IEnumerable* interface, so it too is defined in the *System.Collections.Generic* namespace.

Every *DbSet* property in the EDM has a *ToList()* method that returns a strongly typed *List* collection containing all rows of the defining entity. When the *DbContext* instance references the *DbSet* with the *ToList()* extension method, you really are forcing the results into a collection that implements the *IList* interface. The following definitions show explicit and implicit implementations of *IList* with the *Products DbSet*:

```
IList<Product> results = context.Products.ToList(); // Explicit.
List<Product> results  = context.Products.ToList(); // Implicit.
```

Since *IList* and *List* collections are not lazy loaded, these collections are populated with data from the database as soon as the query is initialized. The act of using the *ToList()* method, even with a lazy-loaded query, will immediately trigger data loading since it forces the collection into a *List*:

```
IEnumerable<Product> productList = context.Products.ToList();
```

LINQPad

To physically demonstrate the difference between lazy loading, deferred execution, and immediate loading of data, we will use a great little freeware tool called LINQPad. LINQPad shows how SQL is generated by LINQ to Entities queries. You can download LINQPad free from www.linqpad.net. LINQPad is developed by Joseph Albahari, who has written several C# books, including *C# 5.0 in a Nutshell*, which he co-authored with Ben Albahari. Joseph Albahari's books are more advanced and in depth than is this book. I also recommend his books if you are looking for advanced material. His work and coverage are excellent.

Example 14-4 Using LINQPad to Observe Query Execution

Now that you have LINQPad, you can use it to observe how different types of queries are executed. LINQPad is an excellent tool for demonstrating which queries are lazy loaded and which queries are loaded immediately.

To add a data connection, launch LINQPad and, in the top-left corner, select Add Connection. In the Choose Data Context dialog that appears, select Default (LINQ To SQL) and then click Next. In the LINQPad Connection dialog that launches, select the Attach Database File radio button in the Database area. Then, click the Browse link so you can navigate to the FoodStore.mdf file. Select the *FoodStore* database from the Specify New Or Existing Database drop-down menu. Also, be sure to uncheck the Capitalize Property Names option to allow LINQPad to recognize table attributes with the same letter case as specified in the database. Then, click OK to finalize the addition of your data connection. Figure 14-10 shows the connection options needed.

After you click OK to accept the connection settings, you will be returned to the main LINQPad window. Select C# Program from the Language drop-down menu. Then, choose the *FoodStore* database from the Connection drop-down menu to establish your database reference. Now, you can write C# code to run queries against your database.

NOTE

The code you write in LINQPad is identical to the code you write in a regular C# application except the database context is not required.

After you have written your code, to run your query (see Figure 14-11), click the green execute button or press F5 when in LINQPad.

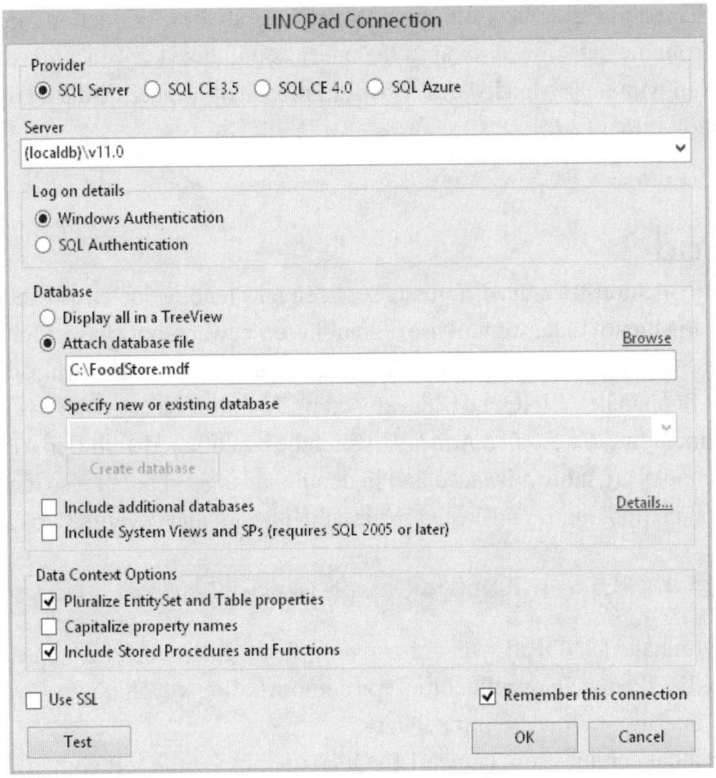

Figure 14-10 Creating a data connection in LINQPad

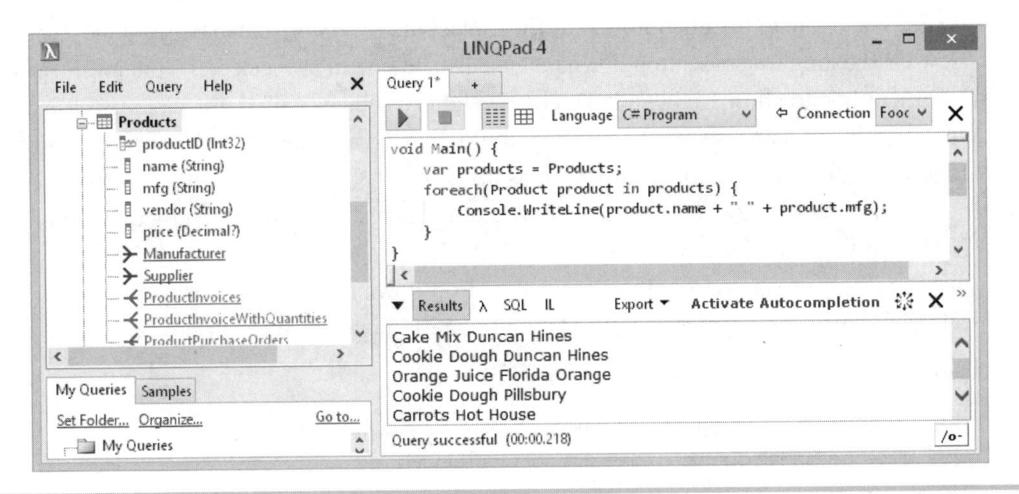

Figure 14-11 Creating and running queries in LINQPad

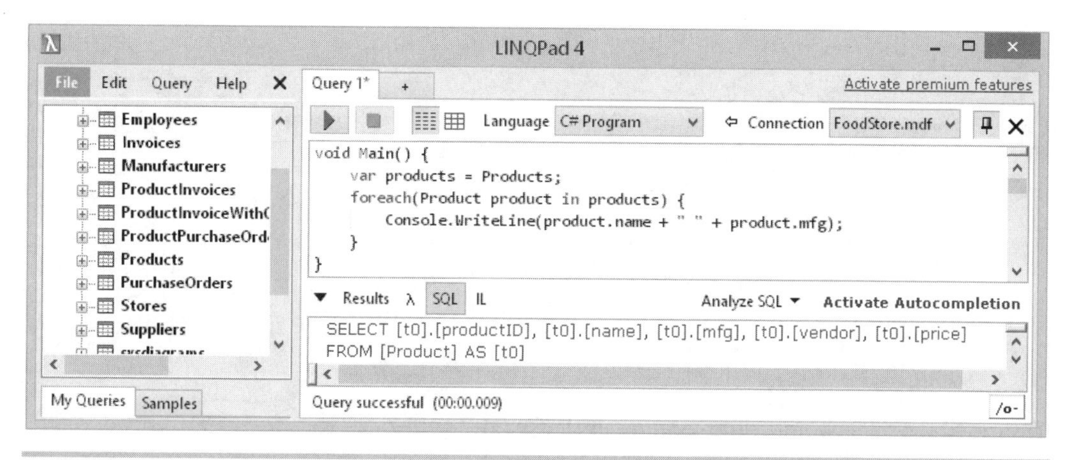

Figure 14-12 Viewing SQL that was executed in the database from LINQPad

You can view the SQL that is generated and sent to the database by clicking SQL in LINQPad, shown in Figure 14-12. When you see the SQL, you know the query was executed.

If you modify the code by removing the *foreach* loop and execute the query again, you will notice that no data is displayed. Also, no SQL is present after these changes (see Figure 14-13). The reason is that the implicit *var* type uses the *IQueryable* interface, which creates the query but does not run it until the data is required.

Things change when you reference the *ToList()* method to the *Products DbSet*. As shown in Figure 14-14, the data is immediately loaded, as indicated by the SQL that is generated. The *ToList()* method is basically forcing the query to use the *IList* interface, which triggers the generation of SQL that is sent to the database for execution.

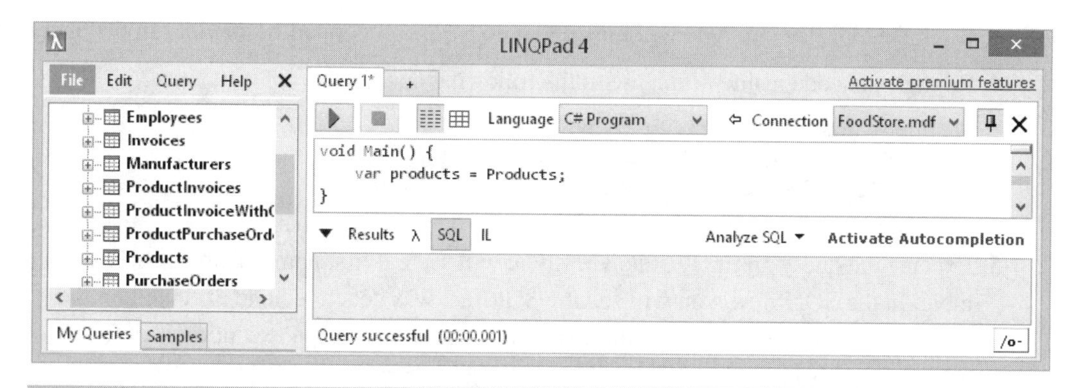

Figure 14-13 Observing lazy-loaded queries in LINQPad

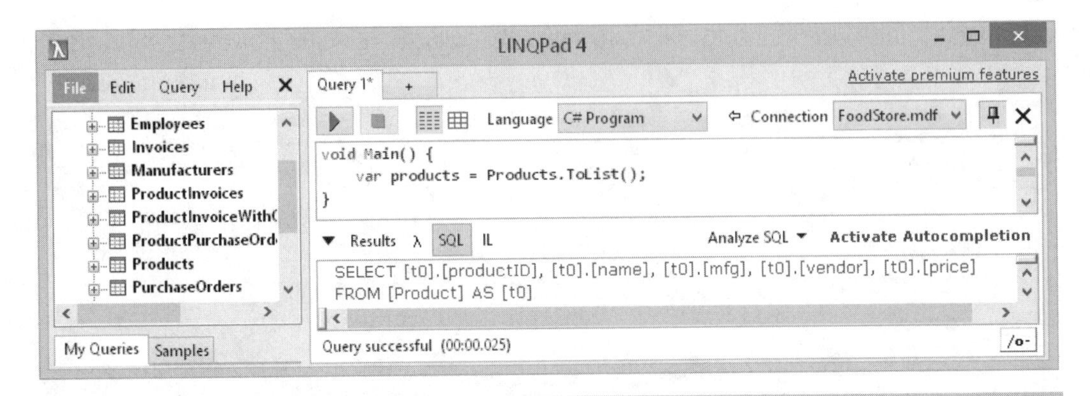

Figure 14-14 Immediate data loading in LINQPad

Try This 14-2 Observing Query Differences with LINQPad

Here is a chance for you to use LINQPad to see how different interfaces determine how and when database queries are run through the Entity Framework.

1. Set up LINQPad with a connection to the *FoodStore* database and choose C# Program in the Language drop-down menu.
2. Enter the following code inside *Main()*:

```
IEnumerable<Employee> employees = Employees;
```

3. Click the SQL tab, and you will notice that no SQL is generated when you run the query.
4. Replace the code inside *Main()* with the following code:

```
IEnumerable<Employee> employees = Employees;
foreach(Employee employee in employees) {
      Console.WriteLine(employee.first_name);
}
```

5. Execute the query. In the Results view, you will see the first names from the *Employee* table. In the SQL view, you will see the SQL that was generated and executed on the database. Since the query is defined as a lazy-loaded query, the execution is deferred until the data is needed.
6. Replace all code inside the *Main()* method with the following code:

```
List<Employee> employees = Employees.ToList();
```

7. Execute this latest query. Notice in the Results view that no data is shown because there are no instructions to write data to the console. However, in the SQL view, you will notice that SQL was generated and sent to the database. This is because the latest query uses the *IList* interface, which forces immediate loading when used with the Entity Framework.

Chapter 14 Self Test

The following questions are intended to help reinforce your comprehension of the concepts covered in this chapter. The answers can be found in the accompanying online Appendix B, "Answers to the Self Tests."

1. Why is the Entity Framework called an ORM framework?
2. Define the following terms as they relate to the Entity Framework:
   A. DbContext
   B. Entity
   C. DbSet
3. This question is intended only for database experts who plan to connect to their own custom databases. Indicate whether each of the following statements is true or false:
   A. ____ A primary key is not required for the table to appear in the conceptual view.
   B. ____ Bridge tables that do not have unique columns aside from columns of the parent tables will not appear in the conceptual view.
   C. ____ During development, if your associations are not updating properly when updating your Entity Data Model, you can try removing the entire Entity Data Model and adding it again.
   D. ____ Before re-adding your Entity Data Model to an existing project, for best results, delete the existing connection string for it in the config file and save the config file.
4. Write a console application that uses the Entity Framework to query the *Store* table of the *FoodStore* database. Show the data that is stored in the *region* and *branch* columns of each row in this table in your query results. For guidance on how to do this, see Example 14-2.

5. Indicate whether the following query declarations are lazy loaded or immediately loaded. If you use LINQPad to verify your answers, be sure to remove the context reference.

   A. ______________ IQueryable<Store> stores = context.Stores;

   B. ______________ var stores = context.Stores.ToList();

   C. ______________ var stores = context.Stores;

   D. ______________ IEnumerable<Store> stores = context.Stores.ToList();

   E. ______________ IEnumerable<Store> stores = context.Stores;

   F. ______________ IList<Product> results = context.Products.ToList();

   G. ______________ List<Product> results = context.Products.ToList();

6. What is the advantage of lazy loading over immediate data loading?

7. Why would you want to define a query that loads data immediately instead of defining a query that is lazy loaded?

Chapter 15

LINQ to Entities: Query Syntax

Key Skills & Concepts

- Read Queries
- Adding Objects
- Updating Objects
- Deleting Objects

This chapter discusses how to implement query syntax with LINQ to Entities for querying and managing data objects. Specifically, the LINQ commands discussed in this chapter enable you to select, filter, sort, group, summarize, insert, update, and delete data. You can actually use LINQ to read the contents of an array, a *List* collection, or really collections of any type. LINQ to Entities is a variation of LINQ that allows you to query database objects through the Entity Framework. LINQ with the Entity Framework is one of the more common ways to use LINQ, but LINQ is an extremely flexible tool for querying other types of objects. Once you are familiar with LINQ to Entities, you will find that transitioning to other forms of LINQ is easy without the Entity Framework layer. This chapter focuses on query syntax that is one of two main syntax flavors for LINQ. Query syntax looks a lot like a Structured Query Language with commands for manipulating data, but at the same time it is very different from SQL.

To keep this content practical, the material covered here presents a typical range of commands that any data-driven application developer needs. More complex queries that join or combine data from different collections, however, are covered in Chapter 17.

Referencing the FoodStore Database

To build any of the code examples in this chapter, begin with a new console application that has an Entity Data Model that references the *FoodStore* database. Then replace the code inside the *Main()* method with the code that is associated with the current example. For a reference on how to set up your projects, see Chapter 14, "Example 14-1: Adding an ADO.NET Entity Data Model to Your Project." Remember also, if you are using the .mdf database file, changes to the data, including adds, updates, and deletes, will not be saved to the database unless the Copy to Output Directory property of the FoodStore.mdf file is set to "Copy if newer".

As well, to ensure your code is working, it is good practice to inspect the data independently of your code. To do this, refer to Chapter 13, "Example 13-3: Browsing Database Content with Visual Studio." Also remember, if you are using the database file as a data source, create a connection to the database file that is copied by the application to the bin folder to inspect the same data that is used by your project.

LINQ query syntax is completely different from the C# code we've worked with so far. It allows little islands of highly verbose, expressive, natural language expressions in our otherwise fairly terse C# syntax. It can be a little jarring at first to make the shift to query syntax. If you are an experienced SQL developer, you might think query syntax looks a lot like SQL, but this is a mixed blessing because the placement of keywords requires a different sequence than SQL. Be prepared for a slight shift in the way you write C# code.

Read Queries

LINQ allows us to query objects of varying types. The classes and methods that enable these operations belong to the *System.Linq* namespace. For any read query, a *from* keyword starts the query definition and a *select* keyword finishes it. The *in* keyword precedes the collection that contains the data. When using the Entity Framework, you reference the collection with the *DbContext* object. To reference each instance of the collection, query syntax uses an alias, which can be any name. Often, C# developers use the first letter of the collection as an alias. When querying any collection, the alias can reference the properties of the object being queried.

Referencing Properties of an Object

This example defines a query that retrieves all column values from every row of the *Product* table:

```
var query = from p in context.Products
            select p;
```

To cut down on data processing overhead, just select the property values that you need from each object. When implicitly declaring a collection with a *var* definition that has a unique column set, you are really defining an *anonymous type*. In the next example, an alias is used to only select *name* and *vendor* column values from each row of the *Product* table in the database. Notice also that when defining the columns to be retrieved, the *new* keyword and opening curly brace start the series. Column values retrieved are separated with a comma, and the series is terminated with a closing curly brace.

```
var query = from p in context.Products
            select new { p.name, p.vendor };
```

With either of these two previous query definitions, you can iterate through the query results to display the selected column values:

```
foreach (var item in query)
    Console.WriteLine(item.name + " - " + item.vendor);
```

Assigning Custom Property Names

You have the option to declare custom property names for columns when defining your queries. In this case, *ProductName* and *Supplier* properties are declared to represent *name* and *vendor* properties of the *Product* entity class:

```
var query = from p in context.Products
            select new { ProductName = p.name, Supplier = p.vendor };
```

When a query uses custom property names, you can reference them later with the query object:

```
foreach (var item in query)
    Console.WriteLine(item.ProductName + " - " + item.Supplier  );
```

Example 15-1 Selecting Specific Columns of an Object

This example demonstrates query syntax to implement an implicitly typed query to retrieve the *name* and *vendor* column values from the *Product* table. For this case, the alias of "p" is created to represent the *Products DbSet*. The alias also allows us to select the columns of each *Product* object in the collection by name.

As with all examples in this chapter, to build this example, start with a new console application. Next, add an entity data model that references all tables in the *FoodStore* database. Then, replace the code inside the *Main()* method with the following:

```
FoodStoreEntities context = new FoodStoreEntities(); // Reference database.
var query = from p in context.Products
            select new { p.name, p.vendor };         // Select columns.
foreach (var item in query)                          // Show rows.
    Console.WriteLine(item.name + " - " + item.vendor);
Console.ReadLine();
```

The output from running this program shows the values for each *name* and *vendor* column in every row of the *Product* table:

```
Cake Mix - Sysco
Cookie Dough - Sysco
Orange Juice - GFS
Cookie Dough - GFS
Carrots - GFS
```

Example 15-2 Selecting All Columns of an Object

This example generates output that is identical to that of Example 15-1, though in this case, all column values are retrieved for every row in the collection. Some of the column data read is not used, so you could say this version of the query is less efficient than the query in Example 15-1. Unlike Example 15-1 though, the *foreach* loop header here defines a *Product* object to store each row of the query, because the query implicitly defines a selection of *Product* objects.

```
FoodStoreEntities context = new FoodStoreEntities(); // Reference database.
var query = from p in context.Products              // Select all columns.
            select p;
foreach (Product product in query)                  // Show rows.
    Console.WriteLine(product.name + " - " + product.vendor);
Console.ReadLine();
```

Try This 15-1 Reading Data with Query Syntax

Here is an exercise to practice reading data from the database with query syntax.

1. Revise the Example 15-1 solution to only retrieve and display *branch* and *region* column data from the *Store* table. This time though, define your own custom property names called *Branch* and *Region*.
2. To verify that the data retrieved by your C# code is correct, use the Server Explorer/ Database Explorer tool to inspect the data that exists in the *Store* table of the *FoodStore* database (refer to Example 13-3 in Chapter 13) and to discover any additional columns that exist in the table.
3. Adjust your code to retrieve and display data for additional columns of the *Store* table. While adjusting your query, use the alias to discover additional properties of the *Store* entity. You can do this by typing "p." and inspecting the properties that appear in the drop-down menu.

Lazy Loading vs. Immediate Data Loading

As mentioned in Chapter 14, implicitly typed queries are defined with the *var* keyword. For implicit queries, the compiler can infer the collection type. Also recall that these implicit queries use the *IQueryable* interface, which means they are lazy loaded. When a query is lazy loaded, the data is not actually retrieved until it is needed. In other words, the execution is deferred. Usually lazy loading is desirable because it allows you to build a query in incremental steps.

You can force immediate data loading, known as eager loading, by forcing the query into a *List* collection. The following query is immediately loaded as soon as it is declared:

```
List<Product> query = context.Products.ToList();
```

In this next case, immediate loading occurs during the second instruction when the query is forced into a *List* collection:

```
var query = from p in context.Products
            select p;
List<Product> products = query.ToList();
```

Filtering

When retrieving rows of data from large collections, you often will not want all rows. To reduce network traffic between your application and the database server, it is best to eliminate unwanted rows with a filter on your query. A filter is really a conditional statement that evaluates to a true or false result. Only rows that satisfy the filter condition are selected.

Basic Filtering

Query syntax provides a *where* keyword to implement a condition to identify desired rows when selecting objects from a collection. The *where* clause is placed after the *from* clause and before the *select* clause. Compound conditions can exist in the *where* clause with "&&" for AND conditions and "||" for OR conditions.

Example 15-3 Applying a Where Filter

This example shows an implementation of the *where* keyword with LINQ to select only data for *Product* objects with a price greater than 0.99 and less than 2.00:

```
FoodStoreEntities context = new FoodStoreEntities(); // Reference database.
var query = from p in context.Products
```

```
            where p.price > 0.99m && p.price < 2.00m // Apply filter.
            select p;
foreach (var item in query) {                        // Show rows.
    decimal price    = (decimal)item.price;
    string priceStr = price.ToString("C");
    Console.WriteLine(item.name    + " - "+ priceStr);
}
Console.ReadLine();
```

When running this program, the *where* filter ensures that rows are selected only when the price is between 0.99 and 2.00:

```
Cookie Dough - $1.25
Cookie Dough - $1.45
Carrots - $1.01
```

Filtering with a Collection of Values

When filtering data rows of a query with matching values in a collection such as an array or *List,* the collection object provides a *Contains()* method that returns a Boolean result to indicate where properties of the query have a matching value in the designated collection.

Example 15-4 Filtering with a Collection

This example shows how to retrieve *Product* objects where the *name* value is either "Cookie Dough" or "Cake Mix". The values "Cookie Dough" and "Cake Mix" are stored in a string array that uses the *Contains()* method to perform the comparison.

```
FoodStoreEntities context = new FoodStoreEntities(); // Reference database.
string[]      productTypes = { "Cookie Dough", "Cake Mix" };

var query = from    p in context.Products
            where   productTypes.Contains(p.name)     // Find array match.
            select  p;
foreach (Product product in query) {                 // Show rows.
    decimal price    = (decimal)product.price;
    string priceStr = "$" + price.ToString("N2");
    Console.WriteLine(product.name + " - " + priceStr);
}
Console.ReadLine();
```

The rows selected have *name* properties that match values in the array of products:

```
Cake Mix - $2.99
Cookie Dough - $1.25
Cookie Dough - $1.45
```

Retrieving Similar Matches

You may want to write queries that search for items that either start with a set of characters or match a pattern. Query syntax in LINQ can easily be combined with a broad selection of C# methods to parse and compare strings.

Example 15-5 Filtering with String Comparison Methods

This example uses query syntax with LINQ to retrieve details for all products that have names either starting with "Car" or containing the word "Juice". In this example, the string object's *StartsWith()* and *Contains()* methods are used to obtain the desired results.

```
FoodStoreEntities context = new FoodStoreEntities(); // Reference database.
var query = from    p in context.Products            // Filter rows.
            where   p.name.StartsWith("Car") ||p.name.Contains("Juice")
            select  p;
foreach (Product product in query)                   // Show rows.
    Console.WriteLine(product.name + " - " + product.vendor);
Console.ReadLine();
```

When you run this example, all product rows retrieved are for product names that either start with "Car" or contain the word "Juice":

```
Orange Juice - GFS
Carrots - GFS
```

Selecting Distinct Rows

When working with data sets, you likely will encounter duplicate rows of data, which is often not desirable. The *Distinct()* extension method eliminates duplicate rows. Note that the *Distinct()* method is applied to the entire query.

Example 15-6 Selecting Distinct Rows

This example shows how to obtain a listing of unique products with the *Distinct()* extension method:

```
FoodStoreEntities context = new FoodStoreEntities(); // Reference database.
var  query = (from p in context.Products             // Get unique rows.
              select p.name).Distinct();
foreach(string productName in query)                 // Show product names.
    Console.WriteLine(productName);
Console.ReadLine();
```

When you run the program, only one instance of "Cookie Dough" appears because the *Distinct()* extension method eliminated the duplicate item:

```
Cake Mix
Carrots
Cookie Dough
Orange Juice
```

Try running the program without the *Distinct()* extension method and notice that "Cookie Dough" appears twice.

Reading One Object Only

When querying for one object only, you can implement the *FirstOrDefault()* method to restrict the query to the first match found. This method allows you to assign the query result to a single class object. If no match is found, *FirstOrDefault()* assigns a null value to the query.

Example 15-7 Reading One Object Only

The query in this example uses the *FirstOrDefault()* method to retrieve the *Product* object that is uniquely identified with *productID* = 1:

```
FoodStoreEntities context = new FoodStoreEntities(); // Reference database.
Product product = (from   p in context.Products      // Get Product object.
                   where  p.productID == 1
                   select p).FirstOrDefault();
if(product!=null)                                    // Show Product detail.
    Console.WriteLine(product.productID + " - " + product.name);
Console.ReadLine();
```

The output displays details for the *Product* object that is selected (unless the object is not null):

```
1 - Cake Mix
```

Sorting

Sorting is performed using LINQ to Entities query syntax with an *orderby* keyword. By default, the sort direction is ascending. You can, however, reverse the sort direction with the *descending* keyword after the column that is specified in the *orderby* clause. The *orderby* clause fits between the *where* and *select* keywords.

Example 15-8 Sorting

This example shows how to implement a descending sort of products by *price*:

```
FoodStoreEntities context = new FoodStoreEntities(); // Reference database.
var query = from p in context.Products
            where p.price > 0.99m && p.price < 2.00m
            orderby p.price descending              // Set order.
            select p;
foreach (Product product in query) {                // Show results.
    decimal price = (decimal)product.price;
    Console.WriteLine(product.name    + " - " + price.ToString("C"));
}
Console.ReadLine();
```

The sorted output from this example shows rows by *price* in descending order:

```
Cookie Dough - $1.45
Cookie Dough - $1.25
Carrots - $1.01
```

Sorting on Multiple Columns

This section explains how to define sort criteria with the *orderby* keyword with two or more columns. The primary sort is on the first column. Additional sort criteria in descending priority are specified with comma-separated column values.

Example 15-9 Sorting on Multiple Columns

This example implements an *orderby* clause to sort *Product* items by vendor and then by *price* in ascending order:

```
FoodStoreEntities context = new FoodStoreEntities(); // Reference database.
var query = from p in context.Products
            orderby p.vendor, p.price               // Set order.
            select p;
foreach (Product product in query) {                // Show rows.
    decimal price    = (decimal)product.price;
    string  priceStr = price.ToString("C");
    Console.WriteLine(product.name + " - " + product.vendor
                    + " - " + priceStr);
}
Console.ReadLine();
```

When running this example, the rows are sorted by *vendor* and then *price*:

```
Carrots - GFS - $1.01
Cookie Dough - GFS - $1.45
Orange Juice - GFS - $4.25
Cookie Dough - Sysco - $1.25
Cake Mix - Sysco - $2.99
```

Subselection

LINQ to Entities queries really shine when you need to perform a subselection from an existing query. Since queries defined with the *IQueryable* interface are lazy loaded, separate queries implementing this interface can be combined to create one complex query before the query is sent to the database. Since only one call is made to the database with the most streamlined query, this process effectively minimizes the data traffic between your application and the database.

Example 15-10 Subselection

This example shows a simplified view of how to combine one *ObjectQuery* instance with another. The first query selects *Product* objects that have the *vendor* name of "GFS". The second query finds all *Product* objects in the first query that have names that start with "C".

```
FoodStoreEntities context = new FoodStoreEntities();  // Reference database.
var gfsProducts = from p in context.Products          // First query.
                  where p.vendor == "GFS"
                  select p;
var query = from p in gfsProducts                     // Combine query.
            where p.name.StartsWith("C")
            select p;
foreach (Product product in query)                    // Show rows.
    Console.WriteLine(product.name + " - "  + product.vendor);
Console.ReadLine();
```

The final output shows the result of the combined query:

```
Cookie Dough - GFS
Carrots - GFS
```

TIP

If you are ever struggling to figure out the logic for writing a complex query, break the query into simple steps with separate queries. Then you can combine the queries as shown previously. When defining each subquery, if you use the *IQueryable* interface, which is implied when you include the *var* keyword, the query will be lazy loaded. The lazy-loaded queries will not execute on the server when they are defined. However, once you make a request to use the data from the combined query, one request will be sent to the database. In the end, you have logic that is separated into simple steps and your application makes only one efficient trip to the database to get the data.

Try This 15-2 Inspecting Combined Queries

We have discussed how to combine lazy-loaded queries into one query. Let's examine how this can be done so that only one trip is made to the database when data is needed by the final query.

1. Open LINQPad and create a connection to the *FoodStore* database (refer to Chapter 14, "Example 14-4: Using LINQPad to Observe Query Execution").
2. Inside the *Main()* method of LINQPad, add the code shown in Figure 15-1.

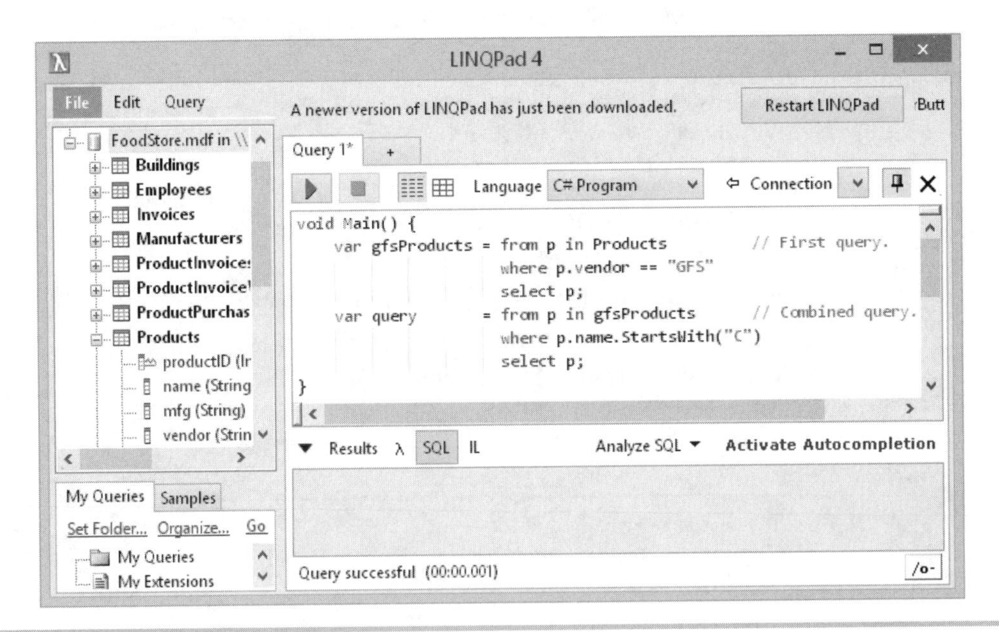

Figure 15-1 Observing a combined query in LINQPad

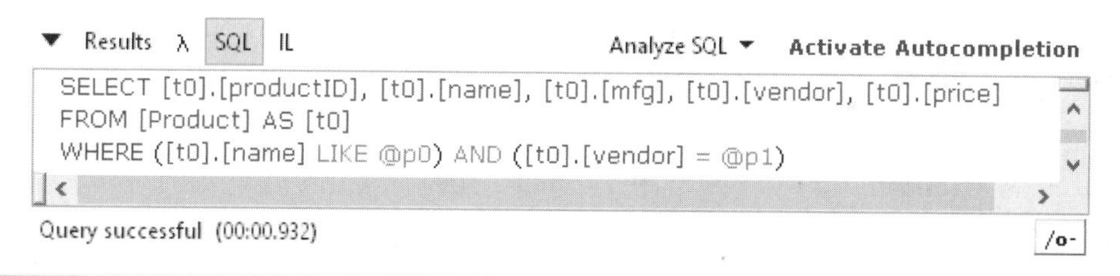

Figure 15-2 Examining the SQL

3. Execute the code in LINQPad by pressing F5.
4. Click the SQL tab in LINQPad and notice in the Results pane that no SQL has been generated (see Figure 15-1). The absence of SQL means both queries did not execute.
5. Add the following lines of code after your existing code inside the *Main()* method within LINQPad:

```
foreach (Product product in query)
    Console.WriteLine(product.name + " - "  + product.vendor);
```

6. Execute the updated version of your code in LINQPad by pressing F5.
7. When executing the code after the code update, notice that SQL is generated because the application needs data from the final query (see Figure 15-2).

Merging Similar Queries with a Union

LINQ provides a *Union()* extension method to merge the results of two queries where the property names, type, and sequence of each query are the same.

Example 15-11 Combining Similar Queries with a Union

This example shows how to merge the results of two separate queries on the *Supplier* and *Manufacturer* entities to generate a listing of affiliates:

```
FoodStoreEntities context = new FoodStoreEntities(); // Reference database.
var suppliers     = from s in context.Suppliers      // Get suppliers.
                    select new { Affiliate = s.vendor };
var manufacturers = from m in context.Manufacturers  // Get manufacturers.
                    select new { Affiliate = m.mfg };
var affiliates    = manufacturers.Union(suppliers);  // Union queries.
foreach (var row in affiliates)                      // Show results.
    Console.WriteLine(row.Affiliate);
Console.ReadLine();
```

The output from this union of manufacturers and suppliers is a combined listing of company names:

```
Duncan Hines
Florida Orange
GFS
Hot House
McCain
Pillsbury
Sysco
```

Aggregate Summary Queries

ObjectQuery instances offer aggregate extension methods to calculate summary information for your queries. Common aggregate methods include *Count(), Sum(), Max(), Min(),* and *Average()*.

Example 15-12 Simple Summaries

This example shows a very simplified view of how aggregate extension methods can provide summary data for a query:

```
FoodStoreEntities context = new FoodStoreEntities();    // Reference database.
var               prices = from p in context.Products // Get prices.
                           select p.price;
Console.WriteLine("Count:   " + prices.Count());       // Show count.
Console.WriteLine("Sum:     " + prices.Sum());         // Show sum.
Console.WriteLine("Max:     " + prices.Max());         // Show max.
Console.WriteLine("Min:     " + prices.Min());         // Show min.
Console.WriteLine("Average: " + prices.Average());     // Show average.
Console.ReadLine();
```

As expected, summary details about all *Product* prices are displayed when running the code:

```
Count:   5
Sum:     10.9500
Max:     4.2500
Min:     1.0100
Average: 2.1900
```

NOTE

Since summary information is generated when performing aggregation, aggregation queries can only retrieve summary columns and designated grouping columns.

Summaries with Grouping

Often, you will want to perform summaries with grouped data. For example, you might want to show the count of items sold per vendor, or show the total stores in each region. When performing aggregation with LINQ, the column that uniquely identifies each group row is called a key. To enable grouping, column values retrieved are stored inside a temporary aggregate table. Summaries can then be performed on each row of the associated table.

When grouping, most aggregate extension methods use a lambda statement as a parameter to identify the column it summarizes. These aggregate methods will be explained in further detail in Chapter 16.

Example 15-13 Summaries with Grouping

This example shows how to generate a query that retrieves all manufacturers that have more than one item listed in the *Product* table. To see how this is arranged, you will notice in this example that the grouping column is designated with a *group* keyword before the alias and a *by* keyword before the actual column reference. Also in this same clause, an *into* keyword designates an object to store the summary query. The *group-by-into* clause fits between the *where* and *from* clauses. Also notice in the *select* clause, the *group* column is selected through a reference to the *Key* property of the *summary* object. Group summaries are also assigned from the aggregate object in the *select* clause.

```
FoodStoreEntities context = new FoodStoreEntities(); // Reference database.
var vendorCounts = from p in context.Products
                   group p by p.mfg into summary
                   where summary.Count() > 1          // Filter the groups.
                   select new {                       // Define columns.
                   Manufacturer = summary.Key,        // Set Key to group.
                   ProductCount = summary.Count() }; // Get count per group.
foreach (var item in vendorCounts)                    // Show count per group.
    Console.WriteLine(item.Manufacturer + ": " + item.ProductCount);
Console.ReadLine();
```

For our example, it turns out only one manufacturer, Duncan Hines, has more than one item listed in the *Product* table:

```
Duncan Hines: 2
```

Adding Objects

When working with the Entity Data Model, if you insert a row of data into a database table, you are really adding an object to a collection. Each entity's *DbSet* set provides an *Add()* method to insert an object into the table. After inserting data into a table using LINQ to Entities, you must call the *SaveChanges()* method of the *DbContext* class to commit the data to the database.

Example 15-14 Inserting Objects

The code in this example declares and initializes a *Product* object to store information about french fries. After initializing the *Product* object, the *Add()* method of the *Products DbSet* inserts the data into the database. Then, the *SaveChanges()* method commits the data to the database. The database only allows *Product* objects with unique *productID* values, so a try-catch block prevents a crash whenever insertion of an object with a duplicate *productID* is attempted.

```
FoodStoreEntities context = new FoodStoreEntities(); // Reference database.
try {
    Product product   = new Product();                // Create Product.
    product.productID = 6;                            // Initialize Product.
    product.price     = 3.33m;
    product.name      = "French Fries";
    product.mfg       = "McCain";
    product.vendor    = "GFS";
    context.Products.Add(product);                    // Add Product.
    context.SaveChanges();                            // Commit changes.
}
catch (Exception e) {
    Console.WriteLine(e.Message  // Inform user if data is not added.
  + " Product objects with duplicate productID values are not permitted.");
}
var productList = context.Products.ToList();          // Show Products.
foreach (Product item in productList)
    Console.WriteLine("ID: " + item.productID + " - " + item.name);
Console.ReadLine();
```

When you run the program, the new *Product* object is inserted in the database table. When querying the database, "French Fries" now appears in the list:

```
ID: 1 - Cake Mix
ID: 2 - Cookie Dough
ID: 3 - Orange Juice
ID: 4 - Cookie Dough
ID: 5 - Carrots
ID: 6 - French Fries
```

Updating Objects

When you update a value within a row of data using the Entity Framework, you are really updating a property of an object since each row of an entity is an object of the entity. After you modify the property of an entity instance, you can make a call to *SaveChanges()* to commit the changes to the database.

Example 15-15 Updating Objects

The following code shows how to update the price of french fries. First, the object is obtained, the *price* property is adjusted if the object is found, and changes are saved with the call to *SaveChanges()*. Before running the program, if you browse the data with the Server Explorer/Database Explorer, you will notice that the price before the update is $3.33.

```
FoodStoreEntities context = new FoodStoreEntities(); // Reference database.
Product product = ( from   p in context.Products     // Get fries object.
                    where  p.name == "French Fries"
                    select p).FirstOrDefault();
if (product != null) {
    product.price = 4.88m;                            // Update price.
    context.SaveChanges();                            // Save to database.
}
foreach (Product row in context.Products) {           // Show results.
    decimal price = (decimal)row.price;
    Console.WriteLine(row.name + " " + price.ToString("C"));
}
Console.ReadLine();
```

After the update, the price becomes $4.88:

```
Cake Mix $2.99
Cookie Dough $1.25
Orange Juice $4.25
Cookie Dough $1.45
Carrots $1.01
French Fries $4.88
```

Deleting Objects

When you delete a row of data with LINQ to Entities, you are really deleting an object from an entity. Each *DbSet* has a *Remove()* method that deletes an object from its collection. To commit the deletion to the database, you must use the *DbContext* object to call *SaveChanges()*.

Example 15-16 Deleting Objects

This example shows the query syntax needed to delete the french fries item that was created earlier. To build this example, create an application that references all tables in the *FoodStore* database. Then, add this code to the *Main()* method:

```
FoodStoreEntities context = new FoodStoreEntities(); // Reference database.
Product fries    = ( from   p in context.Products     // Get Product object.
                     where  p.name == "French Fries"
                     select p).FirstOrDefault();
if (fries != null)                                    // Delete object.
    context.Products.Remove(fries);
context.SaveChanges();                                // Commit changes.
foreach (var product in context.Products)             // Show Products.
    Console.WriteLine(product.productID + " " + product.name);
Console.ReadLine();
```

When you run this program, you will notice the products listed no longer include "French Fries":

```
1 Cake Mix
2 Cookie Dough
3 Orange Juice
4 Cookie Dough
5 Carrots
```

Chapter 15 Self Test

The following questions are intended to help reinforce your comprehension of the concepts covered in this chapter. The answers can be found in the accompanying online Appendix B, "Answers to the Self Tests."

1. Write a program that uses LINQ to select and display only the *invoiceNum* and *branch* columns from the *Invoice* table of the *FoodStore* database.
2. Using query syntax with LINQ, select and display all rows and columns of the *Invoice* table in the *FoodStore* database, but do not specify any columns in your query.
3. If you replace the *foreach* header in Example 15-1 with

   ```
   foreach(Product item in query)
   ```

   why is it not possible to run the project?

4. In Example 15-2, if you replaced the instruction

```
var query = from p in context.Products
            select p;
```

with

```
IQueryable<Product> query = from p in context.Products select p;
```

is the query that is defined with the *IQueryable* interface lazy loaded?

5. Write a program that has a query that only selects *productID, name, mfg, vendor,* and *price* columns from the *Product* table when the *mfg* property is "Duncan Hines".

6. Using the *FirstOrDefault()* method, query the *Employee* table to show the *last_name* and *first_name* values for a person who is uniquely identified with *employee_id* = 9001.

7. Using the *FoodStore* database, write a query to display all *branch* and *region* column values from the *Store* table for stores located in the "BC" region.

8. Using query syntax with the *Contains()* method, write a query to select and display *building_name, branch,* and *region* detail from the *Store* table for stores that are located in "Mission", "Vancouver", or "Seattle".

9. In a new application, use query syntax to select and display all *branch* and *region* column values from the *Store* table. Sort the rows by *branch* in descending order.

10. Using the *FoodStore* database, write a program that uses LINQ with query syntax to select all *region* and *branch* column values from the *Store* table and sort them by *region* and then by *branch.*

11. Using the following code:

```
string[] manufacturers = new string[]
{ "Florida Orange", "California Orange", "California Gold" };

var mfgQuery = from m in manufacturers
               where m.Contains("Orange") select m;
```

write a query that selects *mfg* and *mfgDiscount* values from the *Manufacturer* table where *mfg* names exist in the *mfgQuery* results.

12. Write a program that uses the *Count()* method to obtain and show the count of all manufacturers in the *Manufacturer* table.

13. With query syntax, use a *group-by-into* clause and the *Count()* method to show the total number of stores in each region.

14. Write a program to add a new manufacturer to the *Manufacturer* entity. When doing so, assign "Ichiban" as the *mfg* value and assign 10 as Ichiban's *mfgDiscount* value. Once the new manufacturer object is inserted into the database, display all manufacturers in the database.
15. Using the Server Explorer/Database Explorer, browse the *Manufacturer* table to ensure an entry exists for "Ichiban". Then, write a small program to delete the entry for the *Manufacturer* where *mfg* is "Ichiban". Using a *foreach* loop, iterate through all remaining *Manufacturer* objects in the collection and print their *mfg* values to the console window.

Chapter 16

LINQ to Entities: Method-Based Syntax

Key Skills & Concepts

- Lambda Syntax
- Read Queries
- Inserting, Updating, and Deleting Objects

This chapter covers how to use method-based syntax for performing LINQ commands for database management through the Entity Framework. This syntax is enabled by extension methods. The extension method approach offers an alternative for writing LINQ commands instead of using query syntax, which was covered in Chapter 15.

Referencing the FoodStore Database

As in Chapter 15, to build any of the code examples in this chapter, begin with a new console application that has an Entity Data Model that references the *FoodStore* database. Then replace the code inside the *Main()* method with the code that is associated with the current example. For a reference on how to set up your projects, see Chapter 14, "Example 14-1: Adding an ADO.NET Entity Data Model to Your Project". Remember also, if you are using the .mdf database file, changes to the data, including adds, updates, and deletes, will not be saved to the database unless the Copy to Output Directory property of the FoodStore.mdf file is set to "Copy if newer".

As well, to ensure your code is working, it is good practice to inspect the data independently of your code. To do this, refer to Chapter 13, "Example 13-3: Browsing Database Content with Visual Studio". Also remember, if you are using the database file as a data source, create a connection to the database file that is copied by the application to the bin folder to inspect the same data that is used by your project.

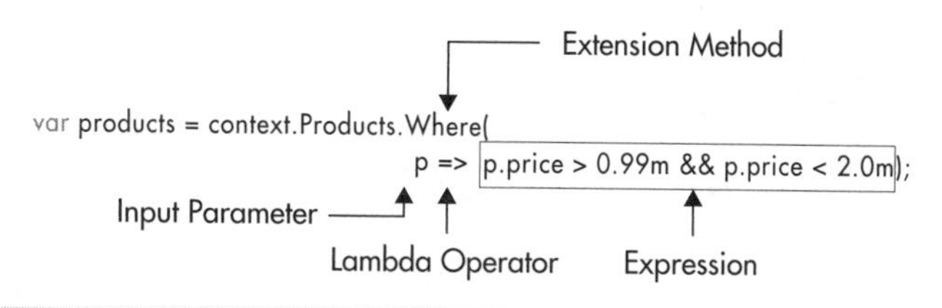

Figure 16-1 Lambda syntax

Lambda Syntax

Method-based syntax is enabled through extension methods that are available from the *System.Linq* namespace. These extension methods receive anonymous functions as parameters. As explained in Chapter 11, the anonymous function body uses lambda syntax to define the input parameters and operations. Figure 16-1 shows a sample of a LINQ command that is defined with a *Where()* extension method. The lambda operator => implies "goes to". The input parameters of a lambda statement are on the left side of the lambda operator and the expression is on the right. Together, the parameters and expression define the anonymous function.

The input parameter type for the lambda statement in Figure 16-1 is inferred. In other words, the compiler can determine the parameter data type in the lambda expression. For Figure 16-1, the input parameter is a *Product* object. The compiler knows the parameter is a *Product* object because the *Where()* extension method is operating on the *Products DbSet*.

Read Queries

To start our discussion on how to use extension methods, let's examine the *Select()* method since it is one of the most basic methods used for querying databases. The *Select()* extension method can be used to define the columns of the data set that is returned from a LINQ query.

Example 16-1 Defining Query Columns with the Select() Method

This example implements *Select()* to retrieve *name* and *vendor* values from the *Products* entity. Like all examples in this chapter, to build this example using a new console application, add an Entity Data Model (EDM) that references all tables in the *FoodStore* database. Then, place this code inside the *Main()* method.

```
FoodStoreEntities context = new FoodStoreEntities(); // Reference database.
var products = context.Products.Select(              // Get Product detail.
               p=> new { Name = p.name, Vendor = p.vendor });
foreach (var row in products)                        // Show Product detail.
    Console.WriteLine(row.Name + " - " + row.Vendor);
Console.ReadLine();
```

When running this program, the *name* and *vendor* values are obtained from each row of the *Product* table:

```
Cake Mix - Sysco
Cookie Dough - Sysco
Orange Juice - GFS
Cookie Dough - GFS
Carrots - GFS
```

For a comparison, it is worth noting that you could replace the previous method-based query declaration with this query syntax to achieve the same result:

```
var products = from p in context.Products
               select new { Name = p.name, Vendor = p.vendor };
```

Filtering

The *Where()* extension method allows you to restrict or filter rows of a query with an expression that gives a true or false result. The *Where()* method is typically placed before the *Select()* method if a *Select()* method exists.

Example 16-2 Applying a Where Filter

The *Where()* method in this example uses a lambda expression to retrieve all products with prices ranging from $1.00 to $1.99:

```
FoodStoreEntities context = new FoodStoreEntities(); // Reference database.
var products = context.Products                      // Define query.
           .Where( p => p.price>0.99m && p.price<2.00m)
           .Select(p => new{Name = p.name, Price = p.price});
foreach (var row in products) {                      // Show detail.
    decimal price = (decimal)row.Price;
    Console.WriteLine(row.Name + " - " + price.ToString("C"));
}
Console.ReadLine();
```

The data that is retrieved and displayed when running the program is within the price range set by the *Where()* method:

```
Cookie Dough - $1.25
Cookie Dough - $1.45
Carrots - $1.01
```

To show the difference, you could swap out the method-based query in this example with the following query syntax to generate the same results:

```
var products = from p in context.Products
               where p.price>0.99m && p.price<2.00m
               select new { Name = p.name, Price = p.price };
```

Try This 16-1 Basic Extension Methods

This exercise gives you some practice writing method-based syntax.

1. Create a console application that references the *FoodStore* database.
2. Using the *Select()* and *Where()* extension methods, create a program to select and display the *branch, region,* and *building_name* column values from the *Store* table of the *FoodStore* database for all stores that are located in the BC region.
3. Check the results that are shown in your program output by browsing the data contained in the *Store* table of the *FoodStore* database with the Server Explorer/ Database Explorer tool (see Chapter 13, Example 13-3).

Filtering with a Collection of Values

The *Contains()* method, from the *System.Linq* namespace, enables filtering against predefined arrays and lists of items. Both collection and array types expose the *Contains()* method. The *Contains()* method can be placed inside the *Where()* method. The *Where()* method receives an anonymous function.

Example 16-3 Filtering with a Collection

This example uses the *Contains()* method to select all invoice numbers for Seattle or Vancouver store branches. In this case, the *Where()* method receives an anonymous function that infers an *Invoice* object as the input parameter and uses the Boolean *Contains()* method in the expression.

```
FoodStoreEntities context = new FoodStoreEntities(); // Reference database.
string[] branchArray      = { "Vancouver", "Seattle" }; // Define array.
var  query = context.Invoices
    .Where(inv=>branchArray.Contains(inv.branch))       // Apply filter.
    .Select(  i => new { InvoiceNum = i.invoiceNum, Branch = i.branch });
foreach (var item in query)                             // Show results.
    Console.WriteLine(item.InvoiceNum + "  " + item.Branch);
Console.ReadLine();
```

When you run the program, the invoice data displayed is limited to the Vancouver and Seattle branches:

```
1001 Vancouver
1002 Vancouver
1005 Seattle
```

Retrieving Similar Matches

During searches, it may be desirable to limit query results to a subset of characters of a column value. For example, you may wish to find a last name that starts with "V" or perhaps "Van". Extension methods are extremely powerful for string comparisons since a wide variety of other C# methods can be applied to parse and isolate search results. As suggestions, the *StartsWith(), IndexOf(),* and *IsMatch()* methods presented in Chapter 6 are helpful for filtering query results from within the *Where()* extension method. *ToUpper()* and *ToLower()* methods can be used to manage case sensitivity if needed.

Example 16-4 Filtering with String Comparison Methods

This example demonstrates how to implement a query to retrieve product names that either start with "C" or contain the word "Juice". For this example, the *StartsWith()* method is used to check the first element of a string, and the *Contains()* method is used to search for the existence of a pattern anywhere in the string.

```
FoodStoreEntities context = new FoodStoreEntities(); // Reference database.
var query = context.Products                         // Filter on names
    .Where(prod => prod.name.StartsWith("C")         // starting with 'C' or
```

```
                || prod.name.Contains("Juice"));      // containing 'Juice'.
foreach (var row in query)                             // Show detail.
    Console.WriteLine(row.name + ", " + row.mfg);
Console.ReadLine();
```

When you run this program, all products that have a name that begins with “C” or that contain the word “Juice” are listed:

```
Cake Mix, Duncan Hines
Cookie Dough, Duncan Hines
Orange Juice, Florida Orange
Cookie Dough, Pillsbury
Carrots, Hot House
```

Selecting Distinct Rows

For some queries, you may need to eliminate duplicate rows. The *Distinct()* method ensures that each row of your query is unique.

Example 16-5 Selecting Distinct Rows

This code example shows how to use the *Distinct()* method to select unique product names. In this example, the *Distinct()* method ensures that the product name “Cookie Dough” does not appear more than once.

```
FoodStoreEntities context = new FoodStoreEntities(); // Reference database.
var query = context.Products                         // Query unique names.
                  .Select(p => new { Name = p.name }).Distinct();
foreach (var item in query)                          // Show detail.
    Console.WriteLine(item.Name);
Console.ReadLine();
```

When you run the program, you will notice that the rows are all unique. However, if you remove the *Distinct()* method and run the program again, you will notice that “Cookie Dough” appears twice.

Sorting

The sequence of a data query can be arranged with the *OrderBy()* and *OrderByDescending()* extension methods to sort rows by a specific column value. *ThenBy()* and *ThenByDescending()* methods offer secondary sorting options for columns that follow the primary sort column. Each of these extension methods receives the object as the input parameter and the sort column in the anonymous function body.

Example 16-6 Sorting

This example arranges *Product* data in ascending sequence by *vendor* and then by *name* in descending order:

```
FoodStoreEntities context = new FoodStoreEntities(); // Reference database.
var products = context.Products                      // Query products.
            .OrderBy(p=>p.vendor)
            .ThenByDescending(p=>p.name);
foreach (var p in products)                          // Show detail.
    Console.WriteLine(p.productID + ", " + p.name + ", " + p.vendor);
Console.ReadLine();
```

The output from this shows the rows listed in alphabetical manner by *vendor* and then product *name*:

```
3, Orange Juice, GFS
4, Cookie Dough, GFS
5, Carrots, GFS
2, Cookie Dough, Sysco
1, Cake Mix, Sysco
```

Subselection

The previous chapter described how to create a second query from a separate query with deferred execution. This ability to combine a series of *ObjectQuery* instances simplifies the steps for assembling query logic before sending one efficient final command to the database. Let's see how to query an existing query with method-based syntax.

Example 16-7 Subselection

This example uses two *ObjectQuery* instances to build a query. The first query named *gfsProducts* retrieves all products that are sold by the vendor named "GFS". The second query named *finalQuery* retrieves all values from *gfsProducts* that start with "C". When the data is needed, the final query is the only one that gets executed on the database.

```
FoodStoreEntities context = new FoodStoreEntities(); // Reference database.
var gfsProducts                                      // Get 'GFS' products
    = context.Products.Where(p => p.vendor == "GFS");
var finalQuery                                       // starting with 'C'.
    = gfsProducts.Where(p => p.name.StartsWith("C"));
foreach (Product p in finalQuery)                    // Show detail.
    Console.WriteLine(p.productID + ", " + p.name + ", " + p.vendor);
Console.ReadLine();
```

In the output, only "GFS" products starting with "C" appear:

```
4, Cookie Dough, GFS
5, Carrots, GFS
```

Merging Similar Queries with a Union

A union is a merge of separate query results where the column sequence, names, and data types of both queries match. The *Union()* extension method allows the one set of query results to be appended to results from another.

Example 16-8 Combining Similar Queries with a Union

This code example shows how to implement the *Union()* method to merge two separate queries. The example retrieves names of supplier and manufacturer companies to generate a list of affiliated companies.

```
FoodStoreEntities db = new FoodStoreEntities(); // Reference database.

// Perform separate queries with identically named columns.
var suppliers     = db.Suppliers.Select(  s=>new {  Affiliate = s.vendor});
var manufacturers = db.Manufacturers.Select( m=>new { Affiliate = m.mfg });

var query = suppliers.Union( manufacturers);     // Combine queries.
foreach (var item in query)                      // Show results.
    Console.WriteLine(item.Affiliate);
Console.ReadLine();
```

The affiliate companies listed include all supplier and manufacturer names:

```
Duncan Hines
Florida Orange
GFS
Hot House
McCain
Pillsbury
Sysco
```

Aggregate Summary Queries

Aggregate queries are database queries that generate tabulated summaries. Common extension methods for generating summaries include *Average(), Count(), Max(), Min(),* and *Sum()*. Rows of data returned by summary queries are categorized with grouping columns that are assigned in the *GroupBy()* method. Each grouping column can then be accessed in the *Select()* method with a *Key* reference.

NOTE

As the summary query is constructed, the only columns that can be retrieved must be either columns that are specified in the *GroupBy()* method or summary values for that group.

Example 16-9 Summaries with Grouping

This example calculates the total quantity of units sold for each product by adding the total units sold on each invoice. The summary is performed for each *productID,* so *productID* is the designated grouping key. The total units sold for each product is generated using the *Sum()* extension method.

```
FoodStoreEntities context = new FoodStoreEntities(); // Reference database.
var query = context.ProductInvoiceWithQuantities
            .GroupBy(product=>product.productID)     // Set grouping key.
            .Select( p =>
            new { ProductID  = p.Key,                // Query columns.
                  QtySold    = p.Sum(prod => prod.quantity) });
foreach (var row in query) {                         // Show results.
    Console.Write("Product:" + row.ProductID + " ");
    Console.WriteLine("Qty Sold:"+ row.QtySold);
}
Console.ReadLine();
```

The values displayed in this query show the total combined invoiced quantities for each product:

```
Product:1 Qty Sold:7
Product:2 Qty Sold:4
Product:3 Qty Sold:3
Product:4 Qty Sold:3
```

Try This 16-2 Aggregate Queries with Simple Grouping

This exercise offers practice writing slightly advanced method-based LINQ queries with aggregation.

1. Create a console application and add an EDM that references the *FoodStore* database.
2. Using method-based syntax, write a query on the *Store* table that counts the total stores per *region.*
3. In your output, display the *region* and store count in it.

Grouping on Multiple Columns

You may want to group on more than one column to generate subcategories within your summary results. To group on multiple columns, you must define grouping columns and a key that represents the object that references the grouping columns. This is different from the previous section, where the key represented only one column. In our new query, the key represents a multicolumn anonymous type that we define in the *GroupBy()* clause. The aggregate query can only show summary values and columns that are associated with the key.

Example 16-10 Grouping on Multiple Columns

This demonstration uses *GroupBy()* to generate summary information for inventory first by *vendor* and then by *mfg*. The total count of products per manufacturer is then generated for each subcategory.

```
FoodStoreEntities context = new FoodStoreEntities(); // Reference database.
var query = context.Products
    .GroupBy(p => new { p.vendor, p.mfg },              // Set grouping columns.
                  ( key, p ) =>                          // Define key.
              new { Vendor = key.vendor,                 // Assign query columns.
                    Mfg    = key.mfg,
                    Count  = p.Count() });
foreach (var row in query)                               // Show results.
    Console.WriteLine("Vendor:" + row.Vendor
    + " Manufacturer:" + row.Mfg + "   Count:" + row.Count);
Console.ReadLine();
```

The output provided in the first portion of this example shows the raw product data with *Product name, vendor, and mfg* values. Then, the products are grouped by *vendor* and then manufacturer, *mfg,* categories. Counts of unique items offered from each manufacturer per vendor are displayed.

```
Vendor:GFS Manufacturer:Florida Orange   Count:1
Vendor:GFS Manufacturer:Hot House   Count:1
Vendor:GFS Manufacturer:Pillsbury   Count:1
Vendor:Sysco Manufacturer:Duncan Hines   Count:2
```

Inserting, Updating, and Deleting Objects

When inserting, updating, and deleting object data with LINQ, you may use either query syntax or method-based syntax to obtain a reference to the object. However, query syntax and method-based syntax use the same extension methods to insert, update, and delete objects. Since there is no difference in how these operations are performed, please refer to Chapter 17 for information on how to implement inserts, updates, and deletes with LINQ to Entities.

NOTE

Chapter 17 also discusses how to perform object inserts, updates, and deletes with junction, bridge, or link tables.

Chapter 16 Self Test

The following questions are intended to help reinforce your comprehension of the concepts covered in this chapter. The answers can be found in the accompanying online Appendix B, "Answers to the Self Tests".

1. Indicate whether each of the following queries uses deferred execution (lazy loading) or immediate loading:

   A. ________

   ```
   var products = context.Products.Select( p => new {Name = p.name });
   ```

   B. ________

   ```
   IList<Product> products = context.Products
                 .Where( p=> p.price> 1.00m).ToList();
   ```

2. Examine the query in question 1A.

   A. What is the name of the inferred parameter?

   B. What is the inferred parameter type?

3. Using extension methods, write a query to retrieve all *first_name* and *last_name* values from rows of the *Employee* table.
4. Using the *Where()* extension method, create a program to select and display the *branch, region, and building_name* column values from the *Store* table of the *FoodStore* database for all stores that are located in the BC region.
5. Using method-based LINQ, create a program to select and display *productID, name, mfg, vendor, and price* column values of the *Product* table from the *FoodStore* database for any product named "Cake Mix" or "Cookie Dough".
6. Write a program that uses *Select()* and *Where()* methods to retrieve all *branch* and *region* column values from the *Store* table where the region is not equal to BC.
7. Revise Example 16-3 so that the *branchArray* values are stored in a *List* rather than in an array.

8. Using the *Contains()* method and the *FoodStore* database, write a program to select and display *productID, name, and mfg* column values of the *Product* table where the *mfg* name is either "Duncan Hines" or "Pillsbury".

9. Write a program that uses method-based syntax to query the *Employee* table of the *FoodStore* database to show *first_name* and *last_name* column values for all employees with a first name starting with the letter "J".

10. Adjust the ordering and column selection in Example 16-6 so the output becomes

```
3 - Orange Juice - GFS - $4.25
2 - Cookie Dough - Sysco - $1.25
4 - Cookie Dough - GFS - $1.45
5 - Carrots - GFS - $1.01
1 - Cake Mix - Sysco - $2.99
```

11. Using method-based syntax, select a list of unique *building_name* columns from the *Building* table in the *FoodStore* database. Browse the data with the Server Explorer/ Database Explorer to determine if duplicate *building_name* values in the *Building* table actually exist.

12. In a new console application with an Entity Data Model that references the *FoodStore* database, replace all code in *Main()* with

```
string[] manufacturers =
new string[] { "Florida Orange", "California Orange", "California Gold" };
var mfgQuery = manufacturers.Where(m => m.Contains("Orange"));
```

Then, write a LINQ query, using method-based syntax, that selects *mfg* and *mfgDiscount* values from the *Manufacturer* table where *mfg* names exist in the *mfgQuery* result set.

13. Explain why you receive an error if you change the *Affiliate* column name in the *suppliers* query of Example 16-8 to *SupplyCompany*.

14. Using LINQ to Entities, write a query to show the *Count()* of all employees in the *Employee* table of the *FoodStore* database.

15. Using LINQ to Entities, write a query to show the total number of stores in a region. Use the data from the *Store* table in the *FoodStore* database.

Chapter 17

Join Queries with LINQ to Entities

Key Skills & Concepts

- Introductory Relational Database Theory
- Navigation Properties
- Equal Joins
- Outer Joins
- Joining More than Two Collections in One Query
- Bridging Many-to-Many Relationships

The aim of this chapter is to give you the control needed to perform a decent range of queries that any data-driven application developer will find useful. When using LINQ to Entities, you often will need to write queries that combine values from more than one table or data set. A query that combines related rows from more than one table is called a *join*. This chapter discusses techniques for implementing joins of all major types. There are many different ways to query values from multiple entities in LINQ, so the methods presented here have been selected for flexibility and simplicity.

Referencing the FoodStore Database

As in the previous few chapters, to build any of the code examples in this chapter, begin with a new console application that has an Entity Data Model that references the *FoodStore* database. Then replace the code inside the *Main()* method with the code that is associated with the current example. For a reference on how to set up your projects, see Chapter 14, "Example 14-1: Adding an ADO.NET Entity Data Model to Your Project". Remember also, if you are using the .mdf database file, changes to the data, including adds, updates, and deletes, will not be saved to the database unless the Copy to Output Directory property of the FoodStore.mdf file is set to "Copy if newer".

As well, to ensure your code is working, it is good practice to inspect the data independently of your code. To do this, refer to Chapter 13, "Example 13-3: Browsing Database Content with Visual Studio". Also remember, if you are using the database file as a data source, create a connection to the database file that is copied by the application to the bin folder to inspect the same data that is used by your project.

Introductory Relational Database Theory

Before we start coding, let's look at some basic terms that describe the relationships between data tables. When working with database tables, relationships between rows of neighboring tables are defined by matching column values.

Primary Keys

A *primary key* is a column or combination of columns that uniquely identifies each row of a table. There is only one primary key declared per table, and its value in each row cannot be null. For example, in a table that contains citizen profiles, a suitable primary key might be a Social Security number (SSN) because this number uniquely identifies an individual person. You could argue that an e-mail address might be a unique identifier for that same person. The e-mail address is an equally valid candidate for being a primary key. In the end though, only one primary key can be chosen for the table, and this choice is made by the database developer.

Composite Primary Key

A primary key that is composed of more than one column is called a *composite key*. A combination of more than one column to create the primary key is only valid if the combination of columns is in *minimal form,* which means that all columns of the composite key are required to create the unique identifier. Consider a case where you store information about rooms within different buildings. The room number and building name combination uniquely identifies each room, so these two columns together could be combined to form the primary key. This composite primary key is in minimal form because there is no excess data and both columns are required to create the unique identifier. Consider another case where a developer wants to use a Social Security number and last name in a composite primary key. The SSN is already a unique identifier on its own, so including the last name in the key is excessive or redundant. Since the last name is not required to create a unique identifier, this combination of columns is not in minimal form and cannot serve as a primary key. Instead, the SSN on its own is in minimal form and is a valid candidate for being the primary key.

Foreign Keys

A *foreign key* is a column or combination of columns in one table that references a primary key in another table. Several rows of a table may contain the same foreign key value. The foreign key column may also be null. When working with the *FoodStore* database, the *branch* column uniquely identifies each row of the *Store* table, so it is the

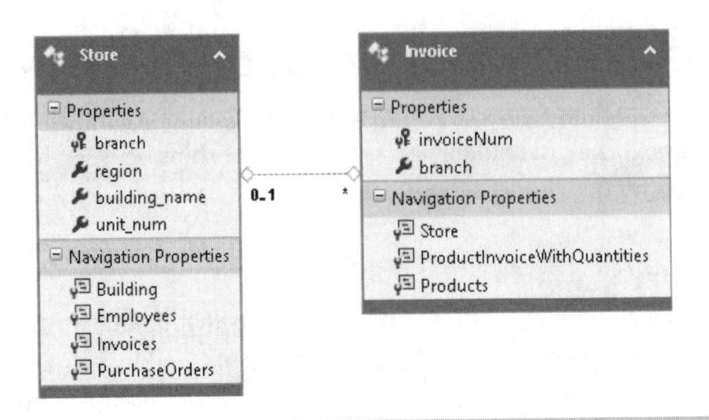

Figure 17-1 Store and Invoice entity association

primary key for the *Store* table. In contrast, the *branch* column of the *Invoice* table is a foreign key to the *branch* column in the *Store* table.

Figure 17-1 shows part of the *FoodStore* Entity Data Model conceptual view. The primary key in the *Store* table is identified with a key symbol beside the *branch* column. The *branch* column also appears in the *Invoice* table because it is a foreign key that matches the primary key of the *Store* table.

Cardinality

Identifying the number of instances of one table to another is really important when writing queries. *Cardinality* is a notation that describes the total instances of one table or entity to another. Cardinality notation for quantity is summarized in Table 17-1.

To observe how cardinality is applied in a database diagram, see Figure 17-1, which shows a subsection of a conceptual view for an Entity Data Model. The combination of the 0..1 symbol beside the *Store* entity and the * symbol beside the *Invoice* entity indicates that a store can have many invoices. This notation also indicates that an invoice can only be generated for zero stores or one store. Since an invoice belongs to 0..1 stores, this implies that the invoice can be created first and assigned to a store later. You may also note that

0..1	Zero or One	0..*	Zero or Many
1	One and Only One	1..*	One or Many
*	Many		

Table 17-1 Cardinality Notation

the *Invoice* and *Store* tables are associated with the *branch* column, where *branch* is the primary key in the *Store* table and *branch* is a foreign key in the *Invoice* table. The parent table hosts the primary key in the relationship, so for this case, the *Store* table is the parent. The parent can have many children, so in this case, the *Invoice* entity is the child table because a store can have many invoices.

To further examine cardinality in terms of a relationship or association, see Figure 17-2, which shows three different types of associations between entities. When examining the association between the *Building* and *Store,* the cardinality makes it clear that a *Building* can have zero or many *Store* instances. However, a *Store* must exist in only one *Building.* Since a building can have many stores, we can say the *Building* table is the parent and the *Store* table is the child.

The association and cardinality for the relationship between the *Product* and *Invoice* entities in Figure 17-2 describe a very different relationship. A *Product* can be listed on many invoices, and an *Invoice* object can list many products. This is a many-to-many relationship. Many-to-many relationships are not actually permitted in relational database design. To avoid this situation, a third table is inserted between the two parent tables. This third table is often referred to by different names, such as a bridge table, a junction table, or a link table. The *ProductInvoice* table in the entity relationship diagram in Figure A-1 of the Appendix is an example of a bridge table that alleviates a many-to-many relationship.

The third association in Figure 17-2 describes the relationship between a *Person* and a *SecurityCode* object. For this example, a *Person* may have either zero security codes or one security code. When reading this association in the other direction, we can also say each security code only belongs to one person. You might suggest that the security code be stored in the *Person* table, and this is a valid possibility. However, a separate table might be used to store this information for reasons that could range from needing to have a different table with a different set of permissions to needing more data without disturbing a preexisting table structure.

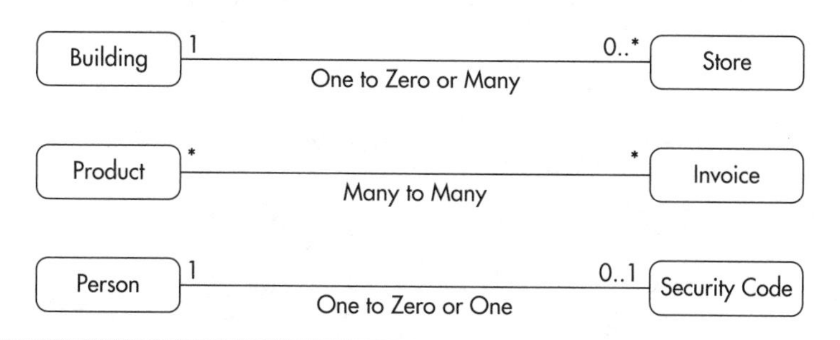

Figure 17-2 Association types

Navigation Properties

When writing LINQ queries that join tables, you will want to know about navigation properties. Navigation properties are exposed in the Entity Data Model to enable easy referencing of associated entities from one to another. As you saw earlier in Figure 17-1, the *Store* entity lists navigation properties of associated *DbSet* collections for *Building, Employees, Invoices,* and *PurchaseOrders*. As well, the *Invoices* entity lists navigation properties for *Store, ProductInvoiceWithQuantitites,* and *Products DbSet* collections. Navigation properties offer simple syntax alternatives, but they will also prove to be an essential feature when we discuss how to bridge many-to-many relationships later in this chapter.

Try This 17-1 Testing Your Knowledge of Database Theory

This exercise gives you some practice using relational database theory. Use Figure 17-3 to answer the following questions:

1. If there are any, identify the property or properties that make the primary key in the *Building* entity.
2. If there are any, identify the property or properties that make the primary key in the *Store* entity.
3. If there are any, identify the property or properties that create a foreign key in the *Building* entity.
4. If there are any, identify the property or properties that create a foreign key in the *Store* table.

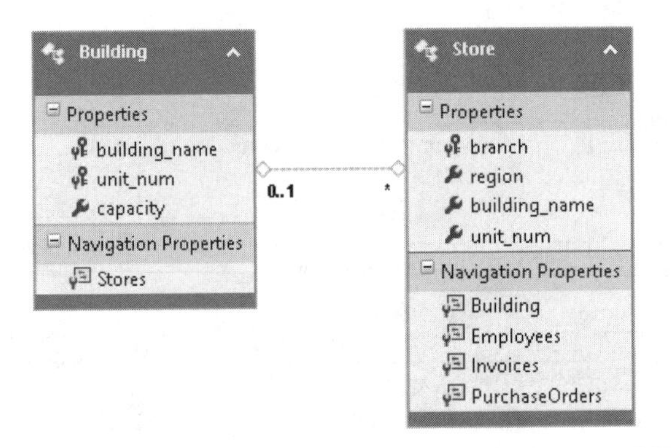

Figure 17-3 Building and Store entity association

5. How many stores can a building contain?
6. How many buildings can be associated with a store?
7. How many primary keys can be designated for each table?
8. Identify the navigation properties for the *Store* entity.
9. Identify the navigation properties for the *Building* entity.

Equal Joins

At the start of this chapter, the term *join* was mentioned to describe the combination of data from rows of related data sets. An *equal join,* also known as an *inner join,* is the most common type of join. Equal joins retrieve data from rows of two tables that have matching primary and foreign key values.

Equal Joins with Query Syntax

There are several different ways to perform equal joins with LINQ query syntax. For simplicity and flexibility, I prefer to use two separate *from* clauses for each *DbSet* while also defining the join column in the *where* clause. The sequence in which each *DbSet* is listed in the query does not matter—query results will be the same regardless of their sequence.

Example 17-1 Inner Join with Query Syntax

This example performs an inner join to display all *invoiceNum* values for invoices associated with each *Store,* along with the related store's branch and region data. To build the example, like all examples in this chapter, create a new console application project and add an EDM that references all tables in the *FoodStore* database. Then, add the following code in the *Main()* method:

```
FoodStoreEntities context = new FoodStoreEntities(); // Reference database.
var query = from  s in context.Stores                // Query Stores.
            from  i in context.Invoices              // Query Invoices.
            where s.branch == i.branch               // Join using the keys.
            select new { s.branch, s.region, i.invoiceNum };
foreach (var row in query)                           // Display results.
    Console.WriteLine(row.branch + " - " + row.region + " - "
                    + row.invoiceNum);
Console.ReadLine();
```

The output shows all invoice numbers that have an associated store branch along with the region:

```
Vancouver - BC - 1001
Vancouver - BC - 1002
Kamloops - BC - 1003
Mission - BC - 1004
Seattle - WA - 1005
```

If you were to inspect the *Store* table data with the Server Explorer/Database Explorer, you would notice that a *branch* value named "Richmond" exists in the *Store* table, but it does not appear in the output of this example. "Richmond" is missing from the output because there are no invoices associated with this branch. On a similar note, if you examine the *Invoice* table data, you will notice an invoice 1006 exists, yet it does not appear in this example's output. Invoice 1006 is missing from the output because a *branch* value has not been assigned to it.

Equal Joins with Method-Based Syntax

When using method-based syntax to perform an equal (inner) join, the *DbSet* provides a *Join()* extension method for this purpose. Inside the *Join()* method, you define the associated *DbSet,* as well as the associated columns. The final parameter defines the entities that are combined by the query: after applying the *Join()* method, extension methods that follow can access an object that represents the joined entities.

Example 17-2 Inner Join with Extension Methods

The query in this example performs an equal join between the *Invoice* and *Store* tables on the *branch* column. A *Where()* extension method has also been added to only select branches from Vancouver.

```
FoodStoreEntities context = new FoodStoreEntities();
var query =  context.Stores.Join(          // Outer DbSet.
                 context.Invoices,         // Inner DbSet.
                 s => s.branch,            // Join columns.
                 i => i.branch,
                 (s, i) => new { s, i }) // Entity references.
    // 'si' is the combined Stores and Invoices DbSet from Join().
    .Where( si => si.s.branch == "Vancouver")        // Apply filter.
    .Select(si => new { Branch     = si.s.branch,    // Define query columns.
                        Region     = si.s.region,
                        InvoiceNum = si.i.invoiceNum });
```

```
foreach (var item in query)
    Console.WriteLine("Invoice "   + item.InvoiceNum.ToString() + ": "
                    + item.Branch + ", " + item.Region);
Console.ReadLine();
```

When running the program, the data set includes columns from both the *Invoice* and *Store* tables through the equal join where the branch is Vancouver:

```
Invoice 1001: Vancouver, BC
Invoice 1002: Vancouver, BC
```

Equal Joins with Navigation Properties

So far in this book, the query and method-based syntax for performing equal joins between two neighboring entities functions correctly, regardless of the entity sequence in the query. This syntax works accurately in either direction for many-to-one or one-to-many relationships. Instead of performing joins in this manner, however, you can use the navigation property of the entity that has only one matching row in the other entity. In the *FoodStore* database, for example, a *Store* object is associated with many *Invoice* objects, but each *Invoice* object is only associated with one *Store* object (see Figure 17-1). Since an *Invoice* object relates to only one instance of the *Store* entity, the *Store* navigation property of the *Invoice* entity can be used to perform the equal join.

NOTE

When performing an equal join between two entities with navigation properties, be sure to check for null values in the join columns; otherwise, the navigation property referring to the parent will be null. This extra step will prevent errors from occurring when you try to access data from a navigation property that is null.

Example 17-3 Equal Join with Query Syntax and Navigation Properties

This demonstration shows how to use query syntax to retrieve values from the *Invoice* and *Store* tables with the *Store* navigation property of the *Invoices DbSet*:

```
FoodStoreEntities context = new FoodStoreEntities(); // Reference database.
var query  = from i in context.Invoices // Invoice belongs to only 1 Store.
             where i.branch != null     // Ensure join column is not null.
             // Get data from Invoice object and 'Store' navigation property.
             select new { i.branch, i.Store.region, i.invoiceNum };

foreach (var item in query)             // Show results.
    Console.WriteLine(item.branch + " - " + item.region + " - "
                    + item.invoiceNum);
Console.ReadLine();
```

The output shows all related *branch, region,* and *invoiceNum* data from the *Store* and *Invoice* tables where matching *branch* column values exist in each table. The output shows the same row data that was obtained from the query in Example 17-1.

Example 17-4 Equal Join with Method-Based Syntax and Navigation Properties

This example performs the exact same query as shown in Example 17-3 while using the navigation property of the *Invoices* data set. This time, though, method-based syntax implements the query.

```
FoodStoreEntities context = new FoodStoreEntities();   // Reference database.
var query  = context.Invoices                         // Invoice has 0..1 matching Store.
             .Where(i => i.branch != null) // Ensure join column isn't null.
             .Select(result => new         // Define query columns.
              { result.branch, result.Store.region, result.invoiceNum });
foreach (var item in query)                // Show results.
    Console.WriteLine(item.branch + " - " + item.region + " - "
                   + item.invoiceNum);
Console.ReadLine();
```

The output from running this example is identical to the output that is generated in Example 17-1 and Example 17-3.

Try This 17-2 Practice with Equal Joins

This exercise provides an opportunity to create some simple join queries using both query syntax and method-based syntax.

1. Create a console application with an Entity Data Model that references the *FoodStore* database.
2. Using query syntax in LINQ, create a program that performs an inner join between the *Employee* and *Store* tables of the *FoodStore* database. Show the *branch* column of the *Store* table and the *first_name* and *last_name* columns of the *Employee* table.
3. Use method-based syntax to achieve the same result as in step 2. Test your results.
4. Add code that uses navigation properties to perform the same query as in steps 2 and 3. Test your results by showing the output from your new query.

Equal Joins on Composite Keys

When a primary key is created with more than one column, it is a *composite key*. Joining on composite keys is slightly more complicated than joining just on one column.

Equal Joins on Composite Key with Query Syntax

When performing an inner join between two entities with a composite key while using query syntax, one approach involves including a *from* clause for each entity while placing the join columns in the *where* clause.

Example 17-5 Joining on Multiple Columns with Query Syntax

This example shows how to retrieve values from the *Store* and *Building* entities by joining on the *building_name* and *unit_num* columns:

```
FoodStoreEntities db = new FoodStoreEntities();      // Reference database.
var query = from s in db.Stores                      // Identify entities.
            from b in db.Buildings
            where s.building_name == b.building_name // Join on key columns.
               && s.unit_num      == b.unit_num
            select new{                              // Set selected columns.
                Branch       = s.branch,
                Region       = s.region,
                BuildingName = b.building_name,
                UnitNum      = b.unit_num,
                Capacity     = b.capacity };
foreach (var row in query) {                         // Show results.
    Console.WriteLine("Branch: "      + row.Branch
                    + ", "            + row.Region);
    Console.WriteLine("Building: "    + row.BuildingName
                    + ", unit #"      + row.UnitNum
                    + ", capacity: " + row.Capacity);
    Console.WriteLine();
}
Console.ReadLine();
```

The output from running this code shows the related *Building* and *Store* column values where matching keys exist. Also, note that the "Richmond" store is absent and unit 2381 at City Center is also absent since there are no matching keys for these entries.

```
Branch: Kamloops, BC
Building: Vineyard Estates, unit #180, capacity: 20400

Branch: Mission, BC
Building: Peaceful Place, unit #226, capacity: 18000
```

```
Branch: Seattle, WA
Building: Fairlane Square, unit #17235, capacity: 45000

Branch: Vancouver, BC
Building: City Center, unit #2380, capacity: 40000
```

Equal Joins on Composite Key with Method-Based Syntax

For performing joins on a composite key when using extension methods, the *SelectMany()* extension method of one *DbSet* receives the *DbSet* of the other entity with filtering on the join columns.

Example 17-6 Joining on Multiple Columns with Extension Methods

This example shows how to use the *SelectMany()* method to perform a join on multiple columns to retrieve data from the *Store* and *Building* tables:

```
FoodStoreEntities db = new FoodStoreEntities(); // Reference database.
var query = db.Stores
    .SelectMany(s =>                // Get Stores
        db.Buildings.Where(b =>     // and Buildings where match exists.
                        s.building_name == b.building_name
                        &&   s.unit_num == b.unit_num)
        .Select(    bldgSubset => // Reference matching Buildings.
            new{    Branch       = s.branch, // Set selected columns.
                    BuildingName = s.building_name,
                    UnitNum      = s.unit_num,
                    Region       = s.region,
                    Capacity     = bldgSubset.capacity }));
foreach (var row in query) {        // Show results.
    Console.WriteLine("Branch: " + row.Branch + ", " + row.Region);
    Console.WriteLine("Building: "    + row.BuildingName
                    + ", unit #"      + row.UnitNum
                    + ", capacity: " + row.Capacity + "\n");
}
Console.ReadLine();
```

The output from running this code is identical to the output for the same join using query syntax in Example 17-5.

Equal Joins on Composite Key with Navigation Properties

To implement navigation properties for equal joins on multiple columns, the *DbSet* used in the equal join query must be for the entity that has only one matching instance in the neighboring entity.

Example 17-7 Equal Joins on a Composite Key with Navigation Properties

This example shows how to implement method-based syntax to perform an equal join between the *Store* and *Building* tables. For this case, to join data from each table, matching *building_name* and *unit_num* values in each table are required. Since a *Store* object only relates to one *Building* instance, the *Building* navigation property of the *Stores DbSet* must be used to retrieve data from the *Building* table.

```
FoodStoreEntities db = new FoodStoreEntities(); // Reference database.
var query = db.Stores.Where(s=> s.building_name != null  // Join columns
                             && s.unit_num      != null) // cannot be null.
.Select( s=> new {                              // Define selected columns.
    Branch       = s.branch,
    Region       = s.region,
    BuildingName = s.building_name,
    UnitNum      = s.Building.unit_num,         // Use 'Building' navigation
    Capacity     = s.Building.capacity }); // property of the 'Store' DbSet.
foreach (var row in query) {                    // Show results.
    Console.WriteLine("Branch: "     + row.Branch
                    + ", "           + row.Region);
    Console.WriteLine("Building: "   + row.BuildingName
                    + ", unit #"     + row.UnitNum
                    + ", capacity: " + row.Capacity + "\n");
}
Console.ReadLine();
```

The output from running this example is identical to the output that is generated in Example 17-5 and Example 17-6.

Outer Joins

An *outer join* is a join on two data tables where all rows of at least one table are selected, regardless of whether there is a match in the other table. Database developers often describe specific types of outer joins as left, right, and full outer joins. LINQ makes no direct distinction for these types of joins, but they are possible in LINQ, so they are described here.

Left Outer Joins

A left outer join selects all desired columns and rows from the left table. The left outer join includes column values from the right table whenever a related row is found. If matching right table rows do not exist, then null values are substituted in their place.

The Venn diagram in Figure 17-4 provides a visual summary of the left outer join. All rows of the left table are selected, regardless of whether matching keys exist in the right table.

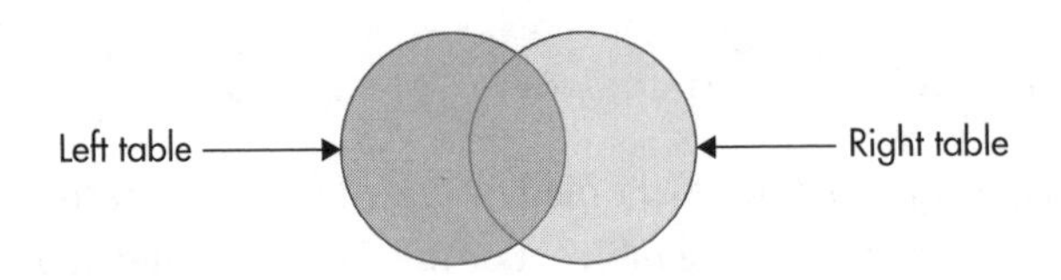

Figure 17-4 Rows selected in a left outer join

Since all rows of the left table are selected, the left table is dark. Matching rows in the right table that are selected are represented by the intersection between the left and right table.

Left Outer Joins with LINQ

A left outer join query can be performed using several different techniques. For simplicity, I use a mixture of query syntax and extension methods to perform this type of query.

Example 17-8 Left Outer Join

The following code example shows how to perform a left join between the *Store* and *Invoice* tables on the *branch* column. The *Store* entity is treated as the left entity. The query retrieves data about each store, regardless of whether it has an invoice or not. Since the *Store* entity is treated as the left table, it is placed in the first *from* clause, which requests all rows from this table. The second *from* clause retrieves rows from the right table wherever there is a match between the primary and foreign key columns. A *DefaultIfEmpty()* extension method is appended to the second *from* clause to allow null values when no match is found in the right table. In the *select* clause, a conditional operator assigns 0 to the right table's *invoiceNum* value whenever null data is encountered.

```
FoodStoreEntities context = new FoodStoreEntities();  // Reference database.
var query = from s in context.Stores     // Get rows from left table.
            from i in context.Invoices  // Get rows from right table.
                     .Where(inv => inv.branch == s.branch)  // Join columns.
                     .DefaultIfEmpty()  // Return null invoice values if
                                        // invoice does not exist for Store.
    select new {
        Branch     = s.branch,
        Region     = s.region,
        // Store invoiceNum value if it exists otherwise assign 0.
        InvoiceNum =  (i.invoiceNum != null)? i.invoiceNum : 0 };
foreach (var item in query)             // Show results.
    Console.WriteLine(item.Branch + " - "
                    + item.Region + " - " + item.InvoiceNum);
Console.ReadLine();
```

As expected, the data set displayed shows all column values from the *Store* table, regardless of whether or not the store has an invoice. For this example, a value of 0 is assigned to the invoice for "Richmond" since the "Richmond" branch does not have an invoice.

```
Kamloops - BC - 1003
Mission - BC - 1004
Richmond - BC - 0
Seattle - WA - 1005
Vancouver - BC - 1001
Vancouver - BC - 1002
```

Right Outer Joins

A right outer join retrieves all rows of the right table plus any matching rows from the left table. Rows are retrieved from the right table, regardless of whether there is a match in the left table. The Venn diagram in Figure 17-5 shows a right table that is dark since all rows are selected from it. The selected rows of the left table are represented by the intersection between the left and right table.

Right Outer Joins with LINQ

Even though LINQ does not allow you to directly distinguish between left and right joins, the right join can be performed indirectly with LINQ by treating the right table as the outer table. In this case, handling for null values must be managed for the inner table. In other words, this query is performed just like a left join except the order of the tables in the query is reversed.

Example 17-9 Right Outer Join

This example demonstrates a right outer join between the *Invoice* and *Store* entities in the *FoodStore* database, where the *Invoice* table is treated as the right entity. The *Invoice* entity therefore is the outer table in the join with the *Stores DbSet*. Column values of the *Store* entity must be adjusted when they are null.

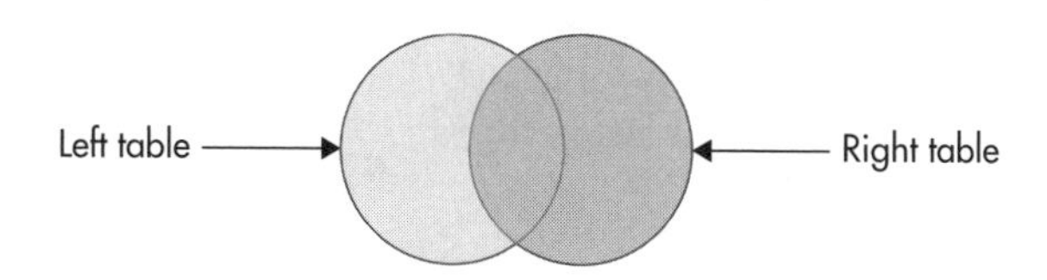

Figure 17-5 Rows selected in a right outer join

When comparing this to Example 17-8, you will notice that the query structure is basically identical except the *DbSet* positions are reversed. Also, handling for nulls is now done for the *Store* columns instead of the *Invoice* columns.

```
FoodStoreEntities context = new FoodStoreEntities(); // Reference database.
var query = from i in context.Invoices                // Outer table.
            from s in context.Stores                  // Inner table.
                .Where(store => store.branch == i.branch)  // Join columns.
                .DefaultIfEmpty() // Set null for inner table if no match.
    select new {
        // If values exist show them, otherwise assign "null".
        Branch     = (s.branch != null)? s.branch : "null",
        Region     = (s.region != null)? s.region : "null",
        InvoiceNum =  i.invoiceNum };
foreach (var item in query) // Display results.
    Console.WriteLine(item.Branch + " - " + item.Region + " - "
                    + item.InvoiceNum);
Console.ReadLine();
```

When running the program, all rows of the outer table, *Invoice,* are selected and values are retrieved from *Store* whenever a match is found:

```
Vancouver - BC - 1001
Vancouver - BC - 1002
Kamloops - BC - 1003
Mission - BC - 1004
Seattle - WA - 1005
null - null - 1006
```

Full Outer Joins

A full outer join retrieves columns from all rows of both associated tables in the join, regardless of whether or not a primary key–foreign key match exists. The Venn diagram in Figure 17-6 shows that all rows of each table are selected from both tables.

Full Outer Joins with LINQ

There is no full outer join operator in LINQ to Entities. However, you can implement a full outer join with a union of the left and right outer join queries for the same two tables.

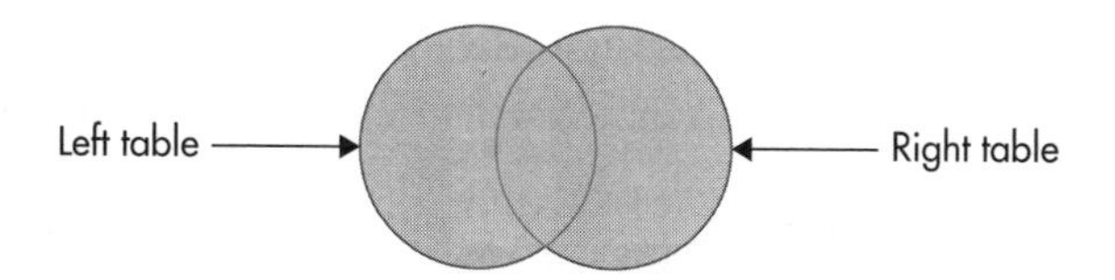

Figure 17-6 Rows selected in a full outer join

Example 17-10 Full Outer Join

This example demonstrates how the query syntax in LINQ performs a full outer join between *Store* and *Invoice* tables. In simple terms, the final query is really an outer join on *Stores* combined through a union with an outer join on *Invoices.*

```
FoodStoreEntities context = new FoodStoreEntities(); // Reference database.

// Outer join on Stores.
var allStores   = from s in context.Stores                       // Outer table.
                  from i in context.Invoices                     // Inner table.
                 .Where(inv => inv.branch == s.branch)           // Join columns.
                 .DefaultIfEmpty() // Set null for inner table if no match.
    select new {
        Branch     = s.branch,
        Region     = s.region,
        // Store invoiceNum value if it exists otherwise assign 0.
        InvoiceNum =  (i.invoiceNum != null)? i.invoiceNum : 0 };

// Outer join on Invoices.
var allInvoices = from i in context.Invoices                     // Outer table.
                  from s in context.Stores                       // Inner table.
                 .Where(store => store.branch == i.branch) // Join columns.
                 .DefaultIfEmpty() // Set null for inner table if no match.
    select new {
        // Set branch and region if values exist. Otherwise assign null.
        Branch     = (s.branch != null)? s.branch : "null",
        Region     = (s.region != null)? s.region : "null",
        InvoiceNum =  i.invoiceNum };

// Full outer join.
var fullJoin = allStores.Union(allInvoices);
foreach (var item in fullJoin) // Display results.
    Console.WriteLine(item.Branch + " - " + item.Region + " - "
                    + item.InvoiceNum);
Console.ReadLine();
```

When you run this code, the results show data from all rows of both tables. Notice how nulls and a zero are assigned when no matching key exists in the neighboring table.

```
Kamloops - BC - 1003
Mission - BC - 1004
null - null - 1006
Richmond - BC - 0
Seattle - WA - 1005
Vancouver - BC - 1001
Vancouver - BC - 1002
```

Joining More Than Two Collections in One Query

When joining multiple collections in one query, for simplicity, it is sometimes easier to join only two neighboring collections at a time. Results from joining two collections can be treated as a single *ObjectQuery* instance, which can later be joined with another *ObjectQuery* instance. You might try to combine more than two tables in one single query definition, but if the query becomes too unwieldy as you figure out the logic, then consider splitting it up. With deferred execution, the final *ObjectQuery* from a series of cumulative joins will contain all of the information needed to generate one efficient command before it is sent to the database.

Example 17-11 Joining More than Two Collections in One Query

This example demonstrates how to show product and invoice detail for all invoices that have orange juice included in the item list. To gather all of this information, a join between the *Products, ProductInvoiceWithQuantities,* and *Invoices* collections is required. To help separate the process of building the query into different subqueries, this query is generated in a cumulative manner. The first query is an inner join between the *Product* and *ProductInvoiceWithQuantity* tables. The second query is an inner join between the first query and the *Invoice* table. You might prefer to write one query that joins all entities together, but this demonstration shows how to separate the logic just in case you need to break your logic into simpler steps.

```
const int    ORANGE_JUICE = 3;
FoodStoreEntities context = new FoodStoreEntities(); // Reference database.

var productQuantity =                          // First query.
    from  p in context.Products                // Entities.
    from  i in context.ProductInvoiceWithQuantities
    where p.productID == ORANGE_JUICE && // Join column.
```

```
        p.productID == i.productID     // Join condition.
    select new{                        // Chosen columns.
        ProductID       = p.productID,
        ProductName     = p.name,
        Mfg             = p.mfg,
        Quantity        = i.quantity,
        InvoiceNum      = i.invoiceNum };

var productInvoice =                   // Join first query and Invoices.
    from pq in productQuantity         // First query result.
    from i in context.Invoices         // Invoices collection.
    where pq.InvoiceNum == i.invoiceNum // Join column.
    select new {                       // Chosen columns.
        Branch          = i.branch,
        ProductID       = pq.ProductID,
        ProductName     = pq.ProductName,
        Mfg             = pq.Mfg,
        Quantity        = pq.Quantity,
        InvoiceNum      = pq.InvoiceNum };

foreach (var item in productInvoice) {   // Show results.
    Console.WriteLine("Product ID:    " + item.ProductID);
    Console.WriteLine("Product Name: " + item.ProductName);
    Console.WriteLine("Quantity:      " + item.Quantity);
    Console.WriteLine("Store Branch: " + item.Branch + "\n");
}
Console.ReadLine();
```

The result from the final query shows data from all three tables to summarize product and invoice information for any invoice that includes orange juice sales:

```
Product ID:   3
Product Name: Orange Juice
Quantity:     1
Store Branch: Vancouver

Product ID:   3
Product Name: Orange Juice
Quantity:     2
Store Branch: Kamloops
```

Bridging Many-to-Many Relationships

The relationships between tables we have queried so far involve joins between tables where one entity relates to many instances of another. It is possible, though, to have a many-to-many relationship. In Figure 17-7, notice that a many-to-many relationship exists

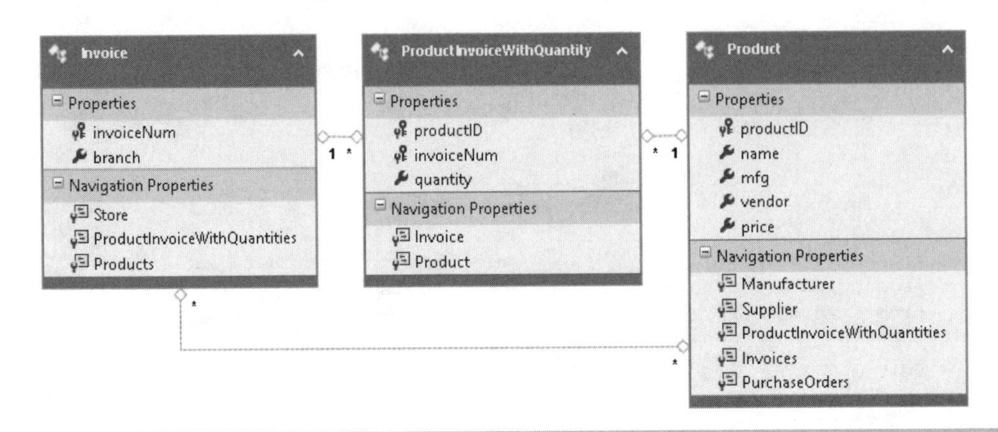

Figure 17-7 Many-to-many relationships

between the *Invoice* and *Product* entities. You can identify this relationship where the cardinality notation for many, *, is located at each end of the associating line between the *Invoice* and *Product* entities.

It is clear that a product can appear on many invoices and that an invoice can have many products. However, many-to-many relationships are not permitted in relational database design because they do not allow uniquely defined relationships between table rows. A way around this is to create a table between the two parent entities wherever a many-to-many relationship exists. This child table contains foreign keys that link to the parents' primary keys. As mentioned earlier in the chapter, this new table is often called a bridge table, a junction table, or a link table. Figure 17-7 actually shows a bridge table named *ProductInvoiceWithQuantity*. This table appears in the conceptual view of the Entity Data Model because it has a unique *quantity* property that does not appear in either parent table. However, if you were to browse the database tables with the Server Explorer/Database Explorer, you would notice that there is a *ProductInvoice* table as well, which also serves as a bridge to the *Invoice* and *Product* tables (see Figure 17-8).

NOTE

Usually, only one bridge table exists between entities. In the preceding example, however, two bridge tables were intentionally added between the *Product* and *Invoice* tables to demonstrate the difference between one that has unique columns and one that is only made up of foreign keys to the parent entities.

The composite primary key in *ProductInvoice* is made up of foreign keys that reference primary keys in the parents, and there are no other unique columns in this table.

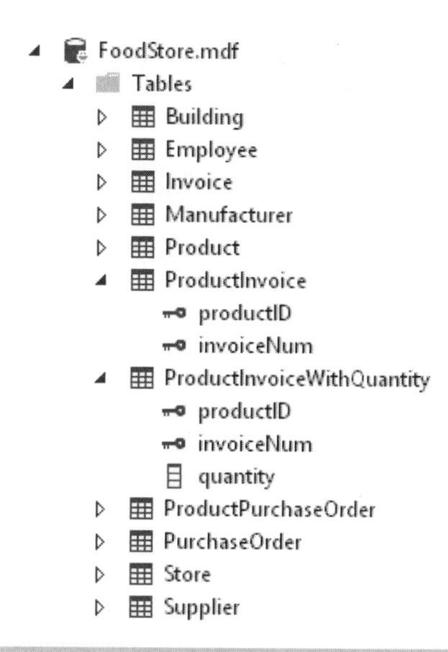

Figure 17-8 Viewing the bridge table in the Server Explorer/Database Explorer

When there are no unique columns in a bridge table, the entity will not appear in the Entity Data Model. This presents a challenge to the way we write our LINQ commands.

Querying Bridge Table Objects

Even if the junction table does not appear in the Entity Data Model, navigation properties allow us to access bridged data when reading data from the database.

Example 17-12 Querying Bridged Table Objects

This example shows how to use navigation properties to show corresponding invoice and product details for invoices where cake mix is ordered.

As previously illustrated in Figure 17-7, the *ProductInvoice* table that bridges the *Invoice* and *Product* tables is absent from the Entity Data Model. However, if you use the Server Explorer/Database Explorer tool, you will notice the table is definitely present. To display the product details for a specific *Invoice* object where there is a bridge between the *Product* and *Invoice* tables, you can use the *Invoices* navigation property of the *Products DbSet* to reference the data. In this query for this example, there are two *from* clauses. The second *from* clause uses the alias of the *Products DBSet* to reference the *Invoices* navigation property. The alias, *i,* is assigned to the *Invoices* navigation property, which can then reference columns of the *Invoice* table.

```
FoodStoreEntities db = new FoodStoreEntities();// Reference database.
var query = from p in db.Products
            from i in p.Invoices // Get Invoices via Products
                                 // Navigation property.
            where p.name == "Cake Mix" // filter on 'Cake Mix'.
            select new {    ProductID   = p.productID,  // from Product.
                            InvoiceNum  = i.invoiceNum, // from Invoice.
                            Branch      = i.branch,     // from Invoice.
                            ProductName = p.name   };   // from Product.
foreach (var row in query) {                            // Show results.
    Console.Write(row.ProductID  + ", " + row.InvoiceNum + ", ");
    Console.WriteLine(row.Branch + ", " + row.ProductName);
}
Console.ReadLine();
```

The final result shows column values from the *Product* and *Invoice* tables that are bridged through the *ProductInvoice* table:

```
1, 1001, Vancouver, Cake Mix
1, 1004, Mission, Cake Mix
```

Inserting Bridge Table Objects

When adding rows to a bridge table that is not exposed in the Entity Data Model, you must first obtain object references to corresponding objects of each parent table. Then, with one of the objects, you may reference the *DbSet* of the other parent table as a navigation property. The *Add()* method of the navigation property inserts the associated object as a parameter to create the link table entry.

Example 17-13 Inserting Bridge Table Objects

This example demonstrates how to add a bridge table entry that contains *productID* = 4 and *invoiceNum* = 1004 to the *ProductInvoice* table. In other words, it takes an existing product and adds it to an existing invoice. This entry is recorded in the *ProductInvoice* table. To start, the associated parent objects of the *Product* and *Invoice* tables are obtained. Then the navigation property of the *Invoice* object is used to add the bridge table instance with the help of the *Product* object. Before running the example, to confirm this entry does not exist initially, view the contents of the *ProductInvoice* table from the Server Explorer/Database Explorer (refer to Chapter 13, Example 13-3).

```
FoodStoreEntities context = new FoodStoreEntities(); // Reference database.
Product product = ( from  p in context.Products      // Get Product object.
```

```
                    where  p.productID == 4
                    select p).FirstOrDefault();
Invoice invoice = ( from   i in context.Invoices    // Get Invoice object.
                    where  i.invoiceNum == 1004
                    select i).FirstOrDefault();
try {
    invoice.Products.Add(product);                  // Add to bridge table.
    context.SaveChanges();                          // Save to database.
}
catch (Exception e) {
    Console.WriteLine("Exception: " + e.Message
            + " A duplicate entry may exist "
            + "or invalid primary-foreign key relationships may exist.");
}

var query = from i in context.Invoices              // Show bridged data if
            where i.invoiceNum == 1004 select i;    // invoiceNum is 1004.
foreach (var i in query)
    foreach (var p in i.Products)
        Console.WriteLine("invoiceNum: " + i.invoiceNum + "  " +
                          "productID: " + p.productID);
Console.ReadLine();
```

When running this program, a new entry for an *invoiceNum* value of 1004 and a *productID* of 4 appears after it is added to the database:

```
invoiceNum: 1004  productID: 1
invoiceNum: 1004  productID: 2
invoiceNum: 1004  productID: 3
invoiceNum: 1004  productID: 4
```

At this point, you may want to confirm the entry actually was saved to the database by browsing the data with the Server Explorer/Database Explorer. Remember, if you are using a database file, changes will only be saved if the Copy to Output Directory property of the FoodStore.mdf file is set to "Copy if newer". To ensure you are browsing the correct database copy, your Server Explorer/Database Explorer connection needs to reference the database file that is copied to the bin folder of your project.

Also note when using the *Add()* method for this example, you could reverse the object and navigation property order to perform the same object insertion. For example, you could replace

```
invoice.Products.Add(product);
```

with

```
product.Invoices.Add(invoice);
```

TIP

When adding an object into a link table with a navigation property, the object does not need to already exist in the parent table. In Example 17-13, you could create and initialize a brand-new *Product* object. Then you could use the instruction *invoice.Products.Add(product)* to add this new object simultaneously to both the *Product* entity and the *ProductInvoice* table.

Deleting Bridge Table Objects

To delete items from a bridge table that are not exposed in the Entity Data Model, you must first obtain references to the parent objects. The *Remove()* method of one object's navigation properties receives the associated object as a parameter. The transaction is committed to the database with the *SaveChanges()* method.

Example 17-14 Deleting Bridge Table Objects

In this example, the code deletes the *ProductInvoice* entry where the *invoiceNum* value is 1004 and the *productID* is 4. The deletion basically removes this item from the invoice but does not delete the invoice or the actual product.

```
FoodStoreEntities context = new FoodStoreEntities(); // Reference database.
Invoice invoice = (from   i in context.Invoices      // Get parent objects.
                   where  i.invoiceNum == 1004
                   select i).FirstOrDefault();
Product product = (from   p in context.Products
                   where  p.productID == 4
                   select p).FirstOrDefault();
if (invoice.Products.Contains(product)) {            // Check for nulls.
    invoice.Products.Remove(product);                // Delete  object.
    context.SaveChanges();
}
var invoices = from i in context.Invoices
               where i.invoiceNum == 1004 select i;
foreach (var i in invoices)
    foreach (var p in i.Products)
        Console.WriteLine("invoice: " + i.invoiceNum  + "  "
                        +"productID: " + p.productID);
Console.ReadLine();
```

When running the program, you will notice that the bridge table item for invoice number 1004 and product number 4 is no longer present:

```
invoice: 1004  productID: 1
invoice: 1004  productID: 2
invoice: 1004  productID: 3
```

When using the *Remove()* method, the order of objects can be reversed to generate the same outcome. To delete the bridge table entry, the instruction

```
invoice.Products.Remove(product);
```

could be replaced with

```
product.Products.Remove(invoice);
```

If you browse the *ProductInvoice* table with the Server Explorer/Database Explorer, you will notice that the entry for an *invoiceNum* of 1004 and *productID* of 4 no longer exists.

Chapter 17 Self Test

The following questions are intended to help reinforce your comprehension of the concepts covered in this chapter. The answers can be found in the accompanying online Appendix B, "Answers to the Self Tests".

1. Examine the conceptual view in Figure A-2 of the Appendix and consider the association between the *Store* and *PurchaseOrder* entities to answer the following questions:

A. Which entity is the parent and which entity is the child in this relationship?

B. Which columns make the primary key in the *Store* table?

C. Which columns make the primary key of the *PurchaseOrder* table?

D. How many purchase orders can a store have?

E. How many stores can be included on a purchase order?

F. What foreign key exists in the *PurchaseOrder* table?

2. Starting with Example 17-1, if you change the following code from

```
var query = from  s in context.Stores
            from  i in context.Invoices
```

to

```
var query = from  i in context.Invoices
            from  s in context.Stores
```

is the final result the same?

3. Write a query to show the purchase orders belonging to each store. In your output show the *branch* and *region* values of the *Store* table along with the *po_num* property of the *PurchaseOrder* table.
   A. Write this query using query syntax.
   B. Write this query using method-based syntax.
   C. Write this query using navigation properties.
4. Modify Example 17-2 so the *Invoices DBSet* applies the *Join()* extension method to obtain the same output.
5. Show all *mfg* and *mfgDiscount* values from the *Manufacturer* table along with their corresponding product *name* value from the *Product* table. Display manufacturer details, regardless of whether they have a related product in the *Product* table. An outer join is required to perform this query. Do this using LINQ.
6. In a one-to-many relationship, why is it not possible to create a full outer join with a union of two outer join queries that use navigation properties?
7. Using query syntax, perform a full outer join between the *Store* and *Building* tables. Show the *branch* and *region* values from the *Store* table and the *building_name* value from the *Building* table, regardless of whether or not the store has an associated *building_name* and regardless of whether or not a building is associated with a *Store branch*. Remember, the join needs to be done on the primary key, which is composed from the *building_name* and *unit_num* columns.
8. *ProductPurchaseOrder* is a bridge/junction table that associates data between *Product* and *PurchaseOrder* tables. *ProductPurchaseOrder* does not appear in the conceptual view of the Entity Data Model, but does appear in the database. Using the Server Explorer/Database Explorer, examine the data inside the *ProductPurchaseOrder* table to ensure that an entry with *productID* = 2 and *po_num* = 102 does not exist. Then, using LINQ with query syntax, insert *productID* = 2 and *po_num* = 102 to the *ProductPurchaseOrder* table. Iterate through the *ProductPurchaseOrder* table items to display the output to verify your new entry exists.
9. Using the Server Explorer/Database Explorer, browse the *ProductPurchaseOrder* table to ensure an entry with *productID* = 2 and *po_num* = 102 exists after completing question 8 in this chapter. Then, create a program to remove this bridge table entry. After removing the entry, iterate through the *ProductPurchaseOrder* table items to ensure this bridge table item has been removed.

Chapter 18

Traditional Database Development

Key Skills & Concepts

- .NET Classes for Managing Database Data
- Referencing Your Connection String in C#
- Memory-Based Database Management with the SqlDataAdapter Class
- Streaming Data with the SqlDataReader Class

This chapter discusses traditional .NET techniques for reading and managing database content with SQL and stored procedures. All examples in this chapter run using either the Microsoft SQL Server Database File or the Microsoft SQL Server version of the *FoodStore* database. While Microsoft databases are used for this material, the general methods presented here are universal for all mainstream relational databases.

SQL

To really appreciate how LINQ to Entities helps to automate development and to understand development alternatives, it is important to have a basic understanding about developing with SQL. SQL is a database scripting language that is used to create, read, insert, and delete database content. SQL (commonly pronounced "sequel") is an acronym for *structured query language*. You can build, manage, and query a database entirely with SQL. SQL executes on the database server. All database vendors have their own unique SQL syntax, but the basic syntax is similar for most vendors.

Prior to the existence of LINQ to Entities, C# developers working with database content would traditionally send SQL commands from their application for execution on the database. The Entity Framework, however, automatically generates and sends SQL to the database to perform the operation so, with the EF, you can avoid using SQL altogether. Even though C# developers now predominately use the Entity Framework to manage database content, there may be times when you will want to work with the SQL directly. You may wish to send SQL database commands from your applications when working with existing legacy systems. In other situations, you may just find it is easier to write your own SQL for really complex queries. At least be aware of this option since it can be helpful in some circumstances.

This book will not discuss how to write SQL since it is outside the C# framework. However, this chapter will demonstrate how to execute simple SQL commands from your C# applications. With the ability to run SQL from your code, you have full access to all of the privileges that are granted to your C# application user for managing and querying the database.

Stored Procedures

Stored procedures are routines, written in SQL, with optional parameters that encapsulate SQL. These routines execute when called by name. Stored procedures are created, stored, and executed on the database server. The syntax for stored procedures may vary significantly for each database vendor. Since stored procedures are outside the scope of the C# library, this book will not discuss stored procedures in detail, but this chapter and the LINQ chapters will show how to execute stored procedures from your C# code.

.NET Classes for Managing Database Data

Before discussing actual database manipulation from code, when executing SQL from your code, you will want to know about three C# classes that offer you dynamic structures to manage database content:

- DataTable
- DataColumn
- DataRow

These three classes are contained inside the *System.Data* namespace.

DataTable

The C# *DataTable* class stores the data returned from a database query. This class is popular with .NET developers because it integrates easily with several different C# libraries that support data-driven application development. A *DataTable* object structure is defined with the data column structures at design time or automatically from the database query results. When declaring a *DataTable* object, you can use the default constructor:

```
DataTable dt = new DataTable();
```

DataColumn

To define columns manually, you can use the *Add()* method of the *DataTable* object's *Columns* collection. The *Columns* collection stores *DataColumn* objects. The *DataColumn* class provides different options to define the column type and name. Here are two common overloads for adding columns to *DataTable* objects:

```
DataColumn Add(string columnName);              // define name only
DataColumn Add(string columnName, Type type); // define name and type
```

When defining the columns of your table, you need to add them in the order they appear in your data table from left to right.

```
DataTable dt = new DataTable();
dt.Columns.Add("ID",      typeof(int));          // define name and type
dt.Columns.Add("Title");                          // define name only
dt.Columns.Add("Salary", typeof(decimal));       // define name and type
```

The first column you add is automatically assigned an index value of zero. The second column has an index of one, the third column an index of two, and so on.

DataRow

After the columns of the *DataTable* are defined, you can then fill the table with data using the *Add()* method of the *Rows* collection. The type and sequence of values supplied to the *Add()* method must match the corresponding *DataTable* object definition of column sequence and type, if applicable:

```
dt.Rows.Add(1, "Manager", 65000m);
dt.Rows.Add(2, "Staff", 45000m);
```

Rows of the table can be accessed sequentially using a *foreach* loop:

```
foreach (DataRow row in dt.Rows) {
}
```

Each row of the *DataTable* can also be accessed with a numeric index:

```
for (int rowNum = 0; rowNum < dt.Rows.Count; rowNum++)
    DataRow row = dt.Rows[rowNum];
```

You can reference each cell within a row using either a numeric index for the row and column:

```
for (int row = 0; row < dt.Rows.Count; row++) {
    for (int col = 0; col < dt.Columns.Count; col++)
        Console.Write(dt.Rows[row][col]);
```

or a named reference for the column with a *DataRow* object:

```
foreach (DataRow row in dt.Rows)
    Console.WriteLine(row["Salary"]);
```

Example 18-1 Working with Data Tables, Columns, and Rows

The code in this example shows how to define a *DataTable* that contains salary information for different job roles. The data in the columns of the *DataTable* rows is displayed using a nested *foreach* loop, numeric indexes, and named references:

```
using System;
using System.Data;

namespace Starter {
    class Program {
        enum JobTitle { admin = 0, manager, staff };
        public static void Main() {
            // Define table.
            DataTable dt = new DataTable();
            dt.Columns.Add("ID",     typeof(int));
            dt.Columns.Add("Title");
            dt.Columns.Add("Salary", typeof(decimal));

            // Add rows containing data.
            dt.Rows.Add(JobTitle.manager, "Manager", 65000m);
            dt.Rows.Add(JobTitle.staff, "Staff", 45000m);

            // Show table contents.
            ShowTableUsingForEeach(dt);
            ShowTableUsingNumericIndex(dt);
            ShowTableWithNamedReference(dt);

            Console.ReadLine();
        }

        // Shows table data with named reference to each column.
        static void ShowTableWithNamedReference(DataTable dt) {
            const string ID     = "ID", TITLE  = "Title";
            const string SALARY = "Salary";

            foreach (DataRow row in dt.Rows) {
                Console.Write(row[ID] + " ");
                Console.Write(row[TITLE] + " ");
                Console.WriteLine(row[SALARY]);
            }
        }

        // Shows data in a nested foreach loop for DataRow and DataColumn.
        static void ShowTableUsingForEeach(DataTable dt) {
            foreach (DataRow row in dt.Rows) {
                foreach (DataColumn col in dt.Columns)
                    Console.Write(row[col] + " ");
                Console.WriteLine();
            }
```

```
            Console.WriteLine();
        }

        // Uses a numeric index to show all column values in each row.
        static void ShowTableUsingNumericIndex(DataTable dt) {
            for (int row = 0; row < dt.Rows.Count; row++) {
                for (int col = 0; col < dt.Columns.Count; col++)
                    Console.Write(dt.Rows[row][col] + " ");
                Console.WriteLine();
            }
            Console.WriteLine();
        }
    }
}
```

When the program runs, after defining the table and adding data to it, row values of the *DataTable* are printed three separate times, each with a different method of reference:

```
1 Manager 65000
2 Staff 45000

1 Manager 65000
2 Staff 45000

1 Manager 65000
2 Staff 45000
```

Try This 18-1 Constructing and Using Your Own DataTable

Here is an opportunity to practice working with data in a *DataTable* object.

1. Write a small program to declare a *DataTable* object to store the bank account data from the following table:

Last Name	First Name	Balance
Alfredson	Alfred	$101.01
Bezos	Bob	$202.02
Carerra	Carly	$303.03

2. After storing data in this new *DataTable* object, use a loop to iterate through the *DataTable* and display the contents of each row with a named reference.

Referencing Your Connection String in C#

Chapter 13 discussed how to create a connection string in the App.config file. When working with database content from your C# code, you need to reference this connection string in your C# code. To retrieve the connection string in your C# code from the App.config file, you can use the *ConnectionStrings* property of the *ConfigurationManager* class:

```
string connection =
        ConfigurationManager.ConnectionStrings["MyConnection"]
       .ConnectionString;
```

The *ConnectionStrings* property references the name attribute value, *MyConnection,* in one of the *add* elements within the *connectionStrings* element that is stored in the App .config file.

NOTE

For information on how to build the connection string named *MyConnection,* refer to Example 13-1 or Example 13-2 in Chapter 13.

The *ConfigurationManager* class is available through the *System.Configuration* namespace. This *System.Configuration* namespace, however, is not included in the default console application. If you wish to use this library reference, you must manually add it to your project. The steps on how to do this are explained next.

Example 18-2 Adding a Reference to the System.Configuration Library

In this example, you will manually add a reference to the library that contains the *System. Configuration* namespace. Depending on how you created your database connection to the *FoodStore* database, begin with the solution from either Example 13-1 or Example 13-2 in Chapter 13. Then, right-click the References folder in the Solution Explorer and select Add Reference from the drop-down menu. In the Reference Manager dialog that launches, expand the Assemblies node and select Framework (refer to Figure 18-1). Then, click OK when these steps are complete.

When you finish, you will see the *System.Configuration* listing in the References folder of your project (see Figure 18-2).

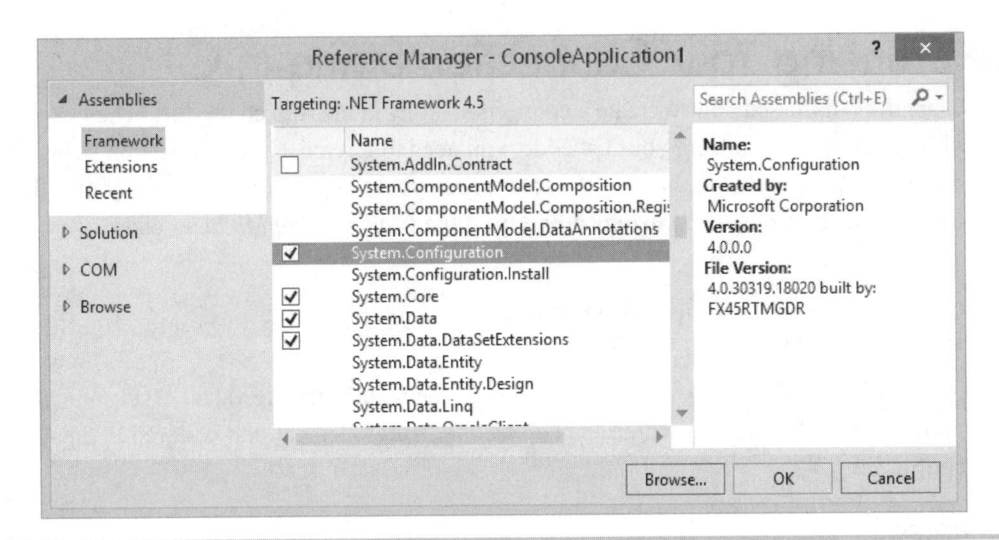

Figure 18-1 Adding a reference to the System.Configuration namespace

Now that your code project is configured, keep it handy. You will use this solution as the starting project for the next series of examples. Before you get to them, though, examine some of the classes used for managing database queries in C#.

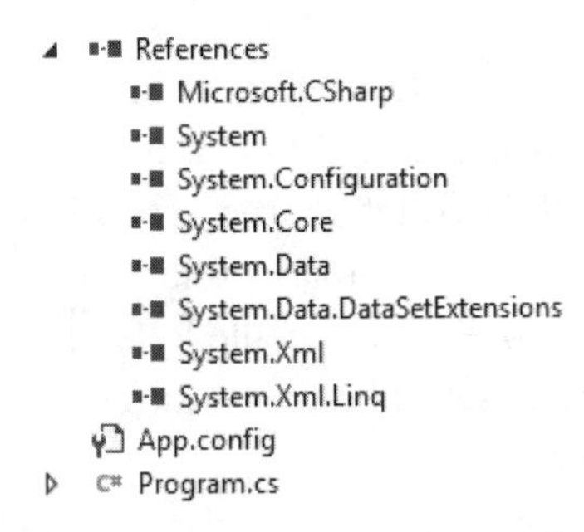

Figure 18-2 System.Configuration reference

Memory-Based Database Management with the SqlDataAdapter Class

The *SqlDataAdapter* class, from the *System.Data.SqlClient* namespace, is a popular C# class that enables the management of both SQL and stored procedure queries in memory.

Initializing a SqlDataAdapter Object

The override used in this book to declare and initialize a *SqlDataAdapter* object receives the SQL string or the stored procedure name and the connection string as parameters:

```
SqlDataAdapter sqlDataAdapter = new SqlDataAdapter (
                                    string procedureNameOrSQL,
                                    string connectionString);
```

Retrieving Data with the SqlDataAdapter Class

The *SqlDataAdapter* object is populated with the *Fill()* method. The *Fill()* method receives a *DataTable* object as a parameter, as shown next. *Fill()* populates the *DataTable* object with data returned from the SQL or stored procedure query. The integer returned by the *Fill()* method indicates how many rows were added to the object.

```
string connection = ConfigurationManager.ConnectionStrings["MyConnection"]
                    .ConnectionString;
SqlDataAdapter adapter = new SqlDataAdapter(sql, connection);
adapter.Fill(table);
```

Timing Out

SQL and stored procedure queries that are managed by a *SqlDataAdapter* object are referenced with the *SelectCommand* property. You have several options for setting and getting *SelectCommand* properties to regulate how the queries are run. You can assign the object's *SelectCommand.CommandTimeout* property (designated in seconds), as shown next, to define the total time the application will wait for a database response during a query. If the database does not respond within this time, the adapter terminates the query and throws an error. The default time is 30 seconds, but the time can be set to a different integer value.

```
int CommandTimeout { get; set; }
```

Example 18-3 Executing SQL with the SqlDataAdapter Class

This example demonstrates how to write C# code to retrieve all rows and columns of data from the *Product* table of the *FoodStore* database. The C# code obtains the data connection from the App.config file and stores it as a string. The connection string and a SQL script, "SELECT * FROM Product", are then passed to the *SqlDataAdapter* object during initialization. "SELECT * FROM Product" tells the database server to select all column values from all rows of the *Product* table. This SQL is sent to the database server for execution. A call to the *SqlDataAdapter* object's *Fill()* method retrieves query results in a *DataTable* object.

As an extra precaution, a try-catch block encloses code that reads the data connection, initializes the *SqlDataAdapter* object, and triggers the query. If an error occurs, the try-catch block prevents a program crash while offering a place to report on reasons why the crash occurred.

To begin this example, start with the solution from Example 18-2, which already contains both a connection string to the *FoodStore* database and the *System.Configuration* namespace reference. Then, replace all code contained in Program.cs with the following:

```
using System;
using System.Data;
using System.Data.SqlClient;
using System.Configuration;

namespace Starter {
    class Program {
        public static void Main() {
            DataTable dt = RunSQL("SELECT * FROM Product");
            ShowOutput(dt);
            Console.ReadLine();
        }

        // Get connection, initialize SqlDataAdapter, and get data.
        static DataTable RunSQL(string sql) {
            DataTable table = new DataTable();
            try {
                string connection
                = ConfigurationManager.ConnectionStrings["MyConnection"]
                                      .ConnectionString;
                SqlDataAdapter adapter = new SqlDataAdapter(sql, connection);
                adapter.Fill(table);
            }
            catch(Exception e) {
                Console.WriteLine("The SQL is either invalid or your "
                                + "connection failed.  Please check your "
```

```
                                + "App.config reference just in case: "
                                + e.Message);
            }
            return table;
        }

        // Iterate through DataTable rows and columns to show data.
        static void ShowOutput(DataTable dt) {
            if (dt == null) {
                Console.WriteLine("Empty dataset: Check your SQL.");
                return;
            }
            foreach (DataRow row in dt.Rows) {
                foreach (DataColumn col in dt.Columns)
                    Console.Write(row[col].ToString() + ", ");
                Console.WriteLine();
            }
        }
    }
}
```

The output from running the application shows database content for all items in the *Product* table:

```
1, Cake Mix, Duncan Hines, Sysco, 2.9900,
2, Cookie Dough, Duncan Hines, Sysco, 1.2500,
3, Orange Juice, Florida Orange, GFS, 4.2500,
4, Cookie Dough, Pillsbury, GFS, 1.4500,
5, Carrots, Hot House, GFS, 1.0100,
```

Try This 18-2 Executing SQL from Your C# Code

For practice, try running some different SQL to query the *FoodStore* database:

1. Modify the SQL in Example 18-3 to select all items from the *Store* table. The required SQL statement is "SELECT * FROM Store", which means retrieve all column values in all rows of the *Store* table.
2. Compare the results from your query of the *Store* table in the last step with the *Store* table data that appears in the Server Explorer/Database Explorer. See Chapter 13, Example 13-3, to review steps on how to browse table data with the Server Explorer/Database Explorer.

Managing Stored Procedures with the SqlDataAdapter Class

This section discusses how to execute stored procedures on the database from your code. When using the *SqlDataAdapter* class to run stored procedures directly from code, all of the steps previously discussed for preparing the *SqlDataAdapter* object are required. However, extra configuration is needed to manage stored procedures.

Setting the CommandType Property

The *CommandType* property of the *SqlDataAdapter* class defines the type of query. By default, the *SqlDataAdapter* object is set to execute raw SQL strings. However, when executing stored procedures, the *SqlDataAdapter* object's *CommandType* property must be set to *CommandType.StoredProcedure*:

```
sqlDataAdapter.SelectCommand.CommandType = CommandType.StoredProcedure;
```

Initializing Procedure Parameters

When a stored procedure has parameters, the *SqlParameter* class defines the stored procedure parameter:

```
SqlParameter sqlParameter
    = new SqlParameter(string paramName, string paramValue));
```

SqlParameter objects are attached with the *Parameters.Add()* method:

```
sqlDataAdapter.SelectCommand.Parameters.Add(
    new SqlParameter(string paramName, string paramValue));
```

Example 18-4 Executing Stored Procedures with the SqlDataAdapter Class

This example shows how to execute both raw SQL and two stored procedures already contained in the *FoodStore* database. First, let's examine the CREATE statements for the two stored procedures used in the example. The first stored procedure, *spProductDetail,* receives two parameters, and the second stored procedure, *spGetAllProducts,* receives no parameters:

```
CREATE PROCEDURE spProductDetail (@name VARCHAR(25), @vendor VARCHAR(25))
    AS SELECT * FROM Product WHERE @name = name
    AND @vendor = vendor;
    GO

CREATE PROCEDURE spGetAllProducts
    AS SELECT * FROM Product;
    GO
```

```
◢ C# ConsoleApplication1
  ▷ Properties
  ▷ References
  ◢ DataAccesssLayer
    ▷ C# DBCommands.cs
    ▷ C# DBEngine.cs
    App.config
  ▷ C# Program.cs
```

Figure 18-3 SqlDataAdapter project structure

To build this example, start with the solution for Example 18-2 since it already contains references to the database and *System.Configuration* namespace. Next, to separate your database logic from your main program, create a folder called DataAccessLayer and then add the files DBCommands.cs and DBEngine.cs to it (see Figure 18-3).

The code inside DBEngine.cs sets up a *SqlDataAdapter* object to run SQL and all stored procedures with and without parameters. It admittedly is a lot of code, but the upside is you can execute any stored procedure or SQL statement with it. Replace any auto-generated code that may exist inside the file DBEngine.cs with the following code. The comments inside the code highlight the role of each method.

```
using System;
using System.Configuration;
using System.Data;
using System.Data.SqlClient;
namespace Starter.DataAccessLayer {
    public class DBEngine {
        // Build the C# adapter for the database command and connection.
        static SqlDataAdapter Adapter(string command) {
            SqlDataAdapter adapter = null;
            try {
                string connection =
                ConfigurationManager.ConnectionStrings["MyConnection"]

                                    .ConnectionString;
                adapter = new SqlDataAdapter(command, connection);
                adapter.SelectCommand.CommandTimeout = 10;
            }
            catch(Exception e) {
                Console.WriteLine("A database connection error occurred. "
                                + "Please check your App.config settings:  "
                                + e.Message);
            }
            return adapter;
        }
```

```
// Add parameter names and values to the stored procedure adapter.
static SqlDataAdapter AddParameters(SqlDataAdapter adapter,
                     string[] parameters, string[] values) {
    if (parameters == null && values == null)
        return adapter;
    else if (parameters.Length != values.Length) {
        Console.WriteLine("Error: " +
        "Total procedure parameter names and values do not match");
        return null;
    }
    for (int i = 0; i < values.Length; i++) {
        adapter.SelectCommand.Parameters.Add(
            new SqlParameter(parameters[i], values[i]));
    }
    return adapter;
}

// Build a SqlDataAdapter for a stored procedure.
static SqlDataAdapter ProcedureAdapter(string procedure,
                  string[] parameters, string[] values) {

    SqlDataAdapter adapter = Adapter(procedure);

    if (adapter == null)
        return null;

    adapter.SelectCommand.CommandType
            = CommandType.StoredProcedure;
    adapter = AddParameters(
                adapter, parameters, values);
    return adapter;
}

// Run the SQL or stored procedure and store results in a DataTable
static DataTable RunCommand(SqlDataAdapter adapter) {
    if (adapter == null)
        return null;
    DataTable table = new DataTable();
    try{
        adapter.Fill(table);
    }
    catch (Exception exception) {
        Console.Write("An error occurred while running the ");
        Console.Write("SQL or stored procedure: ");
        Console.WriteLine(exception.Message);
        return null;
    }
    return table;
}

// Execute stored procedure that has no parameters.
```

```
        public static DataTable ExecParameterlessProcedure(
                                            string procedure) {
            return RunCommand(ProcedureAdapter(procedure, null, null));
        }

        // Execute stored procedure that has parameters.
        public static DataTable ExecProcedure(string name,
                        string[] parameters, string[] values) {
            return RunCommand(ProcedureAdapter(name, parameters, values));
        }

        // Execute SQL.
        public static DataTable ExecSQL(string sql) {
            return RunCommand(Adapter(sql));
        }
    }
}
```

Next, to set up routines that use the *DBEngine* class to execute specific stored procedures or SQL, replace the existing code inside DBCommands.cs with the following code. Each method in the *DBCommands* class defines a SQL or stored procedure command, executes it, and returns results in a *DataTable* object.

```
using System;
using System.Data;

namespace Starter.DataAccessLayer {
    class DBCommands {
        // Execute a stored procedure that has no parameters.
        public static DataTable SpGetAllProducts() {
            return DBEngine.ExecParameterlessProcedure(
                            "spGetAllProducts");
        }

        // Execute a stored procedure that has parameters.
        public static DataTable SpProductDetail(string name,
                                                string vendor) {
            string[] parameterNames  =  { "@name", "@vendor" };
            string[] parameterValues =  { name, vendor };
            return DBEngine.ExecProcedure( "spProductDetail",
                                        parameterNames, parameterValues);
        }

        // Run raw SQL using a parameter.
        public static DataTable RunSQL(string sql) {
            return DBEngine.ExecSQL(sql);
        }
    }
}
```

Next, replace the auto-generated code inside Program.cs with the following code to reference the *DataAccessLayer* namespace for running queries against the database from the *Main()* method:

```
using System;
using System.Data;
using Starter.DataAccessLayer;

namespace Starter {
    class Program {
        static void ShowOutput(DataTable dt) {
            if (dt == null)
                return;

            foreach (DataRow row in dt.Rows) {
                foreach (DataColumn col in dt.Columns) {
                    Console.Write(row[col].ToString() + ", ");
                }
                Console.WriteLine();
            }
            Console.WriteLine();
        }

        public static void Main() {
            ShowOutput(DBCommands.SpGetAllProducts());
            ShowOutput(DBCommands.SpProductDetail("Orange Juice",
                                                  "GFS"));
            ShowOutput(DBCommands.RunSQL("SELECT * FROM Product"));
            Console.ReadLine();
        }
    }
}
```

When you run the program, the output from each of the different commands is displayed in the window:

```
1, Cake Mix, Duncan Hines, Sysco, 2.9900,
2, Cookie Dough, Duncan Hines, Sysco, 1.2500,
3, Orange Juice, Florida Orange, GFS, 4.2500,
4, Cookie Dough, Pillsbury, GFS, 1.4500,
5, Carrots, Hot House, GFS, 1.0100,

3, Orange Juice, Florida Orange, GFS, 4.2500,

1, Cake Mix, Duncan Hines, Sysco, 2.9900,
```

```
2, Cookie Dough, Duncan Hines, Sysco, 1.2500,
3, Orange Juice, Florida Orange, GFS, 4.2500,
4, Cookie Dough, Pillsbury, GFS, 1.4500,
5, Carrots, Hot House, GFS, 1.0100,
```

Streaming Data with the SqlDataReader Class

Whenever your C# application runs really large database queries, you may prefer or need to use the *SqlDataReader* class instead of the *SqlDataAdapter* class. Like the *SqlDataAdapter* class, the *SqlDataReader* class is also part of the *System.Data.SqlClient* namespace. A *SqlDataReader* object, however, executes database queries row by row, so it is less memory intensive. This process of reading row by row is called *streaming*. Streaming with the *SqlDataReader* class allows you to read data in a forward-only manner, so you don't have the same flexibility to navigate a data set as easily when compared with the *SqlDataAdapter* class. Another challenge with the *SqlDataReader* class is that opening, using, and closing the connection requires extra work compared to the *SqlDataAdapter* class, which has some of these steps automated.

Managing the Database Connection

When using the *SqlDataReader* class, you have to manually manage the database connection. A *SqlConnection* class is used for this task. To initialize the *SqlConnection* object, provide the connection string as a parameter to the constructor, as shown next. Once the *SqlConnection* object is initialized, you then have to call the *SqlConnection* object's *Open()* method before running the query.

```
// Get connection string from App.config.
string connection = ConfigurationManager
                    .ConnectionStrings["MyConnection"]
                    .ConnectionString;
// Initialize and open SqlConnection object.
SqlConnection sqlConnection = new SqlConnection(connection);
sqlConnection.Open();
```

Initializing the Command

The *SqlDataReader* class uses the *SqlCommand* class to execute both raw SQL and stored procedures. When used with the *SqlDataReader* class, the *SqlCommand* object is initialized with either the SQL string or the procedure name and the *SqlConnection* object as parameters:

```
SqlCommand sqlCommand = new SqlCommand("spGetAllProducts", sqlConnection);
```

Retrieving Data with the SqlDataReader Class

After initializing the *SqlCommand* object with an open database connection, the *SqlCommand* object's *ExecuteReader()* method is called to return a *SqlDataReader* object:

```
SqlDataReader reader = sqlCommand.ExecuteReader();
```

The *Read()* method of the *SqlDataReader* object enables iteration through the rows of data that are returned from the command. In this first example, each column of the query is referenced using the column name:

```
while (sqlDataReader.Read()) {
    string  stringVar  = (string) reader["name"];
    int     numberVar  = (int)    reader["productID"];
}
```

In the next example, a numeric index references each column of the data set:

```
while (sqlDataReader.Read()) {
    for (int i = 0; i < reader.FieldCount; i++) {
        Console.Write( reader[i].ToString() + "  " );
    }
    Console.WriteLine();
}
```

Closing the SqlDataReader and SqlConnection Objects

Once you finish reading with the *SqlDataReader* object, call its *Close()* method to free up resources that are accessed by the object. Also, when the read is finished, call the *Close()* method of the *SqlConnection* object for the same reason.

```
if(sqlDataReader != null)
    sqlDataReader.Close();
if(sqlConnection != null)
    sqlConnection.Close();
```

Example 18-5 Executing SQL with the SqlDataReader Class

Here is a simple example that uses the *SqlDataReader* class to stream data. The *SqlDataReader* object is first initialized with an opened *SqlConnection* object and SQL string, "SELECT * FROM Product", as parameters. Then, the *SqlDataReader* object sends the SQL query to the database for execution. This SQL query tells the database to select all values in all rows of the *Product* table. The reader retrieves a row from the database just before printing the columns contained in it. To help detect any issues with the data connection or query execution, try-catch blocks are used to trap errors and to prevent the program from crashing.

To start this example, begin with the solution for Example 18-2. Replace all code in Program.cs with the following:

```
using System;
using System.Data.SqlClient;
using System.Configuration;

namespace Starter {
    class Reader {
        SqlConnection        sqlConnection;
        public SqlDataReader Sdr { get; private set; }

        // Build SqlCommand for SQL only and run it.
        public void RunSQL(string sql) {
            Sdr = ExecuteReader(new SqlCommand(sql, OpenConnection()));
        }

        // Run the SqlDataReader and show errors if failure occurs.
        public SqlDataReader ExecuteReader(SqlCommand command) {
            try {
                return command.ExecuteReader();
            }
            catch (Exception e) {
                Console.WriteLine(e.Message);
            }
            return null;
        }

        // Open the connection and show errors if failure occurs.
        public SqlConnection OpenConnection() {
            try {
                string connection = ConfigurationManager
                      .ConnectionStrings["MyConnection"].ConnectionString;
                sqlConnection = new SqlConnection(connection);
                sqlConnection.Open();
            }
            catch(Exception e) {
                Console.WriteLine("Data connection failed: "
                                + "Check the App.config reference. "
                                + e.Message);
            }
            return sqlConnection;
        }

        public void CloseReaderAndConnection() {
            if (Sdr != null)
                Sdr.Close();
            if (sqlConnection != null)
```

```
                sqlConnection.Close();
            }
        }

        class Program {
            public static void Main() {
                Reader reader = new Reader();
                reader.RunSQL("SELECT * FROM Product");
                ShowOutput(reader);
                Console.ReadLine();
            }

            static void ShowOutput(Reader reader) {
                // Retrieve and display rows from database one-by-one.
                while (reader.Sdr!=null && reader.Sdr.Read()) {
                    // Reference database columns by name.
                    int     id          = (int)reader.Sdr["productID"];
                    string  productName = (string) reader.Sdr["name"];
                    decimal price       = (decimal)reader.Sdr["price"];
                    Console.WriteLine("ID: " + id  + "   Name: " + productName
                                    + "   Price: " + price.ToString("C"));
                }
                // Close the reader so you can reopen and use it later.
                if(reader != null)
                    reader.CloseReaderAndConnection();
            }
        }
    }
```

Selected column values from the *Product* table are printed after each row is retrieved with the *SqlDataReader* object:

```
ID: 1   Name: Cake Mix    Price: $2.99
ID: 2   Name: Cookie Dough    Price: $1.25
ID: 3   Name: Orange Juice    Price: $4.25
ID: 4   Name: Cookie Dough    Price: $1.45
ID: 5   Name: Carrots    Price: $1.01
```

Managing Stored Procedures with the SqlDataReader Class

In addition to the steps already discussed in this chapter for initializing a *SqlDataReader* object, extra steps are needed to prepare the *SqlDataReader* object for running stored procedures, as discussed in this section.

The *CommandType* property defines the type of query. By default, the *SqlCommand* object executes SQL strings. However, to prepare a *SqlCommand* object to execute stored procedures, you must set the *CommandType* property to *CommandType.StoredProcedure*:

```
sqlCommand.CommandType = CommandType.StoredProcedure;
```

When executing a stored procedure with parameters, the *SqlParameter* class allows you to define a stored procedure parameter to store the parameter name and corresponding argument value:

```
SqlParameter sqlParameter  = new SqlParameter(paramName, paramValue));
```

To define the *SqlDataReader* object to run a stored procedure that has one or more parameters, attach each *SqlParameter* object to the *SqlCommand* object with the *Parameters.Add()* method:

```
sqlCommand.Parameters.Add(new SqlParameter(parameterName, parameterValue));
```

The reader is then generated with the *SqlCommand* object's *ExecuteReader()* method:

```
SqlDataReader sqlDataReader = sqlCommand.ExecuteReader();
```

Example 18-6 Executing Stored Procedures with the SqlDataReader Class

This example combines the *SqlDataReader* structures and supporting classes to stream queries from the database. This program implements the same SQL and stored procedure queries that were run in Example 18-4. This time, though, the *SqlDataReader* object returns the data set row by row rather than as one *DataTable* object.

To begin, start with Example 18-2, then create the folder and file structure shown in Figure 18-4.

The *ReaderEngine* class in this example creates a database connection, opens it, builds the *SqlCommand* object, and executes the command. Options are provided in the code to build the *SqlCommand* to either execute raw SQL or a stored procedure, with or without

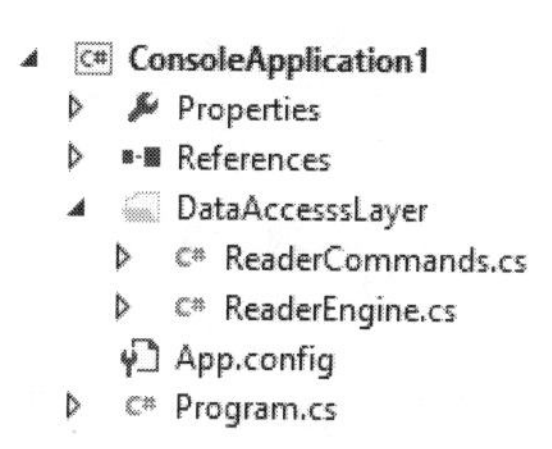

Figure 18-4 SqlDataReader class project structure

parameters. A *SqlDataReader* object is returned by the *ReaderEngine* class from the *ExecuteReader()* method.

```
using System;
using System.Data;
using System.Data.SqlClient;
using System.Configuration;

namespace Starter.DataAccessLayer {
    public class ReaderEngine {
        SqlConnection sqlConnection;

        // Open the connection.
        SqlConnection OpenConnection() {
            try {
                string connection  = ConfigurationManager
                        .ConnectionStrings["MyConnection"]
                        .ConnectionString;
                sqlConnection = new SqlConnection(connection);
                sqlConnection.Open();
            }
            catch (Exception e) {
                Console.Write("An error occurred with the data ");
                Console.Write("connection.  Please check the App.config");
                Console.Write(" reference and ensure the connection ");
                Console.WriteLine("is already open "+ e.Message);
                return null;
            }
            return sqlConnection;
        }
        // Close database connection.
        public void CloseConnection() {
            if (sqlConnection != null)
                sqlConnection.Close();
        }
        // Build SqlCommand for stored procedure.
        SqlCommand ProcedureCommand(string   procedure,
                                    string[] parameterNames,
                                    string[] parameterValues) {
            SqlCommand command  = new SqlCommand(procedure,
                                                 OpenConnection());
            command.CommandType = CommandType.StoredProcedure;

            // Return SqlCommand object as is for parameterless procedure.
            if (parameterNames == null && parameterValues == null)
                return command;

            // Add parameters to SqlCommand for procedures with parameters.
            for (int i = 0; i < parameterValues.Length; i++) {
                command.Parameters.Add(
```

```
                    new SqlParameter(parameterNames[i],
                                     parameterValues[i]));
            }
            return command;
        }
        // Execute the command.
        SqlDataReader ExecuteReader(SqlCommand command) {
            try{
                return command.ExecuteReader();
            }
            // If there are errors show them.
            catch (Exception e) {
                Console.WriteLine(e.Message);
            }
            return null;
        }
        // Build SqlCommand for SQL only and run it.
        public SqlDataReader ExecSQL(string sqlString) {
            return ExecuteReader(new SqlCommand(sqlString,
                                                OpenConnection()));
        }
        // Execute procedure without parameters.
        public SqlDataReader ExecParameterlessProcedure(string procedure) {
            SqlCommand command = ProcedureCommand(procedure, null, null);
            return ExecuteReader(command);
        }
        // Execute procedure with parameters.
        public SqlDataReader ExecProcedure(string   procedure,
                                           string[] parameterNames,
                                           string[] parameterValues) {
            SqlCommand command = ProcedureCommand(procedure,
                                                  parameterNames,
                                                  parameterValues);
            return ExecuteReader(command);
        }
    }
}
```

The *ReaderCommands* class contains methods for executing SQL and stored procedures through a reference to the *ReaderEngine* class. A separate method assembles the parameters required for each SQL query or stored procedure and returns the *SqlDataReader* object needed to perform the iterative read. To run a command, an instance of the *ReaderCommands* class opens the connection, executes the desired command, and returns a reader object. A *CloseReaderAndConnection()* method also exists in the class, so it can be called separately to perform cleanup when you are finished with the reader.

```
using System;
using System.Data;
using System.Data.SqlClient;
```

```
namespace Starter.DataAccessLayer {
    class ReaderCommands {
        public SqlDataReader Reader { get; private set; }
        ReaderEngine readerEngine;

        public ReaderCommands() {
             readerEngine = new ReaderEngine();
        }
        // Execute procedure with no parameters.
        public void SpGetAllProducts() {
            Reader
            = readerEngine.ExecParameterlessProcedure("spGetAllProducts");
        }
        // Execute procedure with parameters.
        public void SpProductDetail(string name, string vendor) {
            const string NAME          =    "spProductDetail";
            string[] parameterNames  = { "@name", "@vendor" };
            string[] parameterValues = { name, vendor };
            Reader = readerEngine.ExecProcedure(NAME, parameterNames,
                                                    parameterValues);
        }
        // Run SQL only.
        public void RunSQL(string sql) {
            Reader = readerEngine.ExecSQL(sql);
        }
        public void CloseReaderAndConnection() {
            if (Reader != null)
                Reader.Close();
            if(readerEngine != null)
                readerEngine.CloseConnection();
        }
    }
}
```

With the supporting structure for executing database commands in place, you can now replace the code in Program.cs with the revised code that follows to trigger the stored procedures and SQL. Inside *ShowOutput()*, the *SqlDataReader* object named Reader iterates through the rows of data that are returned from the command.

```
using System;
using Starter.DataAccessLayer;
using System.Data.SqlClient;

namespace Starter {
    class Program {
        public static void Main() {
            ReaderCommands rc;

            // Execute a stored procedure with no parameters.
            rc = new ReaderCommands();
```

```
            rc.SpGetAllProducts();
            ShowOutput(rc);

            // Execute a stored procedure with parameters.
            rc = new ReaderCommands();
            rc.SpProductDetail("Orange Juice", "GFS");
            ShowOutput(rc);

            // Execute SQL.
            rc = new ReaderCommands();
            rc.RunSQL("SELECT * FROM Product");
            ShowOutput(rc);
            Console.ReadLine();
        }
        static void ShowOutput(ReaderCommands rc) {
            // Retrieve and display rows from database one-by-one.
            while (rc.Reader != null && rc.Reader.Read()) {
                // Reference database columns by name.
                int    id           = (int)rc.Reader["productID"];
                string productName  = (string) rc.Reader["name"];
                string manufacturer = (string) rc.Reader["mfg"];
                string vendor       = (string) rc.Reader["vendor"];
                decimal price       = (decimal)rc.Reader["price"];
                Console.WriteLine(id + ", " + productName + ", "
                                + manufacturer + ", "  + vendor + ", "
                                + price.ToString("C"));
            }
            rc.CloseReaderAndConnection();
            Console.WriteLine();
        }
    }
}
```

The output from this program shows data that is retrieved after executing two stored procedures and one raw SQL command:

```
1, Cake Mix, Duncan Hines, Sysco, $2.99
2, Cookie Dough, Duncan Hines, Sysco, $1.25
3, Orange Juice, Florida Orange, GFS, $4.25
4, Cookie Dough, Pillsbury, GFS, $1.45
5, Carrots, Hot House, GFS, $1.01

3, Orange Juice, Florida Orange, GFS, $4.25

1, Cake Mix, Duncan Hines, Sysco, $2.99
2, Cookie Dough, Duncan Hines, Sysco, $1.25
3, Orange Juice, Florida Orange, GFS, $4.25
4, Cookie Dough, Pillsbury, GFS, $1.45
5, Carrots, Hot House, GFS, $1.01
```

Chapter 18 Self Test

The following questions are intended to help reinforce your comprehension of the concepts covered in this chapter. The answers can be found in the accompanying online Appendix B, "Answers to the Self Tests."

1. When you are creating a *DataTable* object to store data manually, which step must you take first—define rows or define columns? Explain your answer.
2. Create a *DataTable* object that stores the following years and detail for important medical discoveries: ("1895, X-Ray"; "1921, Isolation of insulin"; "1928, Penicillin").
3. What assembly must be added to your procedure to reference the *System.Configuration* namespace? Why do you need this namespace reference in Example 18-3?
4. A. For Example 18-3, modify the *ConnectionStrings* reference inside *RunSQL()* from

   ```
   string connection =
   ConfigurationManager.ConnectionStrings["MyConnection"].ConnectionString;
   ```

   to

   ```
   string connection =
   ConfigurationManager.ConnectionStrings["NewConnection"].ConnectionString;
   ```

   What message is printed to the console from the try-catch block?

   B. After making the change in part A, what change could you make in the App.config file to fix your project?
5. What change must you make to Example 18-3 so that the program retrieves and displays all data from the *Employee* table?
6. Modify Example 18-3 so the code in *ShowOutput()* only uses named references to access column data from the *Product* data table. You can view all official column names of the *Product* table in the Server Explorer/Database Explorer.
7. Compare the advantages and disadvantages of the *SqlDataAdapter* class versus the *SqlDataReader* class.
8. When the *FoodStore* database was created, a stored procedure named *spFindProduct* was created with the following script:

   ```
   CREATE PROCEDURE spFindProduct(@productID INT) AS
       SELECT productID, name, price FROM Product
       WHERE productID = @productID;
       GO
   ```

Modify the DBCommands.cs file for Example 18-4 to include a method that executes the *spFindProduct* stored procedure with the help of the *SqlDataAdapter* class. Since the stored procedure is triggered with a text-based command, your new method in DBCommands.cs must convert the *productID* to a string value and store it in the string array that is passed to the *ExecProcedure()* method. Call your new method from the *Main()* method inside Program.cs to execute *spFindProduct* and to display product details for the product with a *productID* of 1.

9. Modify the ReaderCommands.cs file for Example 18-5 to include a method that executes the *spFindProduct* stored procedure, shown in question 8, with the help of the *SqlDataReader* class. Since the stored procedure is triggered by text, in your new method, you will need to convert the *productID* value to a string and include it in the string array that is passed to the *ExecProcedure()* method. Then, call this new method from the *Main()* method inside Program.cs to execute *spFindProduct* and to display product details for the product with a *productID* of 1. Since all columns of the *Product* table are not present in the result set from *spFindProduct,* you will need to also adjust the *ShowOutput()* method.

Chapter 19

File Input Output

Key Skills & Concepts

- Writing and Reading Plain Text
- Writing and Reading Binary Data
- Reading Buffered Binary Data
- Randomly Accessing Binary Data

This chapter offers a simple introduction to writing and reading file content. The techniques presented vary depending on data format, accessibility, and performance requirements.

Writing and Reading Plain Text

It is likely you will want to read and write human-readable text from many of your applications. Your reasons for doing this could include tasks ranging from logging activity, initializing components of your application from a flat file, and managing simple but persistent data without a database, to creating or even reading spreadsheet data with a delimited format. C# provides the *StreamWriter* and *StreamReader* classes from the *System.IO* namespace to help.

NOTE

Throughout the discussion you will notice several references to data streams. A stream is like a river that is connected to a data source. Data flows through the stream to the destination. The data may be converted to another format by the time it reaches its destination.

StreamWriter

The *StreamWriter* class offers methods to write text to a file. Files that are written in this manner can be read with a simple text editor such as Microsoft Notepad. To initialize the *StreamWriter* object, you can specify the file path with a constructor parameter, as shown next. You may also include a Boolean parameter in one of the constructor overloads to indicate whether you wish to append data to an existing file or overwrite the file contents.

Whenever the *StreamWriter* object is created, if the file in the path specified does not exist, a new file is created.

```
const bool APPEND = true; // Create or add to file.
StreamWriter   sw = new StreamWriter(path, APPEND);
```

NOTE

By default, files are written to the same directory as the application executable. This default location is usually one directory above the bin\Debug directory of your project folder. The substring "../" within a file path means move up one directory.

The *Write()* method of the *StreamWriter* class outputs text while leaving the file pointer on the same line in the file. The *WriteLine()* method, on the other hand, outputs text and advances to a new line in the file. This example uses the *WriteLine()* and *Write()* methods to output content to a file:

```
sw.WriteLine("I say hello."); // Write and go to new line.
sw.Write("You say ");         // Write but leave file pointer at end of line.
sw.WriteLine("good-bye.");    // Write and go to new line.
```

When the previous instructions are implemented with a *StreamWriter* object named *sw*, the output from these instructions would appear in the file as

```
I say hello.
You say good-bye.
```

After writing output, calling the *StreamWriter* object's *Close()* method releases the file so that it can be used by another process:

```
sw.Close();
```

Alternatively, and preferably, you can put the *StreamWriter* object declaration in a *using* statement. With a *using* block, you do not have to manually close the *StreamWriter* object. The *StreamWriter* instance is closed and the file is automatically released for you when the program exits the code block:

```
const bool      APPEND = true;
const string FILE_PATH = "../../fileName.txt"; // 2 folders above bin folder.
using (StreamWriter sw = new StreamWriter(path, APPEND)) {
    // Output contents to file.
}
```

Example 19-1 Outputting to a Text File or Spreadsheet

This example demonstrates how to use the *StreamWriter* class to output comma-separated values to a file that can be read by a simple text editor or by a spreadsheet application such as Microsoft Excel. For this case, budget data is written in comma-separated format to a file named Budget.csv.

```
using System;
using System.IO;

namespace Starter {
    class Program {
        public static void Main() {
            const string FILE_PATH = "../../Budget.csv";
            WriteToFile(FILE_PATH);    // File path and name is two
            Console.ReadLine();        // directories above the 'bin' folder.
        }
        static void WriteToFile(string path) {
            const bool APPEND = true; // Create or add to existing file.
            try {
                // Create writer to add or append to a file.
                using (StreamWriter sw = new StreamWriter(path, !APPEND)) {
                    sw.WriteLine("Category, Transaction Amount, Balance");
                    sw.WriteLine("Food, 123.45, 220.98");
                    sw.WriteLine("Phone, 40.00, 180.98");
                }
            }
            catch (Exception e) { // Show error detail if any.
                Console.WriteLine("Write error:  " + e.Message);
            }
        }
    }
}
```

When running the application, a file named Budget.csv is written in the same directory where the code files of your project are located. This folder is the parent directory to the bin\Debug directory. The file generated contains readable text so it can be opened in Microsoft Notepad or any basic text editor. As well, since the file extension is .csv and the file contents are comma-separated values, you can view the contents in Microsoft Excel or any freeware spreadsheet application (see Figure 19-1).

StreamReader

Chances are, in addition to writing text to external files, you will want to be able to read text into your application from external files. The *StreamReader* class provides methods to

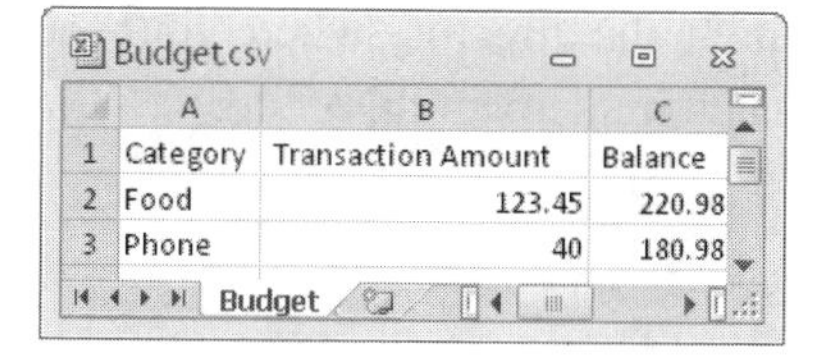

	A	B	C
1	Category	Transaction Amount	Balance
2	Food	123.45	220.98
3	Phone	40	180.98

Figure 19-1 Viewing .csv file contents in Microsoft Excel

do this, and they are easy to use. When creating a *StreamReader* object, the file location is specified as a string parameter of the constructor.

```
const string FILE_PATH = "../../Budget.csv";
StreamReader         sr = new StreamReader(FILE_PATH);
```

To help, the *StreamReader* object's *ReadLine()* method reads a single line of text and advances the file pointer to the start of the next line. If desired, you can also use the *Read()* method to read one character at a time. The *EndOfStream* Boolean property indicates if the end of the file has been reached. This example shows how the reader might iterate through a file and read content one line at a time until the end of the file:

```
sr = new StreamReader(filePath);
while (!sr.EndOfStream) {                    // When not at the file end
    string line = sr.ReadLine();             // read a new line.
}
```

When finished reading from a text file, the *StreamReader* object's *Close()* method must be called to release the file so it can be freed up for use in another process if needed:

```
sr.Close();
```

Similar to the *StreamWriter* class, you may consider placing the *StreamReader* object declaration inside a *using* statement instead. Once the program leaves the *using* block, the *StreamReader* object is closed and the file is released.

Example 19-2 Reading Text from a File

This example reads from the Budget.csv file that was created in Example 19-1. The reading is done line by line until the end of the file and each string is displayed in the console. The purpose of the example is to show that it is easy to load spreadsheet data that is stored in a comma-separated format. The comma-separated data is then split into an array, and each array value is also displayed in the console. To begin, create a new console application and copy the Budget.csv file to the directory where your source files are located in your new console application. Then implement this code:

```
using System;
using System.IO;

namespace Starter {
    class Program {
        public static void Main() {
            const string FILE_PATH = "../../Budget.csv";
            ReadFromFile(FILE_PATH); // File path and name is 2 directories
            Console.ReadLine();      // above the project 'bin' folder.
        }
        static void ReadFromFile(string filePath) {
            try {
                using (StreamReader sr = new StreamReader(filePath)) {
                    while (!sr.EndOfStream) {         // If not at file end
                        string line = sr.ReadLine(); // read a new line.
                        Console.WriteLine("Entire line:   "
                                          + line);          // Show line.
                        string[] contents = line.Split(','); // Fill array.
                        Console.Write("Array values: ");
                        foreach (string data in contents)    // Show array.
                            Console.Write(data + " * ");
                        Console.WriteLine("\n");
                    }
                }
            }
            catch(Exception e) { // Show error detail if any.
                Console.WriteLine("Read error:  " + e.Message);
            }
        }
    }
}
```

The output shows each line of the file followed by data from the array:

```
Entire line:  Category, Transaction Amount, Balance
Array values: Category *  Transaction Amount *  Balance *

Entire line:  Food, 123.45, 220.98
Array values: Food *  123.45 *  220.98 *

Entire line:  Phone, 40.00, 180.98
Array values: Phone *  40.00 *  180.98 *
```

Try This 19-1 Writing, Reading, and Extracting Text Data

This is an opportunity to see firsthand how easy it is to write and read text data, which can also be viewed using a spreadsheet application.

1. Starting with a new console application, write the following text content to a file called Sales.csv:

```
Monthly Sales,Amount
August,23333.25
September,18323.22
October,13344.23
```

2. After writing, close your *StreamWriter* object to release the file.
3. Open the file for reading with the *StreamReader* class.
4. As you read each line, split the contents into an array.
5. Convert the numeric values to decimal objects and keep a cumulative sum.
6. Output the sum of the sales figures for August, September, and October once you calculate this value from the data that is read back into the application.
7. Check to ensure you can open the Sales.csv application with a spreadsheet application such as Microsoft Excel.

Writing and Reading Binary Data

Binary data is digitally encoded data. You cannot read this type of content with a simple text editor. However, the binary format is more machine friendly than raw text because it is more easily read, stored, transferred, and modified by your computer system. Also, since binary data is measured in bytes, the binary format offers significant flexibility for direct access to any portion of the data. In addition to these efficiencies gained, the binary format allows you to create your own proprietary file types, which you can optimize for performance and storage space. Let's now look at how the libraries in the *System.IO* namespace can help you manage your binary content.

Enumerator	Detail	Enumerator	Detail
Append	Opens existing file or creates new one and adds content to the end of it.	Open	Opens existing file and throws an error if it does not exist.
Create	Creates a new file or overwrites an existing file.	OpenOrCreate	Opens file if it exists or creates one if it does not.
CreateNew	Creates a new file. If the file already exists, an error is thrown.	Truncate	Opens an existing file and truncates it to zero bytes.

Table 19-1 FileMode Enumerators

FileMode

Whenever a file is opened for reading or writing, the *FileMode* enumeration is used as a parameter to describe how the stream will be used. Table 19-1 describes the different *FileMode* enumerators.

BinaryWriter

As shown next, a *BinaryWriter* object is initialized with a *FileStream* instance that is returned by the *File.Open()* method. The *File.Open()* method receives a file path and a *FileMode* enumerator as parameters. Once initialized, the *BinaryWriter* class automates the process of converting values of any simple data type to binary format while writing output.

```
using (BinaryWriter writer =
   new BinaryWriter(File.Open(FILE_PATH, FileMode.Create))) {

     writer.Write("ABC");
     writer.Write(123);
}
```

Once again, when a *BinaryWriter* is declared inside a *using* statement, the program disposes of the object after leaving the code block. If the declaration is not inside a *using* statement, a call to the *Close()* method of the *BinaryWriter* object is required to release the file so that it can be used by another process:

```
writer.Close();
```

BinaryReader

For binary input, you can use the *BinaryReader* class. An object of this class is initialized with a *FileStream* object that is returned by the *File.Open()* method:

```
using (BinaryReader reader
 = new BinaryReader(File.Open(FILE_PATH, FileMode.Open))) {
}
```

Method Name	Reads	Method Name	Reads
ReadBoolean()	Boolean	ReadInt32()	4-byte integer
ReadByte()	1 byte	ReadInt64()	8-byte integer
ReadBytes(int count)	Specific # of bytes	ReadSByte()	1 signed byte
ReadChar()	1 character	ReadSingle()	1 float
ReadChars()	Specific # of characters	ReadString()	Complete string
ReadDecimal()	1 decimal	ReadUInt16()	1 unsigned 2-byte int
ReadDouble()	1 double	ReadUInt32()	1 unsigned 4-byte int
ReadInt16()	2-byte integer	ReadUInt64()	1 unsigned 8-byte int

Table 19-2 BinaryReader Methods

If you know the location and format of data segments in a file, the *BinaryReader* class offers several methods to read the binary data and convert it to the required type (see Table 19-2).

In this sample, the *ReadDecimal()* method reads a binary value and converts it to a decimal object:

```
decimal balance = reader.ReadDecimal();
```

When leaving the *using* block, the *BinaryReader* object is disposed and the file is released so that it can be used by another process.

Example 19-3 Writing and Reading Binary Data Sequentially

To see how the classes work together with binary content, this example demonstrates how to sequentially write and read binary values of known simple types to and from a file:

```
using System;
using System.IO;

namespace Starter {
    class Program {
        const string FILE_PATH  = "../../MyBinaryFile.dat";

        public static void Main( ) {
            WriteOutput();
            DisplayInput();
            Console.ReadLine();
        }
        static void WriteOutput( ) {
            try {
```

```
                // Create file and write to it with a BinaryWriter object.
                using (BinaryWriter writer
                 = new BinaryWriter(File.Open(FILE_PATH, FileMode.Create))) {
                    writer.Write(true);
                    writer.Write('A');
                    writer.Write(1.1m);
                    writer.Write(2.2);
                    writer.Write(3.3f);
                    writer.Write(4);
                    writer.Write("Hello");
                }
            }
            catch (Exception e) {
                Console.WriteLine(e.Message);
            }
        }
        static void DisplayInput( ) {
            try {
                using (BinaryReader reader
                 = new BinaryReader(File.Open(FILE_PATH, FileMode.Open))) {

                    // Read known formats in a known order.
                    Console.WriteLine(reader.ReadBoolean());
                    Console.WriteLine(reader.ReadChar());
                    Console.WriteLine(reader.ReadDecimal());
                    Console.WriteLine(reader.ReadDouble());
                    Console.WriteLine(reader.ReadSingle());
                    Console.WriteLine(reader.ReadInt32());
                    Console.WriteLine(reader.ReadString());
                }
            }
            catch (Exception e) {
                Console.WriteLine(e.Message);
            }
        }
    }
}
```

When running the program, a binary file named MyBinaryFile.dat is created, data is stored in it, and then the contents of the file are read, converted back to a useable format, and displayed in the console:

```
True
A
1.1
2.2
3.3
4
Hello
```

This example creates the MyBinaryFile.dat file in the same directory as the source files. If you open the file using Notepad, you will notice that the contents of the file are in an unreadable binary format.

Try This 19-2 Writing and Reading Binary Data

To get some reassurance that the binary write and read techniques actually work properly, try this exercise.

1. Starting with Example 19-3, modify the code to write the first name "James" and last name "Bond" along with the identification number of 7 in binary format.
2. Adjust the code to read the content back in and to display it in the console window.

Reading Buffered Binary Data

When you need to retrieve large amounts of data, either from across a network or from a large file, you may risk overloading the system memory where the reading application resides. To efficiently read large amounts of data, you can retrieve this data in separate blocks. Each time a block is retrieved, it is loaded into a temporary buffer for storage while processing. Often, the buffer is treated as an array of raw bytes, which can be converted to a more useful format by your application. The *Read()* method of the *FileStream* class loads raw byte data into the buffer:

```
int Read(byte[] buffer, int bufferOffset, int totalBytesToRetrieve);
```

When separating your file into chunks for buffering, you can determine the file size, which is readily available from the *FileStream* object's *Length* property:

```
int fileStream.Length;
```

With these structures in mind, a routine that reads buffered data into 4-byte chunks iteratively could look something like the following:

```
const string FILE_PATH   = "../../MyBinaryBuffer.dat";
const int BUFFER_SIZE    = 16; // 16 bytes - 4 bytes per integer.

using(FileStream fileStream = new FileStream(FILE_PATH, FileMode.Open)) {
     int bytesRead       = 0;
```

```
        int totalBytesRead  = 0;

        // Read data into byte buffer as long as there is data to be read.
        while((bytesRead = fileStream.Read(buffer, 0,buffer.Length)) > 0){
            totalBytesRead += bytesRead;
            DoSomethingWithBuffer(buffer);
            buffer = ResetBuffer((int)fileStream.Length, totalBytesRead);
            if(buffer == null)
                break;
        }
    }
```

Example 19-4 Reading Binary Data from a Buffer

This example shows the full application that reads blocks of data into a buffer. To enable this example, a binary file containing integers is created. Segments of this binary file are read into a byte array, which is then converted into integers by the application for display in the console window.

```
using System;
using System.IO;

namespace Starter {
    class Program {
        const string FILE_PATH   = "../../MyBinaryBuffer.dat";
        const int BUFFER_SIZE    = 16; // 16 bytes - 4 bytes per integer.

        public static void Main() {
            GenerateBinaryContent();
            ReadBinaryData();
            Console.ReadLine();
        }

        // Generates data and stores it in a file in binary format.
        static void GenerateBinaryContent( ) {
            try {
                using(BinaryWriter writer
                = new BinaryWriter(File.Open(FILE_PATH, FileMode.Create))) {
                    int[] numberArray   = { 1, 2, 3, 4, 5, 6, 7, 2, 1 };
                    for(int i = 0;i < numberArray.Length;i++)
                        writer.Write(numberArray[i]);
                }
            }
            catch(Exception e) {
                Console.WriteLine(e.Message);
            }
        }
```

```
        // Reads binary data into 4 byte blocks.
        static void ReadBinaryData( ) {
            byte[]    buffer        = new byte[BUFFER_SIZE];
            try {
                using(FileStream fileStream
                = new FileStream(FILE_PATH, FileMode.Open)) {
                    int bytesRead       = 0;
                    int totalBytesRead  = 0;
                    // Read data into byte buffer as long as data exists.
                    while((bytesRead
                         = fileStream.Read(buffer, 0,buffer.Length)) > 0) {
                        totalBytesRead += bytesRead;
                        ShowBufferContents(buffer);
                        buffer = ResetBuffer((int)fileStream.Length,
                                                    totalBytesRead);
                        if(buffer == null)
                            break;
                    }
                }
            }
            catch(Exception e) {
                Console.WriteLine("Read error:  " + e.Message);
            }
        }

        // Extract and show data currently in the buffer.
        static void ShowBufferContents(byte[] buffer) {
            const int BYTES_PER_INT = 4;  // 1 integer = 4 bytes

            // Convert bytes to integers and display them.
            for(int i = 0;i < buffer.Length; i+= BYTES_PER_INT) {
                int intValue = BitConverter.ToInt32(buffer, i);
                Console.Write(intValue + ", ");
            }
        }

        // Clear and size buffer to 4 bytes or remaining bytes if < 4.
        static byte[] ResetBuffer(int fileLength, int totalBytesRead) {
            byte[] buffer  = null;

            // Allocate space if data is left in file.
            if(totalBytesRead < fileLength) {
                if(totalBytesRead + BUFFER_SIZE <= fileLength)
                    buffer = new byte[BUFFER_SIZE];
                else
                    buffer = new byte[fileLength - totalBytesRead];
            }
            return buffer;
        }
    }
}
```

When you run the program, you can see contents of the binary file in the console window after it is read and converted back to integer format:

```
1, 2, 3, 4, 5, 6, 7, 2, 1,
```

Randomly Accessing Binary Data

Sometimes you will want to read only a portion of a binary file, especially if the file is large. You can access the start position you need in the file with the *Seek()* method of the *FileStream* class, which moves the position of the file pointer. *Seek()* receives two parameters. The first *Seek()* parameter sets the offset in bytes for the file pointer. The second *Seek()* parameter receives the *SeekOrigin* enumeration as a parameter. The *SeekOrigin* enumeration sets the file pointer's initial starting point before it is adjusted with the offset. *SeekOrigin*'s enumerated values range from *SeekOrigin.Begin,* which starts the read at the offset from the beginning, to *SeekOrigin.Current,* which begins reading at the offset from the current file position, to *SeekOrigin.End,* which starts reading at the negative offset from the end of the file. Your code to randomly access a section in the file could look like the following:

```
FileStream fileStream   = new FileStream(FILE_PATH, FileMode.Open);
const int OFFSET        = 8;    // Skip first two integers (8 bytes).
fileStream.Seek(OFFSET, SeekOrigin.Begin);
```

Example 19-5 Random Binary Access

This example demonstrates how to adjust the file pointer to directly access and read a specific subsection of a file. In this case, once the required changes are made, the application will begin reading data into a buffer, starting at the third number. The buffer is large enough to contain four integers. To build this current example, begin with the solution for Example 19-4 and replace the *ReadBinaryData()* method with this version:

```
// Reads binary data into 4 byte blocks.
static void ReadBinaryData() {
    byte[]    buffer         = new byte[BUFFER_SIZE];
    try{
        using (FileStream fileStream
                              = new FileStream(FILE_PATH,FileMode.Open)) {
            const int OFFSET = 8; // Skip first two integers (8 bytes).
```

```
            fileStream.Seek(OFFSET, SeekOrigin.Begin); // Start at 3rd int.
            fileStream.Read(buffer, 0, buffer.Length); // Fill the buffer.
            ShowBufferContents(buffer);
        }
    }
    catch (Exception e) {
        Console.WriteLine("Read error:  " + e.Message);
    }
}
```

Note that the starting offset is 8 bytes and that 16 bytes are read. Since each integer is 4 bytes long, this means that the third, fourth, fifth, and sixth integers are read. The output displayed when running the program verifies this:

```
3, 4, 5, 6,
```

Chapter 19 Self Test

The following questions are intended to help reinforce your comprehension of the concepts covered in this chapter. The answers can be found in the accompanying online Appendix B, "Answers to the Self Tests."

1. Whenever you run the code in Example 19-1, the output is always the same. What change can you make so new content is added to the end of the existing file every time the application is run?
2. Write your name in a text editor and then save and close the file. Write a program to read the contents of the file and display it in the console window.
3. Explain in your own words why you receive an error if you revise Example 19-3 by changing the *ReadDecimal()* method to *ReadInt32()*.
4. Modify Example 19-5 by adding one extra *Seek()* and *Read()* method instruction, but leave the existing *Seek()* and *Read()* instructions as they are. The final output after making this change should be

```
3, 4, 5, 6, 2, 1,
```

Chapter 20

XML Handling

Key Skills & Concepts

- XML Introduction
- LINQ to XML Introduction
- Creating XML Elements and Attributes
- Updating XML Elements and Attributes
- Deleting XML Elements
- XML Serialization and Deserialization

This chapter discusses how to use Visual Studio and C# to create, read, update, write, and validate XML. You may already be familiar with XML (Extensible Markup Language), but in case you have not worked with it or need a quick review, the first part of this chapter provides a brief introduction to XML while also describing features of Visual Studio that support and automate development with XML.

XML Introduction

XML is a platform-independent, self-descriptive, reader-friendly language that allows you to create a tag system for marking, storing, and transferring data in a readable text format. Even if you have not worked with XML before, you likely can still read and understand the data in the document because of the descriptive markup (see Example 20-1). These days XML is often used to format software configuration files and is still one of the common formats for transferring data over the Web. Chances are if you are new to C# development, you will not be working with XML very much. However, as you start branching out as a C# developer for Windows, mobile, or web development, you may need to work with XML, so you will want awareness of this topic.

Example 20-1 Creating an XML File

Here is an example of an XML document that stores data about U.S. states. To create the file, type the contents in Notepad and save it as us_states.xml. You will use this file in future examples.

NOTE

XML comments begin with <!-- and end with -->.

```
<?xml version="1.0" encoding="utf-8"?>
<states> <!-- Root element -->
  <state region="West"> <!-- First state element -->
    <name abbreviation="HI">Hawaii</name>
    <population>1295178</population>
    <capital>
      <city>Honolulu</city>
      <population>407018</population>
    </capital>
  </state>
  <state region="East"> <!-- Second state element -->
    <name abbreviation="MA">Massachusetts</name>
    <population>6547629</population>
    <capital>
      <city>Boston</city>
      <population>618656</population>
    </capital>
  </state>
  <state region="West"> <!-- Third state element -->
    <name abbreviation="CA">California</name>
    <population>36457549</population>
    <capital>
      <city>Sacramento</city>
      <population>489488</population>
    </capital>
  </state>
</states>
```

XML Elements and Attributes

An XML document is created from a series of tags called *elements.* These elements are encased in angle brackets. Element values are nested between the opening and closing tags. An element can also have zero to many properties called *attributes.* Attributes of an element are located either inside an opening tag or within a self-contained element tag. Attribute values are contained within quotes. To help clarify where these pieces fit, Figure 20-1 shows three different ways that elements can be written to store *name, population,* and *capital* data of a U.S. state.

Element Hierarchy

Elements in an XML document are often described in terms of family hierarchy, where the root element is the top of the hierarchy. Nested elements are children of the parent element above.

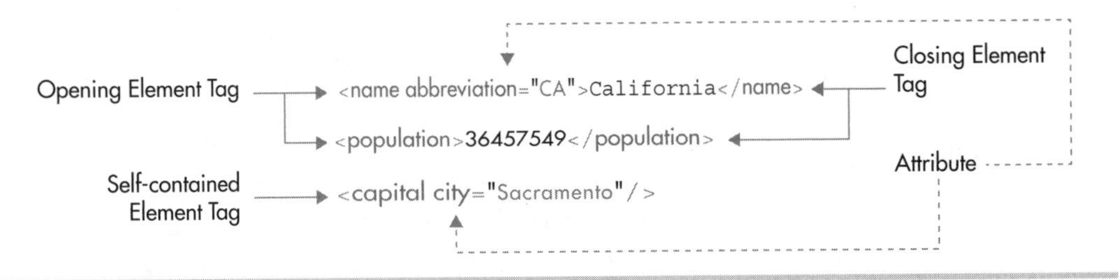

Figure 20-1 XML element and attribute syntax

Elements at the same level in a hierarchy are siblings of each other. Elements that are two levels below a node are grandchildren of the grandparent element. In the XML document displayed in Example 20-1, the *states* element is the root element. Each *state* element is a child of the *states* element. The *name, population,* and *capital* elements are all siblings of each other and are grandchildren of the *states* element.

Adding an XML Document to a Visual Studio Project

The steps needed to include an XML file in your Visual Studio project are similar to those needed for adding any code file.

Example 20-2 Adding an XML Document to a Visual Studio Project

To add an XML document to your project, in the Solution Explorer, right-click the project name and choose Add | New Item. Then, select XML File under the Data Template node. Once the file has been added to your solution, rename the file to us_states.xml and replace whatever code exists in the newly generated document with the code from Example 20-1. When these steps are complete, your solution files will appear in a manner similar to the view presented in Figure 20-2.

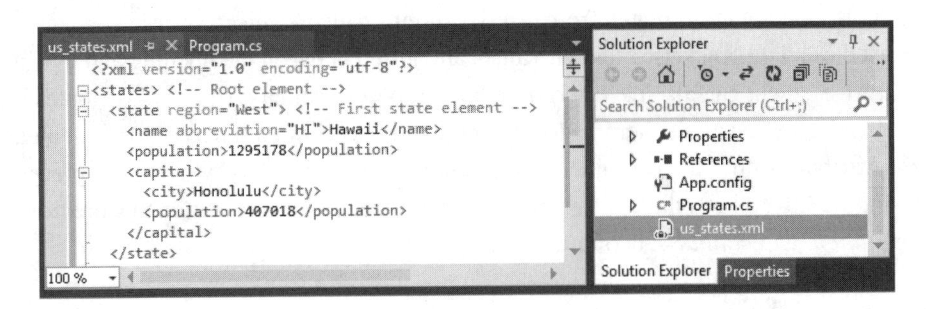

Figure 20-2 Referencing an XML document in Visual Studio

Well-Formed XML

By convention, all XML documents must conform to a universal set of rules for syntax. When in conformance with these rules, XML documents are said to be well formed. XML documents can only be well formed if

- There is only one root tag:

```
<news><title>CNN</title><title>NBC</title></news> <!-- A root tag exists. -->
<title>CNN</title><title>NBC</title>            <!-- No root tag exists. -->
```

- All elements are closed properly:

```
<link>http://www.cnn.com</link> <!-- This element is closed. -->
<link>http://www.cnn.com        <!-- This element is not closed. -->
```

- Elements are properly nested and do not overlap:

```
<news><title>CNN</title></news> <!-- Proper nesting. -->
<news><title>CNN</news></title> <!-- Improper nesting. -->
```

- Attributes are within quotes:

```
<news title="CNN"></news>       <!-- Proper use of quotes. -->
<news title=NBC></news>         <!-- Quotes are missing. -->
```

- Letter case is identical for opening and closing tags:

```
<news>CNN</news>                <!-- Letter case use is correct. -->
<news>NBC</News>                <!-- Letter case use is incorrect. -->
```

When editing XML in Microsoft Visual Studio, the code editor automatically highlights with squiggly lines sections of XML that are not well formed, as shown in Figure 20-3.

TIP

XML can have a higher level of validation with an XML schema that regulates the data types, sequence, and occurrences of XML content. Visual Studio supports auto-generation of XML schema. As well, the XML editor within Visual Studio supports design-time validation when the XML references the schema.

```
<state region=West>                                  <!-- No quotes.-->
  <Name abbreviation="HI">Hawaii</name>              <!-- Unmatched tags/letter case. -->
  <population>1295178<a></population></a>           <!-- Improper nesting. -->
  <capital>
    <city>&Honolulu</city>                           <!-- Invalid characters. -->
    <population>407018</population>
  </capital>
</state>
```

Figure 20-3 Non-well-formed XML errors

LINQ to XML Introduction

When working with XML, if you are comfortable with LINQ, you might consider using LINQ to XML to manage your XML content. LINQ to XML offers a simple and complete in-memory interface to create, read, update, and delete XML. The class structures, methods, and properties that enable LINQ to XML are from the *System.Xml.Linq* namespace.

NOTE

There are interfaces other than LINQ for managing XML. LINQ to XML is used in this book for simplicity. If you wish to explore alternatives, the *System.Xml* namespace provides an *XmlDocument* class for in-memory XML management and an *XmlReader* class for streamed XML document management. Both of these classes enable querying with *XPath*, which is a standard XML query language for most language platforms. As well, both classes provide a rich series of methods and properties to assist in referencing different nodes of an XML document without *XPath*.

Most of the time, LINQ to XML offers everything you need for XML management. LINQ to XML is easy to learn too if you are familiar with LINQ. When coding with LINQ to XML, you will be working with *XElement, XAttribute,* and *XDocument* classes. These structures are simple and intuitive to apply with XML elements and attributes.

XElement

The *XElement* class stores information about an element. We will discuss its constructor in more detail a little later in the chapter. For now, be aware that the *XElement* class offers helpful *Name* and *Value* properties:

```
XElement florida = new XElement("state", "Florida");    // Initialize.
Console.WriteLine(florida.Name + ": "
                 + florida.Value); // Shows 'state: Florida'.
```

The *XElement* object's *Load()* method can read an entire XML file into memory. This example shows how you might load the us_states.xml file presented in Example 20-1:

```
const string FILE_PATH = @"..\\..\\us_states.xml";
XElement root = XElement.Load(FILE_PATH);              // Load entire file.
Console.WriteLine(root.Name);                          // Outputs 'states'.
```

The *XElement*'s *Parse()* method can also load XML contents from a string:

```
XElement e = XElement.Parse("<state>Ohio</state>"); // Load string.
Console.WriteLine(e.Name + ": " + e.Value);         // Outputs 'state: Ohio'.
```

XElement Collections

For managing collections of elements, the *XElement* class provides an *Elements()* method. The *Elements()* method receives the name of the element and returns an *IEnumerable* collection of elements. This example outputs Ace and 3 on separate lines:

```
XElement card
       = XElement.Parse("<cards><card>Ace</card><card>3</card></cards>");
IEnumerable<XElement> cards = card.Elements("card");
foreach (XElement element in cards)
    Console.WriteLine(element.Value);
```

XAttribute

XML attributes are defined and managed with the help of the *XAttribute* class. We will discuss attribute creation in more detail a little later in this chapter. For now though, be aware that every *XAttribute* instance provides a reference to an attribute *Name* and *Value* property. The *XAttribute* instance can be extracted from an *XElement* object with the *Attribute()* method, which receives the attribute name as a parameter:

```
XElement card = XElement.Parse("<card suit='spades'>Ace</card>");
XAttribute  a = card.Attribute("suit");
Console.WriteLine(a.Name + ": " + a.Value); // Outputs 'suit: spades'.
```

XAttribute Collections

The *XElement* class provides the *Attributes()* method to manage an *IEnumerable* collection of attributes for each *XElement* instance. This example outputs the attribute details "suit: spades" and "number: 3" on separate lines:

```
XElement card = XElement.Parse("<card suit='spades' number='3'/>");
IEnumerable<XAttribute> attributes = card.Attributes();
foreach (XAttribute attribute in attributes)
    Console.WriteLine(attribute.Name + ": " + attribute.Value);
```

Querying Elements

When you load an XML document or series of elements, you can query nested elements with LINQ extension methods. LINQ extension methods combined with *Element(), Elements(), Attribute(),* and *Attributes()* methods offer you significant flexibility to query your XML.

Example 20-3 Selecting Elements and Attributes

This code example shows how queries filter values from an XML element hierarchy with the *Attribute()* and *Element()* methods of an *XElement* object along with a *Where()* extension. These methods work together to query the us_states.xml file from Example 20-1. The query selects the *state* element for California along with all of its nested elements. The initial query that isolates this *state* element is conducted with the following code:

```
const string FILEPATH = "..\\..\\us_states.xml"; // Load the file.
XElement root         = XElement.Load(FILEPATH);
XElement state = root.Elements("state")  // Get state element for CA.
        .Where( e=>e.Element("name").Value == "California")
        .FirstOrDefault();
```

The *state* element and nested content that is selected with this query is

```
<state region="West">
  <name abbreviation="CA">California</name>
  <population>36457549</population>
  <capital>
    <city>Sacramento</city>
    <population>489488</population>
  </capital>
</state>
```

Queries on different nodes can be made to show detail about the state region, name, abbreviation, and capital city:

```
state.Attribute("region").Value                        // Gets "West".
state.Element("name").Value                            // Gets "California".
state.Element("name").Attribute("abbreviation").Value // Gets "CA".
state.Element("capital").Element("city").Value);      // Gets "Sacramento".
```

Notice how easy it is to chain up *Element(), Attribute(),* and other LINQ extension methods to get information from the XML. To build this example, use the solution for Example 20-1 and replace the code inside Program.cs with the following:

```
using System;
using System.Linq;
using System.Xml.Linq;

namespace ConsoleApplication1 {
    class Program {
```

```
        static void Main() {
            const string FILEPATH = "..\\..\\us_states.xml"; // Load file.
            XElement root          = XElement.Load(FILEPATH);

            XElement state = root.Elements("state")  // Get California.
                    .Where( x=>x.Element("name").Value == "California")
                    .FirstOrDefault();

            Console.WriteLine("'region' attribute of state:       "
                + state.Attribute("region").Value);  // Show region value.

            Console.WriteLine("'name' element of state:           "
                + state.Element("name").Value);      // Show state.

            Console.WriteLine("'abbreviation' attribute of name:  "
                + state.Element("name").Attribute("abbreviation")
                   .Value);                        // Show state abbreviation.

            Console.WriteLine("'city' element:" + // Show city.
                "                    "
                + state.Element("capital").Element("city").Value);
            Console.ReadLine();
        }
    }
}
```

When running the program, the details for the element for California are retrieved and displayed:

```
'region' attribute of state:      West
'name' element of state:          California
'abbreviation' attribute of name: CA
'city' element:                   Sacramento
```

Try This 20-1 Querying XML with LINQ

Here is a chance to see how nicely LINQ and XML work together.

1. Start with the solution from Example 20-3.

2. Write a program to retrieve and display the population of Boston with LINQ to XML.

Example 20-4 Querying with Method-based Syntax and Query Syntax

As you might have suspected, both query syntax and method-based syntax are easily applied with LINQ to XML to manage content. You will find LINQ to XML is very similar to LINQ to Entities syntax when querying, ordering, filtering, and displaying XML element and attribute content. This example shows all of the code needed to perform queries with both query syntax and method-based syntax to retrieve and display all Western states, in us_states.xml, with a state population of over 1,000,000 people:

```
using System;
using System.Collections.Generic;
using System.Linq;
using System.Xml.Linq;

namespace ConsoleApplication1 {
    class Program {
        static void Main() {
            // Load the file.
            const string FILEPATH = "..\\..\\us_states.xml";
            XElement root         = XElement.Load(FILEPATH);

            // Query syntax.
            IEnumerable<XElement> querySyntax =
            from    e in root.Elements("state")
            orderby e.Element("capital").Element("city").Value descending
            where   e.Attribute("region").Value == "West"
            && (int)e.Element("population") > 1000000
            select e;
            Display(querySyntax, "* Query Syntax *");

            // Method-based syntax.
            IEnumerable<XElement> methodBasedSyntax =
            root.Elements("state").OrderByDescending(
                   e => e.Element("capital").Element("city").Value)
            .Where(e => e.Attribute("region").Value == "West"
                && (int)e.Element("population") > 1000000);
            Display(methodBasedSyntax, "* Method Based Syntax *");
            Console.ReadLine();
        }

        static void Display(IEnumerable<XElement> elements, string title) {
            Console.WriteLine(title);

            // Show the value of the 'name' element.
            foreach (XElement e in elements) {
                Console.Write(e.Element("capital").Element("city").Value);
                Console.Write(", "     + e.Element("name").Value);
                Console.WriteLine(" (" + e.Element("name")
```

```
                        .Attribute("abbreviation").Value +")");
            }
            Console.WriteLine();
        }
    }
}
```

The output displays the capital city, state name, and state abbreviation of the states that are selected in each query:

```
* Query Syntax *
Sacramento, California (CA)
Honolulu, Hawaii (HI)

* Method Based Syntax *
Sacramento, California (CA)
Honolulu, Hawaii (HI)
```

Now that you have queried XML with LINQ, it is worth noting that LINQ is a very versatile language feature—it's not tied to database access or XML. With custom providers, many of which are supplied by third parties, you can use LINQ to query just about any sort of structured data.

Additional Element Selection Methods and Properties

In addition to being able to navigate through an XML document with the methods already presented, several other methods and properties are available to assist you with element selection. If you start the query with

```
XElement root = XElement.Parse("<ids><id>A</id><id>B</id></ids>"); // Load XML
```

you can then use the methods and properties of the *XElement* class to navigate through the XML content. The next code block shows a listing of such methods and properties applied to the *XElement* object retrieved in the previous query. The comments include a description of how each structure works and the contents retrieved.

```
root.AncestorsAndSelf();    // Gets current element and ancestor elements.
                            // <ids><id>A</id><id>B</id></ids>

root.Descendants("id");     // Gets collection of descendant elements.
                            // <id>A</id><id>B</id>

root.Elements("id")         // Gets element at a specific position.
    .ElementAt(0);          // <id>A</id>
```

```
root.Elements("id")           // Gets the parent element.
    .ElementAt(0).Parent;     // <ids><id>A</id><id>B</id></ids>

root.Elements("id")
    .Where(e => e.Value == "A")
    .Ancestors("ids");        // Gets predecessor in family hierarchy.
                              // <ids><id>A</id><id>B</id></ids>

root.Elements("id")           // Takes the first specified number of elements.
    .Take(2);                 // <id>A</id><id>B</id>

root.Elements("id")           // Skips given number of elements and gets others.
    .Skip(1);                 // <id>B</id>

root.Elements("id")           // Inverts the collection sequence.
    .Reverse();               // <id>B</id><id>A</id>
```

Try This 20-2 Querying XML with LINQ, Continued

This exercise offers an opportunity to choose from different extension methods and properties when querying XML with LINQ.

1. Create a project with the following XML file:

```
<?xml version="1.0" encoding="utf-8"?>
<animals>
  <canines>
    <dog>african hunting dog</dog>
    <dog>bat-eared fox</dog>
  </canines>
  <felines>
    <cat>jaguar</cat>
    <cat>leopard</cat>
    <cat>tiger</cat>
  </felines>
</animals>
```

2. Write code that loads the XML.
3. Write queries and show your results so that the output appears as follows:

```
* Dog at Second Position *
 <dog>bat-eared fox</dog>

* Cats in Reverse Order *
<cat>tiger</cat>
<cat>leopard</cat>
<cat>jaguar</cat>
```

Creating XML Elements and Attributes

Now let's look at how to create XML elements and attributes. It is actually easy to do once you get used to working with the *XElement* and *XAttribute* constructors.

Creating Attributes

The *XAttribute* constructor is simple to work with. The constructor receives the attribute name and value as parameters:

```
XAttribute typeAttribute  = new XAttribute("perennial","yes");
```

Creating Elements

To create an *XElement* object, the constructor is very flexible and offers several options. You can create an element with only its name and value as parameters:

```
// Generates "<flower>Iris</flower>"
XElement flower = new XElement("flower", "Iris");
```

Your *XElement* constructor could also receive an element name, value, and an attribute:

```
// Generates "<flower perennial="yes">Iris</flower>"
XElement flower = new XElement("flower", " Iris", typeAttribute);
```

You could also define an *XElement* object with a name and a nested *XElement* object:

```
// Generates "<flowers><flower>Iris</flower></flowers>"
XElement root   = new XElement("flowers", flowerElement);
```

You can even define an *XElement* object with a name, an attribute, and a nested *XElement* object:

```
// Generates "<flowers><flower perennial="yes">Iris</flower></flowers>"
XElement   root   = new XElement("flowers", typeAttribute, flowerElement);
```

With nesting, you have many options available to create complex elements.

Example 20-5 Creating Elements and Attributes

Here is an example of how you could create a *flower* element with nested *name* and *perennial* elements:

```
using System;
using System.Xml.Linq;
```

```
namespace ConsoleApplication1 {
    class Program {
        static void Main() {
            XElement iris = new XElement("flower",
                new XElement("name", "Iris", new XAttribute("color",
                                                             "white")),
                new XElement("perennial", "yes"));

            Console.WriteLine(iris);
            Console.ReadLine();
        }
    }
}
```

The output shows a newly created *flower* element with *name* and *perennial* elements nested inside:

```
<flower>
  <name color="white">Iris</name>
  <perennial>yes</perennial>
</flower>
```

Adding Elements to Existing Documents

Once you have created an element, you might want to add or insert it to an existing XML file. To add XML elements to an existing document, you may use the *Add(), AddFirst(), AddBeforeSelf(),* and *AddAfterSelf()* methods of the *XElement* object. Each of these methods receives an *XElement* object as a parameter. Additions are committed to the file with the *Save()* method of the *XElement* class.

Example 20-6 Creating and Adding Elements

This example uses the *AddBeforeSelf()* method to insert an element that contains data about Florida before the element for Massachusetts. To begin, create a new console application and reference the us_states.xml document from Example 20-1. Then replace the code in Program.cs with the following code:

```
using System;
using System.Linq;
using System.Xml.Linq;

namespace ConsoleApplication1 {
    class Program {
        static void Main() {
```

```
            // Load the file.
            const string FILE_PATH = @"..\\..\\us_states.xml";
            XElement          root = XElement.Load(FILE_PATH);
            XElement massachusetts =
                     root.Elements("state")
                    .Where(n => n.Element("name").Value == "Massachusetts")
                    .FirstOrDefault();

            XElement florida =
                new XElement("state", new XAttribute("region", "East"),
                new XElement("name", "Florida",
                             new XAttribute("abbreviation", "FL")),
                new XElement("population", 19320000),
                new XElement("capital",
                    new XElement("city", "Tallahassee"),
                    new XElement("population", 183900)));

            // Add new state element
            massachusetts.AddBeforeSelf(florida);

            Console.Write(root);  // Display the element.
            root.Save(FILE_PATH); // Commit changes.
            Console.ReadLine();
        }
    }
}
```

After running the program, if you examine the us_states.xml file, you will see the element for Florida above the element for Massachusetts. The Florida element appears as

```
<state region="East">
  <name abbreviation="FL">Florida</name>
  <population>19320000</population>
  <capital>
    <city>Tallahassee</city>
    <population>183900</population>
  </capital>
</state>
```

Updating XML Elements and Attributes

Both *XElement* and *XAttribute* classes provide a *SetValue()* method to update element and attribute values. When updating either an *XElement* or *XAttribute* instance, the *SetValue()* method receives the new value as a parameter and sets it for the object. Once values have been adjusted, the *Save()* method of the *XElement* class commits these changes to the XML source.

Example 20-7 Updating Elements and Attributes

This example shows how to update an element and attribute within the Florida element. First, the program increases the *population* element value from 19,320,000 to 19,400,000. Then, the *name abbreviation* attribute is modified from FL to Fla. To begin, start with the solution for Example 20-6 and then replace the existing code in Program.cs with the following code:

```
using System;
using System.Linq;
using System.Xml.Linq;

namespace ConsoleApplication1 {
    class Program {
        static void Main() {
            // Load the file.
            const string FILE_PATH = @"..\\..\\us_states.xml";
            XElement          root = XElement.Load(FILE_PATH);
            const int   POPULATION = 19400000;

            // Get the 'state' element where abbreviation is 'FL'.
            var florida = root.Elements("state")
           .Where(s => s.Element("name").Attribute("abbreviation")
           .Value == "FL").FirstOrDefault();

            // Update value of the 'florida' element if it exists.
            if (florida != null) {
                florida.Element("population").SetValue(POPULATION);
                florida.Element("name")
                       .Attribute("abbreviation").SetValue("Fla.");
                root.Save(FILE_PATH);          // Commit the changes.
                Console.WriteLine(florida);
            }
            Console.ReadLine();
        }
    }
}
```

After running this example, the Florida element is displayed with the updated values for the *abbreviation* attribute and state *population* element:

```
<state region="East">
    <name abbreviation="Fla.">Florida</name>
    <population>19400000</population>
```

```
    <capital>
      <city>Tallahassee</city>
      <population>183900</population>
    </capital>
</state>
```

Deleting XML Elements

To delete an element, the *Remove()* method of the *XElement* object deletes the selected instance from the tree. The *Save()* method commits the changes to the XML document.

Example 20-8 Removing an Element

This example shows how to remove the element that contains details for the state of Florida. To begin, start with the solution from Example 20-6 and then replace the code inside Program.cs with the following code:

```
using System;
using System.Linq;
using System.Xml.Linq;

namespace ConsoleApplication1 {
    class Program {
        static void Main() {
            const string FILE_PATH = "..\\..\\us_states.xml";
            XElement          root = XElement.Load(FILE_PATH); // Load file.
            var florida = root.Elements("state")          // Get Florida.
                        .Where(s => s.Element("name").Value == "Florida")
                        .FirstOrDefault();
            if(florida != null)                           // Delete element.
                florida.Remove();

            Console.Write(root);                          // Show XML.
            root.Save(FILE_PATH);                         // Save changes.
            Console.ReadLine();
        }
    }
}
```

If you examine the us_states.xml file after running this program, you will notice the element for Florida has been removed.

XML Serialization and Deserialization

XML serialization is the process of converting an object or a list of objects to XML. XML deserialization converts it back. Automating these processes can be especially useful if you are converting database content or other data to XML and vice versa.

Serialization

Let's first look at serialization. The *XmlSerializer* class contains methods for converting C# data objects to XML. When the *XmlSerializer* object is declared, the class or *List* type is specified:

```
XmlSerializer serializer = new XmlSerializer(typeof(ClassName));
XmlSerializer serializer = new XmlSerializer(typeof(List<ClassName>));
```

The *Serialize()* method of the *XmlSerializer* class receives a writer and a data object or list as parameters. You can use a *Stream, TextWriter,* or *XmlWriter* object as the writer parameter. This example uses a *StringWriter* object from the *System.IO* namespace. The *Serialize()* method stores data from the data object into the *StringWriter* object.

```
Employee         employee = new Employee("Arshad", 53);
StringWriter stringWriter = new StringWriter();
XmlSerializer  serializer = new XmlSerializer(typeof(Employee));
// Store XML in StringWriter object.
serializer.Serialize(stringWriter, employee);
```

Once the *StringWriter()* object is populated with data, you can convert it to an *XElement* object:

```
XElement element = XElement.Parse(stringWriter.ToString());
```

When your data is represented as an *XElement* object, you then have the ability to manage it with LINQ.

Example 20-9 Converting Data Objects to XML

This first serialization example shows a complete view of how to generate XML from an *Employee* object:

```
using System;
using System.Xml;
using System.Xml.Serialization;
using System.IO;
using System.Xml.Linq;
```

```
namespace Starter {
    public class Employee {
        public string FirstName { get; set; }
        public int    ID        { get; set; }

        public Employee() {}
        public Employee(string firstName, int id) {
            FirstName = firstName;
            ID        = id;
        }
    }
    public class Program {
        public static void Main() {
            // Convert Employee data object to StringWriter object.
            Employee         employee = new Employee("Arshad", 53);
            StringWriter stringWriter = new StringWriter();
            XmlSerializer  serializer = new XmlSerializer(typeof(Employee));
            serializer.Serialize(stringWriter, employee);

            string xml = stringWriter.ToString();   // Convert to string.
            XElement element = XElement.Parse(xml); // Convert string to XML.
            Console.WriteLine(element);             // Show XML.
            Console.ReadLine();
        }
    }
}
```

When you run this program, the class object is converted to XML and the XML content is displayed in the window:

```
<Employee xmlns:xsi="http://www.w3.org/2001/XMLSchema-instance"
          xmlns:xsd="http://www.w3.org/2001/XMLSchema">
  <FirstName>Arshad</FirstName>
  <ID>53</ID>
</Employee>
```

Here's a tip—you will notice the default XML generation includes a reference in the root element to the document namespace, xmlns:xsi, and the default schema, xmlns:xsd. To remove these references in Example 20-9, replace

```
serializer.Serialize(stringWriter, employee);
```

with

```
XmlSerializerNamespaces ns = new XmlSerializerNamespaces();
ns.Add("","");
serializer.Serialize(stringWriter, employee, ns);
```

Customizing XML Serialization

By default, during serialization, all C# data object properties are converted to elements. Also by default, all auto-generated XML element names are given the same name as the class property. This automation is helpful, but you may need to control the serialization process to store some of the data as XML attributes instead of elements. Or, you might need to customize the XML element and attribute names. To do this, you can use C# attributes. To customize an XML element, you may prefix a class property with the *XmlElement* attribute, which is like a tag that begins and ends with square braces. The *XmlElement* attribute receives the desired element name as a parameter:

```
[XmlElement("firstName")]; // Store data in XML element named "firstName"
public string FirstName { get; set; }
```

NOTE

For more information on C# attributes, see Chapter 22.

By default, serialization generates an element from a C# object property. To override this behavior and generate an attribute instead, place the *XmlAttribute* tag before the C# property. You may also pass a custom name for the attribute as a parameter:

```
[XmlAttribute("id")]        // Store data as XML attribute named "id".
public int    ID        { get; set; }
```

Example 20-10 Customizing XML Serialization

This example shows how you can add attributes to property declarations to customize XML generation. In this case, begin with the solution for Example 20-9. If you replace the *Employee* class declaration with the following:

```
public class Employee {
    [XmlElement("firstName")]
    public string FirstName { get; set; }
    [XmlAttribute("id")]
    public int    ID        { get; set; }

    public Employee() {}
    public Employee(string firstName, int id) {
        FirstName = firstName;
        ID        = id;
    }
}
```

when running the program, the XML generated will take on the element and attribute names that are indicated by the tags in the class. Notice how the new output is different from the output from Example 20-9:

```
<Employee xmlns:xsi="http://www.w3.org/2001/XMLSchema-instance"
          xmlns:xsd="http://www.w3.org/2001/XMLSchema" id="53">
  <firstName>Arshad</firstName>
</Employee>
```

Deserialization

Deserialization is the process of converting XML to a C# data object or a list of C# objects. The deserialization process is actually easier than serialization because you can use LINQ to query the XML to directly retrieve the data in whatever format is required. The following is an example query that extracts *Employee* objects from an XML document and stores them in a list. Every row of the query extracts the required XML content and stores it in a property of the object. Notice a slight difference in the notation compared to the LINQ covered earlier. When defining the columns in the query within the *Select()* extension method, the phrase *new Employee()* ensures that each row of the query is converted to an *Employee* object.

```
List<Employee> employees = xmlDoc.Elements("Employee") // Method syntax.
    .Select(e => new Employee() {                      // Create new object.
        FirstName = e.Element("firstName").Value,
        ID        = Convert.ToInt32(e.Attribute("id").Value)
    }).ToList();
```

NOTE

While this is not covered in the book, be aware that you can also deserialize the XML with the *XmlSerializer.Deserialize()* method.

Example 20-11 Deserialization with LINQ

This example shows how to apply both method-based syntax and query syntax to convert XML content into a list of *Employee* objects. The following XML content is contained in a file named employees.xml. To begin, create a console application. Then, place the employees.xml file with this content in the same folder as your Program.cs file:

```
<Employees>
  <Employee id='53'>
    <firstName>Arshad</firstName>
  </Employee>
```

```
  <Employee id='42'>
    <firstName>Habiba</firstName>
  </Employee>
</Employees>
```

Next, replace the existing code in Program.cs with this version to extract the XML content into a list of *Employee* objects:

```
using System;
using System.Collections.Generic;
using System.Xml.Linq;
using System.Linq;

namespace Starter {
    public class Employee {
        public string FirstName { get; set; }
        public int    ID        { get; set; }
    }
    public class Program {
        public static void Main() {
            XElement xml = XElement.Load(@"../../employee.xml"); // Load XML.

            // Method syntax.
            List<Employee> employeesA = xml.Elements("Employee")
                .Select(e => new Employee() {
                    FirstName = e.Element("firstName").Value,
                    ID        = Convert.ToInt32(e.Attribute("id").Value)
                }).ToList();
            ShowEmployees(employeesA);

            // Query syntax.
            List<Employee> employeesB =  (
                from e in xml.Elements("Employee")
                select new Employee() {
                    FirstName = e.Element("firstName").Value,
                    ID        = Convert.ToInt32(e.Attribute("id").Value)
                }).ToList();
            ShowEmployees(employeesB);
            Console.ReadLine();
        }
        public static void ShowEmployees(List<Employee> employees) {
            foreach (Employee employee in employees)
                Console.WriteLine("Name:" + employee.FirstName
                                + " ID:" + employee.ID);
            Console.WriteLine();
        }
    }
}
```

The output from both queries confirms that each successfully extracts the XML content into a list of *Employee* objects:

```
Name:Arshad ID:53
Name:Habiba ID:42

Name:Arshad ID:53
Name:Habiba ID:42
```

Chapter 20 Self Test

The following questions are intended to help reinforce your comprehension of the concepts covered in this chapter. The answers can be found in the accompanying online Appendix B, "Answers to the Self Tests."

1. Using us_states.xml from Example 20-1, show all capital cities with their corresponding populations:
   - **A.** Using query syntax.
   - **B.** Using method-based syntax.
2. Create a console application and place the following XML content in a separate file within the project:

```
<employees>
  <employee department="accounting" id="25">
    <firstName>Dave</firstName>
    <lastName>Berg</lastName>
    <certifications>
      <certification>CPA</certification>
      <certification>CA</certification>
    </certifications>
  </employee>
  <employee department="accounting" id="33">
    <firstName>Al</firstName>
    <lastName>Jaffee</lastName>
    <certifications>
      <certification>CMA</certification>
      <certification>CA</certification>
    </certifications>
  </employee>
  <employee department="operations" id="121">
    <firstName>Sergio</firstName>
```

```
      <lastName>Aragonés</lastName>
      <certifications>
        <certification>PMC</certification>
      </certifications>
    </employee>
  </employees>
```

Then using C#:

A. Show the total number of employees.

B. List the first and last names of all employees.

C. List the first name and last name of employees who have a CA certification.

Tip: After your filter, append the following method to select the parent *employee* element:

```
.Ancestors("employee");
```

D. Show the first name, last name, and certifications of all employees who work in operations.

E. Add the following employee:

```
<employee department="operations" id="26">
  <firstName>Don</firstName>
  <lastName>Martin</lastName>
  <certifications>
    <certification>BA</certification>
  </certifications>
</employee>
```

F. Remove the employee from part E. When selecting the employee, search for that person by using their *id* attribute.

3. Starting with the original .xml file in "Try This 20-2," add code to insert and save the following element between the leopard and tiger *cat* elements:

```
<cat>lion</cat>
```

4. Starting with the solution from question 3, change the element value of lion to cave lion and save it to the XML file.

5. Starting with the following class declarations:

```
public class Weather {
    public string Day  { get; set; }
    public int    High { get; set; }
    public int    Low  { get; set; }
```

```
    public Weather() { }
    public Weather(string day, int high, int low) {
        Day  = day;
        High = high;
        Low  = low;
    }
}
public class WeatherReport {
    public List<Weather> report { get; set; }
    public WeatherReport() {
        report = new List<Weather>();
    }
}
```

add extra code to create an instance of *WeatherReport* and populate the report list. Then convert the list into XML so the content appears exactly as shown:

```
<WeatherReport>
  <weather day="Monday">
    <high>85</high>
    <low>68</low>
  </weather>
  <weather day="Tuesday">
    <high>88</high>
    <low>71</low>
  </weather>
</WeatherReport>
```

Chapter 21

JSON Handling

Key Skills & Concepts

- JSON Introduction
- Creating Dynamic JSON Objects
- Dynamic Parsing
- Serialization
- Deserialization

JSON is a human-readable text format that is used primarily to transfer data over the Web. Since JSON is mainly used with web technologies, the topic of working with JSON is not usually included in typical beginner C# programming guides. However, JSON has become a very competitive alternative to XML for platform-independent data transfer. The goal of this chapter is to raise your awareness of JSON as an alternative and to serve as a reference in case you pursue some form of JSON development with C#.

JSON Introduction

JSON stands for JavaScript Object Notation, but this notation is not actually a subset of JavaScript. The JSON format is composed of name-value pairs, where the name is an identifying string and the value can be a numeric value, a string, a Boolean, an array, or a JSON object. JSON arrays are enclosed with square brackets. JSON objects are enclosed with curly braces (see Figure 21-1).

NOTE

JSON is not allowed to have comments, by design.

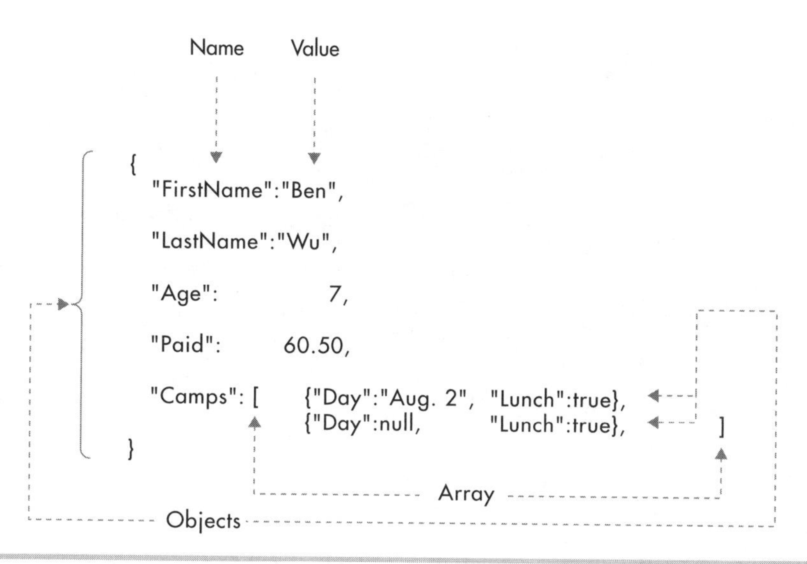

Figure 21-1 JSON sample

Json.NET

The library this book uses to manage JSON is Json.NET, which is one of the more popular C# libraries for this purpose. Json.NET is a third-party library that helps to automate JSON creation, parsing, and conversion to and from C# data objects.

Example 21-1 Adding a Json.NET Reference to Your Project

To include Json.NET in your project, you can download and install it from Visual Studio with the NuGet Package Manager. NuGet is a common interface for including third-party libraries in your .NET projects. To do this, select Tools | NuGet Package Manager | Manage NuGet Packages For Solution. Then, expand the Online node on the left of the dialog that appears (see Figure 21-2). In the search box on the right, enter **Json.Net** and press ENTER. Then, highlight the Json.Net listing and click the Install button. On completing these steps, a *Newtonsoft.Json* listing will appear in the References directory of your project. To use this library with the reference in your project, you will need to include the *Newtonsoft.Json* namespace in your code files.

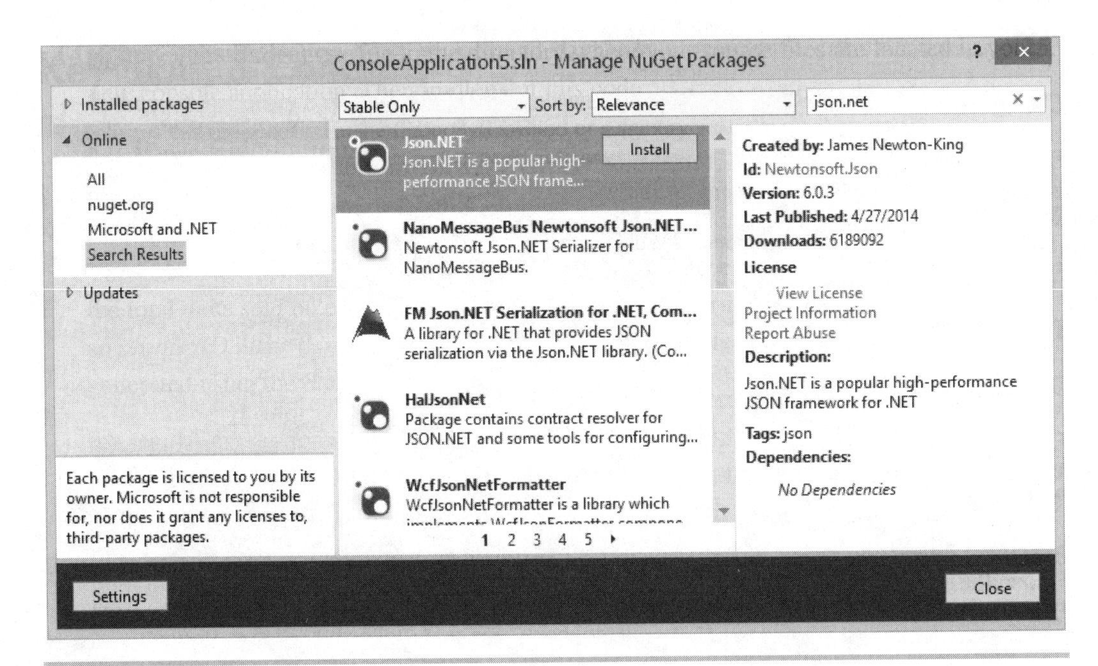

Figure 21-2 NuGet Package Manager

Creating Dynamic JSON Objects

With Json.NET, you can create JSON objects on-the-fly with the *JObject* class. The *JObject* class is flexible, because it allows you to create and query a JSON object without having to undergo the tedious process of converting an entire JSON container to a .NET type.

Dynamic Types

When creating *JObject* instances, use the *dynamic* type for your object so that you can modify the JSON object structure with flexibility while not having to worry about converting it to a .NET type. The *dynamic* type tells the compiler that the object's type is not known until run time. Using a *dynamic* type with JSON objects gives you freedom to append properties or arrays to your object whenever you need to.

TIP

Since your JSON objects are created with string data, your *JObject* instances in Visual Studio will not offer as much IntelliSense support for auto-complete or error checking as other .NET types. Because of this, you will need to be extra careful to spell your property names correctly when working with JSON objects.

Here is a sample *dynamic* JSON object declaration:

```
dynamic registrant = new JObject();
```

To create and add properties to the object, the *Add()* method receives the property name and value pair as a parameter:

```
registrant.Add("FirstName", "Ben");
registrant.Add("LastName", "Wu");
```

The JSON data generated from these instructions is

```
{  "FirstName": "Ben",
   "LastName": "Wu"  }
```

If you prefer, instead of using the *Add()* method you can just make up property names and assign values to them without having to formally declare the property before:

```
dynamic registrant = new JObject();
registrant.FirstName = "Ben";
registrant.LastName  =  "Wu";
```

Creating JSON Arrays

Arrays of similarly typed JSON objects can be created with help from the *JArray* class. This instruction declares an array named *camps*:

```
dynamic camps = new JArray();
```

Once the array is declared, objects can be created, initialized, and appended to the array with the *Add()* method of the *JArray()* class:

```
dynamic aug2 = new JObject();
aug2.Day     = "Aug. 2";
aug2.Lunch   = true;
camps.Add(aug2);
```

Then, the array can be attached to a parent *JObject* instance with a simple assignment. In this case, a *Camps* property is made up on-the-fly and the *camps* array reference is assigned to it:

```
registrant.Camps = camps;
```

After the array has been assigned to the parent object property, it is still possible to add a new object to the array with a reference to the parent object and the *Add()* method of the array property:

```
dynamic aug   = new JObject();
aug.Day       = null;
aug.Lunch     = true;
registrant.Camps.Add(aug);
```

The JSON array that is generated with the previous series of instructions is referenced with the property name *Camps*:

```
"Camps": [
  {
    "Day": "Aug. 2",
    "Lunch": true
  },
  {
    "Day": null,
    "Lunch": true
  }]
```

Example 21-2 Creating a Complex JSON Object

This example creates a JSON object for storing summer camp details in a structure that is identical to the one displayed in Figure 21-1. The structure contains *registrant* properties at the parent level and a *Camps* array that stores multiple sets of *Day* and *Lunch* option properties.

```
using System;
using Newtonsoft.Json.Linq;

namespace Starter {
    class Program {
        public static void Main() {
            // Create parent JSON object.
            dynamic   registrant = new JObject();
            registrant.FirstName = "Ben";
            registrant.LastName  = "Wu";
            registrant.Age       = 7;
            registrant.Paid      = 60.50;
```

```
            dynamic camps = new JArray(); // Create 'Camps' array.
            dynamic aug2 = new JObject(); // Add first day to array.
            aug2.Day      = "Aug. 2";
            aug2.Lunch    = true;
            camps.Add(aug2);

            registrant.Camps = camps;     // Append array to registrant.

            dynamic aug   = new JObject(); // Add second day to array.
            aug.Day       = null;
            aug.Lunch     = true;
            registrant.Camps.Add(aug);

            Console.WriteLine(registrant);
            Console.ReadLine();
        }
    }
}
```

Try This 21-1 JSON Object and Array Creation

This exercise gives you practice working with *JObject* and *JArray* classes.

1. Create the following structure with *dynamic* objects:

```
{
  "Summary": "Shipping Affiliates",
  "ShipLines": [
    {
      "Name": "Hapag-Lloyd",
      "Expertise": "Truck containers"
    },
    {
      "Name": "Seaspan",
      "Expertise": "Raw materials"
    }
  ]
}
```

2. Output your JSON to verify your results.

Dynamic Parsing

Sometimes it is too time consuming to map JSON to .NET types, especially if you are working with a large JSON stream and you only need a small subset of data from it. A *dynamic* type allows you to store the JSON as an object that you can query without the overhead of a major conversion. A dynamic object can be initialized with a JSON string as a parameter in the *JObject.Parse()* method of the *Newtonsoft.Json.Linq* namespace:

```
dynamic jsonObject = JObject.Parse(strJson);
```

Referencing Properties

With a *dynamic* type, you can access the name properties of the JSON object by name:

```
string FirstName = jsonObject.FirstName;
```

Referencing Arrays

To simplify parsing, you can also extract nested arrays from a much larger JSON object. Here, the *Camps* array is being extracted from a larger JSON structure into a separate *dynamic* object:

```
dynamic camps = jsonObject.Camps;
```

After isolating the array data, you can iterate through each object of the array with a *foreach* loop:

```
foreach (dynamic camp in jsonObject.Camps)
    Console.WriteLine(camp.Day + " " + camp.Lunch);
```

As you might expect, arrays are given a *Count* property and JSON objects and their properties within the array can also be referenced with a numeric index:

```
for (int i = 0; i < camps.Count; i++)
    Console.WriteLine(camps[i].Day + " " + camps[i].Lunch);
```

Example 21-3 Dynamic JSON Parsing

This example shows a complete view of how to create a *dynamic* JSON object and how to parse it without converting it to other .NET types. Using the summer camp JSON structure from Figure 21-1, we reference the *FirstName* and *LastName* at the parent level. The *Camps* array is extracted and parsed separately.

```
using System;
using Newtonsoft.Json;
using Newtonsoft.Json.Linq;

namespace ConsoleApplication1 {
    class Program {
        static void Main() {
            string strJson = @"{'FirstName':'Ben','LastName':'Wu','Age':7,"
                            +"'Paid':60.50,"
                            +"'Camps':[{'Day':'Aug. 2','Lunch':true},"
                            +         "{'Day':null,'Lunch':true}]}";
            // Create object and show properties.
            dynamic jsonObject = JObject.Parse(strJson);
            Console.WriteLine("Name: " + jsonObject.FirstName + " "
                                       + jsonObject.LastName);

            dynamic camps = jsonObject.Camps; // Store array separately.
            for (int i = 0; i < camps.Count; i++) {
                string day = "*null*";
                if (camps[i].Day != null)
                    day = camps[i].Day;
                Console.WriteLine(day + " Lunch: " + camps[i].Lunch);
            }
            Console.ReadLine();
        }
    }
}
```

The output is

```
Name: Ben Wu
Aug. 2 Lunch: True
*null* Lunch: True
```

Serialization

Serialization is the conversion of a C# data object to JSON. Conversion is really easy with Json.NET. Given the definition

```
class Person {
    public string FirstName { get; set; }
    public string  LastName { get; set; }
}
```

and instantiation of an object such as *Person,*

```
Person person     = new Person();
person.FirstName = "Ben";
person.LastName  = "Wu";
```

we can pass this *Person* object to the *JsonConvert.SerializeObject()* method as a parameter to transform the data to JSON:

```
var json = JsonConvert.SerializeObject(person);
```

When we display the contents of the JSON that is generated, we get

```
{"FirstName":"Ben","LastName":"Wu"}
```

Example 21-4 Serializing JSON

This example shows how conversion to JSON can be done with a slightly more complex C# data object. In this case, a *Registrant* object stores data about a person in a children's summer camp. The *Registrant* class stores information about the child's name, age, and paid status. This class also contains a *List* of *Camp* objects that store days and lunch order status. When the C# classes are defined, all of the data within the *registrant* object is transformed to JSON with the *JsonConvert.SerializeObject()* method:

```
var json= JsonConvert.SerializeObject(registrant);
```

Here is the program:

```
using System;
using System.Linq;
using Newtonsoft.Json;
using System.Collections.Generic;

namespace ConsoleApplication2 {
    class Camp {
        public string Day { get; set; }
        public bool Lunch { get; set; }
        public Camp(string day, bool lunch ) {
            Day   = day;
            Lunch = lunch;
        }
    }
    class Registrant {
        public string FirstName { get; set; }
        public string  LastName { get; set; }
```

```
        public int          Age { get; set; }
        public decimal     Paid { get; set; }
        public List<Camp>  Camps { get; set;}
        public Registrant(string first, string last, int age, decimal paid) {
            FirstName = first;
            LastName  = last;
            Age       = age;
            Paid      = paid;
            Camps     = new List<Camp>();
        }
    }
    class Program {
        static void Main() {
            Registrant registrant = new Registrant("Ben", "Wu", 7, 60.50m);
            registrant.Camps.Add(new Camp("Aug. 2", true));
            registrant.Camps.Add(new Camp(null,     true));
            var json= JsonConvert.SerializeObject(registrant);
            Console.WriteLine(json);
            Console.ReadLine();
        }
    }
}
```

Running this program generates the output shown earlier in Figure 21-1.

Try This 21-2 Creating JSON Through Serialization

This exercise provides an opportunity to convert a C# data object to JSON through serialization.

1. Create a console application and include the following class declaration:

```
class ShipLine {
    public string Name      { get; set; }
    public string Expertise { get; set; }
}
```

2. Create an object of this *ShipLine* class and assign values to the *Name* and *Expertise* properties.
3. Covert this object to JSON.
4. Display your JSON contents in the console window.

Customizing Property Names During Serialization

When generating JSON from a .NET object, you may wish to customize property names during serialization. You can do this by placing a *JsonProperty* attribute tag above the C# property to be customized. The attribute receives a *PropertyName* parameter that is the name used by the newly created JSON structure.

```
class Person {
    [JsonProperty(PropertyName = "first_name")]
    public string FirstName {get;set;}
}
```

With this custom attribute name in place, the following code:

```
Person person     = new Person();
person.FirstName = "Ben";
var json          = JsonConvert.SerializeObject(person);
```

enables us to generate a JSON structure that uses the custom name instead of *FirstName*:

```
{"first_name":"Ben"}
```

Deserialization

Deserialization of JSON is the conversion of JSON to a C# data object. With Json.NET this is done with the *JsonConvert.DeserializeObject()* method. This method receives the JSON object as a parameter and uses the parent type as the generic type:

```
Registrant r = JsonConvert.DeserializeObject<Registrant>(json);
```

Example 21-5 Deserializing JSON

To see how transforming JSON to a C# data object is done, start with Example 21-4 and replace *Main()* with the code that follows. This code takes a JSON string and converts it to a *Registrant* object with just one instruction.

```
static void Main() {
    string json = "{'FirstName':'Ben','LastName':'Wu','Age':7,'Paid':60.50,"
        +"'Camps':[{'Day':'Aug. 2','Lunch':true},"
        +         "{'Day':null,'Lunch':true}]}";
    // Deserialize.
    Registrant r = JsonConvert.DeserializeObject<Registrant>(json);

    // Show object details with C# and LINQ.
    Console.WriteLine("Registrant:      " + r.FirstName + " " + r.LastName);
    Console.WriteLine("Days Confirmed: ");
```

```
    List<Camp> camps = r.Camps.Where(c => c.Day != null).ToList();
    foreach (Camp camp in camps)
        Console.WriteLine("Day - " + camp.Day + " Lunch - " + camp.Lunch);
    Console.ReadLine();
}
```

Results from the query appear as follows:

```
Registrant:      Ben Wu
Days Confirmed:
Day - Aug. 2 Lunch - True
```

Mapping to Custom Property Names During Deserialization

As shown previously, you may map JSON properties to different C# property names during deserialization. You can do this with the help of the *JsonProperty* attribute and its *PropertyName* parameter. If a C# property declaration has a *JsonProperty* attribute as shown here:

```
class Person {
    [JsonProperty(PropertyName = "first_name")]
    public string FirstName { get; set; }
}
```

A JSON property name that is the same as the *PropertyName* parameter will be mapped to the corresponding C# property:

```
string json = "{'first_name':'Ben'}";
Person p    = JsonConvert.DeserializeObject<Person>(json);
Console.WriteLine("Person:      " + p.FirstName);
```

Chapter 21 Self Test

The following questions are intended to help reinforce your comprehension of the concepts covered in this chapter. The answers can be found in the accompanying online Appendix B, "Answers to the Self Tests."

1. For each of the JSON strings, indicate if the *Prices* property references an object or an array:

A. "Prices": {"Tall": 2.95,"Grande": 3.65,"Venti": 4.15}

B. {"Prices":[{"Price":1.95},{"Price":2.95},{"Price":3.95}]}

2.

A. Build the following JSON structure with the *JObject* and *JArray* classes without creating C# types:

```
{
  "Drinks": [
    {
      "Name": "Coffee",
      "Price": {
        "Tall": 1.95,
        "Grande": 2.55,
        "Venti": 2.95
      }
    },
    {
      "Name": "Frappucino",
      "Price": {
        "Tall": 2.95,
        "Grande": 3.65,
        "Venti": 4.15
      }
    }
  ]
}
```

B. Output your JSON data in its entirety to verify the correctness of your structure.

C. Output the data using properties of the JSON structure so the output appears exactly as

```
Coffee Prices
Tall: $1.95 Grande: $2.55 Venti: $2.95

Frappucino Prices
Tall: $2.95 Grande: $3.65 Venti: $4.15
```

D. Create a representation of the JSON structure in C#. Use the *JsonConvert .DeserializeObject()* method to convert the JSON string into a C# object. To use the *DeserializeObject()* method, you will need to first convert your JSON to a string. Then use the string as a parameter in the *DeserializeObject()* method. Your instructions could look like the following:

```
string json = JsonConvert.SerializeObject(beverages);
Menu drinks = JsonConvert.DeserializeObject<Menu>(json);
```

3. Design the C# classes needed to create the structure that is represented in question 1B. Populate your parent object with the same data and show it.

Part V

Stand-alone Topics

Chapter 22

Attributes

Key Skills & Concepts

- .NET Framework Attributes
- Creating and Implementing Custom Attributes
- Reflection Introduction
- Querying Attribute Targets

Attributes are declarative tags that allow you to associate information, called *metadata,* with classes, structs, types, properties, methods, and other members. You may not need to use attributes much when starting out with C#, but you likely will need them when you advance to Windows and web development.

TIP

The topic of attributes is an important topic for C# developers in ASP.NET and Windows platforms. To simplify your learning, though, if you are new to C#, you might consider skimming through this chapter to gain awareness of attributes and reflection so you can quickly move to topics that are more essential for early stages of learning C#.

Attributes store metadata about a structure. The behavior associated with an attribute is applied independently of the attribute. Structures that are associated with specific attributes can be queried using a technique called reflection at any time during the life of the program.

.NET Framework Attributes

To understand how attributes work, it is helpful to know how to create custom attributes of your own. However, you probably won't need to create custom attributes very often. You are more likely to instead use predefined attributes that are available through the .NET Framework. This section won't list the attributes available, but it will show a few simple attributes so you can get an idea of how they work.

In the following sample, a custom attribute named *Help* is included above a class declaration to describe the class. The class description is passed to the *Help* attribute parameter, and the class version is assigned to the *Version* property of the attribute.

```
[Help("This class manages client contact information.", Version = "1.3")]
class Address { }
```

Here is another sample that uses the *XmlElement* and *XmlAttribute* attributes from the .NET Framework to regulate how class properties are transformed into XML:

```
public class Patent {
    [XmlElement("name")] // Convert property to 'name' element.
    public string Name    { get; set; }    // Stores 'Bread slicer'.

    [XmlAttribute("id")] // Convert property to 'id' attribute.
    public int     PatentID { get; set; } // Stores '1867377'.
}
```

If these properties stored data about Otto Frederick Rohwedder's patent for the world's first bread slicing machine, the XML element and attribute names generated would use the attribute parameter values rather than the property names:

```
<Patent id="1867377">
    <name>Bread slicer</name>
</Patent>
```

It is important to remember here that the attributes store metadata. The transformation behavior is implemented by routines that are run independently of these attributes. Attributes may be associated with an endless range of behavior, which is generally written separately from the attribute.

Try This 22-1 Implementing Attributes Practice

This exercise shows an implementation of the *Obsolete* attribute that is available from the *System* namespace of the .NET Framework. The *Obsolete* attribute can be placed above a structure to warn developers that the structure is deprecated and a more current alternative exists. The program that runs Visual Studio queries the code editor for *Obsolete* attributes and displays warnings or error messages wherever the denoted structure is used. The *Obsolete* attribute receives a string parameter for a *message* input and a Boolean *error* parameter to indicate whether to display an error or warning message in the Error List:

```
const bool SHOW_AS_ERROR = true;
// !SHOW_AS_ERROR means show as warning.
[Obsolete("Use Console.WriteLine() instead.", !SHOW_AS_ERROR)]
```

To observe how the *Obsolete* attribute works in Visual Studio, try these steps:

1. Create a new console application.

2. Replace the code inside Program.cs with the code shown in Figure 22-1.

3. Notice in the Error List that a warning message indicates where the obsolete structure is used. The line of code where the structure is used is underlined with a green wavy line to show where the warning exists. Also notice that the text passed to the attribute's *message* parameter appears in the Error List when the "obsolete" warning is displayed. Since a warning message is raised, the code still compiles and runs.
4. Remove the NOT operator from the attribute *error* parameter in this example so a true value is passed to the *Obsolete* attribute where it is used. With this change, notice that an error message appears in the Error List to highlight the location of the obsolete structure. The line of code in error is now underlined with a red wavy line. As expected, the code will not compile because an error is detected.

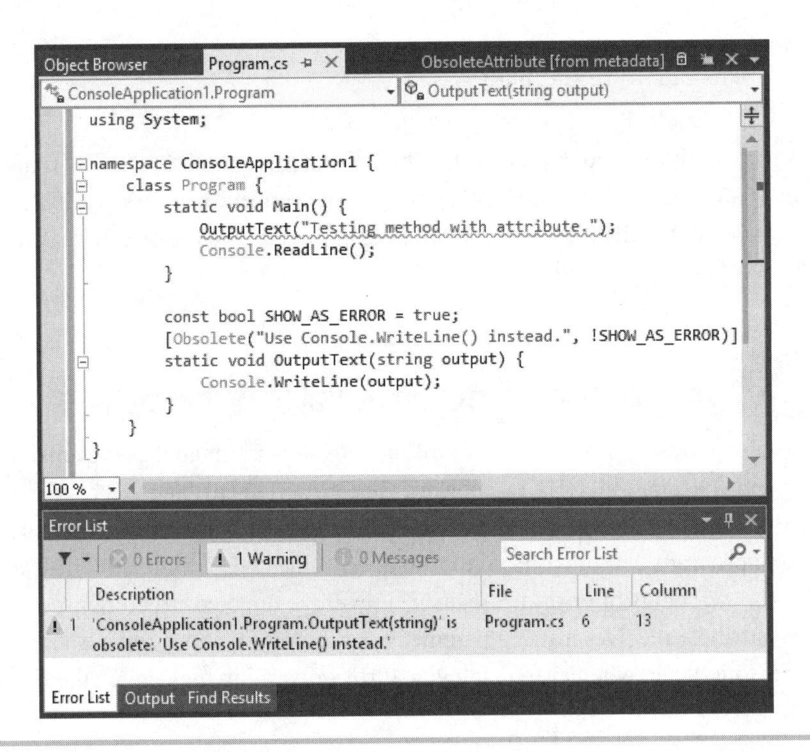

Figure 22-1 Obsolete warning message

Creating and Implementing Custom Attributes

To further understand how attributes work, let's examine how to create and implement an attribute from start to finish.

TIP

Remember you likely will more often use attributes that are defined in the .NET Framework rather than create your own. You may wish to create your own custom attributes, but such cases are unlikely. If you are uncertain whether you should create an attribute, you are probably better off finding another way to implement the feature without an attribute.

Inheriting from the Attribute Class

A custom attribute is declared as a class that inherits from the *Attribute* class. Inside the derived class, an overloaded constructor with parameters and properties can be declared to store metadata for the attribute instance:

```
// Attribute class declaration.
public class Help : Attribute {
    public Help(string description) {
        Description = description;
        Version     = "Undefined";
    }
    public string Description { get; protected set; }
    public string Version     { get; set;  }
}
```

Optional AttributeUsage Attributes

Above the custom attribute class declaration, you may include an optional *AttributeUsage* attribute to restrict how and where the custom attribute is implemented. To specify the type of structure that can apply the attribute, an *AttributeTargets* enumeration allows selection of any structure listed in Table 22-1.

All	Enum	Method
Class	Event	Parameters
Constructor	Field	Return-value
Delegate	Interface	Struct

Table 22-1 Attribute Target Enumerators

The Boolean parameter *AllowMultiple* determines when more than one instance of the attribute can be applied in the same attribute declaration. The Boolean *Inherited* flag indicates whether the attribute is applied in derived classes. Following is an example declaration of a customized attribute class just like the previous sample, but this time the optional *AttributeUsage* attribute is included:

```
// Optional flags.
[AttributeUsage(AttributeTargets.Class, // Target structure.
                AllowMultiple = false,  // 1 instance per target.
                Inherited     = false)] // Won't be inherited.
// Attribute class declaration.
public class Help : Attribute {
    public Help(string detail) {
        Detail  = detail;
        Version = "Undefined";
    }
    public string Detail  { get; protected set; }
    public string Version { get; set;  }
}
```

Implementing Custom Attributes

To apply an attribute, list the attribute in square brackets above the target structure declaration. Parameter values and properties are also included when permitted by the attribute:

```
// Class declarations with 'Help' attributes.
[Help("ClassA - Contains startup methods.")]
public class ClassA {}
[Help("ClassB - Contains shutdown methods.", Version = "1.0")]
public class ClassB {}
```

Querying Attributes

There are many different ways to query for attribute metadata. Regardless, if you implement custom attributes, you will want to determine which attributes are included in your type.

The Type Class

The *Type* class from the *System* namespace is the main class used for extracting information about data types. A *Type* instance for any data type can be obtained with the *GetType()* method of an object:

```
ClassName obj  = new ClassName();
Type classType = obj.GetType();
```

The *Type* instance can also be retrieved with the *typeof* operator when the type name is passed in as a parameter:

```
Type classType = typeof(ClassName);
```

GetCustomAttributes()

Attributes used in a type can be obtained with the *GetCustomAttributes()* method of the *Type* object. The *GetCustomAttributes()* method receives the *Type* object as a parameter along with a Boolean parameter to specify whether or not to search for the attribute in parent classes. The *inherit* parameter is ignored for properties and events.

```
var attributes = classType.GetCustomAttributes(Type attributeType,
                                               bool inherit);
```

Once a listing of attributes is obtained, it is possible to iterate through each *Attribute* instance with a *foreach* loop:

```
foreach(Attribute attribute in attributes) { }
```

Example 22-1 Inspecting Attributes

This example shows how to declare, include, and query a custom attribute named *Help* that stores detail and version information about a class. The query of attributes is run with a call to *GetCustomAttributes()*. All *Help* attributes applied within the *StartApp* and *EndApp* classes are retrieved, and property values of each attribute are displayed.

```
using System;

namespace ConsoleApplication1 {
    static class Program {
        public static void Main() {
            ShowMetadata(typeof(StartApp));
            ShowMetadata(typeof(EndApp));
            Console.ReadLine();
        }

        static void ShowMetadata(Type objectType) {
            // Get all 'Help' attributes.
            var attributes = objectType.GetCustomAttributes(typeof(Help),
                                                            true);

            // Iterate through 'Help attributes'.
            foreach(Attribute attribute in  attributes) {
```

```
                // Cast each attribute as a 'Help' object.
                Help help = (Help)attribute;

                // Display detail and version of 'Help' attribute.
                if(null != help)
                    Console.WriteLine(help.Detail + " Version: "
                                    + help.Version);
            }
        }
    }

    // Define custom attribute.
    [AttributeUsage(AttributeTargets.Class)]
    public class Help : Attribute {
        public Help(string detail) {
            Detail  = detail;
            Version = "Undefined";
        }
        public string Detail  { get; protected set; }
        public string Version { get; set; }
    }

    // Class declarations with 'Help' attribute.
    [Help("Contains setup methods.")]
    public class StartApp {}
    [Help("Contains shutdown methods.", Version = "1.0")]
    public class EndApp {}
}
```

Since the *Help* attribute is applied by both *StartApp* and *EndApp* types, two sets of *Detail* and *Version* properties are displayed when running the program:

```
Contains setup methods. Version: Undefined
Contains shutdown methods. Version: 1.0
```

Try This 22-2 Implementing and Querying Custom Attributes

This exercise offers a chance to get some hands-on practice for creating and querying custom attributes.

1. Add an *Author* property to the *Help* attribute class in Example 22-1.
2. Adjust the *Help* attribute class so you have the ability to assign a value to the *Programmer* property.

3. Modify each area where the *Help* attribute is applied to set your name as the value for the *Programmer* property.
4. Adjust the code so the *Programmer* property value is displayed along with the *Detail* and *Version* properties whenever the *Help* attribute is found when querying the *Type* object.

Reflection Introduction

Searching for attributes is useful, but you also need to know about the members targeted by these attributes. You can use reflection to get this information. *Reflection* is a technique that allows you to obtain metadata about data types. Metadata can include information about a type's members, which might include constructors, methods, enumerations, properties, events, and variables.

NOTE

Reflection can be used to invoke type members, but this topic will not be covered in this book.

Information about a data type is primarily taken from a *Type* object during reflection. There are many methods available to gather information about a *Type* object. Table 22-2 highlights common *Type* methods for getting information about members. The *Type* method return types are available through the *System.Reflection* namespace.

Type Method	Return Type	Description
GetFields()	FieldInfo[]	Returns all the public fields of the current System.Type.
GetProperties()	PropertyInfo[]	Returns all the public properties of the current System.Type.
GetEvents()	EventInfo[]	Returns all the public events that are declared or inherited by the current System.Type.
GetConstructors()	ConstructorInfo[]	Returns all public constructors for the current System.Type.
GetMethods()	MethodInfo[]	Returns all the public methods of the current System.Type.
GetMembers()	MemberInfo[]	Returns all the public members of the current System.Type.

Table 22-2 Type Methods

Example 22-2 Getting Metadata from a Type Object

This example shows how to use reflection to extract information about the structures inside the *StartApp* class. The *System.Type* methods *GetFields(), GetProperties(), GetConstructors(), GetMethods(),* and *GetMembers()* are used to retrieve these relevant structures. After retrieval, the *Name* property of each member in the set retrieved is displayed.

```
using System;
using System.Reflection;

namespace ConsoleApplication1 {
    public class StartApp {
        // Fields, properties, constructors, and methods are all members.
        public int classLevelVariable = 5;                    // Field
        public DateTime Started { get; set; }                 // Property

        public StartApp(DateTime started, int version) {      // Constructor
            Started = started;
        }
        public void ShowStartTime() {                         // Method
            Console.WriteLine(Started);
        }
    }

    static class Program {
        public static void Main() {
            ShowMetadata(typeof(StartApp));
            Console.ReadLine();
        }
        static void ShowMetadata(Type objectType) {
            FieldInfo[] fields = objectType.GetFields();      // Field
            Console.WriteLine("\n* Field data *");
            foreach(FieldInfo field in fields)
                Console.WriteLine(field.Name);

            PropertyInfo[] properties
                              = objectType.GetProperties();  // Property
            Console.WriteLine("\n* Property data *");
            foreach(PropertyInfo property in properties)
                Console.WriteLine(property.Name);

            ConstructorInfo[] constructors = objectType.GetConstructors();
            Console.WriteLine("\n* Constructor data *");      // Constructor
            foreach (ConstructorInfo constructor in constructors)
                Console.WriteLine(constructor.Name);

            MethodInfo[] methods = objectType.GetMethods();   // Method
            Console.WriteLine("\n* Method data *");
            foreach(MethodInfo method in methods)
                Console.WriteLine(method.Name);
```

```
            // Fields, properties, constructors, and methods are all members.
            MemberInfo[] members = objectType.GetMembers();
            Console.WriteLine("\n* Member data *");
            foreach(MemberInfo member in members)
                Console.WriteLine(member.Name);
        }
    }
}
```

The output shows how the *GetFields(), GetProperties(), GetConstructors(), GetMethods(),* and *GetMembers()* methods extract different structures from the *StartApp* class type. Notice that *GetMembers()* combines all fields, properties, constructors, and methods together since each is a member. The *ToString(), Equals(), GetHashCode(),* and *GetType()* methods are present since they are inherent to any C# object.

```
* Field data *
classLevelVariable

* Property data *
Started

* Constructor data *
.ctor

* Method data *
get_Started
set_Started
ShowStartTime
ToString
Equals
GetHashCode
GetType

* Member data *
get_Started
set_Started
ShowStartTime
ToString
Equals
GetHashCode
GetType
.ctor
Started
classLevelVariable
```

Querying Attribute Targets

The previous section shows how *Type* class methods can obtain information about members with reflection. Each member instance can then use the *GetCustomAttributes()* method to determine if it is applying a specific attribute. In the following code example, each member of the *StartApp* class is checked to see if it applies the *BugFixInfo* attribute. Whenever the attribute is applied, property values stored by the attribute for that member are displayed to the console window.

```
// Obtain and iterate through all members.
MemberInfo[] members      = startApp.GetMembers();
foreach (MemberInfo member in members) {
    const bool INHERITED = true;

    // Obtain and iterate through all 'BugFixInfo' attributes.
    var attributes = member.GetCustomAttributes(typeof(BugFixInfo),
                                                INHERITED);
    foreach (Attribute attribute in attributes) {
        // Report on member and related bug fix data.
        BugFixInfo bugfix = (BugFixInfo)attribute;
        Console.WriteLine("\n" + className + ":    " + member.Name);
        Console.WriteLine("Bug ID: "    + bugfix.BugID + "     "
                          +"Fixed by: " + bugfix.ProgrammerName);
    }
}
```

Example 22-3 Tracking Bug Fixes

This example creates and applies an attribute called *BugFixInfo* to track bug fixes in code where the fixes are made. The attribute's *BugID* property stores the bug number that was created when the defect was logged. The person who made the fix is recorded with the *ProgrammerName* property. Reflection is used to extract and report all *BugFixInfo* property values along with the member information where the attribute is applied.

```
using System;
using System.Reflection;

namespace ConsoleApplication1 {
    public class BugFixInfo : Attribute {        // Define custom attribute.
        public string ProgrammerName  { get; set; }
        public int    BugID           { get; set; }

        public BugFixInfo(int bugID, string programmerName) {
            ProgrammerName = programmerName;
            BugID          = bugID;
```

```
        }
    }

    public class StartApp {
        [BugFixInfo(451, "Michael Abrash")]     // Method.
        public StartApp(DateTime started) { }

        [BugFixInfo(488, "Grace Hopper")]       // Constructor.
        public void ShowStartTime() { }
    }

    static class Program {
        public static void Main() {
            // Extract Type for use with Reflection.
            Type   startApp  = typeof(StartApp);
            string className =  startApp.Name;

            // Obtain and iterate through all members.
            MemberInfo[] members      = startApp.GetMembers();
            foreach (MemberInfo member in members) {
                const bool INHERITED = true;

                // Obtain and iterate through all 'BugFixInfo' attributes.
                var attributes = member
                                .GetCustomAttributes(typeof(BugFixInfo),
                                                     INHERITED);
                foreach (Attribute attribute in attributes) {

                    // Report on member and related bug fix data.
                    BugFixInfo bugfix = (BugFixInfo)attribute;
                    Console.WriteLine("\n" + className + ":    "
                                      + member.Name);
                    Console.WriteLine("Bug ID: "   + bugfix.BugID + "    "
                                   +"Fixed by: " + bugfix.ProgrammerName);
                }
            }
            Console.ReadLine();
        }
    }
}
```

The bug fix report shows the class and member name, as well as the bug number and name of the person who fixed it:

```
StartApp:   ShowStartTime
Bug ID: 488    Fixed by: Grace Hopper

StartApp:   .ctor
Bug ID: 451    Fixed by: Michael Abrash
```

Example 22-4 Creating a Validation Attribute

This example shows how to create an attribute to automate regular expression validation. The attribute stores the regular expression pattern for each property where it is applied. For this case, the following attribute inclusion sets a pattern that only allows alphabetical characters:

```
[MyRegex("^[a-zA-Z]+$")]
```

During a validation routine, properties that apply the *MyRegex* attribute are validated with the *Pattern* property value:

```
using System;
using System.Reflection;
using System.Text.RegularExpressions;

namespace ConsoleApplication1 {
    static class Program {
        public static void Main() {
            ShowValidationStatus(new Person("John")); // Valid instance.
            ShowValidationStatus(new Person("7313")); // Invalid instance.
            Console.ReadLine();
        }

        static void ShowValidationStatus(Person name) {
            bool valid = Validation.IsValid(name);
            Console.Write(name.First);
            if(valid)
                Console.WriteLine(" is valid.");
            else
                Console.WriteLine(" is not valid.");
        }
    }

    // Define custom attribute with optional AttributeUsage flags.
    [AttributeUsage(AttributeTargets.Property, // Target structure.
                    AllowMultiple = false,     // 1 instance allowed.
                    Inherited     = true)]     // Can't be inherited.
    public class MyRegex : Attribute {
        public string Pattern { get; private set;}
        public MyRegex(string pattern) {
            Pattern = pattern;
        }
    }

    public class Person {
        [MyRegex("^[a-zA-Z]+$")]            // Apply attribute to only permit
        public string First { get; set; } // upper or lower case letters.
        public Person(string firstName) {
```

```
            First = firstName;
        }
    }

    public class Validation {
        static bool CheckRegex(Object obj, PropertyInfo property) {

            // Select attributes & value where MyRegex attribute found.
            var attributes = property.GetCustomAttributes(typeof(MyRegex));

            // Iterate through 'MyRegex' attributes.
            foreach(Attribute attribute in attributes) {

                // Convert value with 'MyRegex' attribute to a string.
                var  propertyValue = property.GetValue(obj, null);
                string  personName = propertyValue.ToString();

                // Get pattern from MyRegex attribute.
                MyRegex MyRegex    = (MyRegex)attribute;
                string  pattern    = MyRegex.Pattern;

                // Ensure property value conforms to the pattern.
                if(!Regex.IsMatch(personName, pattern))
                    return false;
            }
            return true;
        }

        public static bool IsValid(object obj) {
            var classType  = obj.GetType();
            var properties = classType.GetProperties();  // Get properties.

            // Search properties and apply regex where 'MyRegex' applies.
            foreach (var property in properties) {
                if (!CheckRegex(obj, property))
                    return false;
            }
            return true;
        }
    }
}
```

The following output from this example confirms that the object with the *First* property value of John is valid. The object with the *First* property value of 7313 is invalid. The regular expression is applied in the attribute, but the validation occurs in a routine elsewhere in the program.

```
John is valid.
7313 is not valid.
```

Chapter 22 Self Test

The following questions are intended to help reinforce your comprehension of the concepts covered in this chapter. The answers can be found in the accompanying online Appendix B, "Answers to the Self Tests."

1. Indicate whether each of the following is true or false:

   A. ____ An attribute only stores metadata and it does not contain behavioral logic.

   B. ____ Setting the *error* parameter to true when applying the *Obsolete* attribute to a class member will cause an error wherever the targeted member is invoked.

   C. ____ Given the following object declaration:

   ```
   MyClass myObject    = new MyClass();
   ```

   we can then say

   ```
   myObject.GetType() == typeof(MyClass)
   ```

2. Starting with Example 22-4, add a new property called *Last* that sets and gets the last name inside the *Person* class. Then, place a *MyRegex* attribute above the *Last* property. Add a new constructor that is initialized with both first and last name parameter values. Initialize two new objects with the new constructor and test each object for validity. One object should be initialized with a first and last name that validates. The other object should be initialized with a last name that fails the validation test.

3. Create a new attribute that sets a maximum float value for a property. Implement a validation routine outside the attribute to determine if the property value is a float between 0 and the maximum value stored by the attribute. Do not use regular expressions in your validation routine. Test the attribute in a case where the property is valid and in another case where the property is invalid.

Chapter 23

Operator Overloading

Key Skills & Concepts

- Operator Overloading Introduction
- Operator Overload Method Requirements
- Operators that Can Be Overloaded

This chapter discusses a technique called operator overloading for enabling abbreviated syntax for math operations on complex objects. Operator overloads are more often seen in libraries that apply advanced math, such as with games or graphics programming. If you are programming business applications, you are less likely to develop operator overloads, but sometimes this is called for. In any type of application, though, you may use libraries that have predefined operator overloads, so it is helpful to understand how they are developed and applied.

Operator Overloading Introduction

Operator overloading provides a shorthand way to implement operators such as +, –, *, or / with complex objects.

Before we get started with syntax details, here is an example of a + operator overload that adds *Revenue* and *Expenses* properties for two *Budget* objects:

```
class Budget {
    public decimal Revenue  { get; set; }
    public decimal Expenses { get; set; }
    public static Budget operator +(Budget a, Budget b) { // '+' overload
        Budget combined   = new Budget();
        combined.Revenue  = a.Revenue  + b.Revenue;
        combined.Expenses = a.Expenses + b.Expenses;
        return combined;
    }
}
```

With this + overload, you now have a fast way to add *Budget* object property values:

```
Budget combined = retailBudget + onlineBudget;
```

Calculating totals for sets of two properties isn't too impressive, but the overloaded operator could be really helpful when several properties must be adjusted at once.

Operator Overload Method Requirements

Some guidelines exist around operator overload methods. Operator overload methods must

- Be public
- Be static
- Be located in the struct or class that it operates on
- Receive at least one parameter of the same type as the class or struct it operates on

Operators that Can Be Overloaded

Not all operators can be overloaded. The following table shows common operators that can be overloaded.

++, --, (true, false)	Requires at least one operand as a parameter.
+, −, *, /, %,(==, !=), <, >, <=, >=	Requires two or more operands as parameters.

NOTE

Whenever you are implementing Boolean operators like *true, false*, ==, !=, <, >, <=, or >=, both matching true and false equivalents of the overload must be present. If, for example, you create a > operator overload, you also need to have a < operator overload.

Example 23-1 Operator Overloads for Budget Objects

This example uses a + operator to generate combined totals for *Expenses* and *Revenue* properties of a *Budget* class. It also includes an overload for the *true* operator to check if both *Expenses* and *Revenue* property values are zero. Since the *true* operator is a Boolean operator, a *false* operator overload must also be included in the *Budget* class to satisfy the compiler.

```
using System;

namespace ConsoleApplication1 {
    class Program {
        static void Main() {
            decimal REVENUE = 43000m, EXPENSES = 2030m;
            Budget retail = new Budget(REVENUE, EXPENSES); // Create budget.
            retail.ShowBudget("Retail Budget:");

            Budget online = new Budget(REVENUE, EXPENSES); // Create budget.
            online.ShowBudget("Online Budget:");
```

```
            Budget combined = retail + online; // Combine budgets.
            combined.ShowBudget("Retail and Online Budgets Combined:");

            Budget emptyBudget = new Budget(); // Create budget.
            if (emptyBudget)                   // Ensure balances
                                               // are not zero.
                emptyBudget.ShowBudget("Budget is not empty.");
            else
                Console.WriteLine("Empty Budget.");

            Console.ReadLine();
        }
    }
    class Budget {
        public decimal Revenue  { get; set; }
        public decimal Expenses { get; set; }

        public Budget() { }
        public Budget(decimal revenue, decimal expenses) {
            Revenue  = revenue;
            Expenses = expenses;
        }
        // 'true' operator ensures Budget properties are not zero.
        public static bool operator true(Budget budget) {
            if (budget.Revenue == 0 && budget.Expenses == 0)
                return false;
            return true;
        }
        // 'false' operator only required if 'true' operator is present.
        public static bool operator false(Budget budget) {
            return false;
        }
        // '+' overload adds Budget objects.
        public static Budget operator +(Budget a, Budget b) {
            Budget sum    = new Budget();
            sum.Revenue   = a.Revenue  + b.Revenue;
            sum.Expenses  = a.Expenses + b.Expenses;
            return sum;
        }
        // Show Budget properties.
        public void ShowBudget(string title) {
            Console.WriteLine(title);
            Console.WriteLine("Revenue:  " + Revenue.ToString("C"));
            Console.WriteLine("Expenses: " + Expenses.ToString("C"));
            Console.WriteLine();
        }
    }
}
```

The following output shows revenue and expense totals for retail and online budgets along with their combined totals that are provided with the help of the + operator overload.

A *Budget* object that is not null but has zero revenues and expenses is shown to be empty with the help of the *true* operator overload.

```
Retail Budget:
Revenue:  $43,000.00
Expenses: $2,030.00

Online Budget:
Revenue:  $43,000.00
Expenses: $2,030.00

Retail and Online Budgets Combined:
Revenue:  $86,000.00
Expenses: $4,060.00

Empty Budget.
```

Try This 23-1 Creating and Using a * Operator Overload

Here is a chance for you to try writing overload syntax.

1. Starting with Example 23-1, add to the *Budget* class a * operator overload that, in addition to receiving a *Budget* object as a parameter, receives a decimal parameter named *inflation.*
2. Add code to the body of the new operator overload to inflate the *Revenue* and *Expenses* properties with the parameter value. Then return the adjusted *Budget* object to the calling instruction.
3. In the *Main()* method, just before the *ReadLine()* instruction, test your new overload to inflate the combined object properties by 10 percent. You can use the following instruction:

```
combined *= 1.1m;
combined.ShowBudget("Inflated Budget:");
```

4. Show the new *Revenue* and *Expenses* values that are generated for your combined object with the * operator. If successful, your output should resemble the following:

```
Inflated Budget:
Revenue:  $94,600.00
Expenses: $4,466.00
```

5. Try removing the *false* operator from the program. Notice that you are unable to run the program after this change.

Example 23-2 Implementing a + Operator Overload

For good measure, here is another example that shows how a + operator overload might be used to increment a series of properties. In this case, the + operator simultaneously adjusts first and second quarter fiscal review dates.

```
class Review {
    public DateTime FirstQtr  { get; set; }
    public DateTime SecondQtr { get; set; }

    // + operator adjusts quarterly review dates.
    public static Review operator +(Review review, int days) {
        review.FirstQtr  = review.FirstQtr.AddDays(days);
        review.SecondQtr = review.SecondQtr.AddDays(days);
        return review;
    }
}
```

This operator can then be invoked with the following instruction:

```
review += 45;  // Add days to FirstQtr and SecondQtr properties.
```

```
Here is the full example:using System;

namespace ConsoleApplication1 {
    class Program {
        static void Main() {
            Review review = new Review();
            review.ShowDates("Original Fiscal Review Dates: ");
            review += 45; // Add days to FirstQtr and SecondQtr properties.
            review.ShowDates("Adjusted Fiscal Review Dates: ");
            Console.ReadLine();
        }
    }

    class Review {
        public DateTime FirstQtr  { get; set; }
        public DateTime SecondQtr { get; set; }

        public Review() {
            DateTime startDate = new DateTime(1977, 01, 03);
            FirstQtr  = startDate.AddMonths(3);
            SecondQtr = FirstQtr.AddMonths(3);
        }

        // + operator adjusts quarterly review dates.
        public static Review operator +(Review review, int days) {
```

```
            review.FirstQtr  = review.FirstQtr.AddDays(days);
            review.SecondQtr = review.SecondQtr.AddDays(days);
            return review;
        }

        public void ShowDates(string title) {
            Console.WriteLine(title);
            Console.WriteLine("1st Fiscal Qtr: "
                            + FirstQtr.ToString("M/d/yyyy"));
            Console.WriteLine("2nd Fiscal Qtr: "
                            + SecondQtr.ToString("M/d/yyyy"));
            Console.WriteLine();
        }
    }
}
```

The output displays the original quarterly review dates and the adjusted quarterly review dates after they are moved 45 days ahead:

```
Original Fiscal Review Dates:
1st Fiscal Qtr: 4/3/1977
2nd Fiscal Qtr: 7/3/1977

Adjusted Fiscal Review Dates:
1st Fiscal Qtr: 5/18/1977
2nd Fiscal Qtr: 8/17/1977
```

TIP

If you are uncertain whether developing a custom operator overload is efficient, it is probably best that you not create one. In a case of uncertainty, creating a method to perform the same task is likely a better choice, to ensure code readability.

Try This 23-2 Creating and Using a – Operator Overload

This exercise offers another opportunity to get comfortable with the overload syntax.

1. Starting with Example 23-2, in addition to the already existing + operator, include a – operator overload that deducts days from the *FirstQtr* and *SecondQtr* properties of the *Review* class.
2. Test your new operator by invoking it from the *Main()* method.
3. Display the *FirstQtr* and *SecondQtr* property values with the *ShowDates()* method of your *Review* object after deducting days with the – operator.

Chapter 23 Self Test

The following questions are intended to help reinforce your comprehension of the concepts covered in this chapter. The answers can be found in the accompanying online Appendix B, "Answers to the Self Tests."

1. Indicate whether each statement is true or false:

   A. ____ Overloaded methods must always be static.

   B. ____ Overloaded methods do not always require parameters.

   C. ____ The implementation of a ++ overload also requires the implementation of a -- overload.

   D. ____ Operator overloading is more common in graphics programming than in business application development.

2. Adjust Example 23-1 by adding operator overloads that determines whether the profit level of one *Budget* object is greater than or equal to the profit level of another *Budget* object. Profit equals revenue minus expenses. Test one of your comparison overloads with two *Budget* objects that are initialized as follows:

```
Budget retail = new Budget(88000m, 46700m); // Create budget.
Budget online = new Budget(43000m, 2300m);  // Create budget.
```

   In your output report the outcome of the profit comparison.

Appendix

FoodStore Database Reference

The entity relationship diagram in Figure A-1 shows all tables in the *FoodStore* database. Figure A-2 shows the conceptual view of the *FoodStore* entity data model that is generated by Visual Studio. Notice that the *ProductInvoice* and *ProductPurchaseOrder* bridge tables are absent, yet are present in the entity relationship diagram in Figure A-1.

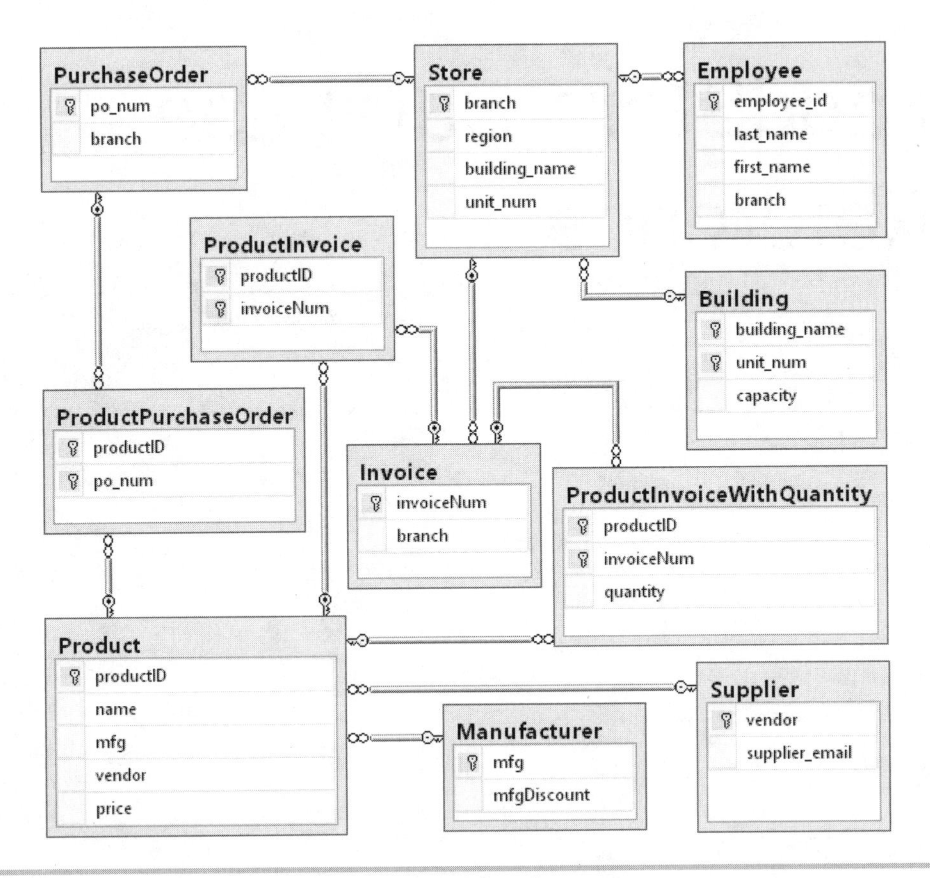

Figure A-1 FoodStore database entity relationship diagram

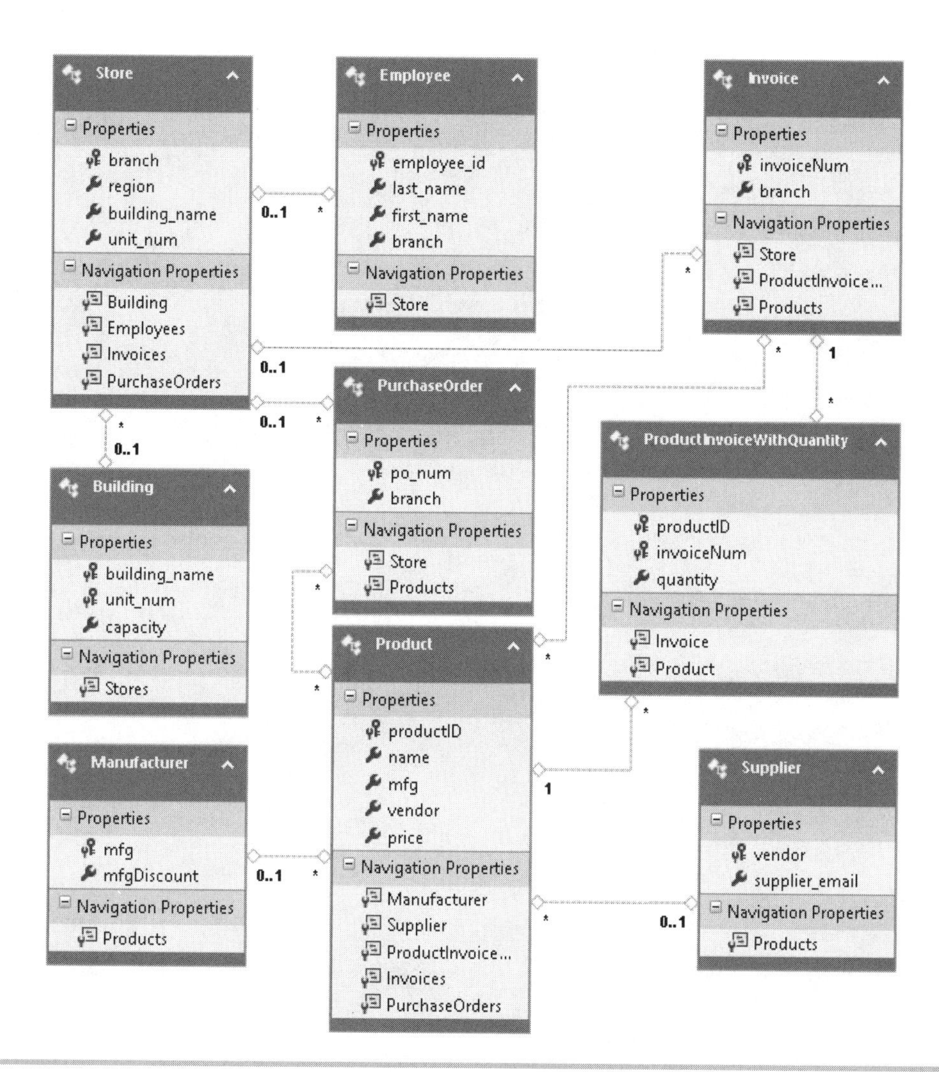

Figure A-2 FoodStore entity data model conceptual view

Index

References to figures are in italics.

A

B

C

D

I

J

K

L

M

N

O

P

R

S

T

U

V

W

X